The Diary of J. J. Grandville
and the Missouri Album

Frontispiece: *Self-Portrait,* circa 1843–46, pencil. Nancy, Musée des Beaux-Arts (Inv. 877.803).

The Diary of J. J. Grandville and the Missouri Album

The Life of an Opposition Caricaturist and Romantic Book Illustrator in Paris under the July Monarchy

Clive F. Getty

Madison • Teaneck
Fairleigh Dickinson University Press

Associated University Presses
2010 Eastpark Boulevard
Cranbury, NJ 08512

The paper used in this publication meets the requirements of the American National Standard for Permanence of Paper for Printed Library Materials Z39.48-1984.

Library of Congress Cataloging-in-Publication Data

Getty, Clive Frank
The diary of J. J. Grandville and the Missouri album : the life of an opposition caricaturist and romantic book illustrator in Paris under the July monarchy / Clive F. Getty
p. cm.
Includes bibliographical references and index.
ISBN 978-0-8386-4200-9 (alk. paper)
1. Grandville, J. J., 1803–1847. 2. Cartoonists—France—Biography. 3. Illustrators—France—Biography. 4. Grandville, J. J., 1803–1847—Notebooks, sketchbooks, etc. I. Title.
NC1499.G66G48 2010
741.944—dc22 2009036186

PRINTED IN THE UNITED STATES OF AMERICA

Contents

List of Catalog Entries

Illustrations

Unless otherwise designated, the works listed below are by Grandville.

Frontispiece: *Self-Portrait,* circa 1843–46, pencil.

Foreword

To dedicate a scholarly career to the work of one artist is an unusual preoccupation. It reveals a fervent dedication, a tenacious commitment to finding out about the thoughts, concerns, and working methods of one individual. When this artist is of the complexity, mystery, and stature of Grandville, then the mission of understanding why certain things were done in certain ways takes on the atmosphere of a crusade. To know an artist well, to find new insights in unusual documents or in the examination of previously dismissed artworks or writings helps enlarge the scope of the original creativity. It is a method that very few scholars pursue as it requires a sense of dogged perseverance that eliminates those who do not have the patience, inclination, or time. But it is just such work that needs to be done if one is to obtain a firm picture—one rooted in history and archival assessment—of an artist about whom much has been written, but that has led in directions not based on historical accuracy or an interpretive basis found in primary documents.

It is, therefore, humbling to find that Clive F. Getty has persevered in his attachment and love of Grandville's work and ideas for close to forty years. His writings have provided new interpretations to Grandville's place as a draughtsman; his new work, presented in the following pages, brings to light insights about Grandville's place and time that have been based on the painstaking reconsideration of the "Missouri Album" found in the Special Collections of the University of Missouri-Columbia Libraries. This document, constructed from works done over many phases of Grandville's career, provides added insight into the ways Grandville thought on a daily basis. In the hands of Professor Getty the album pages are interpreted against the personal and contextual history of Grandville's life and place in society. Since this has never been attempted before, the publication of this material provides a very substantial way to gain an added dimension.

There can be little doubt that this new publication will contribute to our understanding of Grandville's work. More important, the publication of this album demonstrates that archival interpretation of documents and a sympathetic examination of works of art can lead to a higher understanding of connoisseurship. Since this type of study, based on solid and clearly analyzed documentation, has become a lost art that is now only slowly returning to a position of importance, this publication will serve as a tangible model for what can be done by an art historian willing to work and think as a searcher. Professor Getty sees art history as both a cultural study and a way to cultivate sympathetically and systematically "the eye" in the service of historical comprehensiveness and interpretation. There can be no better way to demonstrate a legacy for the future.

Gabriel P. Weisberg
University of Minnesota

Acknowledgments

I am deeply indebted to the numerous people and institutions who offered me encouragement and support during the course of researching and writing this book. First and foremost I wish to thank Marcia Reed who, while Art, Archaeology, and Music librarian at the University of Missouri-Columbia, brought to my attention the existence of the album of Grandville drawings that is the subject of this study. My thanks also to Margaret Howell, former head of Special Collections at the University of Missouri and her successor, Michael Holland, who gave me access to the drawings and arranged for their being photographed. Grandville relatives were a source of steadfast support, most notably the late M. and Mme Pierre Parisot and the late Mme Jean Gutton and her daughters. Equally rewarding was the abiding interest in Grandville and his work on the part of Samuel F. Clapp and Claude Rebeyrat who provided me with invaluable information on more than one occasion.

Since by far the largest part of my research was conducted in France, most of my gratitude goes to French research institutions and their personnel. Those in Nancy, the city of Grandville's birth, deserve special commendation. Former and present staff at the Musée Lorrain, including Claire Aptel and Francine Roze, along with the chief curator, Eric Moinet, have always been as unfailingly gracious as they have been helpful. Equally solicitous have been the staff at the Bibliothèque municipale whose former and present directors, respectively, Guy Vaucel and André Markiewicz, always made every effort to make their collections available to me. Two members of their staff merit special mention: Marie-Claire Mangin and especially Marcelle Moret who obtained slides of needed images in record time. I am also grateful to Claude Pétry, former curator/director of the Musée des Beaux-Arts, who was particularly enthusiastic about the subject of Grandville's diary, and to her successors, notably the present curator/director, Claire Stoullig. Special thanks, however, go to the museum's curator, Clara Gelly-Saldias, for her heroic efforts in locating and having photographed Grandville drawings during the museum's major building and reorganization program. The extensive holdings of the Archives municipales contain a certain number of documents pertaining to Grandville, and I wish to thank Michèle Renson, curator of the archives, for helping to track some of them down. Of the many other people in Nancy who have given me their unstinting support, I need to mention Germaine Meyer-Noirel and Marinette Simon, who gave me access to their collections, as well as the late Gilbert Mangin, many of whose photographs appear in this volume.

Of the many research institutions in Paris, special thanks must be given to the personnel of the Bibliothèque nationale de France whose patience never wavered and whose expertise never faltered despite innumerable queries. Laure Beaumont-Maillet, head curator of the Cabinet des estampes, and members of her staff, Claude Bouret, Giselle Lambert, and Marie-Claire Miessner, merit special commendation as do the ever helpful members of the Service Reproduction. Equally helpful were members of the staff of the Musée Carnavalet, especially curators of the Cabinet des arts graphiques, Jacqueline Lafargue and Brigitte de Montclos; many thanks as well to the ever collegial Philippe Sorel for his steadfast support and for sharing his insights into the relationship between Grandville and the caricatural sculptor Danton jeune. Numerous other institutions and individuals in Paris deserve to be mentioned: Anne-Marie Debelfort of the Fondation Taylor; Philippe Grunchec, curator of the École des Beaux-Arts; Françoise Tetart-Vittu of the Musée de la Mode et du Costume; Françoise Lévèque of the Bibliothèque de l'heure joyeuse; Noëlle Guibert, curator in chief of the collections of the Comédie-Française; Christophe Verneuil, archivist of the École Polytechnique; the staff at the Photothèque des Musées de la Ville de Paris; the Bibliothèque historique de la Ville de Paris; and the Bibliothèque de l'Arsenal. Many thanks as well to Didier Geilbaud for his expertise on Little Red Riding Hood and to Ségolène Le Men and Annie Renonciat for their knowledge of Grandville and the Romantic period in general.

However, there were also people and institutions outside of Nancy and Paris that came to my aid. Most notably, I cannot thank enough Paulette Blampin, archivist for the city of Chatou. Her extensive knowledge of the documents in the collection of the Chatou municipal archives proved invaluable for finding precise information about Chatou when Grandville summered there during his later years. I am also indebted to Philippe Durey, curator in chief at the Musée des Beaux-Arts in Lyon, and Valérie Durey, in charge of the museum's documentation, for their help in obtaining valuable information on the life and work of the painter Joseph Guichard.

Colleagues at Miami University were generous in their support. Jerry Morris, Ralph Raunft, and the late John Michael lent their expertise in children's art. William Pratt and Pierre Sotteau were extremely helpful in the editing of the manuscript. And Robert Wicks's knowledge of desktop publishing proved invaluable.

Equally generous was Beatrice Farwell who made many helpful suggestions during her reading of an early draft of the book's manuscript.

I am especially indebted to the late Lorenz Eitner who patiently guided me through the many revisions of my dissertation on Grandville at Stanford University and, along with the late Albert Elsen, launched my study of this fascinating artist.

My warmest gratitude is extended to Gabriel and Yvonne Weisberg whose friendship, generosity, encouragement, and professional advice have been a constant source of inspiration.

Financial support is crucial for any sustained undertaking, and the present study is no exception. I cannot express enough my gratitude to the American Philosophical Society for providing the grant-in-aid that allowed me to initiate my research. And Miami University has been generous in providing not only subsequent funding, most notably a Summer Research Grant and School of Fine Arts Academic Excellence Grants, but also the time for a project that took somewhat longer than originally anticipated.

To err, alas, is human, and it is quite possible that I have somehow failed to acknowledge each and every one of the numerous individuals and institutions that have generously come to my support during the course of this project. My apologies for any such omissions.

Introduction

Two hundred years ago the early nineteenth-century French caricaturist and book illustrator J. J. Grandville (1803–47) was born. An inventive castigator and moralizing commentator of human foibles, he was hailed by his more discerning contemporaries as the Juvenal of his age.[1] Though somewhat neglected during the later part of the nineteenth century, Grandville was revived in the twentieth century by the surrealists who were drawn to the innovative imagery of his Romantic imagination.[2] The German critic and philosopher, Walter Benjamin, saw him as providing a unique visual commentary on nineteenth-century consumerism and the bourgeois fetish for commodities.[3] Efforts to arrive at a better understanding of Grandville and his artistic originality continue to be made as we celebrate the bicentennial of his birth. The purpose of the present study is to situate Grandville more solidly within the context of his time and place through a systematic examination of the contents of an exceptional album of his drawings at the University of Missouri in Columbia, Missouri, which will be referred to as the Missouri Album.

The Missouri Album is significant for understanding Grandville because it contains a number of excerpts from his diary. Despite their fragmented state, they give us a closer look at Grandville and his world. Amid the trivia of daily existence, we meet his friends, learn about his work habits, and witness surprisingly intimate revelations about both the personal and professional aspects of his life, most notably his distaste for his career as France's leading opposition caricaturist during the early years of Louis-Philippe's July Monarchy. Apart from these private matters, entries also provide us with a first-hand report of life in Paris as experienced by a solidly middle-class artist during the Romantic period. A carnival masquerade ball, a bohemian soirée in Grandville's bachelor apartment, the tricolor fireworks display of the fête du Roi, regular visits to the Jardin des Plantes with friends such as Daumier, strolls in the Tuileries Gardens, theatrical productions (Frédérick Lemaître in *l'Auberge des Adrets,* arguably the most popular French play of the nineteenth century; the incomparable Rachel in Corneille's classic tragedy, *Cinna*), a shadow theater performance (probably chez Séraphin at the Palais-Royal), a benefit ball for the newly founded Association des artistes at the Odéon theater with the visiting Moroccan ambassador in attendance, summer spent in the picturesque suburb of Chatou—all come to life through witty thumbnail sketches and more finished, often exceptionally beautiful drawings that span the major part of his career, from 1830 to 1846. The many diary excerpts from 1846 are particularly important for understanding Grandville's personality. Contrary to the myth that has grown up around the artist, they give no indication of an abnormal state of mind during the year preceding his death. Instead, they reveal the human side of a loving husband and father who was devoted to his family and a tranquil domestic existence.

Although the majority of the drawings in the Missouri Album originate from Grandville's diary, some come from other sources. Several of the more remarkable ones are found on pages from an 1836 sketchbook that include studies for "Little Red Riding Hood" and the legend of Saint Nicholas. These document his interest in book illustration and, more specifically, his contribution to the development of children's literature during the first half of the nineteenth century.

Grandville's life and work have been detailed in three recent publications.[4] The biographical outline that follows provides an orientation for the contents of the Missouri Album by situating the artist within political, economic, and artistic developments during the first half of the nineteenth century in France.

Notes

1. S. Clogenson, "J.-J. Granville [*sic*]," *L'Athenæum français* (March 19, 1853): 273; Charles Blanc, *Les Artistes de mon temps* (Paris: Firmin-Didot, 1876), 283.

2. Pierre Mac Orlan, "Grandville le précurseur," *Arts et Métiers Graphiques,* no. 44 (1934): 19–24; Laure Garcin, "Grandville: Visionnaire, surréaliste, expressioniste," *Gazette des Beaux-Arts* 34 (December 1948): 435–48, 466–70; Jean Adhémar and Romi, "Grandville le maudit," *Bizarre,* no. 2 (1953): 11–16.

3. Walter Benjamin, "Grandville or the World Exhibitions," in *Charles Baudelaire: A Lyric Poet in the Era of High Capitalism,* trans. Harry Zohn (London: NLB, 1973), 164–66. For commentaries on Benjamin's interpretation of Grandville, see Susan Buck-Morss, *The Dialectics of Seeing: Walter Benjamin and the Arcades Project* (Cambridge: MIT Press, 1989), 149–58; Richard Faber, "Paris, das Rom des XIX Jahrhunderts: Eine Metacollage," in *Antike und Moderne: Zu Walter Benjamins "Passagen,"* ed. Norbert W. Bolz and Richard Faber (Würzburg: Königshausen und Neumann, 1986), 53–96; Michele Hannoosh, *Baudelaire and Caricature: From the Comic to an Art of Modernity* (University Park: Pennsylvania State University Press, 1992), 158–72; and "The Allegorical Artist and the Crises of History: Benjamin, Grandville, Baudelaire," *Word & Image* 10 (January–March 1994): 38–54; Marlene Stoessel, "Dans le demi-jour: Le même et le semblable, Deux contes en images de Grandville," in *Walter Benjamin et Paris,* ed. Heinz Wismann (Paris: Les Editions du Cerf, 1986), 433–50.

4. Annie Renonciat, *La Vie et l'oeuvre de J. J. Grandville* (Paris: ACR Edition Internationale, 1985); Musée des Beaux-Arts, Nancy, *Grandville: Dessins originaux* (Nancy: Ville de Nancy, 1986); Staatliche Kunsthalle, Karlsruhe, *J. J. Grandville: Karikatur und Zeichnung; Ein Visionär der französischen Romantik* (Karlsruhe: Staatliche Kunsthalle, 2000). The second of these publications is the reference catalog for an exhibition of Grandville drawings organized by the present author for the Nancy Musée des Beaux-Arts. The exhibition took place first in Nancy (November 17, 1986 to March 2, 1987) and then at the Musée Carnavalet in Paris (October 13, 1987 to January 3, 1988). A point of departure for the catalog was the author's unpublished doctoral dissertation, "The Drawings of J. J. Grandville until 1830: The Development of His Style during His Formative Years" (Stanford University, 1981). The third publication is the catalog for an exhibition held in Karlsruhe at the Staatliche Kunsthalle (September 23 to November 26, 2000) and in Hanover at the Wilhelm-Busch-Museum—Deutsches Museum für Karikatur und kritische Grafik (December 15, 2000 to February 18, 2001) that was based in large part on the Nancy exhibition and catalog. The present investigation builds upon both the author's dissertation and the Nancy catalog. In many ways, it is a sequel to the latter, which is frequently cited.

Abbreviations

Bechtel	Bechtel, Edwin De Turck. *Freedom of the Press and L'Association mensuelle: Philipon versus Louis-Philippe.* New York: Grolier Club, 1952.
Bénézit	Bénézit, Emmanuel. *Dictionnaire critique et documentaire des peintres, sculpteurs dessinateurs et graveurs.* New ed. 10 vols. Paris: Librairie Gründ, 1976.
Blanc	Blanc, Charles. *Les Artistes de mon temps.* Paris: Firmin-Didot, 1876.
Cahiers	*Cahiers de l'Institut d'histoire de la presse et de l'opinion,* no. 7. Tours: Université de Tours, 1983.
Charton	Charton, Édouard. "I.-I. Grandville." *L'Illustration,* March 27, 1847, 49–50.
Chu and Weisberg	Chu, Petra ten-Doesschate, and Gabriel P. Weisberg, eds. *The Popularization of Images: Visual Culture under the July Monarchy.* Princeton: Princeton University Press, 1994.
Clogenson	Clogenson, S. "J.-J. Granville [*sic*]." *L'Athenaeum français,* nos. 11 and 12 (March 12 and 19, 1853): 250–52, 273–75.
Cuno	Cuno, James. "Charles Philipon and La Maison Aubert: The Business, Politics, and Public of Caricature in Paris, 1820–1840." Ph.D. diss., Harvard Univeresity, 1985.
Delteil	Delteil, Loÿs. *Le Peintre-graveur illustré.* 32 vols. Paris: Chez l'auteur, 1906–30.
Dumas	Dumas, Alexandre. *Mes mémoires.* Annotated by Pierre Josserand. 5 vols. Paris: Gallimard, 1954–68.
Hillairet	Hillairet, Jacques. *Dictionnaire historique des rues de Paris.* 9th ed. 2 vols. Paris: Les Éditions de Minuit, 1985.
Missouri	University of Missouri. *The Art of the July Monarchy: France 1830 to 1848.* Columbia: University of Missouri Press, 1990.
Nadar	Nadar [Gaspard Félix Tournachon]. *Quand j'étais photographe.* Paris: E. Flammarion, 1900.
Nancy	Nancy, Musée des Beaux-Arts. *Grandville: Dessins originaux.* Nancy: Ville de Nancy, 1986.
Nollet	Nollet (Fabert), Jules. *Eloge historique de J. J. Grandville.* Antwerp: Max Kornicker, 1853.
Renonciat	Renonciat, Annie. *La Vie et l'oeuvre de J. J. Grandville.* Paris: ACR Édition Internationale, 1985.
Thureau-Dangin	Thureau-Dangin, Paul. *Histoire de la Monarchie de Juillet.* 5th ed. 7 vols. Paris: E. Plon, Nourrit, 1911–14.
Vicaire	Vicaire, Georges. *Manuel de l'amateur de livres du XIXe siècle, 1801–1893.* 8 vols. Paris: A. Rouquette, 1894–1920.

The Diary of J. J. Grandville and the Missouri Album

I

Biography of J. J. Grandville

Biography

1803–25: Early Years in Nancy

Jean Ignace Isidore Gerard Grandville (frontispiece) was born into a modest bourgeois household at 334, rue Callot (today 6, rue de la Monnaie) in the Lorrain capital of Nancy on the 28th of Fructidor in the year XI (September 15, 1803).[1] His parents were Jean Baptiste Mathias Gerard Grandville (1767–1854) and Catherine Emélie Viot (1769–1837). The fourth of six children, he had two surviving older brothers, Nicolas *Ferdinand* (1795–1826) and Alexandre *Hippolyte* (1796–1867), and two younger sisters, Jeanne Françoise *Eulalie* (1804–1836) and *Louise* Charlotte (1806–12). His grieving mother called him Adolphe in memory of a third brother, Joseph Antoine *Adolphe,* born in 1798 who had died only two months earlier at five years of age. He would be referred to as Adolphe within his family during his entire life. The household in the rue Callot also included Grandville's long-lived paternal grandmother, Marie-Anne Charlotte Charpentier, who died in 1830 at the age of 102.

He inherited a family artistic tradition. Under the name of Grandville, his paternal grandparents had been actors at the court theater of Stanislas Leszczyński (1677–1766), deposed king of Poland, father-in-law of Louis XV, and last duke of Lorraine. Both their sons became miniature painters. In order to distinguish himself from his elder brother, Eugène, Grandville's father appended his parent's stage name to the inherited one of Gerard. The two miniature painters had an adopted brother who followed in their parents' footsteps and pursued a brilliant acting career under the name of Fleury at that most prestigious of French theaters, the Comédie-Française in Paris. François Bruno Viot, the brother of Grandville's mother, also appears to have had artistic aspirations, judging from his drawings in the Nancy Bibliothèque municipale (Municipal Library).

In addition to the example set by members of his immediate family, Grandville fell heir to the rich artistic heritage of Nancy itself. The house in the rue Callot where he was born and raised, and in which his father had his studio, was located in the very heart of the provincial capital's picturesque old town. At every turn, he would have encountered imposing medieval monuments such as the late Gothic ducal palace and the massive Porte de la Craffe, sculpted Renaissance doorways, and noble townhouses like the Hôtel des Loups and the Hôtel d'Haussonville. Most impressive of all would have been the nearby Place Stanislas (fig. 1), a superb example of eighteenth-century town planning and one of the most sumptuously decorated Places Royales in all of France. Constructed by the former king of Poland in honor of his son-in-law, the classically symmetrical square boasts finely proportioned civic buildings, a triumphal arch, sculpted fountains, and extensive gilded grills, masterpieces of rococo ironwork produced by the exceptionally talented local locksmith, Jean Lamour. Growing up in the rue Callot, Grandville would also have had the daily reminder of other illustrious artists born in Nancy or its immediate environs. In addition to Jacques Callot, during the sixteenth and seventeenth centuries the proud ducal city nurtured the talents of Jacques Bellange, Israel Sylvestre, Georges de la Tour, and Claude Lorrain.

Grandville's predisposition for the arts announced itself at an early age when he demonstrated a natural inclination for drawing that was fostered by his father. He, however, was not an overly attentive

Fig. 1. Charles Fichot, *Nancy (Meurthe). Place Stanislas-Préfecture,* circa 1850, lithograph. Nancy, Bibliothèque municipale.

student when it came to schoolwork. During his early adolescence in high school, his unruly and lively imagination led him to spend more time sketching than working on required assignments. Private tutoring proved fruitless. Finally, toward the age of fifteen, his parents gave in to their son's wishes and Grandville left high school for his father's studio.

In one year the eager pupil learned practically everything his father could teach him. However, the latter's attempt to make his son into a miniaturist like himself met with less success, for even though he quickly captured the essential features of his clients, the young artist tended to caricature rather than flatter them. His customers were rarely satisfied with the results, and his talents were seldom in demand. Grandville whiled away his ample spare time by drawing sensitive portraits of family members, including the cat, or caricaturing those whom he found ridiculous in nature or grotesque in appearance. Although Grandville's irrepressible penchant for visual satire did not serve him well as an apprentice miniaturist in Nancy, it was to make his fortune in Paris. His father's instructions, however, were not completely for naught. Being trained to work on a small scale would later stand him in good stead as a lithographer and illustrator.

Toward 1825, the Nancy-born Parisian miniaturist, André-Léon Larue, known as Mansion (1785–ca. 1834), made a trip to his native city. During his stay, he visited the studio of his fellow miniaturist and childhood friend, Mr. Gerard Grandville. Impressed with the talent of his colleague's youngest son, Mansion invited him to join his Paris atelier. The idea, once implanted in the youth's mind, proved irresistible. After overcoming his father's initial opposition, he made his way to the French capital like many young, ambitious provincials before him.

1825–1830: Arrival in Paris, Lithographic Albums, and Professional Recognition

Grandville arrived in Paris in 1825, taking in the sights during his first few days. It would have been easy for him to become lost in a city of approximately 890,000.[2] But his father had taken the precaution of arranging contacts. The most immediately useful was Frédéric Leméthеyer (fig. 2), the son-in-law of his brother, Eugène Gerard. Some years older, he and his wife, Grandville's cousin, treated the young arrival like an adopted son. It was probably in order to be close to these relatives, who lived in the recently created rue de la Boule-Rouge, that Grandville rented a room at the Hôtel Saint-Phar on the nearby boulevard Poissonière for the next two years. In addition to making the young provincial feel at home, Leméthеyer, as the general stage manager of a major cultural institution, the Théâtre Royal de l'Opéra-Comique, and future director of the Théâtre Royal de l'Odéon, was in a unique position to introduce his cousin to the Parisian art world (for a more detailed account of Leméthеyer's theatrical career, see cat. no. 3 [recto]). Through him Grandville met such reigning luminaries of the Parisian stage as Talma and Mlle Mars. Thanks to Leméthеyer's policy of giving artists free admission to the theater, he also was able to make the acquaintance of some of the better-known artistic figures of the day, such as the sculptor David d'Angers (1788–1856), who would later model a portrait medallion of Grandville, and the painters Léon Cogniet (1794–1880), Paul Delaroche (1797–1856), Hippolyte Lecomte (1781–1857), Henri Jean Picou (1784–1865), and Horace Vernet (1789–1863). It was probably due to this privileged access during his initial years in Paris, in addition to being raised in a household that included an actress grandmother, that Grandville continued to harbor an interest in the theater for the rest of his life, as references in his diary attest (cat. nos. 3, 6, 15, 23, 52).

Grandville had difficulty establishing himself as a professional artist. Immediately after his arrival in Paris, he entered the studio of Mansion. While there, he brought to fruition an idea he had been thinking about for some time, the creation of an innovative set of playing cards representing different social types. To his dismay, Mansion corrected his designs in order to sign them. The resultant publication, *La Sibylle des salons* (The sibyl of the parlors; Engelmann, 1827), nonetheless gained for Grandville the knowledge that he had marketable artistic ability (fig. 3).[3] Similarly disappointing was a short apprenticeship at around the same time in the studio of the lithographer and history painter, Hippolyte Lecomte, whom he had met at the Opéra-Comique through the well-intentioned Leméthеyer, who thought his cousin's drawing skills could be better put to use on something other than miniatures. But Grandville quickly concluded that his artistic future did not lie in academic painting.[4] His association with Lecomte nevertheless did result in a collaborative publication, *Costumes de théâtre* (Theater costumes; Engelmann, 1826) in which Grandville apparently translated into lithographs Lecomte's drawings of costumes from two popular operas of the day, Meyerbeer's *Il Crociato in Egitto* (The Crusader in Egypt) and Boieldieu's *La Dame blanche* (The White Lady) (fig. 4). Unfortunately, the publication was not the financial success he had hoped it would be. Equally disappointing was the mildly satirical twelve-plate suite of *Les Dimanches d'un bourgeois de Paris, ou les tribulations de la petite propriété* (The Sundays of a Parisian bourgeois, or the tribulations of small ownership; Langlumé, 1826) (fig. 5), which the genial and reasonably successful genre painter Pierre Duval Le Camus (1790–1854; fig. 6) commissioned him to produce (Duval Le Camus had won a second-class medal at the Salon of 1819 and would receive a first-class medal in 1827). The older artist even lent him his studio so that his young protégé would not have to work in the dark confines of his room at the Hôtel Saint-Phar (for Grandville's later association with Duval Le Camus, see cat. no. 47). Frustrated and discouraged, Grandville more than once tearfully expressed his disgust with Paris and wanted to return to Nancy. Each time, however, Leméthеyer persuaded him to stay.

Fig. 2. Bordes, *Frédéric Le Metheyer,* circa 1828, lithograph. Paris, Bibliothèque nationale de France.

Fig. 3. ***Militaire*** **(Military man) from** ***La Sibylle des salons,*** **2nd ed., 1848, lithograph. Paris, Bibliothèque nationale de France.**

Despite these setbacks, Grandville ultimately did find success in the flourishing lithographic print trade. Invented in Munich by Aloys Senefelder in 1796, lithography was first employed for publishing musical scores. However, its potential for reproducing images was soon realized, and by 1816 three lithographic presses were set up in Paris for that purpose. The ease of drawing directly upon the lithographic stone and the numerous prints that could be quickly pulled from it made the new process popular with artists and publishers alike. Lithographic presses proliferated accordingly during the following decade.[5] Being the versatile medium that it was, lithography was used for printing a variety of items besides playing cards and reproductions of theater costumes. It was particularly favored, for

Fig. 4. ***Madame Boulanger as Jenny in La Dame blanche*** **from** ***Costumes de théâtre,*** **1826, lithograph. Nancy, Bibliothèque municipale.**

example, as a vehicle for caricatures. However, perhaps the most prevalent use of lithography during the 1820s was the production of albums. Usually consisting of a dozen or so prints around a common theme, albums were especially popular as *étrennes,* or gifts traditionally exchanged on New Year's Day. Publishers often found themselves in the position of turning to untried talent in order to meet the demand. Thus, many aspiring young artists, often ambitious provincials eager to prove themselves and

Fig. 5. ***1.ère Tribulation: 7 heures du matin, la toilette*** **(1st Tribulation: 7 o'clock in the morning, the grooming) from** ***Les Dimanches d'un bourgeois de Paris,*** **1826, lithograph. Nancy, Bibliothèque municipale.**

impatient to earn money, were tempted to abandon the lengthy regime of academic training for lithography and the more immediately lucrative album trade. The phenomenon became so widespread that it entered into the popular imagery of the day as seen in figure 7 where a young provincial artist, having turned his canvas around on his easel and his back to the plaster cast of an antique bust, leans over a lithographic stone to work on his first album. It could easily represent Grandville himself at this time.

With the exception of several independent prints and covers for sheet music, Grandville concentrated almost exclusively on albums between 1827 and 1830. *Chaque âge a ses plaisirs* (Each age has its pleasures; Gihaut, 1827), a suite of ten mildly satirical prints that illustrated changing interests with

Fig. 6. Leon Noel, *Pierre Duval Le Camus,* 1843, lithograph. Paris, Bibliothèque nationale de France.

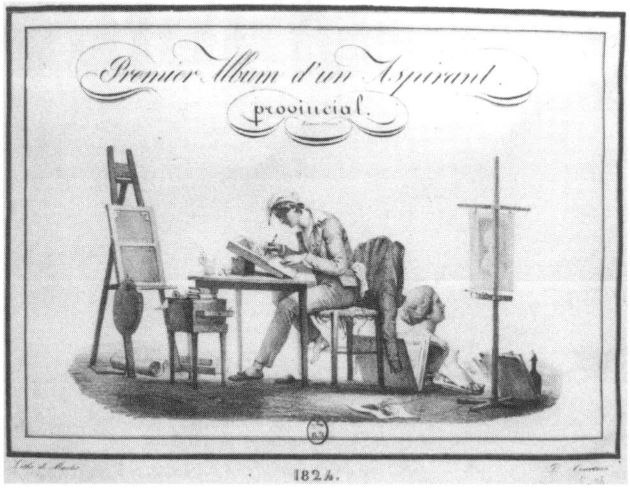

Fig. 7. D. Courtois, *Premier Album d'un Aspirant provincial* (First album of a provincial hopeful), 1824, lithograph. Paris, Bibliothèque nationale de France.

the passage of time—here, the fleshly pleasures of middle age (fig. 8)—first brought Grandville to the attention of editors. But it was *Les Métamorphoses du jour* (Contemporary metamorphoses; Bulla, 1828–29) that first gained him widespread fame. Employing the age-old human/animal analogy, he attached onto human bodies the heads of animals associated with different character traits, for example, a pig for gluttony, a peacock for pride, a sheep for docility, and so on. He then arranged them into situation comedy tableaux reminiscent of vaudeville productions or the light operas staged at the Opéra-Comique. For instance, a ferociously tempered tigress of a wife roars at her sheepish husband who has been caught dallying with the whimpering whippet of a maid (fig. 9). Although most of the metamorphoses dealt with universal human foibles, several were of a political nature and at least one was censored, not being published until after the Revolution of 1830: the anticlerical *Famille de scarabées* (Family of beetles), which likens a procession of ecclesiastics in their elaborate liturgical robes to a parade of brilliantly colored beetles (fig. 10). More than likely *Les Métamorphoses du jour* was

Fig. 8. *Les Jouissances de l'âge mûr* (The pleasures of middle age), plate 2 of *Chaque âge a ses plaisirs,* 1827, lithograph. Paris, Bibliothèque nationale de France.

Fig. 9. ***Ah! elle te plait* [*sic*], *monstre. . . .eh bien je la chasse* (Oh! you like her, monster. . . . well then, I'll send her away), number 18 of *Les Métamorphoses du jour,* 1829, lithograph. Paris, Bibliothèque nationale de France.**

conceived of as an album containing the usual dozen or so plates. That the series eventually included seventy-three is a testament to its immense popularity.

Les Métamorphoses du jour occupies a pivotal point in Grandville's career. In addition to bringing him fame, and probably a certain amount of fortune, the publication incorporated many of those qualities that were to characterize the rest of his oeuvre. His proclivity for satire, already apparent during his youth in Nancy, found a natural outlet in the traditional human/animal analogy that had been used for moralizing commentary since the time of Aesop. Building upon his initial success, Grandville was to use the human/animal analogy over and over again, most notably during his career as a book illustrator, and each time to the applause of his public. This analogy also appealed to Grandville's pronounced predilection for fantasy. Appending animal heads onto human bodies constituted only the first of many subsequent and considerably more fanciful combinations such as those found in his most original work, *Un autre monde* (Another world) of 1843–44. That several plates of *Les Métamorphoses* possessed political overtones, and that one was censored, anticipated his experience as an opposition political caricaturist between 1830 and 1835.

Grandville's use of the human/animal analogy in *Les Métamorphoses du jour* marks the beginning of an obsession with analogies that were popular during the Romantic period thanks to the influence

Fig. 10. *Famille de scarabées* (Family of beetles) from *Les Métamorphoses du jour,* 1830, lithograph. Nancy, Bibliothèque municipale.

of the late eighteenth-century Swiss philosopher and clergyman, Johann Caspar Lavater (1741–1801). Like Lavater's *Essays on Physiognomy* (first published in German between 1775 and 1778), the human/animal analogy implies that there exists a direct correlation between a person's external appearance and inner moral character. Although the concept was scarcely new (e.g., the fourth-century BCE treatise, *Physiognomonica,* by pseudo-Aristotle whom he liberally quoted), Lavater greatly elaborated on it by couching it in both scientific and religious terms. The combination of these two seemingly opposite modes of perception in a single analytic system captivated the nascent Romantic imagination. When the *Essays* were translated into French and English during the 1780s, they quickly became a European best seller and spawned a vogue for "physiologies," or pseudoscientific analyses of individuals through any and all outward manifestations: anatomical features, apparel, mannerisms, and chosen environment. One of the more prolific authors of these early psychoanalytic studies was Honoré de Balzac (1799–1850), Grandville's future colleague on the staffs of the satirical journals *La Silhouette* and *La Caricature.* Lavater's physiognomic theories also had a profound impact on caricaturists, particularly Honoré Daumier (1808–79), another colleague on the same two journals. Grandville naturally followed suit. Lithographic suites from the 1830s, certain of which may have been initially conceived as albums, include *Carte vivante du restaurateur* (The living restaurant menu; Aubert, 1832) where people resemble the food they eat, such as the two pickle-headed men and the brooding hen of a woman in *Cornichon pour deux Volaille froide* (Pickles for two/Cold fowl; fig. 11), and *Les Breuvages de l'homme* (Human beverages; Neuhaus, 1834) which is a sociological study of the relationship between various liquid refreshments and those who consume them, such as freely provided water being drunk by penniless art students (fig. 12). His culminating effort in the genre is *Types modernes, observations*

Fig. 11. ***Cornichon pour deux Volaille froide*** **(Pickles for two/Cold fowl), plate 8 of** ***Carte vivante du restaurateur,*** **1832, lithograph. Paris, Bibliothèque nationale de France.**

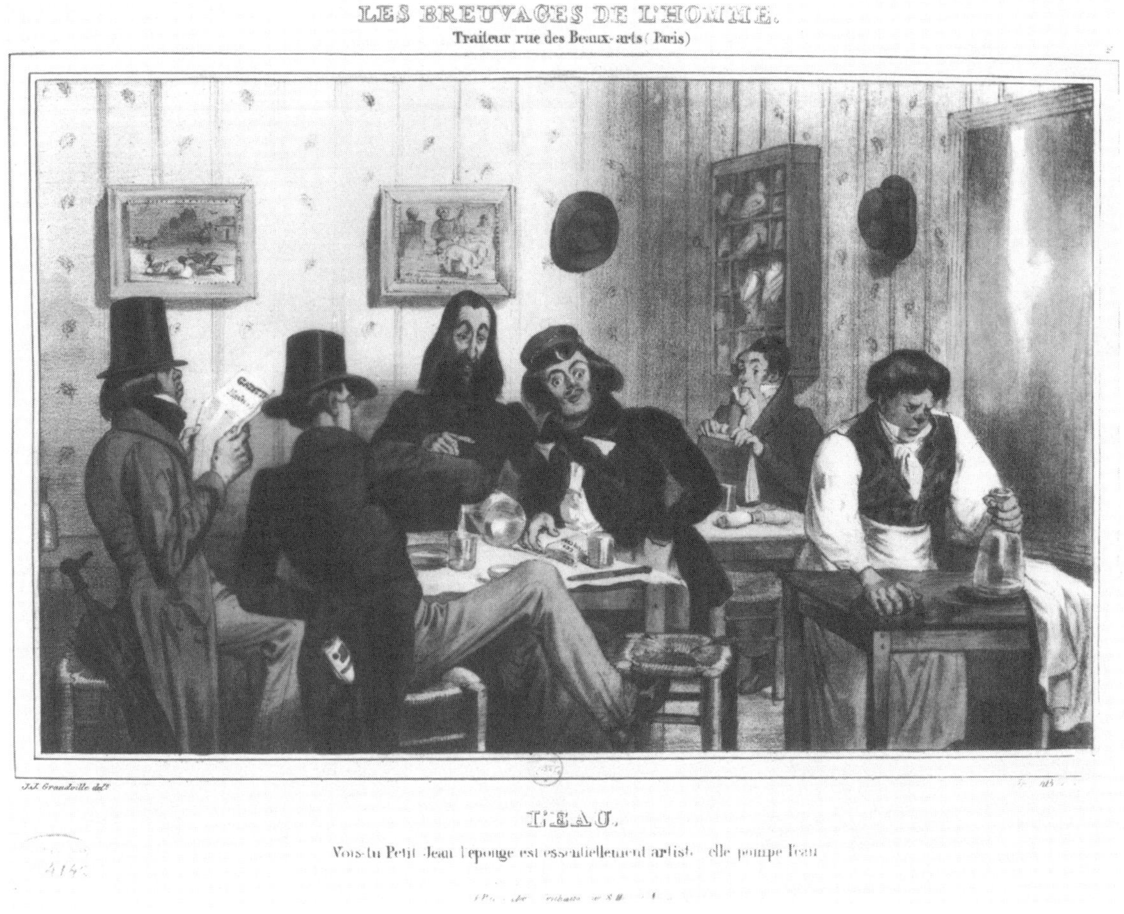

Fig. 12. ***L'eau*** **(Water), plate 2 of** ***Les Breuvages de l'homme,*** **1834, lithograph. Nancy, Bibliothèque municipale.**

critiques, le dedans de l'homme expliqué par le dehors (Modern types, critical observations, the inside of humanity explained by the outside; Neuhaus, 1835) in which he directly pays homage to Lavater and classifies people not only by their physiognomies, but also according to their pets, the manner in which they take snuff, and especially their sartorial accoutrements (cat. no. 7; figs. 50 and 51).[6]

Despite these and other attempted albums, Grandville never replicated the success of *Les Métamorphoses du jour.* In fact, judging from the small or uneven number of their plates, each of his immediately succeeding album projects appears to have been cut short. *Galerie mythologique* (Mythological gallery; Bulla, 1830) a contemporary satire of classical mythology (fig. 13), comprised six plates, while *Principes de grammaire* (Principles of grammar; Senefelder, 1830), which illustrated the different connotations of adjectives when preceding or following a noun, such as *Le repas maigre Le maigre repas* (The light meal, The meager meal; fig. 14), contained only two. The apparent unpopularity of *Voyage pour l'éternité* (Voyage for eternity; Bulla and Aubert, 1830), an updated version of the medieval "dance of Death" in the spirit of Thomas Rowlandson's *The English Dance of Death* from 1815–16, resulted in its termination at nine plates (fig. 15). Drawings from 1829 and 1830 at the Nancy Musée des Beaux-Arts (Museum of Fine Arts) attest to still other album projects that never saw even

Fig. 13. ***Jugement de Paris*** **(Judgment of Paris), plate 6 of *Galerie mythologique,* 1830, lithograph. Nancy, Bibliothèque municipale.**

Fig. 14. ***Le Repas maigre. Le Maigre repas.*** **(The light meal, The meager meal) from *Principes de grammaire,* 1830, lithograph. Nancy, Bibliothèque municipale.**

Fig. 15. ***Vais-je bien?—Vous avancez horriblement.*** **(Am I doing well?—You are running terribly fast.), number 2 of** ***Voyage pour l'éternité,*** **1830, lithograph. Paris, Bibliothèque municipale.**

partial publication (Nancy, cat. nos. 127–44, 148–56). Grandville's next moment of artistic glory would occur only after the Revolution of 1830.

The Latin Quarter and Early Friendships

Grandville's career as a creator of lithographic albums nevertheless established him in the artistic profession and gained him a modest income, which encouraged him to remain in Paris. In 1827, he finally could afford to quit the dark confines of his room in the Hôtel Saint-Phar and rent a better lit, spacious sixth-floor garret at 10, rue des Petits-Augustins (present-day rue Bonaparte). Located across the street from the École des Beaux-Arts (School of Fine Arts) in the colorful Latin Quarter, his new accommodations were often visited by other members of the bohemian set who were struggling to make a name for themselves, such as Alexandre Dumas (1802–70) who had arrived in Paris only three years before Grandville (see cat. no. 21 for Dumas's description of Grandville and his attic abode). As might be expected, a number of young artists lived in the neighborhood, many of whom were his friends. For instance, Paul Delaroche, who was just starting his celebrated career as a history painter and whom Grandville knew through Lemétheyer, lived in an adjoining house on the rue des Marais-Saint-Germain (present-day 17, 19 rue Visconti) with the result that the two saw each other quite frequently at this time. The painter Eugène Lami (1800–1890) also lived at the same address. Other acquaintances in the general vicinity included a future pioneer of iron and glass architecture, Hector Horeau (1801–72), the painter and lithographer Antoine Drulin (1802–69), the miniaturist Pannetier, and the painter of interiors Renou. And then there were some of Grandville's closest friends and future fellow caricaturists, an exceptional group of talented individuals that included Édouard Charton, Gabriel Falampin, Jacques Guiaud, Jules Taschereau, Eugène Forest, and Charles Philipon.

Like most of Grandville's friends, and like Grandville himself, Édouard Charton (1807–90) was a provincial who succeeded in pursuing a professional career in Paris: first as a lawyer, then a publisher, and finally as a politician (fig. 16). Born in Sens, he arrived in the capital in 1824 and became a lawyer in 1827. In 1831 he temporarily fell under the spell of the Saint-Simonians and their utopian doctrines (see cat. no. 8). A man of considerable intellect and wide-ranging interests, Charton was instrumental

Fig. 16. Achille Devéria, *Édouard Charton,* 1848, lithograph. Paris, Bibliothèque nationale de France.

in founding two noted newspapers aimed at educating the literate middle-class public: the *Magasin pittoresque* and *L'Illustration.* Published between 1833 and 1857, the *Magasin pittoresque* was a weekly that covered an inspired combination of artistic, historic, and scientific topics, rather like an early version of *Smithsonian Magazine* and *Scientific American* rolled into one. Charton had sixty-seven of Grandville's drawings reproduced within its pages, including some of the most innovative, such as the famous dream metamorphoses (see figs. 34 and 35 near the end of this chapter); he was also the probable author of a series of important articles on Grandville that appeared in the paper after the artist's death.[7] The aptly named *L'Illustration,* an illustrated weekly dealing with contemporary issues modeled on the *Illustrated London News,* enjoyed a long, successful existence from 1843 until 1945. In addition to publishing seventeen of Grandville's drawings, it advertised his illustrated books. Charton wrote the extensive necrological notice on Grandville that appeared in the paper on March 27, 1847. A steadfast friend, he was among those who visited Grandville during his fatal illness. Shortly after Grandville's death, Charton entered into politics where he stalwartly defended the republican cause. In the aftermath of the Revolution of 1848, he was the elected representative from Yonne at the National Constituent Assembly, which drew up the constitution for the newly proclaimed and short-lived

Second Republic, during which he was a member of the Council of State (fig. 16 portrays Charton one year after Grandville's death, or at the outset of his political career). Having protested against Louis-Napoléon's 1851 coup d'état, Charton was repeatedly unsuccessful in continuing his political career during Louis-Napoléon's reign as Napoléon III. However, with the fall of the Second Empire and the proclamation of the Third Republic on September 4, 1870, Charton was named prefect of Seine-et-Oise, the department comprising Paris and its environs. He later was elected to the Third Republic's National Assembly and then to its senate.

It was in order to be close to Jean Gabriel Falampin, a law student at the time who lived in the rue des Petits-Augustins, that Grandville moved there. His proximity proved to be crucial when Grandville had a close brush with vindictive police in 1831 (see cat. no. 16). Falampin adopted Grandville's coterie of artistic friends as his own, and it was probably through Grandville that he made the acquaintance of Charton. He ultimately became a lawyer and one of the managers of *L'Illustration.* Documentary evidence suggests that he also served as the Grandville family attorney. When in 1853 the artist's widow decided to auction a large portion of her late husband's drawings, Falampin compiled the sale catalog.[8]

Originally from Chambéry, Jacques Guiaud (1811–76) lived just across the Seine at 19, rue de la Monnaie (fig. 17). He shared with Grandville artistic aspirations and became a moderately successful landscape and genre painter. He regularly participated in official Salon exhibitions between 1831 and 1876, receiving medals in 1843 and 1846. A student of Louis Étienne Watelet (1780–1866) and Léon Cogniet, he may have made the acquaintance of Grandville through the latter who, it may be recalled, frequented the Opéra-Comique. Guiaud was also a lithographer.[9] It was in this capacity that at the age

Fig. 17. *Jacques Guiaud,* page 3 from the Carnavalet Album, circa 1830–40, watercolor. Paris, Musée Carnavalet.

of nineteen he collaborated with his older, more experienced friend on caricatures ridiculing the deposed king, Charles X, shortly after the Revolution of 1830. Grandville would give to his young colleague the sketchbook in which he had noted down the ideas for these caricatures. Additional testimony to the particularly close relationship between the two artists may be found in a souvenir album of drawings from throughout Grandville's career that Guiaud compiled and that is today in the collection of the Musée Carnavalet along with the sketchbook.[10] Like Charton, Guiaud faithfully visited the artist's bedside during his fatal illness. He also acted as the liaison between the sculptor Antoine-Laurent Dantan (1798–1878) and the Nancy municipal council when the latter voted, shortly after the artist's death, to place a marble bust of Grandville in the Nancy museum, a commission apparently aborted by the Revolution of 1848 (see cat. no. 32 and Nancy, 415–16); a copy of the plaster model for the bust is reproduced in figure 92. Frequent references are made to Guiaud in diary excerpts from 1830 and 1833 (cat. nos. 2, 5, 20, 29, 30, 32, 33).

Jules-Antoine Taschereau (1801–74) was a native of Tours who arrived in Paris in order to study law, only to pursue, much like Charton, a multifaceted career as author, journalist, publisher, administrator, and politician (fig. 18). He first made a name for himself as the author of erudite publications, such as the *Histoire de la vie et des ouvrages de Molière* (History of the life and works of Molière; Ponthieu, 1825) and the *Histoire de la vie et des ouvrages de P. Corneille* (History of the life and works of P. Corneille; A. Mesnier, 1829). Along with his close friend, the firebrand-liberal Armand Carrel (1800–1836), in 1829 he became an original member on the staff of the famous opposition newspaper, *Le National,* which was instrumental in fomenting the Revolution of 1830. Initially a supporter of the July Monarchy, Taschereau was named secretary general of the prefecture of the Seine. But after approximately one year, he converted to the opposition and quit his administrative post. In 1833, he founded the *Revue rétrospective,* which published original historical and literary documents. Elected to the Chamber of Deputies in 1837, he served as an opposition deputy until 1842. He then returned to journalism, contributing to various newspapers, notably Charton's *L'Illustration.* Like Charton, he was elected to the National Constituent Assembly in the aftermath of the Revolution of 1848; his portrait in figure 18, like Charton's in figure 16, dates from this period. However, unlike Charton, he was a strong supporter of Louis-Napoléon and rose to prominence during the Second Empire. In 1852 he started to serve in several administrative posts at the Bibliothèque Impériale (Imperial Library; today the Bibliothèque nationale de France, or National Library of France) and finally became its director in 1858. In 1855 he began the publication of the library's general catalog. Taschereau was a key figure for Grandville's career as a book illustrator. In 1824, together with Henri Fournier (1800–1888), his close friend and compatriot from Tours, he founded a press that published more of Grandville's illustrated books than any other. Along with their mutual interest in book publication, Grandville and Taschereau would have shared an antipathy for the regime of Louis-Philippe. The close relationship between the two men is attested to by the frequent mention of Taschereau in Grandville's correspondence with his family.

It was probably due in part to their similar backgrounds that Eugène-Hippolyte Forest (1808–?) became Grandville's most important collaborator during his career as a political caricaturist (cat. no. 21; figs. 71, 72, 74, and 76). Born in Strasbourg, Forest, like Grandville, was from the eastern part of France. After arriving in Paris, Forest, again like Grandville and other aspiring young provincial artists, first studied for a short period of time with a painter, in this case the young, emerging Romantic Camille Roqueplan (1803–55), but soon turned to producing prints for the flourishing lithographic trade. His earliest lithographs, dating from 1825, depicted military costumes in a not altogether successful imitation of the nostalgic and enormously popular evocations of lost imperial glory produced by Nicolas-Toussaint Charlet (1792–1845). By 1826 he had taken rooms in the rue des Petits-Augustins, and by

Fig. 18. Alfred Lemoine, *Julès Taschereau,* 1848, lithograph. Paris, Bibliothèque nationale de France.

1829 he had become affiliated with Philipon, producing three caricatures for *La Silhouette,* the satirical journal that directly anticipated *La Caricature.*[11] The earliest artistic collaboration between Grandville and Forest appears to have been a series of pen lithographs done toward 1830 of the mime actor, Alexandre Vattemare (cat. no. 4 [recto]). However, it was after they had worked together on the two plates of *Invocation au Pair éternel* (Invocation to the eternal peer) for the August 18, 1831, issue of *La Caricature* that Grandville began to depend regularly upon Forest for transferring to the lithographic stone his meticulously executed preliminary drawings. Forest, for example, assisted in the creation of every plate Grandville produced for the third volume of *La Caricature,* from November 1831 through April 1832. In addition to their ongoing work for *La Caricature,* Forest and Grandville in 1832 collaborated on the September lithograph for the *Association mensuelle, Sur mon honneur et sur ma conscience [Les Libertés en cour d'Assises]* (On my honor and on my conscience [Liberty on trial in the court of assizes]) and on two lithographic suites published by Aubert, *Petite Macédoine d'Aubert* (Aubert's little macédoine) and *Singeries morales, politiques, etc.* (Moral, political, etc. monkeyshines; for a more detailed discussion of this latter, see cat. no. 10 [recto]). When in 1832 Grandville started to turn his attention to wood engravings and book illustration, so did Forest. Although they did not collaborate on the same prints, they occasionally worked on the same publications. For instance, in 1833 both were involved with the *Journal des enfans* (Children's journal) and the *Musée des familles* (Museum for families) (see cat. no. 21). And in 1840 they both provided illustrations for A. de Savigny's *Historiettes et images* (Short stories and images) published by Aubert. Toward the latter part of his career, Forest concentrated his efforts on painting, participating in Salon exhibitions between 1847 and 1866. Grandville repeatedly refers to Forest in his 1832 and 1833 diaries (cat. nos. 9, 16, 21, 25, 29, and 32).

1830–1835: Philipon, the Revolution of 1830, Political Caricature, and Marriage

Of all of Grandville's friends around 1827, by far the most important for his immediate future was Claude Guillaume Charles Philipon (1800–1862) (fig. 19) who between 1830 and 1835 would engage him in a series of caricatural publications: *La Silhouette, La Caricature,* the *Association mensuelle,* and *Le Charivari.* Philipon not only provided him with steady employment during those years, he also made him into France's most celebrated political caricaturist: Grandville was to become one of the main instruments in Philipon's relentless campaign against the July Monarchy of Louis-Philippe, who emerged from the debris of the Revolution of 1830 as France's new king.

Before his notoriety as a leading opponent of the July Monarchy (so named because of its birth during the aftermath of the Revolution of 1830, which took place in July), Philipon was just another young provincial artist whose early career, like those of his future caricatural colleagues, Forest and Grandville, followed a path similar to that illustrated in figure 7. The son of a prosperous merchant of wallpaper, Philipon studied drawing in his native Lyon. In 1819, he was sent to Paris in order to continue his artistic education in the most prestigious of academic studios, that of Baron Gros (1771–1835), student and successor of the famous formulator of French neoclassic painting, Jacques Louis David (1748–1825). He counted among his fellow students two others who would also become famous as purveyors of popular lithographic prints, Charlet and Henry Monnier (1805–77). It has been speculated that Philipon spent his time in Gros's studio honing his drawing skills, not learning how to paint. For when he retuned to Lyon in 1821, his duties in the family business included the designing and drawing of wallpaper as well as bookkeeping. Such a monotonously placid middle-class existence did

Fig. 19. Achille Devéria, *Charles Philipon,* circa 1831, lithograph. Paris, Bibliothèque nationale de France.

not, however, appeal to Philipon. In 1823, he escaped back to Paris, where he eventually took up residence in the neighborhood of the same rue des Petits-Augustins that Grandville would move to four years later.[12] With little money in his pocket, but possessing a certain amount of talent for drawing, he, like so many other transplanted and bereft young provincial artists, turned to lithography. Philipon specialized in the production of mildly suggestive erotic prints for which there was a ready market during the last years of the Restoration. After six years as a freelance lithographer, he entered into two business ventures involved with the publication of caricatures. On December 5, 1829, he became a founder and principal shareholder of the short-lived caricatural journal, *La Silhouette,* which appeared between January 1830 and January 1831. The paper counted among its main artistic contributors Grandville, Daumier, and Charles-Joseph Traviès (1804–59). Ten days later on December 15, Philipon, together with his half-sister, Marie-Françoise-Madeleine Aubert, and her husband, Gabriel Aubert, who had arrived in Paris only the day before, founded what was to become a very influential print shop, La Maison Aubert. Located in the commercial heart of Paris in one of the more elegant covered passageways that proliferated during the Romantic era, the galerie Véro-Dodat (also referred to as the passage Véro-Dodat), the enterprise prospered by publishing as well as selling prints, including those of Grandville. Only one block away was the Palais-Royal, hereditary residence of Louis-Philippe, duc d'Orléans, and a fashionable promenade frequented by Grandville since his earliest days in Paris (fig. 20; cat. nos. 4 [verso] and 6 [verso]). The Palais-Royal was to become a center of events during the forthcoming Revolution of 1830.

The revolution was precipitated by authoritarian decrees of the reactionary King Charles X. Although a constitutional monarch, thanks to the charter that his brother Louis XVIII had agreed to upon

Fig. 20. ***Le Palais Royal,*** **from** ***Promenades dans Paris,*** **1825, lithograph. Paris, Bibliothèque nationale de France.**

the restoration of the Bourbon monarchy in 1814, Charles X was no friend of democracy. Alarmed by the election at the end of June and beginning of July 1830 of a still more liberal Chamber of Deputies than the one he had dissolved by decree on May 16, he took advantage of the charter's Article 14, which granted the king the prerogative of establishing "all regulations and ordinances necessary for the execution of laws and the security of the State." The infamous ordinances that he decreed on July 25 dissolved the recently elected Chamber, reconvened electors for new elections, modified the electoral law so that there would be fewer electors, and, last but not least, suspended the liberty of the press. Their publication in the official government newspaper, *Le Moniteur universel,* on the following day caused an immediate outcry. Open revolt began one day later on July 27 when workers, students, and young idealists, including Grandville and Daumier, obstructed the narrow Parisian streets with barricades from behind which they fought government troops. The revolution lasted for three days, known as the Trois Glorieuses (Three Glorious Days). By early afternoon of the third day, July 29, all of Paris was under rebel control and fighting had ceased. On August 2, Charles X abdicated. Many victorious insurgents clamored for the establishment of a republic. This idea, however, did not appeal to the members of that one remaining body of government that could claim any legitimacy as the representatives of the people, the Chamber of Deputies.

Under the constitutional monarchies of the Restoration and the July Monarchy, there were two legislative bodies. The upper house was the ineffectual Chambre des Pairs (Chamber of Peers) whose members were appointed by the king. The lower house was the Chambre des Députés (Chamber of Deputies) whose members were elected. The election process, however, was exclusively an upper-middle-class male affair. In order to qualify for the privilege of voting, a man had to pay a minimum of 300 francs, or about 60 dollars, in annual direct taxes at a time when the average annual salary of a rural worker was 477 francs and that of his urban counterpart, 540 francs.[13] The result was an electorate of some ninety thousand voters, or approximately 1 percent of the adult male population. The number of candidates eligible for election was even more restricted. In order to stand for office, a future deputy had to be forty years old and had to pay one thousand francs, or two hundred dollars, in direct taxes. In 1828, for example, these prerequisites limited the field of possible candidates to 14,548.[14] And so, although in theory representatives of the third estate as a whole, deputies were more accurately representatives of their class, the upper bourgeoisie. Liberal opponents of the ultrareactionary Charles X, they became overnight conservative defenders of their own class interests with his abdication. The fact that many deputies were either allied with, or themselves members of, the corporate world indicates where those interests lay: a laissez-faire attitude toward business, which entrepreneurs of France's budding industrial revolution found extremely profitable. The very word "republic" conjured up visions of universal suffrage, the consequent sharing of power with the lower classes, and the possibility of social legislation restraining the free hand with which captains of industry were accustomed to run their enterprises. And so, while grateful to street fighters for dispensing with Charles X, the deputies and the powerful business interests they represented felt that a solution other than a republic was needed for the Revolution of 1830. They decided on a more liberal constitutional monarchy, but one in which members from the restored Bourbon branch of the royal family would not participate.

Thus it was that they turned to Louis-Philippe, head of the cadet, or Orléans, branch of the royal family. On the morning of July 31 he accepted the Chamber of Deputies' invitation to be named lieutenant general of the realm. Later that same day, he was received at the Paris Hôtel de Ville, or city hall, where he was presented to the people by George Washington's former comrade-in-arms and one of the most respected representatives of liberal principles, the marquis de Lafayette. The constitutional charter of 1814 underwent revisions that, among other things, stipulated that the revolutionary tricolor would replace the white Bourbon standard as the national flag and that the reestablishment of censorship would be forbidden. Lafayette publicly proclaimed the new arrangement "la meilleure des républiques" (the best of republics). Louis-Philippe swore allegiance to the hastily revised charter on August 9 before the combined houses of the legislature after which he ascended the throne precipitously vacated by his cousin. He was proclaimed not the King of France like his predecessors, but rather, in an effort to appear more democratic, the King of the French (*Roi des Français*). Because of the revolutionary days that had engendered it, his reign quickly became known as the July Monarchy. It had been suggested that the new regime be legitimized by a national plebiscite, but the idea was brushed aside.[15] This snub was a major miscalculation. Legitimist supporters of the Bourbon dynasty and disappointed republicans alike questioned the legality of Louis-Philippe's rule. And to the less-fortunate members of the population he was not so much the king of the French as the king of the bourgeois interests that had placed him in power—hence the antagonism to the July Monarchy from its very outset. Despised by the far left as well as the far right, Louis-Philippe took what he thought of as a moderate, middle-of-the-road political stance that he termed the "juste milieu," or reasonable middle course. But opposition to his government would not be silenced. In the most extreme cases it registered itself in repeated attempts on the king's life, often on the anniversary of the Trois Glorieuses. The most infamous was that by Fieschi and his "infernal machine" on July 28, 1835: although Louis-Philippe escaped unscathed, forty-one people were wounded, eighteen of them mortally.[16] Eleven years later Grandville would record in his diary another assassination attempt that took place on July 29, 1846 (cat. no. 67). This constant resistance would eventually culminate in another revolution. After nearly eighteen years of triumphant bourgeois values, the July Monarchy ended in the Revolution of 1848, which resulted in the establishment of the short-lived Second Republic, universal male suffrage, and social reforms that favored the working class.

Philipon, along with Grandville, Guiaud, and a host of other caricaturists, lampooned the deposed Charles X. But he was to become known primarily as the opponent of Louis-Philippe. On November 4, 1830, three months after the inauguration of the July Monarchy, appeared the first issue of *La Caricature,* a satirical journal founded by Philipon and published by his brother-in-law Aubert. The weekly paper was modeled after that earlier caricatural publication Philipon had helped to engender, *La Silhouette,* with which it shared writers such as Balzac and artists such as Grandville, Daumier, and Traviès. Intended to be a source of light entertainment, the journal quickly became a vehicle for unrelenting political opposition. The catalyst for this transformation was Philipon's arrest and trial for publishing one of his own prints, *Les Bulles de savon* (Soap bubbles), which criticized Louis-Philippe and was to have appeared in *La Caricature*'s issue for February 24, 1831. Although acquitted on May 23, 1831, Philipon was infuriated by this attempt at press censorship, which was explicitly forbidden by the very charter to which the king had sworn allegiance less than a year earlier. Henceforth, he dedicated *La Caricature* to the freedom of the press. The attacks against Louis-Philippe became increasingly virulent, and the paper was subject to numerous seizures and fines. In due course, Philipon, Daumier, Aubert, and Delaporte (the printer of the journal's lithographs), were all arrested, tried, convicted, and sentenced to both fines and jail terms. Philipon, for example, spent a total of thirteen months in prison and Daumier six. Not surprisingly, Grandville as well came under attack (see cat. no. 16). The besieged journal finally met its demise in 1835 when censorship was reestablished with the "September Laws" promptly drafted in response to Fieschi's attempt on the king's life. Adopted by the Chamber of Deputies in late August, they were promulgated the same day they were passed by the Chamber of Peers on September 9, or six weeks after the spectacularly heinous crime that had precipitated them. The last issue of *La Caricature,* dated August 27, 1835, appeared on September 8.[17]

Grandville produced the jester, a personification of the journal and its satirical spirit, which was used on the poster to advertise *La Caricature* and on the paper's first masthead (fig. 21). He also created its first lithograph, *3e Restauration* (3rd restoration), the latest in his series of caricatures ridiculing Charles X. The focus of his satire was transferred to Louis-Philippe and his government, beginning with *Le Carnaval politique* (The political carnival) which appeared in the paper on February 17, 1831. Of *La Caricature*'s 530 plates, Grandville produced approximately 115 or more than one-fifth of the total, often with the collaboration of other artists, notably Forest. In homage to his preponderant role, the journal included in its April 12, 1832, issue a rhymed "Epitre à Grandville" (Epistle to Grandville), which proclaimed him "Roi de la caricature" (King of Caricature).

In August and December of that same year, Philipon naturally chose Grandville to help launch two more journalistic endeavors, the *Association mensuelle* and *Le Charivari.* The former was described as an "association for the liberty of the press" when Philipon announced it in *La Caricature* on July 26, 1832. The purpose of the publication was to create a reserve fund that would help to defray the mounting expenses of prosecutions and fines leveled against the increasingly embattled journal. For a subscription fee of twelve francs per year, each month associates received one lithograph and its

Fig. 21. Detail, masthead of *La Caricature*, 1830, lithograph. Paris, Bibliothèque nationale de France.

accompanying commentary (the commentaries, written by Philipon also appeared in *La Caricature*). Grandville and Auguste Raffet (1804–60) executed the initial lithograph, *Analyse de la pensée* (Analysis of thought), which attacked Louis-Philippe's *procureur général* (attorney general), Persil, who is shown in a diabolical laboratory where, with the assistance of judges and officials, he transforms the ideas and ideals of the Revolution of 1830 into criminal activity (fig. 22).[18] Grandville, mostly in collaboration with other artists, was the author of seventeen of the *Association mensuelle*'s twenty-four prints that appeared between August 1832 and September 1834.[19]

Le Charivari was a daily newspaper that differed from *La Caricature* not only by its more frequent appearance, but also by its more varied, relatively innocuous content. Each issue included a print. Grandville and Forest provided the lithograph for its inaugural issue of Saturday, December 1, 1832 (fig. 23). Essentially an advertisement, it represents the jester of *La Caricature* as a barker urging people to subscribe to the new publication: *Suivez, suivez, suivez la foule!! c'est l'instant, c'est le moment, c'est la minute, v'la qu'ça commence.* ***365*** *Lithographies par an. On ne paye qu'en s'abonnant.*

Fig. 22. *Analyse de la pensée* (Analysis of thought), plate 1 of the *Association mensuelle,* August 1832, lithograph. Nancy, Bibliothèque municipale.

entrez! entrez! entrez, messieurs et dames!!! entrez (Follow, follow, follow the crowd!! Now's the instant, the moment, the minute that it begins. 365 lithographs per year. You only pay by subscribing. Enter! enter! enter ladies and gentlemen!!! Enter). It was probably as a result of his commitments to *La Caricature* and the *Association mensuelle* that Grandville contributed to *Le Charivari* only irregularly. However, in 1835 he was called upon to create *Le Charivari*'s burlesque response to what was popularly referred to as the "Procès-Monstre" (Monster Trial) of the alleged conspirators behind the famous April 1834 worker insurrection in Lyon. The result was *Le Charivari Monstre* (fig. 24). Printed in advance with the date of July 31, 1835, it was not distributed until August 16, no doubt out of respect for the victims of Fieschi's bloody July 28 attempt on the life of Louis-Philippe. Because of its more general satirical content, *Le Charivari* survived the 1835 September Laws as well as the July Monarchy itself, and continued to be published until 1893.[20] Grandville remained in close contact with *Le Charivari,* which had paid homage to his caricatural prowess by referring to him as "l'Hogarth français" (the French Hogarth) in its issue of December 20, 1834. Members of its staff eventually would write the texts for several of his illustrated books, many of which were advertised within its pages.

Between 1830 and 1835 Grandville was thus a main combatant in Philipon's war against Louis-Philippe, the betrayer of the republican ideals of the Revolution of 1830. The effort monopolized his time, but gained him greater fame in France and the rest of Europe thanks to the international distribution of *La Caricature.* Because of the often vitriolic tone of his prints, many have assumed that he

Fig. 23. ***Suivez, suivez, suivez la foule!!*** **(Follow, follow, follow the crowd!!),** ***Le Charivari,*** **December 1, 1832, lithograph. Paris, Bibliothèque nationale de France.**

Fig. 24. *Le Charivari Monstre,* July 31, 1835, lithograph. Paris, Bibliothèque nationale de France.

shared the same vehement distaste for the July Monarchy as Philipon. Grandville's political opinions, however, were more complex than that.

France's political fortunes fluctuated over the course of Grandville's lifetime. Born under the Consulate in 1803, he spent his boyhood under the Empire established by Napoléon in 1804. As an early adolescent he witnessed in quick succession the first restoration of the Bourbon monarchy in 1814 with Louis XVIII, brother of the guillotined Louis XVI, as king; Napoléon's unsuccessful attempt to reestablish the Empire during the Hundred Days in the spring of 1815; and, after Napoléon's final defeat at Waterloo on June 18, 1815, a second Bourbon restoration. He passed the first years of his manhood in Paris during the reign of Charles X, the last brother of Louis XVI, whose downfall he actively promoted and caricatured. The July Monarchy of Louis-Philippe encompassed his maturity and death.

Early indications of Grandville's political sentiments are as divided as the successive regimes he knew while growing up. The 1820 copy of a Bonapartist caricature from the Hundred Days may indicate early liberal tendencies (Nancy, cat. no. 18). But four years later Grandville drew a not-unsympathetic composition of a youth contemplating a posted bulletin describing the precarious state of Louis XVIII's health three days before the king's death on September 16, 1824 (fig. 25). Whatever their orientation in Nancy, Grandville's political views developed along more radical lines after his arrival in the Paris of Charles X. Given his circle of friends, it is doubtful that he articulated them completely by himself: more than likely he had the help of such young liberals as Philipon. His neighbor during the later years of his life and his biographer, Clogenson, states that by 1830 Grandville was a republican and adds that, rifle in hand, he fought with courage and sangfroid during the revolution of that year.

Grandville's republican sympathies appear to have been motivated at least in part by a profound sense of social injustice. As France entered the industrial age during the first half of the nineteenth century, people moved at an increasingly accelerated pace from the countryside to urban centers unprepared either to house or feed them. Paris, for example, nearly doubled its population in the space of only thirty-five years, from 547,756 inhabitants in 1801 to 909,126 in 1836.[21] Grandville could have encountered daily in the streets of the capital a social by-product of the dislocations brought about by such rapid change: the destitution of the working class, the dispossessed, and the unemployed, who were collectively termed "les misérables," or literally "the miserable ones."[22] He recorded his impressions in a number of drawings from the beginning of the 1830s where he depicted the proletarian poor, or contrasted the disparity between working-class types and members of the bourgeoisie, the former dressed in smocks and coveralls, the latter parading about in the latest fashions (fig. 26; see also Nancy, fig. 4 and cat. nos. 23, 24, 31, 75, 187). Most of these often intimately scaled drawings appear to constitute his own private commentary on those left abandoned by the Revolution of 1830 and on those who most profited from it, including the so-called "bourgeois king" himself, Louis-Philippe. Grandville's republican zeal may have moderated as he grew older—Clogenson observes that he reconsidered certain ideas that he held in 1830 as events "instructed him that it is not good to allow the masses to intervene in affairs of State"—but as his correspondence from 1846 eloquently testifies, Grandville retained his compassion for the disadvantaged and poorer segments of the population until the end of his life (see cat. no. 8 [recto]).

It should be emphasized that Grandville was by no means alone in his sympathy for the working-class poor and antipathy for the bourgeoisie. Rather, he is representative of a broader social consciousness developing in France and the rest of Europe at this time. In the visual arts and literature it frequently manifested itself in a nascent realism of which Grandville's own frank depictions of working-class types are only one example. The lithographer Edme Jean Pigal (1798–1872), his sometime colleague at *La Caricature* and *Le Charivari,* whom he mentions in his 1833 diary (cat. no. 28), specialized, for instance, in depictions of the popular classes. Those works in which he portrayed the

Fig. 25. ***Le Roi est très faible . . . on lui a dit les prières des agonisan*****[ts] (The King is very weak . . . he has been given the last rites), 1824, drawing. Nancy, Musée des Beaux-Arts (Inv. 877.1010 v.).**

Fig. 26. *Worker and Two Bourgeois,* circa 1832, drawing. Nancy, Musée des Beaux-Arts (Inv. 877.230)

meaner aspects of their existence invite comparison with the lithographs of Théodore Géricault (1791–1824) and prints done later by Gavarni (1804–66) and Gustave Doré (1832–1883) that feature the marginalized and downtrodden poor in England's more advanced industrial society. Sympathetic portrayals of working-class types can also be found in the work of other artists associated with *La Caricature:* Charlet,[23] Philippe-Auguste Jeanron (1808–77), Traviès,[24] and, of course, Daumier. Like Grandville, Traviès satirized both middle-class attitudes and types. In fact, his attacks, along with those of Daumier and another Philipon associate, Monnier, were so relentless that Champfleury was moved to label the three artists as "démolisseurs de la bourgeoisie" (demolishers of the bourgeoisie) in his 1865 *Histoire de la caricature moderne* (History of modern caricature).[25]

Similar class-based commentary could be found in the emerging realism of contemporary literature. *La Comédie Humaine* (*The Human Comedy*), initially labeled *Études sociales* (Social studies), begun by Balzac in 1829 and *Le Dernier jour d'un condamné* (*The Last Day of a Condemned Man*) published by Victor Hugo (1802–85) in the same year are early examples of a literary genre popularized in the often melodramatic novels of Jules Janin (1804–74), Paul de Kock (1793–1871), Frédéric Soulié (1800–1847), and Eugène Sue (1804–57). The trend would culminate in Gustave Flaubert's clinical analysis of the "sottise bourgeoise" (bourgeois stupidity), most notably with *Madame Bovary* (1857), and in Émile Zola's trenchant description of working-class misery in books such as *L'Assommoir* (*The Dram-Shop,* 1877) and *Germinal* (*Germinal,* 1885). The 1830s were also characterized by utopian reformers, such as Charles Fourier (1772–1837) and the Saint-Simonians (cat. no. 8), whose theories on economic and social change were later more rigorously developed by the socialist philosophers Pierre Joseph Proudhon, Karl Marx, and Friedrich Engels.

After the Revolution of 1830, it was only natural for Grandville to continue his career as a caricaturist by joining the staff of Philipon's newly founded *La Caricature,* which, as Clogenson emphasizes, did not initially have subversive intentions. However, when the paper started to take a more resolutely opposition stance, Grandville probably approved, since he had his own reasons for criticizing the king and his bourgeois supporters. But it was often Philipon, heart and soul of the publication, who provided his stable of caricaturists with ideas for their increasingly hostile political commentary. As the battle between Philipon and the government intensified, he prodded them in directions where they might otherwise not have gone. This seems to be particularly true of Grandville. A revealing entry from his 1833 diary makes it clear that by April of that year the "Roi de la caricature" was disgusted with his profession (cat. no. 16). Incessant reprisals against other members of *La Caricature*'s staff and threats made against his own person left him thoroughly intimidated. He had already started to explore illustrating books, most notably works for children, as another means of making a living in 1832 (cat. no. 20). It was doubtlessly with a certain amount of relief that he saw the demise of *La Caricature* as a result of the laws of September 1835, which, in spite of the constitutional charter, reestablished press censorship. Freed of his political caricature obligations, Grandville made the final transition to an alternate, comparatively innocuous career: book illustration.

This was a far safer occupation for a family man. In Nancy, on July 22, 1833, Grandville had married his first cousin, Marguerite Henriette Fischer (1810–42), the daughter of his mother's sister, Marguerite Viot. The couple settled down to a quiet domestic existence in a third-floor apartment that overlooked the Seine at 1, rue des Grands-Augustins, not far from Grandville's bachelor quarters at 10, rue des Petits-Augustins. On October 27 of the following year Henriette bore him the first of three sons. Grandville's devotion to his wife and children is reflected not only in the voluminous correspondence with his relatives in Nancy but also in the toys and drawings that he delighted in creating for his small sons' amusement (see cat. nos. 41 and 48). Thus, it was all the more tragic that he was made to suffer their loss in a succession of heart-rending deaths. His first two children died in 1838 and 1841.[26] Then his beloved Henriette died in 1842, following the birth of their third son, Jean Lucien *Georges,* in July of that year. In 1843, Grandville made another trip to Nancy in order to marry Catherine Marceline ("Céline") L'hullier (1819–88), a friend and cousin of Henriette whom the latter solicitously recommended to him shortly before she passed away.[27] Grandville began life anew in the fourth-floor apartment at 26, rue des Saints-Pères where he and Henriette had moved toward the beginning of 1842. In 1845, the only child from his second marriage, Jean-Baptiste *Armand,* was born. Grandville rejoiced in his newfound domestic bliss as both drawings and diary excerpts from 1846 attest (cat. nos. 45–83). He was particularly attached to Georges, who was constantly by his father's side while the artist worked in the room of the apartment reserved for his studio. The children's drawings found in cat. nos. 86–90 may have been done by either Georges or Armand in imitation of their father. Grandville's happiness was not to last. In January 1847 Georges died suddenly at the age of four and a half. Unable to withstand his profound grief, Grandville himself expired two months later.

1835–1847: Book Illustration and the Pursuit of the New

It was in the face of all these personal tragedies that Grandville pursued his successful career as a highly inventive book illustrator from 1836 until his death in 1847.[28] He could not have chosen a better time, for these years coincided with the short-lived but brilliant phenomenon that was Romantic book illustration. During the early 1830s, a special set of circumstances coalesced to give birth to the new art form: industrial advances in printing, bookbinding, and manufacturing paper, the development of wood engraving, and a Romantic love for evocative images. These last two were particularly important.[29]

Perfected by the Englishman, Thomas Bewick (1753–1828), at the end of the eighteenth century, wood engraving possessed a number of advantages over other modes of visual reproduction. It was far superior to the related, traditional woodcut. Instead of being cut into the relatively soft length of the wood grain, images were engraved into the dense, hard end of the grain. This allowed for the creation of considerably more detailed and more clean-cut images than in woodcuts. Because of their sturdiness, endgrain engravings could also withstand far more numerous impressions. Unlike copper engravings or lithographs, which needed to be printed separately and were inserted between pages of text only at the moment of a book's binding, wood-engraved images could share the same page as a text thanks to the capability of incorporating the engraved woodblocks with movable type. This produced another revolution in which Grandville would participate, that of book design (see "Page Design" in "History and Description of the Missouri Album").

Wood engraving did, however, have its drawbacks as far as Grandville was concerned. A source of much irritation was the fact that it was not as direct a medium as lithography where he could see printed exactly what he or a trusted collaborator drew upon the stone. At least three other hands intervened before one of his original drawings became a published print. First there was the hand of an assistant who in pencil patiently transferred the drawing to the woodblock. This was often Auguste Desperet,[30] who earlier had performed a similar service by translating certain of Grandville's political caricatures to the lithographic stone. Even though it meant an extra expenditure of time, a transferred drawing could be, and often was, corrected by the perfectionist artist. Infinitely more trying was the actual process of engraving, which required the specialized skill of a well-trained hand. Among the wood engravers Grandville worked with were the father-and-son team of Lacoste, referred to in cat. no. 27, Adolphe Best (1808–60), on whose name he makes an unflattering pun in cat. no. 51, and Chevauchet who is mentioned in the letter in the appendix. Like all Romantic book illustrators, Grandville was at the mercy of the engraver, for whatever was carved on the woodblock was what got printed and, consequently, was what the public saw. Last, there was the hand of the printer. A block improperly inked with either too much or too little ink could further distort the artist's original idea. All too often Grandville felt betrayed by the intervening hands, especially those of the engraver and printer. And he vented his frustration in a famous prefatory letter addressed "to the present or future possessor of this album," which he appended to the collected and bound drawings of his illustrations for the fables of La Fontaine (a major purpose of the exercise was to demonstrate to the viewer just how superior his original drawings were to the published wood engravings). The letter is a long lamentation in which he details the trials that he was forced to undergo once a drawing left his hands.[31] Despite his misgivings about the medium, Grandville became one of the brightest stars of a veritable constellation of artists who produced the phenomenon that was Romantic wood engraving: Hippolyte Bellangé (1800–1866), Charlet, Achille Devéria (1800–1857), Gavarni, Jean-François Gigoux (1806–1894), Alfred (1800–1837) and Tony Johannot (1803–52), Ernest Meissonier (1815–91), Célestin Nanteuil (1813–73), and Auguste Raffet. Together, they attempted to meet the demand of their contemporaries' seemingly insatiable appetite for illustrated books.

From the time of the Roman poet Horace (65–8 BCE) and his famous formula, *ut pictura poesis* (as in painting, so in poetry) images have been valued for their evocative qualities. This was never more true than during the Romantic period. Surpassing the role of mere description, a book's wood engravings did not simply provide visual complements for what was read. Instead, in the process of interpreting a text an artist often greatly elaborated upon it. Consequently, books were often purchased not because of the author's reputation, but rather that of the artist providing the illustrations, a phenomenon summed up by one contemporary who bluntly observed as early as 1831, "a book is bought today not for the text but for the vignettes."[32] This circumstance resulted in another innovative development, the creation of books through an active collaboration of artist and writer. Significantly enough, the trend first announced itself in a work commissioned from Grandville: *Scènes de la vie privée et publique des animaux* (Scenes from the private and public life of animals; Hetzel et Paulin, 1842). The idea originated with Pierre-Jules Hetzel (1814–86), future editor of Jules Verne, who engaged luminaries of the contemporary French literary scene such as Balzac, George Sand, and Alfred and Paul de Musset to write short stories that were to serve specifically as the vehicles for Grandville's well-known talent for anthropomorphizing animals (fig. 27). The outstanding success of what was often referred to simply as *Les Animaux* (The animals), today still regarded as one of the apogees of Romantic book illustration, prompted other editors to follow suit. Henri Fournier, Taschereau's publishing associate, had the author Émile Forgues (1813–83), whose nom de plume was Old Nick, and Grandville collaborate on the creation of *Petites misères de la vie humaine* (Little misfortunes of human life, 1843; figs. 37 and 61). It was also Fournier who allowed Grandville to reverse the traditional mode of book production in another work on which the artist was then focused, *Un autre monde:* Grandville first created his inimitably inventive images, after which a text was written for them. The result was the most fantastic of all Romantic illustrated books and the one for which he is best known in the twentieth century (figs. 28, 29, 58 and 109).

The images that so entranced the Romantic generation were vignettes, invented by Bewick at the end of the eighteenth century as he was perfecting wood engraving. Ultimately derived from the tendrils and little vines (in French, *vignettes*) that graced the margins of medieval illuminated manuscripts, vignettes differed from earlier book illustrations in that they were not surrounded by a frame that would have separated them from the rest of the page upon which they were printed. Charles Rosen and Henri Zerner best describe the novelty of the vignette, equating its intimate relationship with the sheet of paper on which it appeared with a Romantic penchant for blurring the distinctions between art and life:

> Apparently unassuming as an artistic form, the vignette launches a powerful attack on the classical definition of representation, a window on the world. The vignette is not a window because it has no limit, no frame. The image, defined from its center rather than its edges, emerges from the paper as an apparition or a fantasy. The uncertainty of contour often makes it impossible to distinguish the edge of the vignette from the paper: the whiteness of the paper, which represents the play of light within the image, changes imperceptively into the paper of the book, and realizes, in small, the Romantic blurring of art and reality.[33]

Unencumbered by a frame, the vignette became another symbol on the printed page like letters and words. Its very nature contributed to its parity with, or superiority over, the text it embellished.

Fig. 27. ***Un Hibou philosophe et oiseau de lettres*** **(A philosophical owl and bird of letters) from** ***Scènes de la vie privée et publique des animaux,*** **1842, wood engraving. Private collection.**

One other aspect of Romantic book illustration merits brief consideration: its marketability. Whether specially printed on China paper and hand-bound in stamped leather or fabricated in a more economical and mechanical fashion, illustrated books were luxury items. They were produced for a restricted public that was both literate and fortunate enough to possess varying amounts of discretionary income. In short, Romantic book illustration, like the July Monarchy, itself, was a bourgeois phenomenon.

Whatever his qualms about the finished wood-engraved product, Grandville's new profession suited him perfectly. It provided him with a comfortable income (in 1843, at a time when annual basic living expenses for the family of an average skilled worker in Paris were 950 francs, his net worth was 53,765 francs),[34] and the medium of wood engraving with its crisply defined images complemented the detailed precision of his graphic style, which reflected his early training as a miniaturist. With its typically Romantic expectations of originality, book illustration also allowed him the freedom to continue his artistic program of inventive form and satiric content found in his most successful lithographic albums and political caricatures.

His first illustrated book, *Oeuvres complètes de P. J. de Béranger* (Complete works of P. J. de Béranger; Fournier aîné et Perrotin, 1836), done in collaboration with Raffet, served as a transition between his recently abandoned career and the new one he had begun, for the political content that was often to be found in Béranger's satirical songs complemented perfectly the talents of the former

Fig. 28. ***C'est Vénus en personne!*** **(It's Venus in person!) from** ***Un autre monde,*** **1844, wood engraving. Private collection.**

opposition caricaturist. Upon completion of the *Béranger,* Grandville embarked on a series of projects that demonstrated a continued interest in children's publications, an area he had previously explored in 1832 and 1833 when four of his drawings, including the two original images of Louis Desnoyers's Jean-Paul Choppart, were published as wood engravings in the *Journal des enfans* (see cat. no. 20). The installments for the first volume of *Le Livre des enfants* (The children's book; Paulin, 1836–38), which contained five of his illustrations for "Little Red Riding Hood" (preliminary studies for four of these scenes as well as three unpublished ones are to be found on the pages from an 1836 sketchbook in cat. nos. 39 and 40), appeared at the end of 1836 and the beginning of 1837; subsequent volumes contained his illustrations for three other children's stories by Perrault: "Tom Thumb," "Puss in Boots," and "Bluebeard." He entertained children of all ages with his illustrations to *Voyages de Gulliver dans les contrées lointaines* (*Gulliver's Travels;* Fournier aîné et Perrotin, 1838) and *Aventures de Robinson Crusoë* (*The Adventures of Robinson Crusoe;* Fournier aîné, 1840).

Of equal universal appeal were his most famous illustrations done with a juvenile public at least partly in mind, those for the *Fables de La Fontaine* (Fables of La Fontaine; Fournier aîné et Perrotin, 1838; Fournier aîné, 1840), originally dedicated to Louis XIV's six-year-old son, the dauphin. The moralizing animals of the fables provided a sequel to the satirical animal-headed humans of *Les Méta-*

Fig. 29. ***Les Métamorphoses du sommeil*** **(Dream transformations) from** ***Un autre monde,*** **1844, wood engraving. Paris, Bibliothèque nationale de France.**

morphoses du jour, and met with the same success (fig. 30). Grandville's edition of La Fontaine's fables, which is still being published and sold in French bookstores, solidified his reputation as a moralizing *artiste animalier* or "animal artist," which his editors did not hesitate to exploit. Illustrations to the *Fables de Lavalette* (Fables of Lavalette; Hetzel et Paulin, 1841) and the *Fables de Florian* (Fables of Florian; Dubochet, 1842) followed in due course. The height of Grandville's *animalier* fame as well as his celebrity as a book illustrator were simultaneously reached with *Scènes de la vie privée et publique des animaux* on which he had begun work in 1840. Both Grandville's images and the short stories accompanying them present parables of contemporary French society with the result that the work appears as a sophisticated updating of La Fontaine for adults. Concurrent with his work on *Les Animaux,* Grandville participated in another celebrated publication of the period, *Les Français peints par eux-mêmes* (The French portrayed by themselves), published between 1840 and 1842 by one of the most ambitious Romantic book editors, Léon Curmer (1801–70). The work, which analyzes a cross-section of social types, marks a culminating point in the period's fascination with Lavaterian-inspired "physiologies."

The astonishing success of Grandville's illustrations to the *Fables de La Fontaine* and *Scènes de la vie privée et publique des animaux* lay not simply in his continued exploitation of the ever-popular human/animal analogy and its attendant Lavaterian overtones. What intrigued his contemporaries was

Fig. 30. ***Le Loup et la Cigogne*** **(The Wolf and the Stork) from** ***Fables de La Fontaine,*** **1838, wood engraving. Private collection.**

Grandville's ability to make his moralizing animals appear so convincingly real. This is what distinguished, for example, the animal-headed humans of *Les Métamorphoses du jour* from those of numerous other Restoration caricaturists. There is some debate as to whether or not Grandville found his inspiration for *Les Métamorphoses* in actual animals or the illustrations to an edition of Buffon's pioneering multivolumed *Histoire naturelle* (Natural history, 1749–89). However, the fidelity to nature evident in his book illustrations resulted from numerous directly observed and precisely detailed animal studies that themselves were worthy of illustrating a text in the fledgling science of natural history (for examples of these remarkable drawings, see Nancy, cat. nos. 210–52). As with Lavater, Grandville's combination of scientific exactitude with moralizing content captivated the Romantic imagination. Equally fascinating was his talent for anthropomorphizing his scrupulously researched animal studies so that they became convincing surrogates for the human species they satirized. His moralizing animals serve to demonstrate that Grandville's inventive fantasy world was oftentimes grounded in a closely observed realism every bit as frank and direct as his depictions of working-class types.

As mentioned earlier, the success of *Scènes de la vie privée et publique des animaux* encouraged other editors to follow Hetzel's example and create new books specifically for Grandville. Appearing in an almost annual succession were *Petites misères de la vie humaine* (1843), *Un autre monde* (1844), *Cent proverbes* (One hundred proverbs; Fournier, 1845) (fig. 31), and *Les Fleurs animées* (The animated

Absent le Chat, les Souris dansent.

Fig. 31. ***Absent le Chat, les Souris dansent.*** **(When the cat's away, the mice play.) from** ***Cent proverbes,*** **1845, wood engraving. Paris, Bibliothèque nationale de France.**

Fig. 32. ***Narcisse*** **(Narcissus) from** ***Les Fleurs animées,*** **1847, steel engraving. Paris, Bibliothèque nationale de France.**

flowers; de Gonet, 1847), this last a series of poetic floral personifications (figs. 32, 112, 113, and 118) based on closely observed studies of flowers just as scientific in their exactitude as those previously done of animals (e.g., Nancy, cat. nos. 290–314). The texts for all of these publications were written by affiliates of Philipon's *Le Charivari.* Grandville apparently had become so accustomed to the new arrangement that when it came to illustrating Louis Reybaud's preexisting text of *Jérôme Paturot à la recherche d'une position sociale* (Jérôme Paturot in search of a social position; Dubochet, Le Chevalier et Cie, 1846), a satirical account of a young Romantic's climb toward bourgeois respectability first published in 1842 (figs. 47 and 52), he grew bored with the dated material.

After completing *Les Fleurs animées* on October 21, 1846 (see his diary entry for that date in cat. no. 75), Grandville spent the final months of his life working on three major projects, all of which were published posthumously. While obligated to follow Cervantes' classic text in his illustrations for *L'Ingénieux Chevalier Don Quichotte de la Manche* (The ingenious gentleman Don Quixote of La Mancha; Mame, 1848) (fig. 124), he had complete freedom in developing those for *Les Étoiles* (The stars; de Gonet, 1849) (fig. 33) the stellar counterparts of his popular personified flowers in *Les Fleurs*

Fig. 33. ***L'Étoile du berger*** **(The shepherd's star) from** ***Les Étoiles,*** **1849, steel engraving. Nancy, Bibliothèque municipale.**

animées. Equally free flights of Grandville's imagination were to be found in his two famous dream metamorphoses, sent to Charton on February 26, 1847, and published in the July 1847 issue of the *Magasin pittoresque* (figs. 34 and 35).

Of all the works from his final years, *Un autre monde* and the dream metamorphoses are the most innovative. *Un autre monde,* we have seen, marked a new and seemingly inevitable stage in the production of illustrated books during an era obsessed with images. Instead of commencing with a text or having artist and author working simultaneously together, the publication started with Grandville's images around which was then written a narrative. The task of writing fell to Taxile Delord (1815–77), editor in chief of *Le Charivari* at various intervals between 1842 and 1858, who was aided by Grandville's own outlines for a story and, as a last resort, undoubtedly by the artist himself. A satire on contemporary society similar to Jonathan Swift's *Gulliver's Travels,* with which Grandville was thoroughly acquainted as a result of having illustrated the English classic several years earlier, both images and accompanying text describe the fantastic adventures of three neo-gods as they explore the land, air, and sea. The unrelenting succession of verbal and visual puns, eccentric analogies, suites of

Fig. 34. ***Crime et expiation*** **(Crime and atonement),** ***Magasin pittoresque,*** **July 1847, wood engraving. Paris, Bibliothèque nationale de France.**

MAGASIN PITTORESQUE. 213

P. SOYER.

(Second rêve.— Une promenade dans le ciel.)

Fig. 35. *Une promenade dans le ciel* (A walk in the sky), *Magasin pittoresque,* July 1847, wood engraving. Paris, Bibliothèque nationale de France.

analogous shapes, monstrous hybrids, anthropomorphized objects, plants and animals, mirror distortions, and other visual artifices that Grandville went at great lengths to produce did indeed make of *Un autre monde* another world.[35] It best represents an artistic program of visual metamorphoses that Grandville retrospectively outlined at the end of his life: "J'ai imaginé quoi des monstruosités gracieuses, pour l'homme auquel il faut à tout prix du nouveau" (I have imagined graceful monstrosities for the person who needs, above all, the new).[36] In short, it was Romantic escapism from humdrum conventionality at its most calculated and most imaginative. However, his contemporaries found this surfeit of extravagant images not so much entertaining as visually disorienting and therefore psychically disturbing. Unwittingly, Grandville had stumbled upon what the future surrealists would try so hard to achieve: psychic dislocation caused by the irrational or the totally unexpected. As installments of the book appeared in 1843, it became apparent that few appreciated, much less took the time and mental effort to understand, the imaginary new world that he had so carefully constructed for them.

Baudelaire's devastating criticism is a case in point. Although an eloquent defender of Delacroix's apocalyptic visions, he found that Grandville's transformation of reality into a topsy-turvy fantasyland went beyond the permissible limits of Romantic imagining and inventiveness. Mistakenly referring to *Un autre monde* as *Le Monde à l'envers* (The world turned upside down), he wrote in his *Quelques caricaturistes français* (Some French caricaturists), first published in 1857:

> With superhuman courage this man devoted his life to refashioning creation. He took it in his hands, wrung it, rearranged it, explained it and annotated it; and Nature was transformed into a fantasmagoria. He turned the world upside down. Did he not, in fact, compose a picture-book called *Le Monde à l'envers?* There are some superficial spirits who are amused by Grandville; for my part, I find him terrifying. For unfortunately it is the artist in whom I am interested, and not his drawings. When I open the door of Grandville's works I feel a certain uneasiness, as though I am entering an apartment where disorder was systematically organized —where preposterous cornices were propped up against the floor, where the pictures showed their faces through an optician's distorting-glass, where all the objects elbowed each other about obliquely, the furniture stood with its feet in the air, and the drawers slide inwards instead of out.[37]

Baudelaire was not alone in his disapproval. Charles Blanc in his admiring and otherwise excellent 1854 essay on Grandville does not so much as mention *Un autre monde.*[38]

Equally disturbing were those precocious anticipations of surrealist oneiric imagery, the dream metamorphoses. Although repeatedly exposed to the quintessentially Romantic subject of dreams (e.g., Henry Fuseli's painting *The Nightmare,* 1781; the nightmare in Victor Hugo's *Le Dernier jour d'un condamné,* 1829; the dream imagery of Hector Berlioz's *Symphonie fantastique,* or *Fantastic Symphony,* 1830), the public was unprepared for the novelty of different objects that seemed to change into one another. However, seen within the context of Grandville's artistic development, the dream sequences represent the culmination of a concept with which Grandville had been experimenting since before 1830: series of disparate objects visually related to one another by their analogous shapes (see Nancy, cat. no. 106). He perfected this mode of visual punning in an image that directly anticipates the dream metamorphoses, *Les Métamorphoses du sommeil* (Dream transformations) from *Un autre monde* (fig. 29). Grandville was convinced that these transformations of one object into another accurately duplicated similar metamorphoses that take place during the process of dreaming. But they did not appear convincing to Baudelaire, who in his *Quelques caricaturistes français* disparagingly remarked, "Before his death, [Grandville] applied his always stubborn will to the noting of his successive dreams and nightmares in a plastic form, with all the precision of a stenographer writing down an orator's speech."[39] Harsh as it is, Baudelaire's criticism was not unique. During the decade following Grandville's tragically early death, other critics, including those favorably disposed to triumphant realism, further discredited the artist and, along with Baudelaire, helped to create the Grandville myth.

An Uncertain Legacy: The Grandville Myth

The unusual circumstances of Grandville's death proved particularly deleterious to his reputation. Following the sudden and unexpected passing in January 1847 of Georges, his last link to his beloved first wife, Henriette, the grieving artist apparently lost the will to live. He suffered a series of maladies, finally succumbing to the last. At first Grandville was stricken with an inflammation of the eyelids. No sooner did that heal than he came down with an abscess. Cured of that, he was confined to his bed with a sore throat on March 1. Although his doctor was not alarmed at his condition, Grandville firmly predicted that the illness would be fatal. Eight days later, what apparently was an angina infection had spread to his brain, which brought on a series of fits, necessitating his removal on March 10 from the apartment in the rue des Saints-Pères to a hospice at Vanves, on the outskirts of Paris. He died one week later on March 17 after three days and nights of agony. Certain newspapers misrepresented the nature of his death by reporting that it had been brought on by insanity instead of an infected brain.[40] Such accounts were seized upon by his detractors as proof that Grandville had been unbalanced all along and that his most inventive imagery, such as that encountered in *Un autre monde* and the dream metamorphoses, was indeed crazed. Through countless repetitions, this more sensational version of events took on a life of its own, hence the myth that has grown up around both the artist and his work.

One of the most outspoken critics who contributed to the Grandville myth was Paul de Saint-Victor (1825–81) who found the artist's originality more eccentric than amusing, and took the lead in questioning his mental equilibrium. In *D'après nature,* an 1858 book featuring the work of Grandville's fellow caricaturist, Gavarni, he unfavorably contrasts the "clumsy and petty fantasy" of Grandville with the clarity and comparative realism of Gavarni, whose art he compares to daguerreotypes:

> Quant à Grandville, qu'y a-t-il de commun entre sa fantaisie pesante et mesquine et l'*humour* sagace et expressif de Gavarni? Grandville ne se place pour observer ni dans la réalité, ni dans l'idéal, mais dans je ne sais quelle *chambre noire* de physique amusante, où toutes les figures grimacent et se déforment, comme si elles étaient reflétées par des miroirs oblongs ou concaves. Sa gaieté est baroque, son esprit est un logogriphe, sa moquerie une parodie. La vraisemblance, le goût, la justesse lui sont aussi étrangers qu'à un peintre chinois les lois de la perspective.
>
> Par la clarté de son coup d'oeil, la finesse de son tact et l'originalité d'une exécution qu'on définirait en l'appelant un daguerréotype spirituel, Gavarni est et restera le seul peintre fidèle des moeurs de ce temps. Si j'avais un titre général à donner à son oeuvre, j'inscrirais sur son frontispice: "Mémoires de la vie privée du dix-neuvième siècle."
>
> [As for Grandville, what is there in common between his clumsy and petty fantasy and the discerning and expressive *humor* of Gavarni? As he observes, Grandville places himself neither in reality nor in the ideal, but in I don't know what fun-house dark room where all the faces grimace and are distorted, as if they were reflected in oblong or concave mirrors. His gaiety is bizarre, his wit a logogriph, his ridicule a parody. Verisimilitude, tastefulness, and sound judgment are as alien to him as the laws of perspective are to a Chinese painter.
>
> With the lucidity of his glance, the subtlety of his tact, and the originality of an execution one might describe by calling it a witty daguerreotype, Gavarni is and will remain the only artist faithful to the customs

of this time. If I had to give a general title to his work, I would write on his frontispiece "Memoirs of the private life of the nineteenth century."][41]

Unflattering as it is, this appraisal is considerably more moderate than the invective he had used four years earlier when, while assessing the dream metamorphoses of the *Magasin pittoresque,* he casts aspersions on Grandville's sanity:

> Certes le Démon de la folie était debout derrière le pauvre artiste et lui poussait le coude, lorsqu'il esquissait d'une main égarée ces incohérentes fioritures. Quelques jours après en effet, il s'empara de lui pour ne plus le rendre qu'à la Mort. Mais il me semble que la démence même de ces brouillons fatidiques n'est que la conséquence excessive du talent de Grandville. Vous y retrouvez grossis au microscope toutes les infirmités et tous les défauts de sa manière: la subtilité mesquine, le mysticisme trivial, le sceau de plomb du lieu commun, appliqué aux choses les plus délicates de l'imagination et de la pensée; une aptitude singulière à rétrécir l'infini et à vulgariser l'idéal: si bien que, si je voulais définir en lui l'artiste par un mot qui le contienne et qui le résume, je dirais que c'est un visionnaire qui ronfle en rêvant.
>
> [Surely the demon of insanity was standing behind the poor artist and nudged him along as he sketched with a stray hand these incoherent fripperies. In fact, several days later he grabbed hold of him to no longer release him except to Death. But it seems to me that the very lunacy of these fateful scribblings is simply the result of Grandville's intemperate mind. There you will find magnified under a microscope all the weaknesses and all the deficiencies of his manner: the petty subtlety, the vulgar mysticism, the leaden stamp of the commonplace applied to the most refined matters of the imagination and thought; a singular ability to shrink the immeasureable and vulgarize the ideal: to the extent that if I were to define the artist in him in a phrase that would encompass him and sum him up, I would say that he is a visionary who snores while dreaming.][42]

Saint-Victor, unfortunately, was by no means the only critic to question the artist's mental equilibrium. In his *Quelques caricaturistes français* of 1857 Baudelaire observes, "A philosopher or a doctor would find material for a very pretty psychological or physiological study in Grandville" and concludes that "it is the lunatic side of his talent that makes Grandville important."[43]

What is especially surprising is that one of Grandville's closest friends, Edouard Charton, the very person who published the two dream metamorphoses in the *Magasin pittoresque,* appears to have harbored a realist bias, similar to that of Saint-Victor, as he too wondered about the artist's state of mind toward the end of his career. In the obituary that he wrote for *L'Illustration,* he stated, "On se concertait pour le ramener à des compositions plus positives, plus près de la réalité de moeurs actuelles, plus accessibles à l'intelligence de tous" (Together they [his friends] would work to bring him back to more down-to-earth compositions, closer to the reality of current conventions of appropriateness, more accessible to everyone's understanding). It was also undoubtedly Charton who later wrote the following caricatural appraisal of the artist's work habits in one of the articles dedicated to Grandville in the *Magasin pittoresque* between 1855 and 1857:

> Dès le lever du jour, il était assis devant sa table, le crayon à la main; il ne sortait jamais, ne se permettait aucune promenade, aucune visite, aucune récréation; . . . Ces habitudes laborieuses et sédentaires à l'excès eurent à la longue des conséquences regrettables à la fois sur la direction de l'esprit de Grandville et peut-être même sur la portée de son talent.
>
> [From the crack of dawn, he was seated at his desk, pencil in hand; he never went out, allowed himself no walks, no visits, no recreation whatsoever; . . . These excessively laborious and sedentary habits had in the

long run regrettable consequences for both the direction of Grandville's mind and perhaps even the range of his talent.][44]

The reason behind this slanted appraisal and the obituary comment would appear to be a vague sense of guilt. Even as he mourns his friend's passing, Charton self-righteously attempts to convince the reader (and reassure himself) that if only Grandville had followed his advice and treated more wholesomely real subjects, he would not have fallen victim to his own imaginative excesses.[45]

As noted in the introduction, it is only with those latter-day Romantics, the twentieth-century surrealists, that the reputation of a discredited and all-but-forgotten Grandville began to be rehabilitated. In his work, certain of them recognized a precursor to their own bizarre dream imagery. Max Ernst even drew an homage to the artist for the frontispiece of a 1963 facsimile edition of *Un autre monde* (Paris: Librairies associés).[46] And Walter Benjamin brought him to the attention of Marxist critics by finding in his work a precocious pictorial commentary on "the enthronement of the commodity" and the bourgeois pursuit of materialism in an age of mechanical reproduction.

In view of the adverse opinion of Grandville at the time of his death and his later appropriation by surrealists and Marxists, it is time for a more balanced judgment of his life and work. The primary purpose of the present study is to publish in extenso the drawings in the Missouri Album. Special emphasis is given to the diary fragments, which constitute the major portion of the album's contents. They provide us not only with an intimate glance of middle-class life during the Romantic period, but also with valuable biographical information on Grandville. In the process, they help to dispel the mythological account of the artist's life left by certain of his contemporaries. For example, contrary to what Charton would have us believe, they eloquently attest to the fact that Grandville led anything but a completely sedentary existence either during his youth or later years. Similarly, nowhere is there any evidence of a deranged mind.

A collateral purpose of this study is to make known the existence of Grandville's diary. For the moment, only those excerpts in the Missouri Album are known to have survived. With their publication, perhaps other segments of the diary will come to light and help in furthering a better understanding of Grandville and his art.

Notes

In addition to primary documents, the biography is based on Blanc, Charton, Clogenson, Nollet, and a series of four articles in the *Magasin pittoresque* that were most likely also authored by Charton: "J.-J. Grandville: Dessins inédits" 23, no. 45 (November 1855): 356–58; "J.-J. Grandville: Dessins inédits" 23, no. 48 (December 1855): 380–82; "Une scène de bal: Dessin inédit de J.-J. Grandville," 24, no. 52 (December 1856): 407–8; "Dessins inédits de J.-J. Grandville," 25, no. 14 (April 1857): 111–12. Details on Grandville's family background were taken from Pierre Boyé, "Les Grands-Parents paternels de J.-J. Grandville," *Le Pays Lorrain* (1931): 281–89. Much of the information on Grandville's friends and colleagues comes from Bénézit and other standard references such as the *Dictionnaire de biographie française.* The source of information on Philipon is Cuno.

1. There is some confusion as to how Gerard should be spelled: it is often given as Gérard, with an accent. However, it consistently appears without the accent on Grandville's birth certificate (which includes his father's unaccented signature), in an 1807 census, and on the family gravestone. Moreover, Grandville himself spells the family name without an accent in a letter dated August 18, 1847, and sent to his father-in-law, Antoine Fischer. As a result, I have opted for Gerard sans accent.

2. To be exact, the population of Paris in the following year of 1826 was 890,095, according to the *Statistique de la France* (Paris: Imprimerie Royale, 1837), 210.

3. The original edition of *La Sibylle des salons* carried only the images of various types. The emblems for playing whist were added in a later 1848 edition, as in the example illustrated here.

4. Although somewhat forgotten today, Lecomte enjoyed a certain celebrity during the Restoration and July Monarchy. He had married the daughter of Carle Vernet (1758–1836), and, according to Bénézit, it was probably as a result of his connections with the eminent Vernet dynasty that Lecomte received a large number of commissions for Louis-Philippe's pictorial gallery of French history at Versailles. Unfortunately, we do not know when Grandville entered Lecomte's studio, but his stay there must have been very brief indeed. For Philippe Grunchec, curator at the École des Beaux-Arts, was unable to find any mention of Grandville among the lists of Lecomte's students.

5. For accounts of lithography's early days, see Henri Bouchot, *La Lithographie* (Paris: Ancienne maison Quantin, 1895) and Michael Twyman, *Lithography, 1800–1850* (London: Oxford University Press, 1970).

6. Much has been written concerning the influence of Lavater on early nineteenth-century culture. For a study of physiognomic theory on French caricaturists in general and Daumier in particular, see Judith Wechsler, *A Human Comedy: Physiognomy and Caricature in 19th Century Paris* (Chicago: University of Chicago Press, 1982); a parallel study in the field of literature is Graeme Tytler's *Physiognomy in the European Novel* (Princeton: Princeton University Press, 1982). A more detailed discussion of Lavater's influence on Grandville may be found in Nancy, 14–19, and in my article, "Physiognomy, Science and Romantic Visual Satire," in *Correspondances: Studies in Literature, History, and the Arts in Nineteenth Century France,* ed. Keith Busby (Atlanta, GA: Rodopi, 1992), 71–102.

7. For a well-documented account of the professional relationship between Grandville and Charton, see Philippe Kaenel, "J.-J. Grandville et le *Magasin pittoresque* d'Edouard Charton," *Gazette des Beaux-Arts,* 6th ser., 115 (February 1990): 77–98.

8. Clogenson spells Falampin's name as Falempin. But Falampin without an "e" is to be found in Blanc, in the contract for *Les Étoiles* dated August 17, 1849, and in Charles de Meixmoron de Dombasle, "J.-J. Grandville," *Mémoires de l'Académie de Stanislas* 11 (1893): 303n1.

9. For a listing of Guiaud's prints in the Cabinet des estampes at the Bibliothèque nationale de France, see Jean Adhémar and Jacques Lethève, *Inventaire du fonds français après 1800* (Paris: Bibliothèque nationale, 1955), 9:473–76.

10. Both the sketchbook (D.6424) and the souvenir album (D.6423) were purchased by the museum in 1926 from a Mr. Guiaud, surely a direct descendent of Grandville's friend. Although Grandville was in the habit of keeping his drawings for future reference, he would occasionally give some to friends. Guiaud's souvenir album probably was compiled as drawings were given to him. It is equally probable that he received the sketchbook well after 1830 when it was no longer needed as an artistic aide-mémoire. For more detailed descriptions of these two albums, see André Desfeuilles, "Les dessins de J. I. Grandville du Musée Carnavalet," *Le Vieux Papier,* no. 212 (1965): 249–54, and Ségolène Le Men, *Grandville au Musée Carnavalet* (Paris: Paris-Musée, 1987).

11. Cuno, 155. For a more complete listing of Forest's print production, see Jean Adhémar and Jacques Lethève, *Inventaire du fonds français après 1800* (Paris: Bibliothèque nationale, 1954), 8:100–107.

12. Dumas, 5:76

13. Paul Louis, *Histoire de la classe ouvrière en France de la Révolution à nos jours* (Paris: Librairie Marcel Rivière, 1927), 51–52.

14. Guillaume de Bertier de Sauvigny, *The Bourbon Restoration,* trans. Lynn M. Case (Philadelphia: University of Pennsylvania Press, 1966), 295.

15. Thureau-Dangin, 1:13–44.

16. Ibid., 2:312–13.

17. Cuno, 107–08; Robert Justin Goldstein, *Censorship of Political Caricature in Nineteenth-Century France* (Kent, OH: Kent State University Press, 1989), 153–54.

18. Bechtel, 44.

19. The *Association mensuelle* (Monthly association) has undergone a number of name changes. In the facts of publication on the prints, they are variously labeled as belonging to the "association," the "Souscription mensuelle" (Monthly subscription), the "Souscription" (Subscripiton), the "association mensuelle" (Monthly association), and the "Lithographie mensuelle" (Monthly lithograph). Depending on the author, the collected prints are referred to as either the *Association mensuelle* or the *Lithographie mensuelle* (Delteil and Bechtel, for instance, use the former title and Vicaire the latter; I have chosen to follow the example of Delteil and Bechtel). For a more detailed discussion of the publication, see Bechtel as well as Ségolène Le Men, " 'Ma muse, ta muse, s'amuse . . .' Philipon et l'*Association mensuelle,*" in *Cahiers,* 62–102.

20. Additional accounts of Grandville's career as a political caricaturist may be found in Cuno, 148–58; Nancy, 205–79; and Renonciat, 66–97. For an overview of the caricatural opposition to the July Monarchy, see Gabriel P. Weisberg, "The Coded Image: Agitation in Aspects of Political and Social Caricature," in Missouri, 148–91. An excellent in-depth study is David S. Kerr, *Caricature and French Political Culture, 1830–1848: Charles Philipon and the Illustrated Press* (Oxford: Clarendon Press, 2000).

21. *Statistique de la France,* 210.

22. Long before his famous 1862 novel of the same name, Victor Hugo gave a wrenching description of these "misérables" in his 1832 preface to *Le Dernier jour d'un condamné* (1829). Robert Bezucha, in his essay, "Discourses on Misery" (*A New History of French Literature,* ed. Denis Hollier [Cambridge, MA: Harvard University Press, 1989], 687–92), observes that during the July Monarchy the term "les misérables" was used in reference to what was recognized as a separate social category. He also notes that in 1840 the fledgling field of social science saw the publication in Paris of three particularly devastating studies devoted to it: Eugène Buret, *De la Misère des classes laborieuses en Angleterre et en France,* 2 vols. (Paulin); H.-A. Frégier, *Des Classes dangereuses de la population dans les grandes villes,* 2 vols. (J.-B. Baillière); Dr. Louis-René Villermé, *Tableau de l'état physique et moral des ouvriers,* 2 vols. (J. Renouard). Additional discussions of the plight of the Parisian working class at this time may be found in Edouard Dolléans, *Histoire du mouvement ouvrier, 1830–1871,* 7th ed. (Paris: Librairie Armand Colin, 1967), 1:13–48 and in Hilde Rigaudias-Weiss, *Les Enquêtes ouvrières en France entre 1830 et 1848* (Paris: F. Alcan, 1936). For an exploration of the correlation between widespread poverty and crime in an overpopulated Paris, see Louis Chevalier, *Laboring Classes and Dangerous Classes in Paris during the First Half of the Nineteenth Century,* trans. Frank Jellinek (New York: Howard Fertig, 1973).

23. Michael Paul Driskel, "The Proletarian's Body: Charlet's Representations of Social Class during the July Monarchy," in Chu and Weisberg, 58–89.

24. Gabriel P. Weisberg, "Early Realism," in Missouri, 101–15; and "Proto-Realism in the July Monarchy: The Strategies of Philippe-Auguste Jeanron and Charles-Joseph Traviès," in Chu and Weisberg, 90–112.

25. Weisberg, "The Coded Image," in Missouri, 149.

26. Antoine-Gustave *Ferdinand* was born on October 27, 1834, and died of a cerebral congestion on July 5, 1838, a few months before his fourth birthday. A second son, Jean-Baptiste *Henri,* was born toward the autumn of 1838 and suffocated on a piece of bread lodged in his throat during the first half of 1841, or before his third birthday.

27. Charles Blanc has led scholars to believe that the surname of Grandville's second wife was Lhuillier (305). However, in their marriage certificate, dated October 28, 1843, Céline's surname is given as L'hullier; furthermore, the signatures of both Céline and her mother affixed at the end of the document use this same spelling. An alternate way of writing L'hullier was without the apostrophe, or "Lhullier." This latter spelling was used in both Céline's marriage contract with Grandville, dated October 24, 1843, and in a posthumous *déclaration du comparant,* or court deposition, dated September 1, 1888. All the above-cited documents are to be found in the Archives Départementales de Meurthe-et-Moselle, Nancy.

28. Detailed discussions of Grandville's career as a book illustrator may be found in Nancy, 281–401 and Renonciat, 150–285 as well as in two studies by Philippe Kaenel: "Autour de J.-J. Grandville: Les Conditions de production socio-professionnelles du livre illustré romantique," *Romantisme* 43 (1984): 45–61; *Le Métier d'illustrateur, 1830–1880: Rodolphe Töpffer, J.-J. Grandville, Gustave Doré* (Paris: Editions Messene, 1996).

29. The sources for this and much of the background information that follows concerning Romantic book illustration are Robert Bezucha, "The Renaissance of Book Illustration," in Missouri, 192–213; Pierre Gusman, *La Gravure sur bois en France au XIXe siècle* (Paris: Editions Albert Morancé, 1929); Michel Melot, "Le texte et l'image," in *Le Temps des éditeurs: Du Romantisme à la Belle Époque,* ed. Henri-Jean Martin and Roger Chartier, vol. 3 of *Histoire de l'édition française* (Paris: Promodis, 1985), 287–311; Ségolène Le Men, "La vignette et la lettre," ibid., 313–27; Charles Rosen and Henri Zerner, "The Romantic Vignette and Thomas Bewick," in *Romanticism and Realism* (New York: Viking Press, 1984), 71–96. Additional information may be found in Charles Blanc, *The Grammar of Painting and Engraving,* trans. Kate Newell Doggert (New York: Hurd and Houghton, 1874); Henri Bouchot, *Les Livres à vignettes du XIXe siècle* (Paris: E. Rouveyre, 1891); Jules Brivois, *Bibliographie des ouvrages illustrés du XIXe siècle, principalement des livres à gravures sur bois* (Paris: L. Conquet, 1883); Jules Champfleury, *Les Vignettes romantiques* (Paris: E. Dentu, 1883); Gordon N. Ray, *The Art of the French Illustrated Book, 1700–1914,* 2 vols. (New York: Pierpont Morgan Library, 1982). See also Philippe Kaenel's *Le Métier d'illustrateur, 1830–1880,* cited in the previous note.

30. Born in Lyon, Desperet, like Grandville, Forest, and Philipon was yet another provincial who sought fame and fortune in the French capital. A talented caricaturist and lithographer, he was employed throughout his career by his fellow Lyonnais, Philipon (see Cuno, 155). As Vicaire points out, his name was spelled "sometimes Desperret, sometimes Deperret, sometimes Desperet" (2:55). Like Vicaire and Béraldi (*Les Graveurs du XIXe siècle*), I have chosen the last spelling.

31. Both volumes of bound drawings and the prefatory letter are in the collection of the Nancy Bibliothèque municipale. A full transcription of the letter may be found in Nancy, 1–6. It should be emphasized that Grandville was by no means the only Romantic book illustrator who felt betrayed by intervening hands. Jean Gigoux and Tony Johannot, among others, complained about their dependence upon wood engravers of varying skill (Gusman, 33).

32. Bezucha, 210. This quotation in Régnier-Destourbet, *Un bal sous Louis-Philippe* (Paris: Dumont, 1831) is cited by both Gusman, 26, and Melot, 295.

33. Rosen and Zerner, 81–84. Bezucha cites this same passage in Missouri, 193.

34. A detailed inventory of Grandville's fortune, drawn up on October 10, 1843, at the time of his second marriage, is preserved at the Archives Départementales de Meurthe-et-Moselle in Nancy. The annual expenditures for the household of a Parisian skilled worker in 1840, cited by Driskel in Chu and Weisberg, 70, may be found in Paul Louis's, *Histoire de la classe ouvrière en France de la Révolution à nos jours,* 68. For the amounts Grandville was paid for various book illustration projects, see Renonciat, 147–49.

35. For a more complete analysis of the origin and iconography of *Un autre monde*'s imagery, see Nancy, 340–41 and Stanley Appelbaum, *Bizarreries and Fantasies of Grandville* (New York: Dover, 1974).

36. Clogenson, 275.

37. Charles Baudelaire, *The Painter of Modern Life and Other Essays,* trans. and ed. Jonathan Mayne (London: Phaidon Press, 1964), 181.

38. Grandville, *Les Métamorphoses du jour,* Accompagnées d'un texte par MM. Albéric Second, Louis Lurine, Clément Caraguel, Taxile Delord, H. de Beaulieu, Louis Huart, Charles Monselet, Julien Lemer, précédées d'une notice sur Grandville par M. Charles Blanc (Paris: Gustave Havard, 1854). Blanc's account of Grandville was later reprinted in 1855 as a small book and in 1876 as part of his *Les Artistes de mon temps.*

39. Baudelaire, 182. Baudelaire's assumption that the dream metamorphoses recorded Grandville's own dreams and nightmares is erroneous. For a more detailed discussion of their origin in the artist's experiments with analogous shapes, see Nancy, cat. no. 324.

40. This was the source of much chagrin for family members. Before she died in 1888, his widow, Céline, left the following note intended for the couple's only child, Armand:

> [je] l'adjure en toute vérité de ne pas croire quelques journaux qui ont dénaturé le caractère de la mort de son père . . . qu'il s'est alité le 1er mars 1847, souffrant d'une angine, qu'il a été pris le huitième jour d'un transport au cerveau, qui nécessita son entrée à l'hospice de Vanves où il mourut après trois jours d'agonie, le 17 mars. (Nancy, *Inauguration du monument de J.-J. Grandville* [Nancy: Imprimerie Coopérative de l'Est, 1893], 16)

> [(I) beseech him in all truth not to believe some journals that have distorted the nature of his father's death . . . that he took to his bed March 1, 1847, suffering from an angina, that he was seized by delirium on the eighth day, which necessitated his entering the hospice at Vanves where he died on March 17 after three days of agony]

According to the note of another relative, Madame Marguerite Parisot Cordier, the great-niece of Grandville's first wife, Henriette, "Grandville est mort d'une esquinancie mal soignée qui lui a amené une crise d'urémie, avec délire, les derniers jours" (Grandville died from a poorly treated case of severe tonsillitis, which in the last days led to an attack of uremia, with delirium).

41. Paul de Saint-Victor, "2e Dizain," in Gavarni, *D'après nature* (Paris: Morizot, 1858), 16. A respected author, Saint-Victor was the drama and literary critic for the Parisian newspaper, *La Presse.* His criticism could be witty as well as devastating, and Grandville was by no means his only victim. Another example is the Barbizon School artist, Jean-François Millet (1814–75). It was Saint-Victor who, in his review of the Salon of 1857 for *La Presse,* coined the phrase "the Three Fates of Pauperism" when describing the three peasant women in Millet's famous painting, *The Gleaners,* exhibited that year.

42. Paul de Saint-Victor, "Revue dramatique," *Le Pays: Journal de l'Empire,* September 18, 1854. Saint-Victor belonged to a clique of artists and writers who socialized with and admired Gavarni. Other members of the group were Théophile Gautier (1811–72) and Charles Augustin Sainte-Beuve (1804–69). In his necrological notice on Grandville published in the March 29, 1847, issue of *La Presse,* the former, while praising his moralizing animals, is generally unappreciative of the rest of Grandville's oeuvre, which he finds lacking in clarity, the result of a mind characterized by "a belabored weirdness and a complicated fantasy." Like Saint-Victor, he unfavorably compares him to Gavarni:

> Grandville, quand il abandonnait la critique de l'homme par l'animal, était un esprit plus bizarre qu'original, plus chercheur que primesautier, d'une étrangeté laborieuse et d'une fantaisie compliquée; nature à la fois craintive et audacieuse, hardie dans la pensée, timide dans l'exécution, il s'est souvent mépris sur la portée et les moyens d'expression de son art. Il a voulu faire parler au crayon le langage de la plume; mais, n'ayant pas la ressource des piquantes légendes qui servent d'âme aux croquis de Gavarni, il manque souvent de clarté et ne présente aux yeux que des rébus difficiles à deviner. (*Portraits contemporains* [Paris: Charpentier, 1874], 231–32)

> [When he abandoned the critique of humanity through the use of animals, Grandville's mind was more bizarre than original, more searching than quick-witted, of a belabored weirdness and a complicated fantasy; possessing a temperament both fearful and bold, daring in thought, timid in execution, he was often mistaken about the scope and the means of expression of his art. He wanted to make the pencil speak the language of the pen; but not having recourse to the piquant captions which serve as the soul of Gavarni's drawings, he often lacks clarity and only presents to the eyes rebuses difficult to decipher.]

Circumstantial evidence suggests that these negative assessments of Grandville by Saint-Victor and Gautier were not simply a question of aesthetics. The vitriolic tone of Saint-Victor's article, in particular, seems to be rooted in an antipathy for Grandville as a person as well as an artist. The source of this animosity may have been Gavarni. As Sainte-Beuve relates, when Émile Forgues (Old Nick), the author of *Petites misères de la vie humaine* and an intimate of Gavarni, arranged a meeting between the two artists, it was a fiasco:

> Grandville était un sauvage. Quand Gavarni voulut le connaître, il en fut très-flatté, mais il s'en fit une affaire . . . Le dîner à trois se fit. Grandville s'y prépara comme à un événement; il se pommada, se parfuma et crut n'en avoir jamais fait assez pour être à la hauteur. Gavarni en fut pour ses frais de naturel et ne réussit point à le familiariser. Ce dîner trop laborieux ne recommença pas. (*Nouveaux Lundis,* 7th ed. rev. [Paris: Calmann Lévy, 1890–94], 6:193.)
>
> [Grandville was impossible. When Gavarni wanted to make his acquaintance, he was very flattered but turned the whole thing into an affair . . . The dinner for three took place. Grandville prepared himself as though for an event; he pomaded his hair, perfumed himself, and did not think that he could ever do enough to measure up to the occasion. Gavarni wasted his time trying to be down-to-earth and did not succeed in familiarizing himself with him. This too laborious dinner was not repeated.]

Sainte-Beuve's scarcely concealed contempt for Grandville parallels the negative reactions of Saint-Victor and Gautier.

Gavarni was generally supportive of other artists' efforts. However, in a note to Forgues he explains why he cannot abide Grandville's illustrations to the *Petites misères* and berates his friend for having collaborated on the publication:

> laissons l'art d'écrire . . . mais la vie humaine, vieux diable! c'est une autre chanson et je ne souffre pas aussi bonnement qu'on me désenchante la vie! . . . Vraiment, il te fallait la traîteuse bonhomie de Grandville, Old Nick, il fallait cette naïveté rare du comique dans la forme pour faire passer cette amertune [*sic*] de l'idée. Grandville a t-il été assez moqueur! assez hypocrite et impitoyable! Mais vers la fin, sa joie ne se contient plus; le masque tombe: il lui faut achever ce pauvre bourgeois, ce pauvre grand seigneur, ce pauvre merveilleux, ces pauvres femmes, jusqu'au chat, jusqu'au chien! Il fait souffrir tout cela, brise tout cela, puis il empile ces martyrs dans un wagon pour les envoyer on ne sait où. On croit que tout est dit; mais pour le bouquet, bon Dieu! il fait sauter la chaudière! Oh! vous pouvez vous donner la main. Vous n'avez eu de pitié pour personne, ni l'un ni l'autre; pas une de nos misères n'aura échappé à ce martyrologe . . . Quant à ton collaborateur, si j'avais, comme juré, à le déclarer coupable des dessins de tes "*Petites Misères*", je voudrais faire condamner Grandville à *illustrer* le parfait Cuisinier ou le Mérite des Femmes. (Paul-André Lemoisne, *Gavarni, peintre et lithographe* [Paris: H. Floury, 1924–28], 2:233n2)
>
> [let's leave the art of writing . . . but human life, old devil! that's another story and I am not as good-naturedly tolerant when one disenchants me with life! . . . Really, you had to have the false bonhomie of Grandville, Old Nick, you had to have that singular comical naïveté of form in order to sugarcoat the bitterness of the idea. Was Grandville sarcastic enough! hypocritical and merciless enough! But toward the end, his glee no longer contains itself; the mask falls away: he has to finish off this poor bourgeois, this poor great nobleman, this poor dandy, these poor women, right down to the cat and the dog! He makes all of them suffer, smashes all of them, then crowds these martyrs into a coach in order to send them off to who knows where. You think that everything has been said; but for the finale, good God! he blows up the boiler! Oh! you can congratulate yourself. Neither one of you has had pity on anyone; not a one of our misfortunes will have escaped this martyrology . . . As for your collaborator, if I had to, as a juror, declare him guilty of the drawings for your "Little Misfortunes," I would like to have Grandville condemned to *illustrate* the perfect Cook or the Merit of Women.]

It is not impossible that Saint-Victor's, Gautier's, and Sainte-Beuve's bias against Grandville was grounded to a certain degree in their friendship and admiration for Gavarni. If this were indeed the case, the Grandville myth in large part would have been the result of what has all the appearances of a cabal of influential writers closely affiliated with Gavarni.

43. Baudelaire, 181, 182.

44. "J.-J. Grandville. Dessins inédits." *Magasin pittoresque* 23, no. 48 (December 1855): 380.

45. Grandville would not have been alone in being a victim of midcentury realist prejudice on the part of well-meaning friends. One of the more fascinating episodes in nineteenth-century French literature occurred in 1849, just two years after Grandville's death, when Flaubert gave an initial reading of his wildly Romantic *La Tentation de saint Antoine* (*The Temptation of Saint Anthony*) to Louis Bouilhet and Maxime Du Camp, the latter a champion of realism in literature. Like Charton's advice to Grandville, the two friends urged Flaubert to abandon his visionary "divagations" for a more down-to-earth subject. He temporarily did, and the result was *Madame Bovary* (1857). (See Maxime Du Camp, *Souvenirs littéraires* [Paris: Hachette, 1892], 1:299–317.)

46. For a more detailed analysis of the link between Max Ernst and Grandville, see my essay, "Max Ernst and J. J. Grandville," in *Twenty-First-Century Perspectives on Nineteenth-Century Art: Essays in Honor of Gabriel P. Weisberg,* ed. Petra ten-Doesschate Chu and Laurinda S. Dixon (Newark: University of Delaware Press, 2008), 116–23.

II

History and Description of the Missouri Album

Introduction

There once existed a collection of Grandville documents that included a sketchbook, apparently several letters, and diaries from the years 1830, 1832, 1833, and 1846. At some undetermined date, though probably toward the end of the nineteenth century, someone culled illustrated pages from the sketchbook and cut up the letters and the diaries for the drawings contained in them. These were then glued onto the pages of a scrapbook or souvenir album.[1] This twenty-five-page album is now in the Special Collections of the University of Missouri-Columbia Libraries.

The importance of the Missouri Album lies in the diary fragments, which contain the majority of the drawings and provide significant new information about Grandville's life and work. The drawings in the album have never been published and are examined here in catalog format. Since most are from Grandville's diary, the commentary accompanying them forms a biographical narrative. This study complements in many ways that done in 1986 on the extensive collection of Grandville drawings at the Nancy Musée des Beaux-Arts, *Grandville: Dessins originaux.*

Bound volumes of Grandville drawings are rare. Presently, only seven are known to exist. As noted in the biography, two of them previously belonged to Grandville's close friend, Jacques Guiaud, and are now at the Musée Carnavalet in Paris. One of these is the only Grandville sketchbook known to have survived intact. Along with numerous studies for the lithographic suite, *Voyage pour l'éternité,* it contains satirical commentaries on the fall of Charles X during the Revolution of 1830. The other is a type of *liber amicorum,* composed of drawings that were presumably given to Guiaud by Grandville over the course of their long friendship. Four other volumes of drawings are to be found in the Nancy Bibliothèque municipale. Two of them form a set comprising nearly all the preliminary studies for the *Fables de La Fontaine,* which Grandville himself had bound. A third volume contains human/animal metamorphoses and the fourth, a collection of studies for *Les Fleurs animées.*

Given the fact that the six other known volumes of drawings are to be found in French public collections, it is rather surprising to learn that a seventh is located outside of France at an American university. The provenance of the University of Missouri album remains somewhat unclear. According to the former head of Special Collections, Mrs. Margaret Howell, Dr. Hellmut Lehmann-Haupt, a professor in the School of Library and Informational Science, purchased it for the Special Collections from his former employer, the New York book dealer H. P. Kraus, in what was probably November 1970. Mr. Kraus in turn had purchased the album in 1966 from a Parisian book dealer, Despina Rousseau-Girard, who had obtained it from an undisclosed source.

Establishing the authenticity of the drawings is less problematic. Stylistically, they present numerous parallels with the extensive collection of drawings kept by the artist's family and given to the Nancy Musée des Beaux-Arts upon the death of Grandville's son, Armand.[2] Furthermore, the writing that accompanies many of the drawings is identical to that found in Grandville's correspondence. Last, the persons and events mentioned in the diary fragments leave no doubt as to their author.

The album itself appears to be of commercial manufacture. It is half black leather with gold stamping in an oblong twelvemo format (162 × 215 × 42 mm) with end pages of heavy construction paper faced in a simulated silk pattern. The twenty-five blue flocked cardboard pages, each measuring approximately 150 × 182 mm, are attached to the spine by cloth hinges. It has all the appearance of a fairly ordinary nineteenth-century scrapbook or souvenir album.

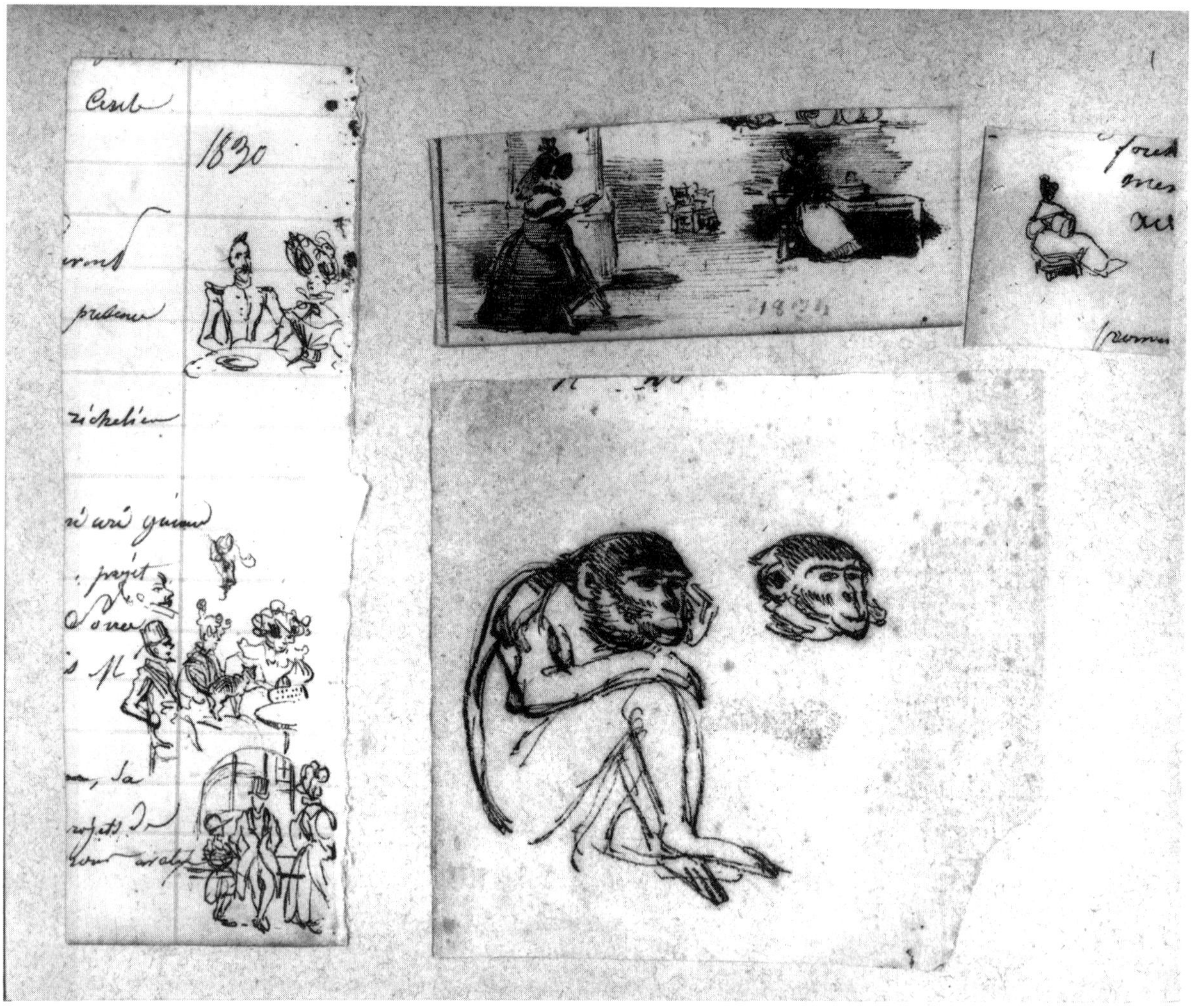

Fig. 36. Page 1 from the Missouri Album, 1830–34, drawings. University of Missouri-Columbia Libraries.

What is not ordinary, of course, is the album's contents. Glued to its pages on paper hinges are seventy-nine pieces of paper of varying sizes containing on their rectos and versos thirteen wash or watercolor-tinted drawings, seven pencil sketches, and approximately one hundred pen and ink sketches by Grandville (fig. 36).[3] Two additional drawings are also probably by Grandville (cat. nos. 84 and 85). Six children's drawings (cat. nos. 86–90) and what appears to be a collaborative effort on the part of Grandville and his son, Georges (cat. no. 82), complete the set. Many of the pieces of paper are postage-stamp size. Most were originally part of diaries from the years 1830, 1832, 1833, and 1846 (the diary of 1834 may or may not be represented by three drawings on two very small paper fragments). Three seem to have been cut out of letters (cat. nos. 81, 84, 85). Seven appear to be full-size pages from a dismantled sketchbook (cat. nos. 38–44). The weights of the paper naturally differ from one group of drawings to the next. For the most part, drawings from the same year were arranged together, thereby dividing the album into three main sections: (1) excerpts from the 1846 diary (pp. 2–7), (2) excerpts from the 1833 diary (pp. 8–14), and (3) remnants of the dismantled sketchbook (pp. 15–21). Excerpts from the 1830 and 1832 diaries and the presumed 1834 diary are scattered, apparently being glued to pages where they best filled in leftover spaces (pp. 1, 6, 7). Two sheets from the 1833 diary have been placed out of sequence at the end of the album (pp. 23 and 24). Several miscellaneous drawings and those from letters dating from 1830 to 1846 are scattered in the same fashion as the excerpts from the 1830, 1832, and 1834 diaries, appearing wherever they best serve to complete the systematic grid arrangement of the slips of paper on a page.

Subjects of the Drawings

The subjects of the drawings vary. Those cut out of the diaries depict a multiplicity of different events, from the commonplace to the unexpected or unusual, that occurred during the course of a day. Equally disparate in subject matter are the drawings found on what appear to be letter fragments. Most of the drawings on the seven leaves from the dismantled sketchbook center around projects for the amusement of children: studies for a pictorial alphabet, seven illustrations to "Little Red Riding Hood," and another illustration depicting an episode from the legend of Saint Nicholas, the patron saint of Grandville's native province of Lorraine. On the back of or attached to these same leaves are three children's drawings as well as the one that appears to be a collaborative work by Grandville and his son, Georges.

The most intriguing drawings are those from the diaries of 1830, 1833, and 1846 (as with the presumed diary of 1834, there are only two tiny fragments from the 1832 diary). The drawings, themselves, especially those from 1833, are often exquisite. But perhaps even more significant are the revelations to be found in the written entries surrounding them. For these diary fragments provide rare and at times surprisingly intimate glimpses into the day-to-day activities of Grandville during three particularly significant years of his life. The year 1830, for instance, witnesses the artist's transition from an author of popular lithographic albums, such as *Les Métamorphoses du jour,* to a full-blown opposition caricaturist as a result of the liberalization of the press in the wake of the revolution of that same year. And the year 1833 is equally critical for Grandville's professional and private life. It marks both the midpoint in his career as a political caricaturist and his change in status from a bachelor to a husband. Excerpts from the diary record preparations for his wedding in July and document his close ties with Daumier, a junior colleague and occasional collaborator on the staff of *La Caricature.* Most importantly, they reveal Grandville's severe reservations about his career as an opposition caricaturist whose work had attracted the unwelcome attention of the police, a particularly disturbing development for someone contemplating marriage and raising a family. They imply that there were reasons other than the severe censorship laws of September 1835 for Grandville's decision to abandon the field of political caricature and to embark upon a new career in book illustration. As mentioned in the introduction, the diary entries from 1846 provide an intimate and poignant glance into the domestic tranquillity enjoyed by Grandville during the last full year of his life. Surrounded by his second wife, Céline L'hullier, and his two small sons, Georges and Armand, he records the simple pleasures of family life he loved so much. This idyllic existence, we have seen, was to be shattered in January 1847 with the sudden and unexpected death of Georges, which was followed by the artist's own demise two months later.

Types of Drawings

The drawings from the diaries fall into three categories: (1) sketches from life, (2) daily events drawn from memory, and (3) miniature copies of larger-scale drawings. Many from 1830 and 1833 appear to be sketches from life, indicating that Grandville was in the habit of carrying his diary with him and occasionally using it as a supplementary or substitute sketchbook. Those from 1846 seem to be for the most part drawn from memory and often border on doodling, recording such mundane matters as changing weather conditions. Only rarely will a drawing replicate in miniature a larger, more finished composition, such as the portrait of Grandville's neighbor at Chatou, Charles Duval (cat. no. 54).

The drawings on what appear to be letter fragments were probably done from memory. And the illustrations for "Little Red Riding Hood" and the legend of Saint Nicholas display Grandville's talent for composing imaginary scenes.

Page Design

Because of the tiny pieces of paper on which they are found and because of their small number, it is not possible to discuss the arrangement of the drawings on the assumed letter fragments. And that of the illustrations for children's stories is perfectly conventional, with the vignettes centered or symmetrically arranged on the sheets that support them.

However, several relatively large fragments from 1830 and 1833 demonstrate that the disposition of drawings on pages in the diaries was often anything but commonplace. This is not totally unexpected given the different nature of the drawings and the likelihood that they, as well as the written entries, were entered into the diary at different times of the day. The interrelationship of drawings, text, and page that results can be exceedingly varied, following no set formula. For example, the drawings may depict in sequence the events of a day, one following the other in chronological order like the registers in a comic book (cat. no. 3). Or their arrangement may be less rigid with image and text casually flowing into one another in an apparently random pattern (cat. no. 16). In either case, their placement is not totally haphazard. To be sure, chance undoubtedly played a major role in any given page's appearance, with Grandville unable to predict which entries, either written or drawn, would occur during the course of the day. But it is equally apparent that his innate sense of visual order took advantage of these chance encounters on the page in order to create extremely varied, yet harmonious compositional wholes. Moreover, it should be emphasized that there is no sense of hierarchy between word and image: as with vignettes, no artificial frames separate image from text, with the result that neither one is privileged over the other in its distribution on the page. Instead, the two merge imperceptibly into one another. Thus, from one page to the next, as he added words to images and images to words like separate pieces in an evolving puzzle, Grandville created a seemingly endless variety of distinctive compositional arrangements. There is every reason to believe that the daily casual experience of working out experimental page designs in his diary was a fortuitous but decisive first step toward the calculated inventiveness of page designs for illustrated books such as *Petites misères de la vie humaine* and *Un autre monde* where image and text are treated as equal partners in an innovative book design adventure (fig. 37).

Graphic Style

Grandville habitually worked out compositions lightly in pencil, saving pen and ink for fixing their definitive forms. Numerous examples of this procedure appear in the drawings from Nancy as well as in the diary drawings, notably those from 1830 and 1833, where unerased pencil lines may be glimpsed beneath those drawn in pen and ink. Occasionally Grandville would highlight a composition with gouache, shade it with wash, or tint it with watercolor. However, it is not so much the medium of pen and ink that distinguishes Grandville's work as the manner in which it is used.

Il se pose enfin sur ta poitrine où ton cœur cesse de battre
Alors les prestiges qui forment son cortége bizarre s'emparent à l'envi de leur proie.
Tu es emporté, par une puissance inconnue et redoutable, dans la spirale d'un escalier dont tes pieds ne touchent pas les degrés.
Ton lit, devenu chaloupe et jouet d'une mer houleuse, court,
10

Fig. 37. Page 73 from *Petites misères de la vie humaine,* 1843, wood engraving. Paris, Bibliothèque nationale de France.

The distinctive clarity and minute precision of Grandville's linear style may be traced to his formal training in the studio of his miniaturist father. However, Grandville's contemporaries often criticized his obsession with the precise rendering of descriptive detail. Baudelaire reproached him for lacking "souplesse" (lissomeness), and, as we have already seen, likened the artist's graphic style to "the precision of a stenographer writing down an orator's speech." Even an admirer such as Charles Blanc characterized the form in Grandville's work as "correcte et positive, aride même" (accurate and matter-of-fact, even dry).[4] True, Grandville's graphic style lacks the verve and robust eloquence found in Daumier, and it does not possess the elegant fluidity of Ingres. But it is neither as dry and lifeless as Blanc would have it nor as pedestrian as Baudelaire pretends. Considered within the context of Grandville's nearly manic obsession with precision, it possesses its own mesmerizing charm, captivating the viewer who takes the time to investigate and at length appreciate the detailed images Grandville so painstakingly achieved. Furthermore, Grandville's graphic style is not totally devoid of a certain elegance, nor does it remain the same. We know that Grandville admired both Ingres and Daumier,[5] who no doubt served as models in his attempt during his later years to create a certain graceful liveliness within his own very linear style. And throughout his career he experimented with different visual effects, which tempered his compulsion for laborious exactitude.

The drawings in the Missouri Album, particularly those found among the diary excerpts from 1830, 1833, and 1846, provide an excellent opportunity to observe these changes, which are much less apparent in the secondhand interpretations of Grandville's published lithographs and wood engravings. The drawings from the 1830 diary represent the culmination of a luminous style, characterized by strongly outlined figures silhouetted against blank backgrounds, which Grandville had been developing since his arrival in Paris in 1825. They offer numerous parallels with the very accomplished pen and ink drawings from 1829–30 depicting dance halls and prostitutes in the collection of the Nancy Musée des Beaux-Arts (Nancy, cat. nos. 127–41). Robust lines of varying thickness shape figures in strong, yet graceful contours. Modeling within these firm contours is minimal, often limited to those lines needed to indicate the folds in the fall of a dress or the outline of a lapel. There is also equally robust hatched and crosshatched shading, but it is used primarily to provide value contrast as Grandville colors the darkness of a man's suit or a brunette's hair. Cast shadows are nearly nonexistent. The resultant drawings possess a brilliant clarity reminiscent of neoclassic line engravings, even though Grandville's lively play of differently calibrated lines differs markedly from the coldly uniform outlines of neoclassic silhouettes. Also like neoclassic engravings, these earlier works tend to appear flat. This flatness is due not just to their linear modeling and general lack of shadows, but also to Grandville's consistent use of classic bas-relief compositions where figures are arranged close to the frontal plane, silhouetted against a blank or nearly blank background.

By 1833 Grandville's graphic style had changed radically. If his style in 1830 may be described as bright and clear, that of 1833 may be characterized as dark and atmospheric. While retaining their rhythmic flow, robust contour outlines have become thick, heavy, and somewhat blurred, often fusing with an extensive use of wash and an elaborate network of hatched and crosshatched shading both inside and outside an object's profile. As a result, figures appear to possess dark halos that blend with an equally dark, all-enveloping, foglike atmosphere. In another marked departure, they now also cast solid, dark shadows, giving more depth to what are still essentially bas-relief compositions.

The reason for so drastic a stylistic change within such a brief span of time can be traced to Grandville's interest in the theater: figures in these drawings often appear as though at the front of a stage, brightly illuminated by footlights, emerging out of the darkness like apparitions. The first artist to use this type of high-contrast lighting was Caravaggio, who became famous for his *tenebroso,* or "dark manner," style of painting during the seventeenth century. Tenebroso may also be used to describe

Grandville's own "dark manner" of 1833. The first indications of Grandville's tenebrous style appear in depictions of theatrical productions from around 1829, such as the *Last Scene from Lancastre* in figure 40. Simultaneously, Grandville started to experiment with tenebroso effects in other drawings. In the next few years, dramatically dark shading gradually established itself within his graphic style: the drawings from the 1833 diary represent a culminating point in this process. Drawings after 1833 just as gradually become less tenebrous. On occasion, Grandville even reverted back to the brilliant clarity of his earlier style.

The drawings from the 1846 diary demonstrate that by the end of his career Grandville had formulated a synthesis of the two earlier styles described above. Although more delicately thin, lines once again firmly contour objects, but they are livelier and more sinuous, creating a fluidity at times reminiscent of Ingres. Shading is present in hatching and crosshatching that convincingly model forms in a carefully rendered chiaroscuro. Similarly, cast shadows create the illusion of spatial depth with the result that figures project more from what are still mostly blank backgrounds. Thus, despite their often postage-stamp size, the drawings from the 1846 diary illustrate the last stage in the development of Grandville's graphic style.

It should be emphasized, however, that the drawings in the Missouri Album present more than a convenient outline of Grandville's stylistic changes. They are first and foremost a delight to the eye. Since most of them were executed in his diary for his own private viewing and amusement, they are the purest manifestation of Grandville's talents as a draftsman that we are likely to encounter. Unlike his highly finished compositions destined for publication, which at times betray studied or even fretful effort, these images appear to flow effortlessly from the artist's mind onto the paper, hence their charm. Spontaneous and fresh, their unassuming casualness first disarms and then totally captivates the viewer. This is especially true of the drawings from the 1833 diary which are among the most beautiful Grandville ever produced.

Notes

1. The identity of the individual, or possibly individuals, who committed this questionable act will probably never be known. The epilogue explores the possibility that the compiler of the Missouri Album may have been Armand Grandville, the artist's only child to reach maturity and his last direct descendant.
2. For an account of this donation, see Nancy, 417 and 419.
3. Many sheets contain multiple pen and ink sketches, some of which may be counted either separately or as belonging to a related adjacent sketch, hence the approximate number.
4. Blanc, 275.
5. *Les Etoiles* (Paris: de Gonet, 1849), vi.

III
Catalog

Introduction

The catalog reproduces in chronological sequence all the drawings in the Missouri Album along with, whenever possible, their versos. Those versos that could not be photographed are either described or have their annotations transcribed. The first line of each entry identifies the drawing according to the number of the page in the album on which it is found as well as to its placement on that page, reading from top to bottom and left to right. The number of the page appears first, followed by a slash, after which appears the number designating the placement of the drawing on the album page: for example, drawing 7/3 (cat. no. 4) is located on page seven of the album and is the third drawing on the page, counting from top to bottom and left to right. Sheets that have drawings or annotations on both sides are normally listed twice under the same catalog number, with the identification number followed by recto or verso. However, when other diary entries chronologically fall between the recto and verso of a diary fragment, or when drawings have been attached to the back of another drawing, then both the recto and verso of a sheet have been given their own catalog numbers. Below the catalog number appear in italics any Grandville annotations. Respecting his orthographical and grammatical errors, they are transcribed as faithfully as possible letter for letter and line for line as they appear on the drawing. Crossed-out words that are legible appear between brackets; fragments of words have been completed, where feasible, with bracketed letters. Also between brackets are descriptions of annotations, such as lists of numbers, which are so fragmentary as to elude any meaningful decipherment. Immediately following Grandville's annotations are their English translation between parentheses (uncompleted fragments of words have been left in the original French). The next line indicates the documented or assumed date of the drawing, while the second to the last line provides its dimensions in millimeters, height followed by width. The last line gives the medium. In most cases it is pen and brown ink, often over pencil, as was Grandville's usual practice. Occasionally it is designated by the French term, *crayon noir* (literally, "black crayon"), a drawing material that Grandville frequently employed during his early years.[1] Where space permits, the drawings are reproduced in their actual size.

Because they constitute the major part of the album, fragments from the 1830, 1833, and 1846 diaries provide the basis for the catalog's chronological framework and appear in as strict a chronological sequence as possible. Consequently, when either printed or written dates justify it, the verso of a diary fragment that has been glued arbitrarily to an album leaf may appear before the recto.

Diary of 1830

Those fragments from the diary of 1830 that have survived appear to date from February and March, or before the revolution of that year. It was a time when Grandville first enjoyed a certain celebrity as a result of the successful publication of *Les Métamorphoses du jour,* whose penultimate plates were registered with the state-mandated *dépôt légal* (copyright registration) some seven months earlier, on June 6, 1829.[1] According to Charles Blanc, the satirical lithographs became the talk of the town: "on les trouvait sur tous les guéridons, dans toutes les mains" (they were found on all the side tables, [and] in everyone's hands).[2] However, despite this success, Grandville continued to live in his one-room garret apartment at 10, rue des Petits-Augustins, which he had been renting since 1828 and which he would inhabit until his first marriage in July 1833.

An article in the *Magasin pittoresque,* undoubtedly authored by Edouard Charton, describes the ambivalent attitude of more "serious" aspiring young artists toward the nascent fame of their caricaturist colleague during what was probably the winter of 1829–30:

> Je rencontrai Grandville pour la première fois dans un atelier d'architecte où se réunissaient chaque soir, en hiver, de jeunes artistes. Seul d'entre les habitués, il avait déjà une réputation: les *Métamorphoses du jour,* son chef-d'oeuvre, l'avaient mis au premier rang de nos dessinateurs satiriques. Je remarquai son air de modeste défiance: je fus plus étonné de voir que la jeune réunion ne paraissait pas tenir en bien grande estime son talent et son succès. Les élèves en peinture y dominaient: ils se préparaient aux concours de l'école et avaient en perspective le prix de Rome; ils aspiraient à continuer Gérard, Gros, Girodet; ils rêvaient la poésie et la gloire. Pour eux, Grandville, prenant place, dès son début, à un des degrés inférieurs de l'art, et paraissant résolu à s'y tenir, s'était volontairement limité, amoindri: on était presque tenté de le plaindre; c'était un homme classé, fini, un caricaturiste. Où sont aujourd'hui ces jeunes enthousiastes? Que sont-ils devenus? Jusqu'où leurs fières espérances ont-elles fleuri? Leurs noms planent-ils bien haut au-dessus de celui de Grandville? Je les cherche. Hélas! la plupart d'entre eux ne sont point sortis de l'obscurité.
>
> [I encountered Grandville for the first time in an architect's atelier where young artists met every evening in winter. He alone of the habitués already had a reputation: the *Métamorphoses du jour,* his masterpiece, had placed him in the first rank of our satiric artists. I noted his air of modest diffidence: I was more surprised to see that the young assembly did not seem to hold in very high esteem his talent and his success. Painting students predominated: they were preparing themselves for the competitions at the École des Beaux-Arts and had in view the *prix de Rome* [the Rome prize]; they aspired to continue Gérard, Gros, Girodet [students of Jacques Louis David trained in the grand manner of neoclassic painting]; they dreamed of poetry and glory. For them, Grandville, staking out from the outset one of the inferior levels of art and seeming determined to remain there, had voluntarily restricted and downgraded himself: one was almost tempted to feel sorry for him; he was a marked man, finished, a caricaturist. Where are these young enthusiasts today? What has become of them? To what extent have their proud hopes born fruit? Do their names rise well above that of Grandville? I search around for them. Alas! most of them have not emerged from obscurity.][3]

Aside from documenting the derogatory attitude of painters toward caricaturists, this quotation, along with the entries in the 1830 diary, corroborates that Grandville seems to have led an active social life during his early bachelor years in Paris. The subjects of the drawings, typical of those done in 1830, include street scenes, theatrical performances (notably that of *Hernani* [cat. no. 3]), elegant soirées, costume balls, diners in restaurants, and attractive young women.[4]

The manner in which these subjects are presented often reflects the early nineteenth-century fad for viewing humanity through the eyes of Lavater. Like the Swiss clergyman and his "science" of physiognomy, Grandville analyzes and categorizes social types by concentrating on a detailed description of gesture and outward appearance. Many 1830 diary fragments and another drawing from around that same year (cat. no. 7) are the visual equivalents of the Lavaterian-inspired "physiologies" written by Grandville's colleague on the staff of *La Silhouette* at the time, Balzac, and constitute his own precocious *Comédie humaine.*

The annotations that accompany the drawings provide additional information, listing expenses for gambling—"perte au Jeu" (cat. no. 4 [verso])—and naming two of his friends and frequent companions, Jacques Guiaud and a certain Chardard. The versos of most of the drawings contain lists of numbers, sometimes with words or fragments of words next to them. From all appearances, they record Grandville's expenses and indicate that his diary also served as his account book. The diary of 1846 will also serve this same double function, leading to the conclusion that Grandville was as meticulous in keeping track of his money as he was in his draftsmanship.

Cat. no. 6, dated "28 Mars 1830," exemplifies the thin-gauge lined paper used for the pages of the 1830 diary. Off-white in color, the paper is printed with what probably were red but now are faded brown horizontal and vertical lines. The pages are divided by horizontal lines that are 8 mm apart and by margins of an undetermined width at both the top and bottom. Each sheet appears to have carried two vertical lines 17–18 mm apart on the left and a third vertical line 82–83 mm farther to the right.

According to a perpetual calendar, the annotations on the versos of certain drawings, such as "Diman 14" (cat. no. 4) and "21 Dimanche" (cat. no. 5), indicate that they date from either February, March, or November 1830. However, given the date of "28 Mars 1830" in cat. no. 6 and the absence of any reference to the Revolution of 1830, it is likely that these as well as the other 1830 fragments date from before the revolution and originate from the same section of the diary: March or the month preceding it, February. Most would appear to date from March. The Sundays of the 14th and 21st in cat. nos. 4 and 5 more than likely directly precede the Sunday of March 28 in cat. no. 6. Other diary fragments that carry the dates of "15," "20," and "21" (cat. nos. 1 and 2) have been assigned to the month of February, where they fit very well.

1. 6/3 recto

15 *Je*
(15 I)

February 15, 1830
94 × 29
Pen and brown ink over pencil, crayon noir

Grandville appears to have corrected the numeral of the day's date from "14" to "15" in crayon noir.

Judging from the first of the three scenes portrayed, this diary entry is from the month of February. The winter of 1830 was a particularly cold one during which the Seine River froze over not once but twice, with two consequent fractures of the ice, or *débâcles,* something that had not occurred since the winter of 1789. The ice broke up for the second time on February 11.[5] Grandville recorded this unusual

Fig. 38. ***Parisians Observing the Rising Waters of the Seine,*** **1830, drawing. Nancy, Musée Lorrain.**

phenomenon in two highly finished drawings where he depicts curious Parisians leaning over the walls along the quays in order to observe the rising waters and ice floes. Both of these drawings are in Nancy, one at the Musée Lorrain (fig. 38) and the other at the Nancy Musée des Beaux-Arts (Nancy, cat. no. 26). The diary sketch most closely resembles the drawing in the Musée Lorrain where we see not only people from the back as they peer over the edge of the embankment, but also, to the left, others viewed full-face and in profile, who appear to be positioned on a bridge. It is interesting to note that the people portrayed are different in all three drawings. As usual, Grandville has taken great care to differentiate between their silhouettes, determined by the cut and contour of their garments as well as by their physiques. The diary drawing is the only one to include, at the far right, a member of the gendarmerie, omnipresent on the streets of Paris during the last years of the Restoration and ever suspicious of any crowd. Together, the three drawings of the same event illustrate one of Grandville's favorite pastimes during his early years in Paris, that of observing the everchanging kaleidoscope of people to be found in the streets of the capital. The snapshotlike quality of the diary drawing and the fact that it differs from the other two indicates that it is a directly observed composition.

Equally spontaneous in appearance are the two accompanying drawings. In contrast with the public street scene at the top of the sheet, they appear to provide an intimate glimpse into Grandville's private life during his bachelor years. The one in the middle presents a scene from later in the day, and features a woman wearing one of the distinctive puffed gigot, or leg-of-mutton, sleeved dresses so popular in 1830 and a typical maid's bonnet (cf., Nancy, cat. nos. 28 and 66). She is seen from the back as she peers out into the darkness of the night between the parted curtains of a tall window with large panes of glass. In titillating fashion, she lifts the hem of her dress up to her knees. To her right are two cats, one standing on a sofa and the other on a table. The scene invites any number of possible interpretations, all of which hinge on her identity. Is she a maid or a prostitute in maid's costume such as Sophie, Mlle Deniza, la Champenoise, and la Picarde in Nancy, cat. nos. 140 and 141? Is she the same young woman as in cat. nos. 2 (verso) and 3 (recto)? Is she Grandville's mistress? While no certain answer can be given, it seems apparent that she is a close acquaintance of the artist, for she reappears at the bottom of the sheet with the same frilly maid's bonnet in a portrait where Grandville has carefully captured the pretty features of her face. He has also contrasted the effect of an artificial light, probably a lamp, which spotlights the woman's face while casting a dark shadow on the wall behind her. A clue to her relationship with Grandville may be found in the glass of water containing a rose, a standard symbol of love, positioned on what appears to be a mantelpiece behind her. However, the juxtaposition of the woman with a rose also suggests an analogy with which Grandville had been experimenting since at least 1828 (see Nancy, cat. no. 106): the overlapping frills of the woman's bonnet are likened to the heavy, overlapping petals of a fully blossomed rose. This analogy of women with flowers will be perfected in a study of *ombres portées* (cast shadows) later in 1830 (Nancy, cat. no. 175), in the chapter "La Mort d'une immortelle" (The death of an immortelle) from *Un autre monde,* and ultimately in *Les Fleurs animées.*

6/3 verso

[Fragment of a list of numbers]

February 1830
94 × 29
Pencil, pen and brown ink

2. 9/1 verso

19 [illegible crossed-out words]
Compts in de
Chez Gaugain [illegible crossed-out words]
[illegible crossed-out words]
20
[illegible crossed-out word] *de Mrs [Guiaud] Chardard*
21 *[Simeon]* [illegible crossed-out words]
(19 [ ]
Balance in from
the House of Gaugain [ ]
20
[ ] of Messrs. Guiaud Chardard
21 Siméon [ ])

February 19–21, 1830
65 × 138
Pen and brown ink

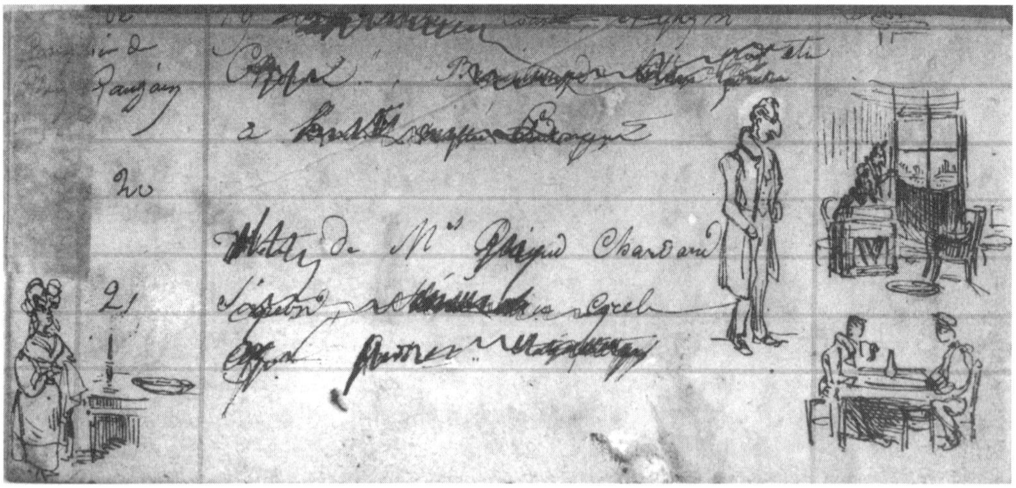

The niceties of chronology were not uppermost in the mind of the compiler of the Missouri Album. Not only were excerpts from different years mixed together, but even the fragments themselves were at times glued to the pages in reverse manner, with the front part of a diary page glued face down, leaving the back of the page face up. The reason for this reversal is apparently simple: the drawing on the back of a given diary page was judged by the compiler of the Missouri Album to be visually more interesting than its front. Such is the case with the first diary fragment on page 9 of the album. What has become the recto (originally the back of the sheet) does, in fact, present a more attractive appearance than the obliterated entries on the verso. However, it stands to reason that the days of February 20 and 21, inscribed on the verso precede those of February 23 and 24, whose events are depicted on the recto.

While the compiler of the Missouri Album found the verso of this diary fragment of secondary importance, it nonetheless provides an informative listing of Grandville's friends and acquaintances from the beginning of 1830. Curiously, certain passages have lines drawn through them as though in an effort to expunge them. Assuming that the diary excerpt is from February, it is possible that at the time that Grandville was participating in the Trois Glorieuses of July 27, 28, 29, 1830, he scratched out the names of his friends as a precautionary measure in the event that the revolution did not succeed and he was taken into custody by the police of Charles X.

"Compts in de Chez Gaugain" undoubtedly refers to a financial transaction with Armand-Pierre-Henri Gaugain (1799–?), the wealthy scion of a prominent Rouen family, who from 1827 to 1829 attempted to establish himself in the flourishing Parisian lithographic print market.[6] The publishing house established by Gaugain specialized in the production of "literary lithographs" or illustrations for preexisting texts, most notably the fables of La Fontaine, the *Chroniques de France* (Annals of France) of Madame Amable Tastu, and the novels of Sir Walter Scott. Gaugain's literary interests included plays, and along with Mme Tastu and his sometime copublisher Lambert, in 1827 he published *Souvenirs du théâtre anglais à Paris, dessinés par MM. Devéria et Boulanger avec un texte de M. Moreau* (Souvenirs of the English theater in Paris, drawn by Messrs. Devéria and Boulanger with a text by Mr. Moreau), which featured scenes from English plays presented on the Parisian stage, such as Ophelia's famous mad scene from act 4 of Shakespeare's *Hamlet.*[7] Gaugain's proclivity for illustrating Romantic literature or literature that appealed to Romantic tastes was matched by his patronage of young artists who, like himself, belonged to the Romantic generation. In addition to Louis Boulanger (1806–67) and

Fig. 39. Achille Devéria, *Henri III,* 1829, lithograph. Paris, Bibliothèque nationale de France.

Achille Devéria, this latter's brother, Eugène Devéria (1805–65), Delacroix (1798–1863), and Camille Roqueplan created many of his illustrative prints.

Gaugain may have entertained the idea of producing a complement to the *Souvenirs du théâtre anglais* with a *Souvenirs du théâtre français,* again by calling upon young artists of the Romantic generation to provide the compositions. For in 1829 he published a lithograph by Achille Devéria depicting act 3, scene 5 from Alexandre Dumas's *Henri III et sa cour* (Henri III and His Court; figure 39). Registered with the dépôt légal on March 17, 1829, the print appeared approximately one month after the play's debut at the Comédie-Française on February 11. At exactly the same time Grandville was in the process of executing a large-scale drawing of the climatic last scene (act 5, scene 6) from Violet d'Épagny's *Lancastre ou l'Usurpation* (Lancaster or the usurpation), which debuted at the Odéon on January 31, 1829, and had its last presentation on March 3 (figure 40; for a more detailed analysis of this drawing and the play it depicts, see Nancy, cat. no. 42). Both the dimensions of the drawing, 168 × 289 mm,

Fig. 40. ***Last Scene from Lancastre,*** **1829, drawing. Nancy, Musée des Beaux-Arts (Inv. 877.586).**

and its highly finished, carefully detailed execution in ink indicate that it was intended for eventual publication as a large format pen lithograph. Perhaps the drawing was commissioned by Gaugain as part of an ongoing series of prints depicting scenes from contemporary French avant-garde (i.e., Romantic) theater, but like the rest of the series, it was never published.[8]

Gaugain certainly would have been aware of Grandville at the beginning of 1829, or at the very moment when the artist was enjoying his first major success with *Les Métamorphoses du jour,* published by Bulla in installments between August 1828 and June 1829. It would have made good business sense to profit from the popularity of this new artistic talent as well as to take advantage of Grandville's privileged access to the theatrical world (the director of the Odéon during the 1828–29 theatrical season, we will recall, was Grandville's cousin by marriage, Lemétheyer) as he contemplated the possibility of publishing a series of prints on contemporary French plays.

Admittedly hypothetical, the above nevertheless provides a plausible background for the mention of Gaugain in Grandville's diary entry one year later on February 19, 1830. The fact that the reference to him has to do with money is particularly intriguing. For Gaugain's short-lived career as a print publisher was plagued by financial difficulties that even his independent 20,000–pound annual income could not surmount. After one of Gaugain's workers, Marie-Etienne Ardit, took over the business in 1829, Bioche de Misery in 1830 filed a breach of contract suit against Gaugain, claiming that the publisher owed him 25,000 francs. Ardit himself was forced to declare bankruptcy in 1831.[9] Perhaps Gaugain also owed Grandville money for works commissioned but never published.[10] Should this have been the case, "Compts in de Chez Gaugain" could refer to a settling of Gaugain's account with Grandville.

Although partially crossed out, the name of Guiaud is perfectly legible. The reference here is to Grandville's younger friend, Jacques Guiaud, who will collaborate with him six months later in the production of caricatures about the fall of Charles X.

The identity of Chardard is more problematic. It is possible that he was among the contingent of fellow Lorrains whom Grandville knew in Paris.[11] However, it appears that by 1833, Chardard was back home, for in a letter dated October 20, 1833, and addressed to his sister-in-law in Nancy, Catherine "Minette" Fischer (1800–1885), Grandville asks her to tell Chardard to be patient: he will send him a letter and drawings in a couple of weeks. Perhaps Grandville and Chardard grew up together in Nancy. Whatever the case, there is every indication that they were the best of friends. Chardard's name reappears two more times in diary entries from 1830 (cat. nos. 4 [recto] and 5 [recto]), and he is referred to again in the diary of 1833 (cat. no. 24). Most tellingly, Grandville corresponded with Chardard after he returned to Nancy and even sent him drawings, a signal honor. The fact that Chardard's name has not been crossed out suggests that he was not engaged in questionable political activities.

Perhaps the most intriguing personage mentioned is "Siméon" who is sketched twice on the right margin of the sheet. Siméon, of whom there are two portraits at the Nancy Musée des Beaux-Arts (figs. 41 and 42) has been tentatively identified as Viscount Joseph-Balthazar Siméon (1781–1846).[12] A dedicated patron of the arts and a talented painter and printmaker in his own right (as a child, he had started his artistic studies with François Granet [1775–1849]), Siméon was named director of Fine Arts within the Department of the Interior under Martignac in January 1828, remaining in that post until August 1829 when the government of Martignac was replaced by that of Polignac. Siméon, however, did not leave public office. Head of the Court of Appeals since 1821, he had been named a member of the Conseil d'État (Council of State), a post he continued to hold even after the Revolution of 1830. During his directorship of Fine Arts, Siméon gained a reputation for doing whatever he could for artists and was elected to the Academy of Fine Arts in recognition of his efforts on behalf of the artistic community. As adroit as his father, Count Joseph-Jérôme Siméon (1749–1842), in navigating the political currents of the time, Viscount Siméon unhesitatingly gave his support to the Revolution of 1830.

It is very tempting to see Siméon as a supporter of an up-and-coming artistic talent such as Grandville whose first real success, *Les Métamorphoses du jour,* was published during Siméon's directorship of Fine Arts. Perhaps he was. But at the same time it is very difficult to see in the profile of the Viscount Siméon, "académicien libre," portrayed ten years later in 1840 by Horace Vernet (fig. 43) the same Siméon of grandly arched nose found at Nancy and in Grandville's diary of 1830.[13] Even given the caricaturist's propensity for exaggeration and distortion, it is hard to reconcile these widely divergent profiles, each dominated by an equally large yet distinctive proboscis, as belonging to the same person.

If Grandville's Siméon is not the Viscount Siméon, who then is he? The two carefully observed sketches in the diary, more than likely done directly from life, perhaps give us a clue. The first sketch represents Siméon standing alone, dressed in long pants, a vest, frock coat, and with what appears to be a lace scarf at his throat. He possesses a studious, dignified air, which is enhanced by glasses. The second sketch represents Siméon in what appears to be his office. Still standing, he is shown half hidden behind a young man seated at a small desk, no doubt his secretary, who cocks his head and looks up, listening attentively as Siméon dictates something to him. The room appears to be oval in shape: through the window are glimpsed the roofs of the Parisian skyline. The furnishings of the room are Spartan: an armchair and a small rug are placed opposite the secretary's desk, the bottom part of the window is draped with a cloth. While all the above could describe a member of the Conseil d'État attending to the affairs of state with his secretary, it could also represent any established bourgeois businessman going over his books. While the identity of Siméon still remains problematic, there is no doubt that he was a close acquaintance of Grandville around 1830.

There are two other drawings on the sheet. The one in the lower right-hand corner, directly below those of Siméon, represents two young men seated at a table with no apparent tablecloth in some cheap

Fig. 41. ***Siméon,*** **circa 1829, drawing. Nancy, Musée des Beaux-Arts (Inv. 877.514).**

restaurant. This vignette may well depict the restaurant that Grandville frequented in the rue Saint-Benoît, not far from Grandville's garret apartment at 10, rue des Petits-Augustins. The owner was particularly sympathetic to the plight of indigent, aspiring young artists living in the neighborhood of the nearby École des Beaux-Arts and served them meals at a special discount rate of thirteen sous.[14] Such slice-of-life scenes often served as sources of inspiration for Grandville's published work. Inconsequential

Fig. 42. ***Siméon,*** **circa 1830, drawing. Nancy, Musée des Beaux-Arts (Inv. 877.350).**

Fig. 43. Horace Vernet, *Viscount Siméon,* 1840, drawing. Paris, Bibliothèque nationale de France.

as it may appear, this scene, lodged in the artist's memory and sketched in his diary, anticipates that of the penniless art students with their carafe of water at an equally cheap restaurant in *L'Eau,* plate 2 of *Les Breuvages de l'homme,* reproduced in figure 12. The drawing in the lower left-hand corner represents one of the innumerable coquettish maids or nannies whom Grandville tirelessly sketched during his bachelor years. With a cloth in her hand, she stands next to a table on which are to be found a candle and a basin. Like the young woman in cat. no. 1, whom she resembles, her identity and relationship to Grandville remain uncertain.

9/1 recto

Lundi	*dejeuner*	*29*
(Monday	lunch	29)

February 22–24, 1830
65 × 138
Pen and brown ink

As already noted, Grandville's 1830 diary doubled as an account book where he recorded his daily expenditures. However, while numerical amounts are given, they unfortunately are not accompanied by monetary designations. The penciled annotation here reveals that he spent presumably either twenty-nine centimes or twenty-nine sous for Monday's lunch.

The pen and ink drawing that partially obscures this annotation indicates that the Monday in question was probably February 22, the day before Mardi Gras, for the drawing appears to represent one of the fancy dress or masquerade balls traditionally held the evening of Mardi Gras, in one final fling of the pre-Lenten carnival season. Grandville two years earlier had portrayed a similar carnival ball at the Odéon theater (Nancy, cat. no. 39) when its director was his well-placed "cousin," Lemétheyer. He would also depict a "Soirée de l'Odèon" in his diary of 1846 (cat. no. 47). Since these other two drawings indicate an ongoing association with this particular Parisian theater, it is quite possible that the ball represented here took place at the Odéon as well.

For Grandville, a ball such as this was more than just an entertaining social event. It was an opportunity to examine firsthand the infinite number of ways clothing simultaneously masks and transforms the human anatomy. It also allowed him to study how character is revealed through outward appearances. Hence, even though the drawing is in a very small format, he records in detail both the costumes and the gestures of the festive crowd. The woman at the far left wears an extravagantly plumed chapeau. Two young women dance at the center of the composition as they daintily lift the hems of their stylish leg-of-mutton sleeve dresses. Both of them wear a distinctive vertical hairdo known as the "coiffure à la girafe," part of the giraffe mania that resulted from that exotic animal's being sent as a gift to Charles X by the Egyptian viceroy, Mohammed Ali Pasha in 1826.[15] A resident of the Jardin des Plantes since her (the animal was female) arrival in Paris June 30, 1827, the giraffe continued to inspire both feminine and masculine hairdressers until the mid-1830s.[16] (For Grandville's sketch of the giraffe at the Jardin des Plantes, see cat. no. 16.) To their right are two men in disguises that recall recent theatrical productions, entirely appropriate for an Odéon fancy dress ball.[17] The one on the immediate right is dressed in Renaissance hose and doublet, a costume much in favor with young Romantics since the debut on February 11, 1829, of Alexander Dumas's *Henri III et sa cour* at the Comédie-Française, where it was still on the program one year later. Judging from a plate in Vizentini's *Costumes de théâtre* (fig. 44), the man in the distinctive feathered hat farther to the right appears to be impersonating Beppo, one of Fra Diavolo's gang of bandits, from Scribe and Auber's popular comic opera of the moment, *Fra Diavolo ou l'Hôtellerie de Terracine* (Fra Diavolo, or The Inn of Terracina), which had opened at the Opéra-Comique only a few weeks earlier on January 28, 1830. In the right foreground stands a woman wearing a bird-beaked mask and another flamboyantly plumed coiffure, and at the far right, a woman in a close-fitting riding habit, veiled hat, and riding crop. As he was often fond of doing, Grandville includes a droll commentary on human behavior: at the far left, while a pretty waitress leans forward to present refreshments on a tray, a gangly young man behind her expectantly cranes his neck to get a better look at what is being served.

These carefully observed renderings of stylish silhouettes and body language are more than mere descriptions. Like Lavater, Grandville explores the analogous relationship between outward appearance and inner moral character. Simultaneously, his comparison and contrast of differing sartorial silhouettes parodies the systems of physiological classification upon which were founded the nascent fields of natural history and comparative anatomy, pioneered respectively by Buffon and Cuvier at the end of the eighteenth and the beginning of the nineteenth centuries (for a more detailed discussion of Grandville's relationship to natural history and comparative anatomy, see cat. no. 12). Grandville has translated into art topical ideas of the day, even as he makes a witty commentary on them and on human nature in general.

Juxtaposed to the festive scene in the upper portion of this diary fragment is the religious one below. Assuming that the costumed revelers evoke the last day of carnival, the kneeling worshippers would then depict the first day of Lent on the following day, Ash Wednesday, February 24. This contrast between opposing scenes of revelry and repentance is heightened by the further contrasts of age and social rank. The pleasure-loving crowd of young people at the top (probably students or young professionals just starting out their careers, like Grandville himself) provides a foil for the more sedate congregation at the bottom, which represents the two main pillars of the Restoration establishment, Church and Crown, the latter evoked by a group of dignitaries, possibly court officials, seated in a separate box protected by a Swiss guard on the right. Grandville would have found this multiplicity of contrasts particularly fascinating since they provided real-life parallels to a series of caricatural contrasts he had embarked upon several years earlier (Nancy, cat. nos. 71–82). Another contrast surely intended is that between the brims of the hats worn by the two stylish ladies conspicuously (and one suspects self-consciously)

Fig. 44. Anonymous, *Monsieur Belnie as Beppo in Fra Diavolo* from *Costumes de théâtre,* 1830, lithograph. Paris, Bibliothèque nationale de France.

on display in the front row of the assembled worshippers as they kneel in prayer. Ever sensitive to the constant and arbitrary changes in fashionable attire that modify the appearance of individuals from one year to the next, Grandville has taken pains to differentiate between the slightly outdated, long horizontal brim of the hat from 1829 worn by the woman to the right and the up-to-date, more vertically oriented brim of the hat from 1830 worn by the woman to the left. As a result, the heads of the women appear as two distinct shapes. Three years later, Grandville would elaborate upon the progressive upward sweep of hat brims in a satire on the milliner's art entitled "inclinaison du chapeau dans l'espace de 4 ans" (gradient of the hat in the space of 4 years; Nancy, cat. no. 80). However, the women are not alone in their coquettish pursuit of the latest fashion. The men seated in their separate, guarded box all sport the stylish masculine version of the coiffure à la girafe, which will become a permanent feature of Louis-Philippe's pear-shaped silhouette during the July Monarchy.

Fig. 45. ***Three Young Women and a Young Man at a Fancy Dress Ball,*** **page 30 recto from the Carnavalet Sketchbook, 1830, drawing. Paris, Musée Carnavalet.**

The two scenes on this sheet provide insight into Grandville's method of working, thanks to their relationship to drawings in his 1829–30 sketchbook preserved at the Musée Carnavalet. The Carnavalet Sketchbook contains notes and drawings for a number of projected publications in addition to the two dozen pages of studies for *Voyage pour l'éternité.* It also contains several studies from life. Among these is a detailed pencil sketch of three young women and a young man at a fancy dress ball on the recto of page 30 (fig. 45). The woman at the right and the man in Renaissance costume next to her are nearly identical to the corresponding figures in the central right portion of the ballroom scene from the diary. This comparison exemplifies how Grandville repeated in his diary larger compositions that recorded particularly memorable events of the day. At first glance, it would appear that he initially drew from life his fellow ball-goers in the sketchbook and then repeated them somewhat more schematically and in smaller format in the diary. But the diary drawing does not simply duplicate the one in the sketchbook. It is a more elaborate composition, possibly the replica in miniature of a third, unknown large-scale drawing intended for the thriving lithographic album trade, and for which the Carnavalet drawing served as a study. Indeed, in theme and composition, as well as in draftsmanship, the costume ball invites comparison with a series of dance hall scenes from 1829 and 1830 (Nancy, cat. nos. 127–35),

Fig. 46. *Seated Woman, Standing Woman, and Woman Kneeling in Prayer,* page 30 verso from the Carnavalet Sketchbook, 1830, drawing. Paris, Musée Carnavalet.

undoubtedly full-scale studies for a projected lithographic album, where the same bas-relief arrangement of people lined up two or three deep within a shallow space is to be found.

The Ash Wednesday church service can also be linked to the Carnavalet Sketchbook. On the verso of page 30 of the sketchbook appears the pencil study of a fashionably dressed woman, complete with stylish broad-brimmed chapeau, who kneels in prayer (fig. 46). Although in reverse position to the kneeling women in the diary, she assuredly is related to them just as the costumed couple on the opposite side of the page are related to the ballroom scene at the top of the diary fragment. However, the "Ash Wednesday" drawing is very different from the carnival ball above it. Smaller in scale and far more schematic in execution, it more than likely was drawn directly in the diary, loosely based upon sketches such as that in the Carnavalet Sketchbook.

The comparison between these two drawings from the diary fragment and related ones in the Carnavalet Sketchbook help us to follow Grandville's procedure as he arrives at two different types of drawings. Sketches, presumably from life, were first done in the sketchbook. They were then either elaborated upon in larger-scale compositions produced with an eye toward eventual publication and then documented in miniature in the diary, or they were elaborated upon directly in the diary where they served as visual records of the day's events and, one suspects, probably as artistic aide-mémoire as well.

3. 6/1 recto

February 26(?), 1830
111 × 37
Pen and brown ink over pencil

The drawing at the top of this diary fragment depicts the final scene of the most celebrated play in the annals of the Romantic theater, Victor Hugo's *Hernani ou l'Honneur castillan* (*Hernani, or The Pledge of Honor*). The drama, a veritable manifesto of Romanticism, provoked during its first performance at

Fig. 47. ***Les Romains échevelés à la 1re représentation d'Hernani*** **(The disheveled Romans at the first performance of *Hernani.*) from *Jérôme Paturot à la recherche d'une position sociale,* 1846, wood engraving. Paris, Bibliothèque nationale de France.**

the Comédie-Française on February 25, 1830, the famous battle between the classicists and Romanticists, which Louis Reybaud described and Grandville sixteen years later illustrated in *Jérôme Paturot à la recherche d'une position sociale* (fig. 47). The double arcade of Moorish arches identifies the action as taking place on the terrace of the palace of Aragon during the last act. In front of the arches stand the drama's three principals: Doña Sol de Silva (Mlle Mars in what was to become one her most acclaimed roles), the twenty-year-old hidalgo and bandit, Hernani (interpreted by Firmin), whom she has just married, and her elderly uncle and former fiancé, Don Ruy Gomez de Silva (Joanny). Along with the stage décor, their costumes announce the play's final act: Doña Sol wears her elaborate white wedding gown, Hernani a black velvet doublet, and Don Ruy Gomez a domino. Judging from Doña Sol's histrionic gesture, Grandville has portrayed the moment when she threatens the unmasked don with a dagger, "Voyez-vous ce poignard?—Ah! vieillard insensé, Craignez-vous pas le fer quand l'oeil a menacé?" (See this dagger?—Ah! you old fool, Don't you fear the blade when the eye has threatened?). This is precisely the same action portrayed by Raffet in a contemporary lithograph (figure 48). Doña Sol's wrath stems from the fact that the newly wedded couple has just learned that the aging grandee insists upon Hernani honoring a rashly sworn oath from act 3, scene 7: "Je te vengerai, duc.—Après, tu me tueras!" (I will avenge you, duke.—Then you will kill me!). The jealous don's intransigence irrevocably leads to a fatal climax in the corpse-littered stage tradition of Shakespeare with the suicides of Doña Sol and Hernani as well as his own.[18]

Fig. 48. Denis-Auguste-Marie Raffet, *Hernani,* 1830, lithograph. Paris, Bibliothèque nationale de France.

Closely associated with the theatrical world and acquainted with such emerging literary talents of the rebellious Romantic generation as Balzac and Alexandre Dumas, Grandville might very well have witnessed the opening performance of *Hernani* and participated in the battle that ensued. As outlined earlier in the biography, Grandville's interest in the theater had been cultivated from an early age. His paternal grandparents had been actors at the court of Stanislas Leszczyński during his reign in Nancy as Duke of Lorraine from 1737 until his death in 1766. It was no doubt due to the influence of his paternal grandmother, who lived with his family in Nancy up until her death in 1830, that the artist adopted his grandparents' stage name, Grandville, for his own artistic pen name. Upon his arrival in Paris in 1825, Grandville immediately made contact with his cousin by marriage, Frédéric Lemétheyer, who at the time was general stage manager of the Opéra-Comique. Lemétheyer had previously served as the director of the theaters of Le Havre and Nîmes and of the Théâtre Feydeau in Paris (also referred to as the salle Feydeau), which was home to the Opéra-Comique from 1805 until 1829. He also had been a drama correspondent. During the 1828–29 season, he would become director of the Odéon.[19] Given these close ties with the theatrical world and his identification with the young, rebellious Romantic generation, it would be very suprising if Grandville had not seen *Hernani* on its opening night or very soon thereafter. The drama remained deeply rooted in the artist's memory. Sixteen years later, in his diary of 1846, he parodied the tragic last scene portrayed here in a lament over the death of a young mouse (cat. no. 62).

The drawing below the final scene from *Hernani* depicts two men conversing in the street. Their silhouettes provide a comical contrast. In top hat and frock coat, the man on the left is suited in the conventional fashion of the day, whereas the one on the right wears a full-sleeved garment and sports a coiffure à la girafe. The flamboyant attire of the latter identifies him as a Romantic, possibly one of the young, extravagantly dressed artists and writers, such as the eighteen-year-old Théophile Gautier in his pale-green trousers and red velvet pourpoint, made specially for the occasion, who had been solicited by Hugo to serve as defenders of *Hernani* during the play's initial performances instead of the traditional claque.[20] One can easily imagine that the conversation of the two men revolves around the play, which had the effect of pitting Romanticist against classicist and producing a revolution in the theatrical world five months before that other, even more convulsive one in the political realm. A similar confrontation between proponents of the Romantic and classic schools drawn by Grandville at around this same time may be found in Nancy, cat. no. 63.

Another conversation, this time indoors and of a more intimate nature, occurs at the bottom of the sheet. An amorous young couple, the man seated on a chair and the woman standing in front of him, hold hands and stare intently into one another's eyes. Note-sized pieces of paper (billets-doux? discarded drawings?) litter the floor. Behind the woman, who wears a dress with leg-of-mutton sleeves and a bonnet similar to the "maids" in cat. nos. 1 (recto) and 2 (verso), a basin rests on a table. Is she the same young woman? Is the young man a self-portrait of the artist, or one of his friends? Again, it is impossible to say. But the scene eloquently attests to the very real interest the twenty-six-year-old Grandville took in the opposite sex during the years leading up to his first marriage in 1833.

The rigidly formal arrangement of the three drawings on this diary fragment suggests that they were done from memory as Grandville chronologically recorded in comic-strip fashion the previous somewhat hectic twenty-four hours: the performance of *Hernani* the evening of February 25, the discussion between classicist and Romanticist the following day, and an amorous rendezvous later on. All three drawings repeat in what appears to be a calculated fashion the same symmetrical composition of figures confronting one another on either side of a central axis: Don Gomez and Doña Sol with Hernani, classicist and Romanticist, man and woman.

6/1 verso

[Fragment of what appears to be a list of expenses]
February 1830
111 × 37
Pencil, pen and brown ink

4. 7/3 recto

depart [illegible crossed-out word]
Alexandre
promenade avec Chardard
(departure [ ]
Alexandre
walk with Chardard)

February or March 1830
66 × 71
Pen and brown ink

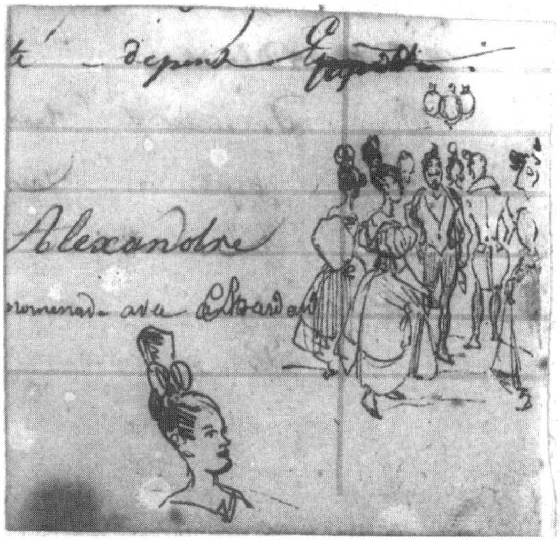

Along with previous diary fragments, this one bears witness to Grandville's active social life. Although it is difficult to read whose departure has been recorded at the top of the sheet, we once again find at the bottom Chardard with whom Grandivlle went out walking.

In between these two casually written entries is the name Alexandre elegantly written at a slanted angle in a calligraphic style known as *à l'anglaise.* The Alexandre in question is the famous mime artist, Alexandre Vattemare (or Wattemare), who specialized in portraying all the different roles of a given play himself. Alexandre's talents first came to the attention of the public at the auditorium of the École royale de déclamation (Royal School of Declamation) and at the Théâtre de Madame. He later was called upon to give private performances to such distinguished personalities of the day as Sir Walter Scott at Abbotsford, Scotland, in 1824 and members of the royal family, including Charles X, at Saint-Cloud in 1826.[21] The entry may either refer to a performance Alexandre had recently given or to a series of pen lithographs of the actor with captions written *à l'anglaise* that Grandville and Forest were working on or had just completed. Published in 1830, the three prints depict Alexandre in the various guises he assumed in three different stage presentations: *Le diable boiteux* (The limping devil),

Fig. 49. ***Walter Scott (schériff) Lisant le Riot act à Alexandre-rassemblement*** **(Walter Scott [sheriff] reading the Riot Act to Alexandre-crowd), 1831, lithograph. Paris, Bibliothèque nationale de France.**

L'homme à dix visages, ou l'art de sortir de prison (The man with ten faces, or the art of getting out of prison), and *Le paquebot, ou seul pour sept* (The packet boat, or one for seven). In July 1831, Grandville would dedicate a fourth pen lithograph to Alexandre that ultimately was published in Alexandre's *Album cosmopolite* (Cosmopolitan Album): *Walter Scott (schériff) Lisant le Riot act à Alexandre-rassemblement* (Walter Scott [sheriff] Reading the Riot Act to Alexandre-crowd), where Alexandre is depicted in the company of the various characters he portrayed onstage, including many of those found in the three former prints (fig. 49).[22] This work was reproduced in the May 8, 1839, issue of *Le Charivari* along with its accompanying commentary from the *Album cosmopolite,* which explains its iconography: after the performance before the famous novelist, Scott was inspired to write a short impromptu in which he facetiously threatened to read the Riot Act to the host of characters the mime had conjured up, ordering them to disperse. Grandville gives his own admiring tribute to Alexandre when signing the lithograph: "Souvenir d'amitié donné a [*sic*] M Alexandre et Compagnie par un de ses admirateurs sans nombre Marly le Roi 1 Juillet 1831" (Memento of friendship given to Mr. Alexandre and Company by one of his innumerable admirers Marly le Roi, July 1, 1831). Grandville's esteem for Alexandre is not surprising. Changing costumes constantly as he played up to twenty characters in one performance, Alexandre was a living example of those chameleonlike metamorphoses of the human body effected by fashion, which Grandville never tired of satirizing. Similarly, each time he assumed a different personality appropriate to a given costume, Alexandre acted out the Lavaterian analogy between outward appearances and inner character, another of Grandville's favorite caricatural themes.

Immediately to the right of Alexandre's name appears a festive gathering similar to the ball in cat. no. 2 (recto). Young women in the same distinctive coiffures and stylish balloon-sleeved frocks of 1830 again daintily lift the hems of their dresses as they dance. The head of one woman has been enlarged at the bottom of the sheet in order to better portray her elaborate coiffure à la girafe: hair pulled back, piled in a bun at the back of the head and held in place by a tall, vertical comb that sports a large bow at the front of its base. At the center of the composition a young Romantic proudly displays the masculine equivalent of 1830 sartorial splendor: high-collared, broad-lapelled, wide-breasted frock coat worn open in order to give a full view of the contrasting vest underneath, narrow-legged pants tightly stretched by trouser straps, and hair combed forward into yet another vertical crinose tribute to Mohammed Ali Pasha's famous giraffe at the Jardin des Plantes.

7/3 verso

	1/12	*Diner*
	id–	*Dejeuner (Trois*
	13	*perte au Jeu*
	id	*Dejeuner*
Diman[che]	*14*	*Dejeuner*
		Diner
	(1/12	Dinner
	idem	Lunch (Three
	13	gambling loss
	idem	Lunch
Sunday 14		Lunch
		Dinner)

February or March 12–14, 1830
66 × 71
Pen and brown ink

This diary fragment lists Grandville's expenses for three consecutive days, Friday the 12th, Saturday the 13th, and Sunday the 14th of either February or March 1830. The significance of the "1" and the slash in front of the 12 remains unknown. Unfortunately, the amounts Grandville has spent have been cut off at the right. Nonetheless, this diary excerpt contains a surprise. The annotation "perte au Jeu," or gambling loss, can only mean that Grandville was no stranger to games of chance. Given his frugality and what we know of his sober, middle-class existence, it is doubtful that he gambled on a regular basis when he was young. And yet, during his leisure hours on a weekend, as is the case here, gambling may have served as an occasional form of entertainment. It should be noted that gambling was a popular pastime in Paris during the Restoration. The most notorious gambling establishments were located at the Palais-Royal, around whose extensive gardens Louis-Philippe's father, the ever-impecunious Philippe-Égalité (1747–93), had constructed a series of elegant arcaded shops and dwellings as a commercial venture. As we have already seen in the biography, Grandville frequented this favorite Parisian promenade, which he represented in a lithograph from 1825, soon after his arrival in the capital (fig. 20).

5. 1/1 recto

Cercle
1830
[. . .]rand
presence

richelieu

[Char]dard Guiaud
projet
Soiree
[. . .]s M

, Sa
[p]rojets de
[. . .]rour avatix
(Circle
1830
[ ]*rand*
presence

Richelieu

[Char]dard Guiaud
project
Soirée
[. . .]*s* Mr

, His [?]
[p]rojects of
[. . .]*rour avatix*)

March 1830
134 × 47
Pen and brown ink

Judging from the numbered days of the week on the verso of this diary fragment, it dates from either February or March 1830. However, since February 20 and 21 have already been accounted for in cat. no. 2 (verso), the 18th, 19th, and 21st here automatically fall within the month of March. As a result, this excerpt helps to complete the sequence of days between what may be Friday, March 12 in cat. no. 4 (verso) and Sunday, March 28 in cat. no. 6 (recto).

Despite their being incomplete, the annotations reinforce what we already know from the other diary fragments about Grandville's life at the beginning of 1830. The "richelieu" is no doubt a reference to the street of that name, and confirms that Grandville was an habitué of the neighborhood in and around the Palais-Royal. For instance, we have just learned in cat. no. 4 (verso) of Grandville's losses at a game of chance, probably in one of the gambling houses at the Palais-Royal, and in cat. no. 6 (verso) we learn that he had dinner in the adjacent rue de Valois on March 22. Although the Palais-Royal itself had lost some of its glamour since the time of Philippe-Égalité, the area immediately surrounding it constituted the most elegant and most important center of activity in Paris during the last years of the Restoration. Its many shops, bustling crowds, and prostitutes all provided Grandville with an unending parade of varied social types whom he loved to record and caricature during his first years in the capital.[23] That he found the prostitutes particularly alluring during his bachelor years is evidenced by his detailed drawings of them (Nancy, cat. nos. 138–41) and by the gallant episode recorded in cat. no. 16.

In 1830 the Palais-Royal district also would have been the place where Grandville would be called on business. The offices of *La Silhouette,* to which Grandville contributed in 1829 and 1830, were located in the nearby rue des Fossés-Saint-Germain-L'Auxerrois (today rue Perrault) at No. 24. And only one block from the Palais-Royal was the galerie Véro-Dodat, in which was located the print shop of Aubert, who at the time was copublisher with Bulla of *Voyage pour l'éternité* (registered with the dépôt légal between March 8 and July 15, 1830). After the Revolution of 1830, Grandville would frequent the galerie Véro-Dodat regularly. In addition to La Maison Aubert, it housed the offices of *La Caricature* and the *Association mensuelle,* as well as the press where *Le Charivari* would be printed.

The rue de Richelieu, however, calls to mind not just the immediate environs of the Palais-Royal but also, at its opposite extremity, the rue Feydeau and its theater, the salle Feydeau, home of the Opéra-Comique. Grandville would have been intimately acquainted with the salle Feydeau and the Opéra-Comique where Leméthever had served in various administrative capacities before becoming director of the Odéon in 1828. One can easily imagine Grandville shuttling back and forth along the rue de Richelieu, which served as the main conduit between two important aspects of his life: his nascent career as a political caricaturist and his inherited love of the theater.

Beneath "richelieu" appears the name of Jacques Guiaud and more than likely that of Chardard. These two names had been mentioned together in cat. no. 2 (verso), and we have seen Chardard reappear in cat. no. 4 (recto). The frequent recording of these names suggests that Grandville, Guiaud, and Chardard were a closely knit trio of companions at the beginning of 1830.

On the following line there is mention of a "project" and later on what appears to be that of "projects." We know from the Carnavalet Sketchbook of 1829–30 that Grandville was experimenting with ideas for any number of lithographic albums at this time, hoping to find one that would repeat the success of *Les Métamorphoses du jour* (see Nancy, 146–47). His obsession with potential "projects" appears to be reflected in this diary excerpt. However, none of Grandville's subsequent albums were nearly as popular as *Les Métamorphoses du jour.* Although he was not aware of it at the time, his next big success was to be as a political caricaturist for Philipon's *La Caricature,* which began publication some eight months later, on November 4, 1830. The mention of a soirée attests once more to Grandville's active social life in 1830.

The drawings as well, which include two restaurant scenes, reflect Grandville's busy life outside his one-room, sixth-floor garret apartment at 10, rue des Petits-Augustins. These scenes and the frequent mention of money paid for meals in the 1830 diary establish the fact that during his early years in Paris Grandville regularly ate in restaurants: kitchen facilities, if they existed at all, would have been rudimentary at best in his bachelor quarters. Given the amount of time he was obliged to spend in restaurants, it is not surprising to find him sketching his fellow diners while waiting to be served or handed his bill. Restaurants fascinated Grandville. They provided him with an opportunity to study a wide range of social types who, obliged to remain in one place for a period of time, became perfect models for the artist's scrutiny. The numerous restaurant scenes produced around 1830 no doubt were the point of departure for those two somewhat later lithographic suites where Grandville analyzed and caricatured various social types according to the food they ate and the beverages they drank: *Carte vivante du restaurateur* of 1832 and *Les Breuvages de l'homme* of 1834.

The restaurant scene at the top of the sheet portrays a uniformed officer, his hair styled in the popular coiffure à la girafe, stiffly seated at a round table in the company of a fashionably dressed young woman. They provide a contrast with the more informal group below sitting casually at another round table, probably in the same restaurant. The man with a bonnet on his head, arm slung over the back of his chair, the woman in the middle with a cat on her lap, and the woman to the right with her frilly hat and collar constitute a cozy if somewhat frumpy circle of petit bourgeois shopkeepers whose circumscribed and parsimonious existence Grandville satirized on more than one occasion (Nancy, cat. nos. 60, 68, and 69). As he often did in working studies, Grandville repeats on a larger scale the heads of the man and the woman on the left in order better to study their physiognomies.

The street scene at the bottom of the sheet is as typical of 1830 as the two restaurant scenes above. A man, elegantly attired in frock coat and top hat, nonchalantly leans against a bar in front of a shop's display window. On the left stands a young boy in a tunic and on the right a woman wearing a stylish gigot-sleeved dress who turns her head to look through the window at something that has caught her eye. Characteristically, Grandville has concentrated on the differing silhouettes of the various garments, but he has taken special delight in describing the wildly divergent headgear: the boy's duck-billed visored cap, the man's top hat, and the woman's extravagantly beribboned chapeau.

The astutely observed mannerisms and snapshotlike quality of all three drawings on this diary fragment, along with the enlarged and repeated heads in the middle one, indicate that they were sketched from life.

1/1 verso

	Dejeun[er]	
18		
idem	*Fait*	
idem	*dénes*	
19	*dejeun[er]*	
G. Ch . . .	*pap . . .*	
21	*Dimanche*	*Son*
	Grois	*Cra.*
		2 Dim
		Gas
		. . .

Dej[euner]
bas
bou..
(Lunch
18
idem Do
idem *dénes*
19 lunch

G. Ch . . . *pap . . .*

21 Sunday His [?]
Grois *Cra.*
2 *Dim*
Gas
. . .
Lunch
bas
bou..)

March 18–21, 1830
134 × 47
Pencil, pen and brown ink

This list of daily expenses is so badly fragmented as to elude any meaningful commentary. The one bit of information it reveals is that the 21st of the month was a Sunday. In 1830, Sunday fell on the 21st during the months of February, March, and November. In cat. no. 2, we have already encountered the 21st of a month, which was more than likely February. Therefore this Sunday the 21st is from either March or November, most probably March.

6. 6/2 verso

Mars 1830
22 *Dîner Rue de Valois* *40*
Dejeuner *20*
Violette *10*
(March 1830
22 Dinner Rue de Valois 40
Lunch 20
Violet 10)

March 22, 1830
41 × 139
Pencil, pen and brown ink

Grandville again has used his diary as a register of his daily expenses. We learn here that on March 22, 1830, he spent either twenty centimes or twenty sous on lunch and forty on dinner in the rue de Valois, the street bordering the east side of the Palais-Royal. He also spent ten of the same amount on what presumably is a bouquet of violets. Who might have been the recipient of the flowers is a matter of conjecture. But given Grandville's avid interest in the fair sex at the time, we can assume that it was for one of his female acquaintances, possibly one whom we have already encountered.

As is the case with drawing 9/1 in cat. no. 2, this particular diary fragment was glued to the album without any regard for proper chronological sequence. The verso with the date of March 22, while possessing no artistic interest, was originally on the front of the diary page and the recto with the date of March 28 on the back.

6/2 recto

28 Mars 1830

29 Soirée chez Gueras [*sic?*]
(28 March 1830

29 Soirée at the home of Gueras [*sic?*])

March 28–29, 1830
41 × 139
Pencil, pen and brown ink

It is this dated fragment that allows us to identify the distinctive pattern of printed lines on the pages of the 1830 diary.

The date refers to the drawing directly beneath it. On Sunday, March 28, 1830, just four months before the Revolution of 1830's "three glorious days" of July 27, 28, and 29, a command performance ("Spectacle demandé") of Beaumarchais's famous 1784 antiaristocratic comedy, *Le Mariage de Figaro* (*The Marriage of Figaro*), took place at the Odéon.[24] The decor, with its backdrop of chestnut trees and stage-front garden seat, announces the play's fifth and final act. As he had done earlier in his portrayal of *Hernani* in cat. no. 3, Grandville depicts the action leading up to the climax. In scene 7, Count Almaviva is duped into believing that his secret rendezvous under cover of darkness is with his wife's servant, Suzanne, when actually it is with the countess, herself, dressed in Suzanne's clothes. The purpose of the encounter is to allow the count the opportunity to exercise his outdated droit de seigneur (the lord of the manor's right to have first access to the bed of a bride within his dominion) with Suzanne before her marriage to Figaro. The countess stands to the left wearing Suzanne's distinctively tall toque, while the count beside her leans on his cane and lifts his monocle in order to better examine his disguised wife's charms in the shadowy light. The head of the countess and her fashionable coiffure are studied in more detail in two pencil sketches farther to the left. The indication of the curving edge of the stage and the angle at which the action is viewed suggest that Grandville has recorded the scene from a stage box. The same perspective and indication of curving stage edge can be found in Nancy, cat. no. 41, which depicts another play at the Odéon "Vu du Cabinet du Directeur" (viewed from the director's box) while Lemétheyer was the director there. Although it had been just over a year since he had vacated his post, Lemétheyer may have been invited by his successor, Charles-Jean Harel, to view the special performance of *Le Mariage de Figaro* from the director's box, which Lemétheyer in turn shared with his cousin. Should this have been the case, it would explain the similar perspectives in the present drawing and the one in Nancy.

The amusing vignette of a young man climbing out of a bathtub typifies the seemingly mundane events that often appear in the 1830 diary. Today, the taking of a bath probably would not merit special attention. However, for a young, struggling artist living in a garret apartment before the age of modern plumbing, it might have been, especially when taken in the elegant surroundings depicted here: a commodious room containing a large tub equipped with dolphin-shaped spigots, draped windows, and a mirror above a console-supported shelf. The bather in question is undoubtedly the bushy-haired Grandville himself, who luxuriates in the amenities to be found at the home of some well-off friends, most likely the Lemétheyers, who all but adopted the artist when he arrived in Paris. The bath being taken is probably in preparation for a night out on the town: to attend the special command performance of *Le Mariage de Figaro* at the invitation of Lemétheyer or to enjoy a soirée at the home of a certain Gueras.

The placement of the drawings in chronological order on the sheet once again exemplifies how Grandville at times would arrange them in comic-strip fashion. Reading the three here as one would normally, from left to right, the viewer automatically understands that the taking of a bath precedes the two events documented at the right.

Notes

Introduction

1. A number of drawings executed in this medium from around 1824 are to be found at the Nancy Musée des Beaux-Arts, whose 1909 catalog designates it as crayon noir. More crisply precise than charcoal, crayon noir lacks the greasy quality of conté crayon. In the absence of laboratory tests, a positive identification of the substance cannot be made.

Diary of 1830

1. The censored *Famille de scarabées* was not registered with the dépôt légal until after the Revolution of 1830 on August 16, 1830. For the history of the dépôt légal, see Georges Picot, *Le Dépôt légal et nos collections nationales* (Paris: A. Picard, 1883); Henri Lemaître, *Histoire du dépôt légal* (Paris: A. Picard et fils, 1910).
2. Blanc, 284.
3. "J.-J. Grandville. Dessins inédits," *Magasin pittoresque* 23, no. 45 (November 1855): 356–58. The architect in whose studio the young artists met may have been Hector Horeau, one of Grandville's friends from his early years in Paris who lived in the vicinity of the rue des Petits-Augustins and the École des Beaux-Arts.
4. These same themes are well represented in drawings from around 1830 in the Nancy Musée des Beaux-Arts. For a representative sampling, see Nancy, 59–203.
5. "Seconde débâcle à Paris," *Le Moniteur universel,* February 12, 1830, 168.
6. Beth S. Wright, "Henri Gaugain et le musée Colbert: L'Entreprise d'un directeur de galerie et d'un éditeur d'art à l'époque romantique," *Nouvelles de l'estampe,* no. 114 (December 1990): 24–31. Although Wright does not give a date for

the founding of Gaugain's enterprise, she does mention that by 1826 he had garnered several years of business experience as a result of having worked for the publishers Lambert et Noël who entrusted him with a position of some responsibility. Given that Gaugain first appears as a *déposan,* or "depositor," of prints with the dépôt légal on July 12, 1827, it can be assumed that he established his own publishing house in that year. Wright states that one of Gaugain's workers, Marie-Etienne Ardit, took over the business in 1829. Indeed, last mention of Gaugain as a *déposan* with the dépôt légal occurs on November 6, 1829.

7. Reproduced in Wright, 25.

8. There are any number of possible reasons why Grandville's drawing was never published by either Gaugain or anyone else. But the fact that *Lancastre* was not a hit surely was a primary one. What little success the play may have had was quickly forgotten with the opening less than two weeks later of Dumas's immensely popular *Henri III et sa cour,* which was celebrated in prints by not only Devéria, but by other artists as well.

9. Wright, 24–26.

10. There is no record of Gaugain ever having published anything by Grandville. He is not listed as one of the artist's publishers in any oeuvre catalog. And no works by Grandville figure among the few prints cataloged under Gaugain in the printers series of the S.n.r. at the Cabinet des estampes of the Bibliothèque nationale de France.

11. Nollet states on pages 15 and 16, "En 1825, année de son arrivée à Paris, il comptait 16 compatriotes; en 1835, il n'en avait plus que 3 près de lui; tous les autres étaient morts" (In 1825, the year of his arrival in Paris, he counted 16 compatriots; in 1835, only 3 were left at his side; all the others were dead). A drawing from around 1829–30 at the Musée Lorrain annotated "nous etions huit lorrains nous ne sommes plus que Sept" (we were eight Lorrains now we are only seven) also documents Grandville's friends from Lorraine in Paris and the frightening death toll among them. Grandville may have depicted Chardard in this group portrait where he includes himself.

12. Nancy, 118.

13. The pen and ink drawing reproduced in figure 43 may be found in the Réserve of the Cabinet des estampes at the Bibliothèque nationale de France. What is possibly an autographic duplicate of this drawing, accompanied by a portrait of the architect Antoine Laurent Thomas Vaudoyer (1756–1846), another member of the Academy of Fine Arts, is in a private collection and carries the dated signature "H Vernet 30 mai 1840."

14. Clogenson, 252.

15. In his book of souvenirs, *Quand j'étais photographe,* Nadar describes on page 285 the giraffe craze instigated by the animal's arrival in France:

> La girafe qu'on vient d'amener pour la première fois en Europe fait fureur au Jardin du Roi, qui s'appelle maintenant le Jardin des Plantes parce qu'on y va voir des animaux. Modes, enseignes, tout est "à la Girafe."
>
> [The giraffe that has just been brought to Europe for the first time is all the rage at the Jardin du Roi [Garden of the King], which is now called the Jardin des Plantes [Garden of the Plants] because you go there to see animals. Fashions, signs, everything is "à la giraffe."]

Mohammed Ali Pasha (1769–1849) was the founder of the dynasty that ruled Egypt until 1952. He was a master politician who knew how to curry favor with the European powers, particularly France. After the Revolution of 1830 and the fall of Charles X, in 1831 he presented a more permanent and infinitely more prestigious gift to Louis-Philippe: the obelisk of Luxor, which five years later was erected in the middle of the Place de la Concorde where it continues to be admired.

16. Gabriel Dardaud, "L'extraordinaire aventure de la girafe du Pacha d'Egypte," *Revue des Conférences Françaises en Orient,* 15th year, no. 1 (January 1951): 26.

17. In his book on nineteenth-century Parisian balls, François Gasnault notes that dancers often found inspiration for their costumes in political and literary topics of the day (*Guinguettes et lorettes: Bals publics et danse sociale à Paris entre 1830 et 1879* [Paris: Aubier, 1986], 164).

18. Grandville and Raffet were not the only artists of the young Romantic generation to be inspired by *Hernani.* Achille Devéria represented the fatal climax in his own lithograph, which accompanied a review of the drama in the eleventh issue of *La Silhouette:* Hernani lies on the floor dead and Doña Sol, half reclining, delivers a lament with her last dying breath while Don Ruy stands ominously at the left.

19. Paul Porel and Georges Monval, *L'Odéon, histoire administrative, anecdotique et littéraire de second Théâtre français* (Paris: Alphonse Lemerre, 1882), 2:111–12, 119.

20. Victor Hugo, *Oeuvres complètes* (Paris: Ollendorff, 1912), 1:716ff. Gautier's pourpoint is often erroneously referred to as a *gilet rouge,* or red vest. The picturesque costumes of the young Romantics were intended as a provocation to the Classicists. Gautier outlines the aesthetics behind their rebellious sartorial stance:

> Pour nous, le monde se divisait en *flamboyants* et en *grisâtres.* Nous voulions la vie, la lumière, le mouvement, l'audace de pensée et d'exécution, le retour aux belles époques de la Renaissance et à la vraie antiquité, et nous rejetions le coloris effacé, le dessin maigre et sec, les compositions pareilles à des groupements de mannequins, que l'Empire avait légués à la Restauration. (ibid., 718.)

[For us the world was divided into *flamboyants* and *greys*. We wanted life, light, movement, boldness of thought and execution, the return to the grand eras of the Renaissance and true Antiquity, and we rejected the faded color, thin and dry drawing, compositions similar to groupings of mannequins that the Empire had bequeathed to the Restoration.]

21. *Le Moniteur universel,* October 3, 1826; *Le Charivari,* May 8, 1839. Judging from the *Album cosmopolite,* Alexandre gave performances at royal courts throughout Europe where he was warmly received by, among others, the Crown Prince of Prussia (father of Kaiser Wilhelm II) and the Duchess of Kent (mother of Queen Victoria), both of whom served as patrons for the publication of the *Album* (for more details on the *Album cosmopolite,* see the note that follows).

22. The full title of the *Album cosmopolite* outlines its artistic program: *Album cosmopolite, ou choix des collections de M. Alexandre Vattemare, composé de sujets historiques et religieux, paysages, marines, intérieurs, costumes et scènes de moeurs, fleurs, médailles, portraits, manuscrits, vitraux, etc., tous originaux, dessinés par les principaux artistes de l'Europe: Angleterre, Autriche, Bavière, Belgique, Cassel, Dusseldorf, France, Pays-Bas, Prusse, Russie, Saxe, Suisse, etc., accompagné de textes et fac-simile d'autographes de Souverains, Princes, Princesses, Ministres, Savants, Poètes, Artistes et autres personnages distingués soit dans les Sciences, les Arts, ou par leur haute position sociale; gravé et lithograhié par les plus habiles artistes, et publié sous la direction de M. P. Henrichs, attaché au Ministère des Affaires Etrangères, rédacteur des Archives du Commerce, de l'Annuaire universel diplomatique, & membre de plusieurs Académies & Sociétés savantes. Dédié aux artistes de tous les pays* (Cosmopolitan album, or a selection from the collections of Mr. Alexandre Vattemare, composed of historical and religious subjects, landscapes, seascapes, interiors, costumes and genre scenes, flowers, medals, portraits, manuscripts, stained-glass windows, etc., all original, drawn by the principal artists of Europe: England, Austria, Bavaria, Belgium, Cassel, Dusseldorf, France, Holland, Prussia, Russia, Saxony, Switzerland, etc., accompanied by texts and facsimile autographs of sovereigns, princes, princesses, government ministers, scholars, poets, artists and other personages distinguished either in the sciences, the arts, or by their social position; engraved and lithographed by the most skilled artists, and published under the direction of Mr. P. Henrichs, attaché in the Ministry of Foreign Affairs, editor of the Archives of Commerce, of the Universal Diplomatic Register, & member of several academies & learned societies. Dedicated to artists of all countries). As the introduction to the *Album* further explains, its contents consisted of the artistic souvenirs and autographed tributes collected by Alexandre during his numerous performance tours:

Certes, il était dû à celui qui sur la scène prenait toutes les allures, peigneit les êtres et les choses du geste et de la voix, imitait la nature avec ses harmonies et ses contrastes, d'être admiré de ceux dont le magique pinceau pouvait produire les mêmes illusions. Aussi, l'amour de M. Vattemare pour les beaux-arts l'a rendu cher aux artistes; tous se sont empressés de le fêter et ont voulu qu'en les quittant il emportât des preuves de leur confraternité. Des esquisses, croquis, dessins, peintures, autographes, compositions de tous les genres offertes en souvenir de ses joyeuses soirées, grossissaient journellement son bagage. Les personnages les plus illustres ont désiré le voir et l'entendre; aux suffrages de tant d'autres ils ont aussi ajouté le leur. Ces marques d'une bienveillance particulière se sont souvent répétées. A chaque succès de l'artiste de nouveaux tributs venaient enrichir la collection de l'amateur. C'est ainsi qu'on peut s'expliquer cette abondante récolte d'autographes et de dessins de choix que M. Alexandre Vattemare a réunie dans ses tournées dramatiques, et les différentes sources qui continuent d'alimenter son album.

[Surely it was fitting for him who onstage took on all appearances, affected creatures and things with gesture and voice, imitated nature with its harmonies and contrasts, to be admired by those whose magic paintbrush could produce the same illusions. In addition, Mr. Vattemare's love for the fine arts endeared him to artists; they all were eager to honor him and wished that, when leaving them, he take with him tokens of their brotherhood. Sketches, preliminary studies, drawings, paintings, autographs, compositions of all kinds offered in remembrance of his merry evening performances made his baggage swell daily. The most illustrious personages eagerly wished to see and hear him; to the high regard of so many others they added their own. These indications of personal goodwill frequently repeated themselves. With each success of the artist came new tributes to enrich the collection of the amateur. This then accounts for this abundant harvest of autographs and select drawings that Mr. Vattemare has put together during his dramatic tours, and for the various sources which continue to augment his album.]

Grandville's contribution to Alexandre's album combines an artistic souvenir with an autographed tribute for a performance, which appears to have taken place at Marly-le-Roi on July 1, 1831. No effort was spared to impress potential subscribers with the number and quality of persons in high places who admired Alexandre's talents, and who supported the publication of his souvenir album as a token of friendship. A published list of early subscribers included the reigning monarchs of Austria, Belgium, France, Great Britain, Holland, Portugal, Prussia, Russia, and Spain in addition to other dignitaries such as the Duchess of Kent and the Crown Prince of Prussia, who served as the *Album's* official patrons. The first of the *Album's* twenty installments was announced in the *Bibliographie de la France,* July 1, 1837. Grandville's lithograph appeared in the fifth installment in 1838.

23. For a more detailed description of the Palais-Royal district during the last years of the Restoration, see Louis-Gabriel Montigny, *Le Provincial à Paris, esquisses des moeurs parisiennes* (Paris: Chez Ladvocat, 1825), 1:129–33.

24. "Spectacles," *Figaro,* March 28, 1830, 4.

1830

Although drawing 7/1 appears to be from 1830, there are no indications that it originally belonged to the diary of that year, and so it is presented separately.

7. 7/1 recto

Varieté des Colets de Chemises

Le regard de mepris par degradation
Le regard de Convoitise
(Variety of shirt collars

The contemptuous look brought on by decadence
The covetous look)

1830(?)
73 × 145
Pen and brown ink

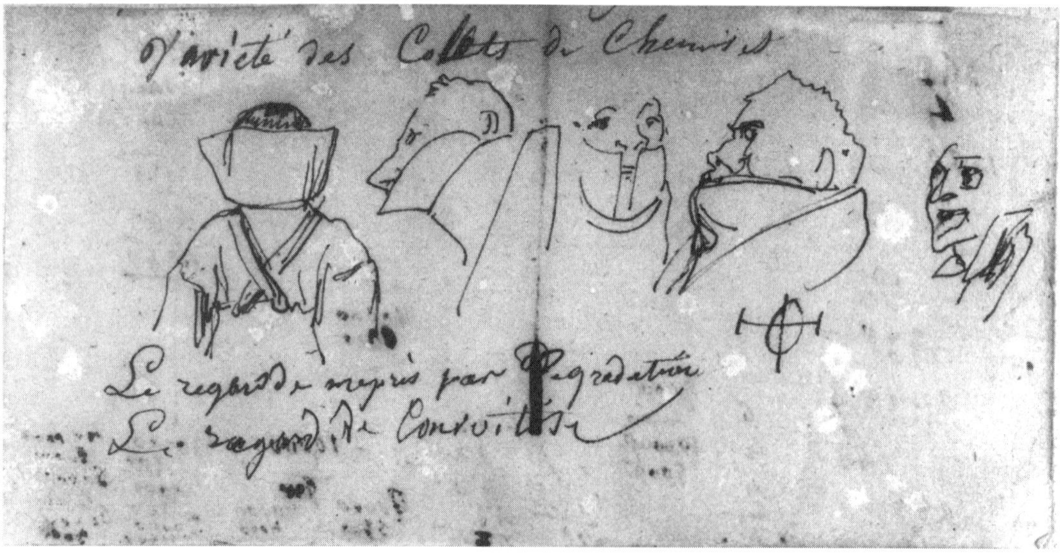

Establishing a date for this drawing is somewhat problematic. The paper does not resemble that of the 1830 diary or of any other diary represented in the Missouri Album: it may be either an independent sheet or part of an unidentified sketchbook. Its subject matter is directly related to the lithograph, *Etude Phrénologique et Col-logique des Français en 1834* (Phrenological and collar-ological study of the French in 1834; fig. 50). This print was registered with the dépôt légal on December 29, 1834, along with the cover, frontispiece, and three other plates of the album entitled *Types modernes. 1835. Observations critiques. Le dedans de l'homme expliqué par le dehors* published by Neuhaus just in time to serve as an *étrenne,* or New Year's Day present, at the beginning of 1835.[1] However, its graphic style,

Fig. 50. ***Etude Phrénologique et Col-logique des Français en 1834*** **(Phrenological and collar-ological study of the French in 1834) from** ***Types modernes,*** **1834, lithograph. Private collection.**

which is characterized by the use of strong linear contours with little or no interior modeling of figures, recalls that employed by Grandville toward 1827–30 (cf., Nancy, cat. nos. 56–58, 115–26). This chronological discrepancy is not as incongruous as it might first appear. For, as a comparison between the drawing and the print quickly demonstrates, the former is an early preliminary study for the latter. It may very well belong to a fairly large group of drawings from 1829–30 in which Grandville experimented with a number of different ideas for possible lithographic albums. The fate of these projects varied. For example, *Voyage pour l'éternité,* although published as an album, was never completed, supposedly because the subject of death was deemed too lugubrious. An announced *Histoire de Mr Mayeux* (History of Mr. Mayeux) seems to have been aborted by the Revolution of 1830, with apparently three of its twelve scheduled lithographs being published separately in *La Caricature.* Other album projects, such as "Les Bals de Paris" (The balls of Paris) and "La Marchande" (The tradeswoman) never saw the light of day.[2] Certain of these projects were listed and described along with still others in the Carnavalet Sketchbook from these same years of 1829 and 1830. Included among these are "Singeries" (p. 1 recto) and "la nouvelle Carte des restaurateurs" (p. 12 verso), which were eventually published as lithographic suites by Aubert in 1832 with the respective titles of *Singeries morales, politiques, etc.* and *Carte vivante du restaurateur.* Seen within this context, the present drawing would represent one of these exploratory ideas initiated around 1829–30, which, like the "Singeries" and "la nouvelle Carte des restaurateurs," was altered and elaborated upon for publication several years later.

As the subtitle of *Types modernes* indicates, the satire of the album revolves around the Lavaterian concept that a person's moral character can be ascertained by his or her physical appearance: "the inside of humanity explained by the outside."[3] Among the distinguishing external features depicted in the album are hats, canes, and pipes. Grandville even drew analogies between a person's character and the manner in which he took snuff or the pet he chose to own. In the present drawing and its related lithograph, he focused on the shape of the head and the choice of collars. The "étude phrénologique" refers to the German doctor Franz Josef Gall's pseudoscience of phrenology, or the study of the analogy between the shape of the skull and a person's psyche, which was directly inspired by Lavater's "science" of physiognomy. The parallel adjectival construction "col-logique" parodies "phrénologique" and takes aim at the dubious logic of a recent sartorial invention, the *faux col* (false collar) or *col amovible* (detachable collar), of which Nadar gave the following jaundiced view:

> A propos de toilette, voilà du nouveau aux vitres des lingères: jusqu'ici on y voyait des chemises avec des cols, maintenant on y voit des cols sans chemises. On changeait de chemise quand il était besoin, quitte, à la rigueur, pour se rattraper sur la lessive du Gascon, en retournant sur soi l'objet: maintenant on dissimulera la chemise sale avec un faux-col propre. Pourquoi pas tout à l'heure des faux-devants et des fausses manchettes? Je n'ai pas goût à ces faussetés.
>
> [With regard to dress, there's something new in haberdashery shop windows: up to this point you saw shirts with collars, now you see collars without shirts. You changed your shirt when it was necessary, if only, in a pinch, to catch up with the wash à la Gascon, by turning the object inside out on yourself: now you'll disguise the dirty shirt with a clean false collar. Why not soon false shirt-fronts and false cuffs? I don't like these falsities.][4]

Although different cranial configurations appear in the drawing and the lithograph, three of the collars depicted in the early study reappear with minor modifications in the print: the oversized collar worn by the boy bottom row center, the nostril-level collar in the middle row second from the left, and the mufflerlike collar in the top row fifth from the right. The boy in the oversized collar again appears in another, more finished preliminary study that stylistically appears to be from 1834 (fig. 51).

The annotations at the bottom of the sheet, "The contemptuous look brought on by decadence. The covetous look," seem to indicate that Grandville initially had the idea of incorporating Lavater's physiognomical analysis with the seventeenth-century French academician Charles Le Brun's theory of expression and with personifications of the Seven Deadly Sins for what eventually developed into *Types modernes.* All three would be combined so that, for instance, in "The contemptuous look brought on by decadence" the viewer could read in a particular individual's facial features both an expression of contempt à la Le Brun and a debased character à la Lavater. And in "The covetous look" could be found a personification of one of the Seven Deadly Sins in addition to an expression of envy à la Le Brun and a covetous character à la Lavater.[5]

While Grandville's interest in Lavater has been established and that in Le Brun documented elsewhere (Nancy, 27–29), his preoccupation with depicting the Seven Deadly Sins toward 1829–30 is attested to by the Carnavalet Sketchbook in which he twice outlines projects entitled "Les Sept pechés Capitaux" (The Seven Deadly Sins; pp. 7 recto and 13 recto). A drawing that stylistically appears to date later elaborates upon this same theme (Nancy, fig. 14).

Fig. 51. Study for *Etude Phrénologique et Col-logique des Français en 1834,* circa 1834, drawing. Present location unknown.

7/1 verso

[Arithmetical calculations]

1830(?)
73 × 145
Pen and brown ink

Notes

1. The date "1834" also appears between the two figures in the lower right-hand corner of the plate. The lithograph was subsequently reprinted, presumably so that the date in its title would coincide with that on the album's cover. Consequently, there exists a second state of this print entitled *Etude Phrénologique et Col-logique des Français en 1835.* The other three plates deposited with the dépôt légal on December 29, 1834, were *Variété des Priseurs* (Variety of snuff-takers), *Variété des Cannes* (Variety of canes), and *Chapellerie au XIXe Siècle (Ire Série) Chapeaux civils* (The hat-trade in the 19th century [1st series] Civilian hats). Three later plates in the album were not registered with the dépôt légal until December 30, 1836: *Les Laïs de Paris au 19me Siècle (année 1836)* (The Laises of Paris during the 19th century [the year 1836]; Lais was the name of

several ancient Greek courtesans), *L'Animalomanie, ou la prédilection sympatico-logico-physique de l'homme pour la bête. Planche 1ère* (Animalmania, or man's sympathetic-logical-physical predilection for animals. 1st plate), and *L'Animalomanie, ou la prédilection sympatico-logico-physique de l'homme pour la bête. Planche 2me* (Animalmania, or man's sympathetic-logical-physical predilection for animals. 2nd plate). There appears to be no record of when the eighth plate in the album, *Variété des Pipes et de leurs Fumeurs* (Variety of pipes and their smokers), was deposited with the dépôt légal.

2. For a more detailed account of these and other album projects from circa 1829–30, see Nancy, 145–49.

3. The Lavaterian inspiration behind *Types modernes* is elaborated upon in Nancy, 14–19. This inspiration was made more explicit when Aubert republished the lithographs in 1842 as an album of twenty-four smaller format plates entitled *L'Homme, son esprit, ses goûts et ses habitudes jugés par son physique* (Man, his disposition, his tastes and his habits judged by his physique). Unlike the original edition, the figures were captioned as either personifying a particular personality trait or representing a particular social type and mentality, such as *Un vaniteux* (A conceited person) and *Le bureaucrate* (The bureaucrat). Thus labeled, the modified *Types modernes* better fit in with the physiological fad that culminated in the 1840s. For the key role played by La Maison Aubert in publishing "physiologies," see James Cuno, "Philipon et Desloges: Éditeurs des 'physiologies' (1841–1842)" in *Cahiers,* 137–55.

4. Nadar, 298.

5. Grandville's character studies invite comparison with Géricault's 1822–23 series of paintings depicting monomanias. "The covetous look," for example, automatically calls to mind the latter's *Monomane de l'envie* (Monomaniac of envy) at the Lyon Musée des Beaux-Arts.

Diary of 1832

Only one drawing can, with any certainty, be identified as belonging to Grandville's diary from 1832: 6/6, which depicts Saint-Simonians on its recto and contains typical diary annotations on its verso. At first glance, the paper appears to be the same as that found in the 1830 diary with similar faded reddish-brown lines printed 8 mm apart. However, the paper has a smoother finish. Also, the graphic style is different: the lines are heavier and more confidently drawn. A second drawing, 1/3, which is stylistically related to 6/6 and executed on similar paper has also been included as possibly belonging to the 1832 diary.

8. 6/6 recto

[ ]issuer

(belleville des St Simoniens)

([*]issuer*

Belleville of the Saint-Simonians)

1832
33 × 58
Pen and brown ink

On the basis of its reference to Saint-Simonians, this diary fragment may be dated 1832. Claude Henri de Rouvroy, Comte de Saint-Simon (1760–1825), one of the founders of modern socialism, optimistically advocated a society where the exploitation of the masses by an elite of inherited wealth would disappear. Instead, a benevolent state would control the means of production, both agricultural and industrial, and distribute goods according to the fundamental principle of "à chacun selon sa capacité, à chaque capacité selon ses oeuvres" (to each according to his ability, to each ability according to its works). Perfect social harmony would result.

On April 20, 1832, one of Saint-Simon's disciples, Prosper Barthélemy Enfantin (1796–1864), the son of a wealthy banker and a graduate of the elite École Polytechnique, founded a model community ostensibly based on Saint-Simon's ideals. It was housed in a small mansion on a country estate that Enfantin had inherited from his father located at Ménilmontant, part of a suburban working-class community known as Belleville just northeast of Paris (Belleville would be annexed by the expanding capital in 1860). For the most part, the forty or so Saint-Simonians who participated in this short-lived social experiment with Enfantin were, like their leader, scions of well-to-do, upper-middle-class, bourgeois families. Many went on to become successful in professions such as engineering, banking, and publishing after the community's final dispersal some eight months later in December 1832.[1]

The community possessed the overtones of a religious sect. Enfantin, like some latter-day guru, was addressed as "Père-Enfantin" (Father Enfantin) and his followers were referred to as "apôtres" (apostles). Daily life was regulated according to an almost monastic routine, and members were dressed in a distinctive uniform consisting of white trousers, white vest, blue tunic or violet frock coat, and red beret. The front of each vest displayed the name of its wearer; Enfantin's simply carried the words, "LE PERE" (The Father). Buttoned from the back instead of the front, the vest symbolized fraternity inasmuch as it could be worn only with the help of a fellow Saint-Simonian. Each member of the community worked for the common good with the result that the well-heeled, well-educated, upper-middle-class liberals indulged themselves in such activities as gardening and polishing boots.[2] This latter activity, satirized by Louis Reybaud in *Jérôme Paturot,* was also lampooned by Grandville in an accompanying illustration (fig. 52). Solidarity with the working class was demonstrated not only by their manual labor, but also by their singing songs such as the following while working:

> Allons bourgeois et prolétaires
> Le travail nous a fait égaux
> Ensemble remuons la terre
> Montrons à tous l'Homme nouveau!
>
> [Let's go bourgeois and proletarians
> Work has made us equal
> Let us move the earth together
> Let us show to all the New Man!][3]

The simplistic working-class role-playing and operatic costumes of these *fils de bourgeois* (sons of the middle class) were not appreciated by their economically less fortunate and socially less elevated neighbors. One can well imagine that they considered such fatuous posturing as an insult to their all-too-real hand-to-mouth existence. Nadar recounts in his souvenirs their indignant reaction:

> A Ménilmontant, les aborigènes traitent un peu vif à coups de pierres les Saint-Simoniens par trop coquets, décolletés comme des danseuses, le buste étranglé sous la coupe rituelle de redingotes collantes largement ouvertes à la poitrine, le pantalon étroit sanglé par le sous-pied sur la botte vernie.
>
> [At Ménilmontant, the natives treat a little sharply with thrown stones the overly stylish Saint-Simonians, low necklined like dancers, the bust choked under the ritual cut of close-fitting frock coats widely open at the chest, narrow pants tightly fitted by the trouser-strap on the polished boot.][4]

Grandville's portrayal of the "belleville des St Simoniens" evokes the social confrontation described by Nadar. One of Enfantin's costumed followers, seen from the back and sporting a beret, has attracted the attention of a fashionably dressed female admirer (Enfantin's Saint-Simonians advocated the eman-

Fig. 52. ***Apôtres dans l'exercice de leurs fonctions sacerdotales*** **(Apostles in the discharge of their sacerdotal duties) from** ***Jérôme Paturot à la recherche d'une position sociale,*** **1846, wood engraving. Paris, Bibliothèque nationale de France.**

cipation of women as well as that of the working class) in the company of a top-hatted escort. This bourgeois trio contrasts with the gawking proletarian locals: a woman wearing wooden shoes and a plain dress with apron at the far left and a man in a day laborer's loose-fitting pants and smock second from the right.

It is difficult to assess Grandville's real attitude toward the Saint-Simonians from this small sketch or from his satirical illustration to *Jérôme Paturot.* Given certain drawings from around this same time in which he pointedly contrasts the misery of the working-class poor with the haughty and callous attitude of the bourgeoisie (fig. 26 and Nancy, cat. no. 187), there is no doubt that Grandville shared with the Saint-Simonians a concern for social reform.[5] However, he may have had the same jaundiced view of Saint-Simonian religion as his friends and colleagues. Balzac lampooned the Saint-Simonians in two articles for *La Caricature.*[6] And one of Grandville's most steadfast friends and supporters, Edouard Charton, formerly a prominent Saint-Simonian, in November 1831 had broken with the utopians over the ascendancy of Enfantin and his mystical "doctrine secrète," or secret doctrine, which promoted a new moral standard based on free love. The following month, he published an account of his life as a Saint-Simonian and the reasons for his rupture with the group in a pamphlet entitled, *Mémoires d'un prédicateur saint-simonien* (Memoirs of a Saint-Simonian preacher).[7] It is entirely possible that, like Balzac's articles and Charton's tract, Grandville's sketch both satirizes the Saint-Simonians and criticizes the questionable turn Saint-Simonian doctrine had taken under the mesmerizing leadership of Enfantin.

6/6 verso

Lundi promenade avec

Recu De madame A
(Monday walk with

Received from madame A)

1832
33 × 58
Pen and brown ink

As we have already seen in cat. no. 4 and will see again in diary excerpts from 1833, Grandville frequently enjoyed walking around Paris in the company of friends. Although the name(s) of Grandville's companion(s) on the particular Monday mentioned here will never be known, Chardard and Guiaud, along with Eugène Forest, who appears in the following catalog entry, are among the likely candidates.

Even more disappointing is that we will probably never know the sum of money Grandville received from "madame A," certainly Madame Aubert, Philipon's half sister and the wife of the famous print publisher, who appears several times in the 1833 diary (cat. nos. 16, 20, and 32). Although it can be assumed that the payment was for a recent political caricature, we can only guess which one.

9. 1/3 recto

fores[t]
mes
Act

prome[nade]
(Fores[t]

my
Act

walk)

1832
34 × 32
Pen and brown ink

Identical in graphic style to the preceding drawing, this diary fragment representing a woman seated on a stool may also be from the 1832 diary. The absence of printed lines suggests that it originally may have been part of an unlined margin. Although badly cropped, two of the words that accompany the vignette can be plausibly reconstituted. The first one surely refers to Eugène Forest, Grandville's closest collaborator at the time who, like Grandville, lived in the rue des Petits-Augustins. The last fragmented word more than likely once more refers to the walks Grandville was in the habit of taking.

1/3 verso

[fragment of writing]

1832
34 × 32
Pen and brown ink

The annotations on the verso of this fragment are too disfigured to allow for any commentary.

Notes

1. Simon Lacordaire, *Vie et histoire du XXe arrondissement* (Paris: Editions Hervas, 1987), 91–93.
2. Ibid., 92.
3. Ibid.
4. Nadar, 282.
5. Grandville's sympathy for the poorer segments of French society was very real. In a letter to his editor, Fournier, postmarked November 24, 1846, he defends their protestations against the deleterious effects that the French Corn Laws had on the price of bread: "Je veux parler de votre émeute à propos des *Corn Laws* de France..de la cherté du pain. Comment c'est vous qui osez écrire que cette augmentation si considerable, d'un aliment si indispensable ne soit que de prétexte au tumulte . . . je trouve au contraire moi que la classe pauvre qui est si cruellement atteinte par ce rencherissement [illegible word] pour elle est bien moderé, bien patient bien héroïque de ne pas mettre sens dessus dessous les quatre coins de la france (ce qui serait un triste moyen j en conviens d'arranger les choses)" (I want to talk about your riot in connection with the Corn Laws of France..of the high price of bread. How can it be you who dare write that this so considerable augmentation of such an indispensable food be only a pretext for turmoil . . . on the contrary, me, I find that the poorer class which is so cruelly hit by this rise in price [illegible word] is very moderate, very patient, very heroic for not having turned things upside down in the four corners of France [which, I admit, would be a sad way to settle the matter]). I wish to thank Annie Renonciat for sharing a copy of this letter with me.
6. *Oeuvres complètes de Honoré de Balzac* (Paris: Conard, 1938), 39:314–16, 472–74. The first article, "Saint-Simonien et Saint-Simoniste," was published in the March 10, 1831, issue of *La Caricature* under the pen name of Le Comte Alex. de B. . . . The second, "Religion Saint-Simonienne," appeared January 19 and 26, 1832, under the pen name of Alfred Coudreux.
7. Paris: Au Bureau de La Revue encyclopédique, 1831. For additional analyses of Charton's break with Enfantin's visionary reorientation of Saint-Simonian dogma, see Kaenel, "J.-J. Grandville et le *Magasin pittoresque* d'Edouard Charton,"

77–78; Marie-Pierre Dupin, "Un publiciste et homme politique saint-simonien: Edouard Charton," *Versailles, Revue des Sociétés des Amis de Versailles,* no. 62 (1976): 24–26. A succinct account of Enfantin's controversial free love doctrine and the divisions it caused within the Saint-Simonian movement may be found in Thureau-Dangin, 1:272–75.

1832

Done in the spirit of the lithographic suite *Singeries morales, politiques, etc.,* which was published by Aubert in 1832, the following drawing is also possibly from that year. The paper on which it has been executed has a smoother finish than that of the presumed 1832 diary. Also, although it is printed with similar faded reddish-brown horizontal lines 8 mm apart, the lines are thinner. On the recto of the sheet is printed a heavy vertical line of the same color; two other vertical lines, 18 mm apart, appear on the verso.

10. 10/4 recto

Les Gardes de l'oc[troi]
(The toll tax guards)

1832(?)
38 × 71
Pen and brown ink

Their close resemblance to humans and their ability to ape human behavior had long made monkeys a traditional vehicle for caricatural commentary. During the eighteenth century there developed a veritable mania for *singeries,* or monkey scenes, which continued to be popular in the print trade at the beginning of the nineteenth century.[1] *Artiste animalier* that he was, Grandville naturally wished to produce his own *singeries,* and with the help of Forest he did. His suite of six lithographs entitled *Singeries morales, politiques, etc.* was registered with the dépôt légal between April 10 and May 9, 1832 (figs. 82 and 83 reproduce plate 6 and a detail from it). It was probably in an effort to publicize the new series that two of the *Singeries* simultaneously appeared as double plates (154, 155 and 158, 159) in *La Caricature* on April 19 and May 3, 1832.

The monkey in the drawing bears a strong resemblance to those in the *Singeries morales, politiques, etc.* and may belong to studies for a sequel that never saw publication. According to the annotation, it represents one of the guards responsible for enforcing the *octroi,* the hated toll tax levied on goods entering Paris. Grandville and Forest attacked the *octroi* in plate 199 of *La Caricature*'s September 13, 1832, issue, *Il faut céder à l'octroi et comment s'en défendre* (You must yield to the toll tax and how to defend yourself against it; fig. 53). The journal's republican sympathies surface in the accompanying commentary, which criticized the social inequity of a tax that hit hardest those who could least afford it:

> L'octroi est un monstre qui suce le peuple; il n'est qu'un moyen de lui échapper, c'est de faire fortune, car l'octroi aime les riches; il ne prend ni leurs laquais, ni leurs chiens, ni leurs carosses [*sic*], mais il se jette

Fig. 53. ***Il faut cèder à l'octroi et comment s'en défendre*** **(You must yield to the toll tax and how to defend yourself against it), plate 199 of** ***La Caricature,*** **September 13, 1832, lithograph. Paris, Bibliothèque nationale de France.**

> sur les misérables; leur nourriture, leurs boissons, leur paille, le poussier qui les chauffe en hiver, à défaut de bois; tout est sa proie, tout lui paye un tribut. L'octroi est un digne soutien de la meilleure des républiques.
>
> [The toll tax is a monster that sucks the people dry; there is only one way to escape it, and that is to make a fortune, for the toll tax likes the rich; it takes neither their footmen, nor their dogs, nor their carriages, but it pounces upon the poverty stricken; their food, their drink, their straw, the coal dust that warms them in the winter for lack of wood; everything is its prey, all pay tribute to it. The toll tax is a worthy prop for the best of republics.]

The phrase "la meilleure des républiques" is, of course, an ironic reference to Lafayette's famous August 7, 1830, assessment of the nascent July Monarchy. Some eight months later Grandville again attacked the *octroi* by depicting it twice in the tenth, May 1833 print for the *Association mensuelle, Le Peuple livré aux impôts suceurs dans la grande fosse du budjet* [*sic*] (The people delivered to the bloodsucker taxes in the great pit of the budget; fig. 57).

10/4 verso

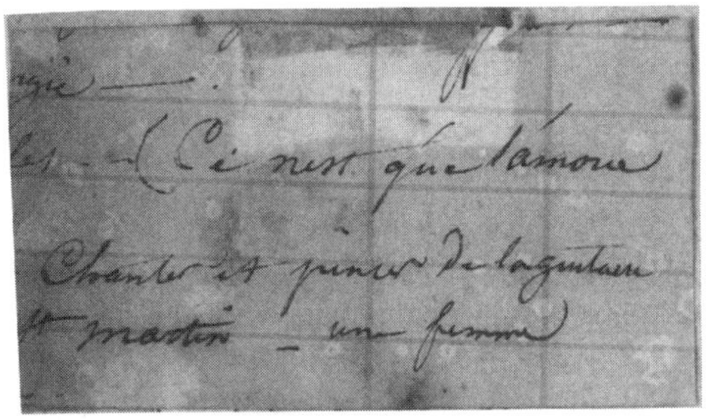

rgie—.
les..(Ci nest que l'amorce
Chanter et pincer de la guitarre
St Martin—une femme
(rgie—.
les..[This is only the priming
To sing and to strum on the guitar
St Martin—a woman)

1832(?)
38 × 71
Pen and brown ink

Like certain drawings in the 1830 diary and references to amorous encounters in the 1833 diary (cat. nos. 16, 22, 24, and 32), this fragmented gallant annotation, in which he appears to suggest how to initiate a seduction, once again attests to Grandville's active interest in the opposite sex during his bachelor years. "St Martin" may be part of the aristocratic-sounding nom de guerre of a brothel madam.[2]

Serenading the object of one's affections to the accompaniment of a guitar was not exactly a new idea. It long had been a traditional first step in the genteel art of courting, and in the eighteenth century often figured as part of rococo *fêtes galantes.* During the Romantic period, guitar playing and singing, whether with a group of friends or in the private company of one's beloved, was a popular recreation that paralleled the contemporaneous vogue for the "style troubadour" in both painting and literature. An 1857 article in the *Magasin pittoresque* evokes this phenomenon as it describes a musical soirée attended by Grandville during his younger years:

> En ce temps-là, le goût de la musique n'était pas encore arrivé à ce degré de délicatesse qui nous rend presque insupportables les talents médiocres, même dans les réunions de parents et d'amis...Les oreilles, moins exercées, étaient donc peu difficiles. La guitare, grattée tant bien que mal, sans qu'on eût jamais appris à en jouer, passait pour un instrument fort agréable, surtout lorqu'elle venait en aide à une voix qui n'était pas absolument fausse. Le soir, quelques familles de peintres et de dessinateurs se donnaient rendez-vous dans un atelier ou dans une modeste chambre, qu'on n'oserait plus appeler aujourd'hui un salon. Au milieu était une grande table couverte de papiers, de crayons, de pinceaux, d'encre de Chine. Pour se reposer du long travail du jour, on s'amusait à faire des esquisses, des croquis, des caricatures. Pendant ce temps, quelques-unes des jeunes dames (sans se faire prier!) chantaient des romances nouvelles ou des airs d'opéra-comique et même de vaudeville, et quelqu'un des dessinateurs, se détachant de la table, les accompagnait en tirant hardiment de la guitare les premier accords qui se rencontraient sous sa main; parfois, de plus plaisants jugeaient nécessaire d'intervenir et d'ajouter à l'intensité des sons un accompagnement de quelque espèce de triangle ou de tambour de basque; souvent aussi le solo ou le duo se transformait en choeur: basses, ténors, barytons, contralti, soprani, tous très-naturels et très-confiants, s'élançaient librement à tout risque, comme à une course au clocher. On s'animait, on s'exaltait, et puis on riait aux éclats; mais, tout en se moquant chacun de soi-même et des autres avec la meilleure grâce du monde, on n'était pas toujours bien persuadé au fond que l'on n'eût pas fait de la fort bonne musique. Il y avait telles notes que l'on avait senti sortir de soi avec étonnement, et l'on en était tout ému.
>
> [In those times, the taste for music had not yet reached that degree of refinement that renders mediocre talents almost unbearable for us, even in gatherings with relatives and friends . . . Ears less trained were consequently not hard to please. The guitar, which one picked at after a fashion without ever having learned

how to play it, passed for a most agreeable instrument, especially when it helped out a voice that was not completely off key. In the evening, several communities of painters and draftsmen met together in a studio or in a modest room that today one would no longer dare call a salon. In the middle was a large table covered with papers, pencils, brushes, India ink. In order to relax after a long day's work, you amused yourself by drawing sketches, doodles, caricatures. During this time, several of the young ladies (without being asked!) sang new love-songs or light opera or even vaudeville tunes, and one of the draftsmen, getting up from the table, accompanied them by boldly plucking on the guitar the first chords that his hand happened to find; sometimes the more droll ones thought it necessary to intervene and add an accompaniment of some sort of triangle or tambourine to the vibrancy of the sounds; the solo or duo was also often transformed into a choir: basses, tenors, baritones, contraltos, sopranos, all very unaffected and very confident, threw themselves into it with abandon risking everything, as in a steeplechase. You came to life, you grew excited, and then you burst out laughing; but, while everyone as gracefully as possible made fun of themselves and of the others, you weren't always in the end fairly well convinced that you hadn't made some very good music. There were those notes that you felt with surprise come out of you, and you were quite moved by it.][3]

The singing and guitar strumming advocated by Grandville in this diary entry would have taken place in more intimate surroundings, similar to those that he depicted in a contemporaneous drawing belonging to the Musée Lorrain where the guitar in this case is being played by a woman (fig. 54). The vase next to her and the phallic fire stoker by her admiring beau symbolically suggest that the evening promises more than a cozy fireside serenade.

Notes

1. See for instance Tf26 pet. fol., *Caricatures, Animaux, Singeries: 1821 à 1831,* in the Cabinet des estampes at the Bibliothèque nationale de France.
2. In his contemporaneous guidebook for provincials visiting Paris, *Le Provincial à Paris, esquisses des moeurs parisiennes* (Paris: Chez Ladvocat, 1825), Louis-Gabriel Montigny observes that it was very fashionable for a madam in a brothel to use the aristocratic particle "de" followed by the name of a saint as her professional alias:

> Le *de,* qu'on ajoute aujourd'hui si facilement à tous les noms, est un ornement obligé de celui de la souveraine du lieu; presque toujours l'ambitieuse particule est suivie d'un nom de saint. On n'a pas d'idée de la consistance que cela donne dans un certain monde: Madame de Saint-Elfride, de Saint-Georges, de Saint-André; c'est d'un effet sûr. (1:70–71)

> [The *of,* that is so easily added to all names today, is an indispensable embellishment of the person who is the sovereign of the place; the ambitious particle is almost always followed by the name of a saint. You have no idea of the impression that makes in certain quarters: Madame of Saint-Elfred, of Saint-George, of Saint-Andrew; it has an unerring effect.]

3. "Dessins inédits de J.-J. Grandville," *Magasin pittoresque* 25, no. 14 (April 1857): 111–12.

Diary of 1833

The remnants of the 1833 diary make us regret all the more that it and the other mutilated journals represented in the Missouri Album have not survived intact, for they give us the best idea of what Grandville's diaries originally looked like. At times nearly complete pages, containing altogether remarkable drawings and extensive written entries that artfully complement one another, chronicle his day-to-day activities in inventive page layouts: promenades, visits to the Jardin des Plantes, theatrical performances, and other aspects of his active social life. They also reveal that Grandville treated his diary as a confidant, recording in the privacy of its pages the most intimate details of his life and his innermost

Fig. 54. *Serenade,* circa 1830, drawing. Nancy, Musée Lorrain.

thoughts: amorous adventures (cat. nos. 16, 22, 24, and 32), a letter written to his "cousine," who he will marry a few months later (cat. no. 28), and most notably, his real feelings toward his highly successful career as France's leading opposition political caricaturist (cat. no. 16). This last bit of invaluable information helps to explain Grandville's motivations for abandoning the field of political caricature in favor of a new career as a book illustrator following the repressive censorship laws of September 1835.

Another intriguing aspect of the 1833 diary excerpts is what they reveal about Grandville's circle of friends and his work habits. Friendships often develop among people with whom one works. That this was apparently the case with Grandville is indicated by frequent references to various colleagues on the staffs of *La Caricature, Le Charivari,* and the *Association mensuelle:* Louis Desnoyers, Honoré Daumier, Eugène Forest, Menut, and Charles Philipon. Grandville, of course, mentions other friends and acquaintances, such as Jacques Guiaud and Alexandre Dumas. But even they share with him a common interest in the arts.

By piecing together annotations from two diary fragments (cat. nos. 26 and 27), we get some idea of Grandville's daily routine in the midst of his career as a political caricaturist: work at home in the morning, a walk around noon, lunch in a restaurant, entertainment in the evening. Other diary entries (cat. nos. 16, 22, 23, and 24) indicate typical weekend activities before his marriage. Friday evenings, it would seem, were reserved for intimate encounters with the fair sex while a Saturday evening might find him at the theater. Sunday could be spent receiving visits from friends, going on yet another walk, or dining with a female companion. We also learn something about the process of producing one of his caricatures and his relationship with La Maison Aubert. Given the information provided in cat. nos. 11, 16, and 20, it appears that once having finished a drawing, he took it to one of his lithographic interpreters and roughed out the composition on the stone. He then left the drawing and verbal instructions with his collaborator, who completed the transfer of the drawing onto the stone. Grandville oversaw the printing of the lithograph. Once the caricature was published, he submitted his bill to Madame Aubert, who in exchange would return his original drawing. He subsequently would be paid by Madame Aubert.

The drawings in the 1833 diary are among the most striking that Grandville produced. Virtual miniature masterpieces, they represent a high point in his experimentation with a tenebroso style in which two technical innovations occur. Instead of being starkly separated by a well-delineated contour outline as seen in his earlier work, image and ground frequently blend together through the use of a wash "halo," whose edges gradually blend into the page and act as a feathery zone of transition between the dark, shadowy drawing and the whiteness of the sheet. Also, diagonal hatching, already present in certain drawings from 1830, predominates. Often used along with the edges of the ink wash as a zone of transition between the image and the surrounding blank support, it contributes to the richly textured, atmospheric play of light and dark so characteristic of these moody and often mysterious compositions. Their dark, brooding presences appear to be the visual equivalent of Grandville's psychological state at a particularly stressful point in his life as he weighed the risks of his career as a political caricaturist and pondered how its continuance might affect not only his own well-being, but also (an additional source of anxiety) that of his future wife and children. A last feature of the 1833 diary, which only serves to enhance the mysterious quality of Grandville's tenebroso style, is the presence of "ghost" images. Because of either the porous quality of the paper or the quantity of ink used in the distinctively dark drawings, or both, images from one side of a sheet have often bled through to the other, where they appear as shadowy, ghostlike apparitions.

The 1833 diary measured approximately 350 × 115 mm. The first page of the diary was printed on China paper; from all appearances, the rest of the diary consisted of a less luxurious, heavier gauge paper. Each page contained spaces for three entries with wide margins at both the top and bottom. The distance from the top of the page to the bottom of the first entry was approximately 133 mm; space for the middle entry measured 100 mm and that for the third entry, which continued uninterrupted until the bottom of the page, was approximately 117 mm. Printed at the top of each page was the name of the month. The date, the day of the week, the day's saint or religious holiday, and the number of days left in the year were printed at the beginning of the space for each entry. Lettering established a hierarchy among the days: major saints and the most important days of the liturgical calendar appeared in all capitals while the names of lesser saints had only the first letter of the name capitalized. The diary also included a printed list of lunar and solar eclipses for 1833. Most of the diary fragments from 1833 contain certain of these printed indications, which allow for their precise dating. Both printed and written text have been transcribed as closely as possible line for line: the printed text appears in bold type, imitating its appearance in the diary; Grandville's entries appear, as usual, in italics, followed by their English translation between parentheses.

11. 12/2 recto

Je vais Chez menut
J'ebauche ma pierre
du sas— mr. samir—
(I go to Menut's place
I sketch out my stone
of the riddle— Mr. Samir—)

January 1 or 2, 1833
65 × 65
Pen and brown ink

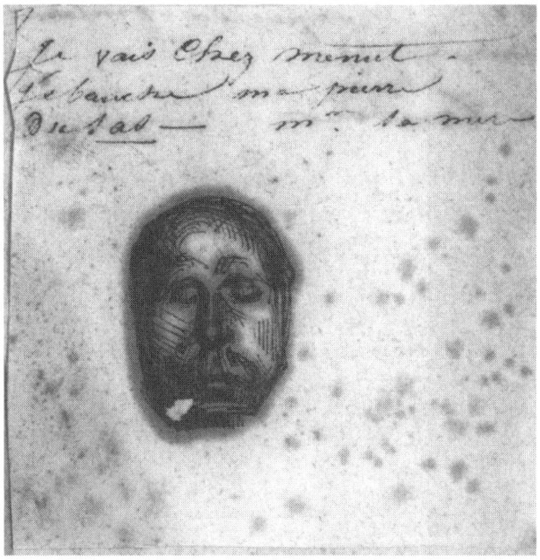

Although this diary fragment is undated, it may be situated at the beginning of January. For it is from the same sheet of China paper as the following catalog entry, which is printed with the date of January 3 and on whose verso is printed the date of January 6 (cat. no. 14). That it is from this particular sheet of China paper and not another that may have appeared in the 1833 diary is corroborated by the fact that it exhibits the same pattern and color of foxing as cat. nos. 12 and 14. Like cat. no. 12, this catalog entry is from the smoother felt side of the sheet and therefore is the recto of its particular diary fragment. Since cat. no. 12 is dated January 3 and there was space for only three diary entries on each side of a page, this diary excerpt must be from either of the two previous days, January 1 or January 2, probably January 2, as it is doubtful that even Grandville worked on New Year's Day.

Grandville goes to the home of Menut and blocks out a composition featuring a riddle, or coarse sieve, on his lithographic stone. Menut is the pseudonym of one of Grandville's artistic collaborators, Marie-Alexandre Alophe (1812–83), a native Parisian and lithographer who contributed two plates to *La Caricature* during the first year of its existence.[1] Like Grandville, Menut will be affiliated with the *Journal des enfans, Musée des familles,* and *Gazette des enfans* (see cat. no. 21). Both men also contributed work to *L'Artiste* (a lithograph by Menut that appeared in an 1833 issue of the journal is reproduced in figure 89). Menut worked with Grandville on the November 1832, December 1832, and January 1833 plates of the *Association mensuelle.* Were it not for the mention of the riddle, one might reasonably conclude that the rough sketch mentioned here is for the January 1833 plate of the *Association mensuelle, L'Echenillement et les semailles* (The season for destroying the pests and sowing new seed), which was registered with the dépôt légal on January 29. But there is no riddle in this print. A riddle, however, does figure as the central image in *Le Triage populaire* (The people's choice), a lithograph cosigned by Desperet that appeared some eight months later as plate 305 of *La Caricature* on August 22, 1833. It is possible that *Le Triage populaire* was originally conceived as the January 1833 plate for the *Association mensuelle,* but, for whatever reasons, *L'Echenillement et les semailles* was substituted instead. Should this be the case, it is equally possible that Menut's work on *Le Triage populaire* had not advanced very far before the switch was made, leaving Desperet with the task of completing the interrupted composition at a later date.

Despite the uncertainty regarding the print, this entry allows us to hypothesize how work proceeded on a collaborative project during Grandville's career as a political caricaturist. Once having finished the drawing for a caricature, he went to the home of an artistic collaborator where he sketched out the main outlines of the composition on a lithographic stone, and no doubt gave a running commentary on how to realize the final product that he envisioned.[2] The interpreter then was left to fill in the details, following both the verbal instructions and the meticulously precise drawing that Grandville would have given to him.

Unfortunately, the identity of Mr. Samir remains a mystery. Equally mysterious in its own way is the drawing of a mustachioed mask hanging on a wall, possibly a recent acquisition purchased in anticipation of carnival. The strong value contrasts that give it a hauntingly eerie quality result from a nearby source of artificial light. Grandville may have used the mask as a wall decoration in a fashion similar to the deer mask in Nancy, cat. no. 7 or the plaster mask depicted in cat. no. 31.

12. 24 recto

3 Jeudi. STE. GENEVIÈVE. 3–362.
(3 Thursday. St. Genevieve 3–362.)

January 3, 1833
114 × 110
Pen and brown ink

Fig. 55. Louis Français, *On recommande aussi aux curieux de ne point trop agacer les nouveaux hôtes du Jardin-des-Plantes. Ceci pouvant, malgré les précautions qu'on a prises, n'être point sans danger!* (It is also recommended that spectators not tease unduly the new denizens of the Jardin des Plantes. Despite precautions that have been taken, this could be not without danger!) from *Scènes de la vie privée et publique des animaux,* 1842, wood engraving. Private collection.

Grandville made frequent visits to the Jardin des Plantes. In those relatively few entries from the 1833 diary that survive, he mentions going there with Daumier on April 20 (cat. no. 16) and again a few weeks later on May 3 in the company of Forest and Guiaud (cat. no. 29). Even though he has not written it down, it is evident from the drawings here and in cat. no. 34 (recto) that he also went to the Jardin des Plantes or, more specifically, its *ménagerie* (menagerie) on January 3 and December 13. For it was the menagerie, or zoo, and not so much the extensive botanical gardens after which it was named that drew Grandville and crowds of his contemporaries to the Jardin des Plantes. This fact is confirmed by Nadar in his ironic observation that the former Jardin du Roi (Garden of the King) "is now called the Jardin des Plantes [Garden of the Plants] because you go there to see animals." Compulsive draftsman that he was, Grandville inevitably left pictorial records of his visits there. We can easily imagine his capturing on paper the menagerie's inhabitants as Louis Français depicted him in the whimsical world-turned-upside-down plate at the end of *Scènes de la vie privée et publique des animaux* (fig. 55).

Grandville has sketched here two of the menagerie's star attractions, the tiger and one of the bears in the *fosse aux ours,* or bear pit.[3] The bear pit was particularly popular with the public thanks to one of its recently deceased inhabitants, the beloved Martin who over a decade later was still remembered as "la perle des ours, l'ours modèle, l'ours dont on parlera encore pendant plusieurs générations, tant

Fig. 56. ***La Fosse aux ours*** **(The bear pit) from** ***Le Jardin des Plantes,*** **1842, wood engraving. Paris, Bibliothèque nationale de France.**

il avait de grâces naturelles" (a jewel of a bear, the model bear, the bear who will be talked about for several generations, so many natural graces did he have).[4] Grandville visited the bear pit regularly and featured it in an illustration for Pierre Boitard's *Le Jardin des Plantes* (Dubochet, 1842; fig. 56).[5] As usual, he could not resist incorporating such a well-known subject into his caricatural program. After several months, he transformed it into "the great pit of the budget" filled with parasitic, bloodsucking hybrid monsters for the May 1833 plate of the *Association mensuelle* (fig. 57). An even more fantastic metamorphosis will take place a decade later in *La Fosse aux doublivores* (The doublivore pit) for the "Une après-midi au Jardin des Plantes" (An afternoon at the Jardin des Plantes) chapter of *Un autre monde* (fig. 58).

The popularity of the Jardin des Plantes's menagerie in general during the Romantic period and Grandville's fascination with animals in particular may be explained to a certain extent by the scientific climate of the time. The end of the eighteenth and the beginning of the nineteenth century saw the emergence of the modern sciences of natural history and comparative anatomy thanks to the pioneering work of French savants such as Buffon (1707–88), Lamarck (1744–1829), Cuvier (1769–1832), and Geoffroy Saint-Hilaire (1772–1844). As a result, the Muséum national d'histoire naturelle (National Museum of Natural History) at the Jardin des Plantes became the leading research institution in

Fig. 57. ***Le Peuple livré aux impôts suceurs dans la grande fosse du budjet*** **[*sic*] (The people delivered to the blood-sucker taxes in the great pit of the budget), plate 10 of the *Association mensuelle,* May 1833, etching. Nancy, Bibliothèque municipale.**

the field of natural history during the nineteenth century. The menagerie, administered by the Muséum, accordingly was equally famous for its collection of rare and exotic living specimens. When Mohammed Ali Pasha's giraffe arrived at Marseilles, the Muséum sent one of its own distinguished members, no less than Geoffroy Saint-Hilaire, to act as the animal's official escort during the long walk to Paris.[6] The exploits, physical as well as intellectual, of the Muséum's professors piqued the public's curiosity about natural history. Grandville reflected this popular interest. We know that he admired Cuvier and used illustrations to Buffon as a reference for his own work. He probably was also acquainted with the theories of Geoffroy Saint-Hilaire. Typically, he recognized the satirical potential of their concepts and parodied them in his caricatures.[7] In the months that follow, he and Forest will be inspired by both Cuvier's magisterial four-volumed *Le Règne animal distribué d'après son organisation, pour servir de base à l'histoire naturelle des animaux et d'introduction à l'anatomie comparée* (*The Animal Kingdom, Arranged After its Organization, Forming a Natural History of Animals, and an Introduction to Comparative Anatomy*), first published by Deterville in 1817, and the Muséum's collection of stuffed animals to create their own *Règne animal. Cabinet d'Histoire naturelle* (Animal kingdom. Natural history collection), a series of three double-plate lithographs published in *La Caricature* between April 18 and May 23, 1833 (figs. 73–75). The immediate catalyst for this illustrated parody of Cuvier may have been a concurrent publication by Achille Comte, *Règne animal de M. Cuvier disposé en tableaux*

Fig. 58. ***La Fosse aux dublivores*** **(The doublivore pit) from** ***Un autre monde,*** **1844, wood engraving. Private collection.**

méthodiques (Animal kingdom of Mr. Cuvier arranged in methodic tables; Crochard, 1832–41).[8] Interestingly enough, five years earlier Comte had written an introduction to Grandville's *Les Métamorphoses du jour.*[9]

But there also exists a more personal reason for Grandville's interest in animals. Like many Romantics, he felt a great deal of respect for the natural world. This led to what has been described as "a type of vague pantheism" that manifested itself in an almost religious regard for animals.[10] He constantly sought their company, and not just at the Jardin des Plantes. While living in his garret apartment at 10, rue des Petits-Augustins, he maintained his own small menagerie of pets, for when Alexandre Dumas would visit him there, he often found the artist "tenant dans sa main un lézard, sifflant un serin dans une cage, ou émiettant du pain dans un bocal de poissons rouges" (holding a lizard in his hand, whistling to a canary in a bird cage, or crumbling bread into a bowl of goldfish).[11]

To be sure, there is one last and overarching reason for Grandville's fascination with animals: their potential for satire. Like Aesop and La Fontaine, he made his own moralizing commentary on the human condition by employing the age-old human/animal analogy. Possessing an uncanny ability to recognize the animal side of humans and the often humanlike qualities of animals, he breathed new life into this standard caricatural theme. As we have seen, Grandville's mastery of the idiom made his reputation and fortune. From his first popular success with *Les Métamorphoses du jour* to *Scènes de la vie privée et publique des animaux,* his contemporaries, also conditioned by the scientific tenor of the times, applauded each successive parallel he drew between themselves and other members of the animal kingdom. The three double-plate *Règne animal* lithographs that he produced several months later exemplify his ongoing interest in the motif.

Grandville's numerous animal studies often display a scientific type of detailed precision. However, the execution of the tiger and the bear sketched here is singularly clumsy, possibly due to the January cold, which did not make for optimum drawing conditions. More accomplished diary drawings of the menagerie's inhabitants resulted from his subsequent visits during the warmer months of April and May when he depicted a monkey, a stork, an elephant, a leopard, a marabou, an ostrich, a peacock, and a goat along with the famous giraffe (cat. nos. 16 , 17, and 29).

13. 12/2 verso

[word fragments]

Tambour
(Drum)

January 4 or 5, 1833
65 × 65
Pen and brown ink

Just as the recto of this sheet dates from either January 1 or January 2, the verso of necessity follows the January 3 entry of the previous catalog number and precedes the January 6 entry that follows. Even though there is mention of a drum, this diary excerpt is so fragmented that it eludes any meaningful commentary.

14. 24 verso

6 Dimanche. L'EPIPHANIE. 6–359.
B—au porteur de Journal
[crossed out line]
[crossed out line]
[crossed out line]
Visite au Tableau de mr Guichard
(6 Sunday. Epiphany. 6–359.
B—to the newsboy
[ ]
[ ]
[ ]
Visit to the painting of Mr. Guichard)

January 6, 1833
114 × 110
Pen and brown ink

As was customary at the beginning of a new year, Grandville gave a present to the boy who delivered the newspaper. The incomplete word that begins with a "B" is probably *bourse* (money). The three lines that follow, for whatever reason, have been crossed out and are totally illegible.

Fortunately, the last line of this diary entry can be read, allowing us to identify yet another of Grandville's artistic acquaintances during his early years in Paris, the painter Joseph-Benoît Guichard (1806–80). A native of Lyon, Guichard first studied with Pierre Henri Revoil (1776–1842) at the École des Beaux-Arts in Lyon. Admitted to the École des Beaux-Arts in Paris in 1819, he eventually became the student of Ingres, the leader of the linear, neoclassic school of painting. However, he simultaneously frequented the studio of Delacroix, who was the acknowledged head of the painterly Romantic school of painting, and, as he later put it, went from one artist to the next "comme on passe du foyer conjugal au boudoir d'une maîtresse" (just as one passes from the conjugal hearth to the boudoir of a mistress).[12] As a result his mature work, in the words of Bénézit, was "tantôt classique tantôt romantique" (sometimes classic, sometimes romantic).

Guichard debuted at the Salon of 1831 with portraits. But he first came to the general attention of the public in 1833 when he submitted to the Salon *Rêve d'amour* (Dream of love; fig. 59), along with three other paintings, *La bonne pensée* (The good thought), *La mauvaise pensée* (The bad thought), and *Portrait de l'auteur* (Portrait of the author). Although he received a second-class medal for his

Fig. 59. Joseph-Benoît Guichard, *Rêve d'amour* (Dream of love), 1833, oil on canvas. Lyon, Musée des Beaux-Arts.

self-portrait, it was *Rêve d'amour,* an ambitious Salon machine measuring 2.605 × 3.260 meters, that elicited the most comment. Around it swirled the controversy of whether elements of the two opposing schools of painting, neoclassic and Romantic, could be successfully combined in the same work. The review in the *Journal des Artistes* typifies the debate:

> M. *J. Guichard* . . . a fait sous le nom Rêves [*sic*] d'amour, un grand tableau qu'on ne comprend pas, tableau où le dessin, quoique correct, n'est pas d'un bon choix, surtout dans la femme endormie, mais où la couleur domine par une chaleur qu'il n'a pas puisée à son école, et aussi par des tons enfumés qu'il a puisés dans une école toute différente. Il est pourtant assez difficile de peindre à la fois à la manière de M. Ingres et à la manière de M. Deveria [*sic*], de M. Decaisne ou de M. Decamps.
>
> [Mr. *J. Guichard* . . . has made under the title of Dreams [*sic*] of love a large painting that you don't understand, a painting where the drawing, although accurate, is not well considered, especially in the sleeping woman, but where color dominates through a warmth that he has not gotten from his school, and also through smoky tonalities that he has gotten from an entirely different school. It is, however, rather difficult to paint simultaneously in the manner of Mr. Ingres and in the manner of Mr. Devéria, Mr. Decaisne or Mr. Decamps [representatives of the Romantic school of painting].][13]

Ingres was not at all pleased with the painting, and *Rêve d'amour* precipitated a rupture between the master and his errant student.[14]

Apparently rumors about the controversial aspect of *Rêve d'amour* had already set the younger members of the artistic community abuzz before the painting's official showing at the Salon. For it was surely this particular "painting of Mr. Guichard" that Grandville stopped by to see on January 6, two months before the opening of the Salon of 1833 on March 1.

It is difficult to determine how well Grandville knew Guichard. But some three months later the two artists went together on a walk during which they talked about "various profound and philosophical subjects" that may have included dreams and the mysterious functioning of the human mind (cat. no. 19).

15. 13/1 verso

[words cut in half]
du grand monde . . . . .. Jai mal au nerfs
dans une loge etroite. Certes les lions
et les ours doivent horriblement souffrir
dans leur Cage. ! Sans rancune
vous vous trompiez [crossed out words]
[crossed out words]
[crossed out words]
([ ]
a big crowd . . . . . I'm ill at ease
in a cramped box. Surely lions
and bears must suffer horribly
in their cages. ! No offense
you were mistaken [ ]
[ ]
[ ])

April(?) 1833
92 × 103
Pen and brown ink

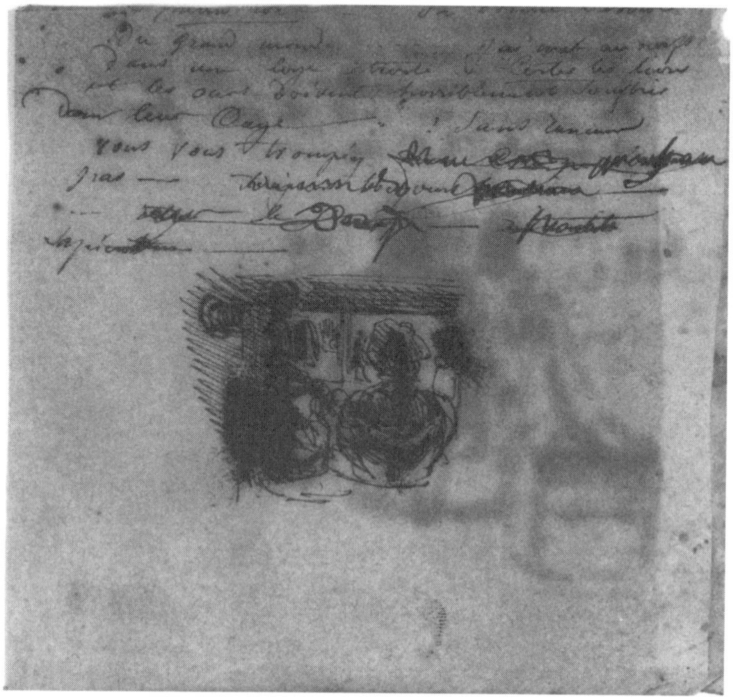

Even though this diary fragment carries no date, circumstantial evidence suggests that it may belong to the month of April. The following catalog number begins a virtually unbroken sequence of diary entries from April 19 to May 6, 1833 (only the entry for April 22 is missing). In the diary entry for April 28 (cat. no. 24), Grandville records the departure from Paris of a certain Thomassin, possibly a friend from Nancy. Above the drawing on the opposite side of the present sheet, seen here in a particularly strong ghost image, he mentions having taken a walk with "Thom et / Thom," quite possibly a reference to Thomassin. Should this be the case, the diary excerpt would consequently date from before Thomassin's departure as well as from before the nearly unbroken sequence of diary entries beginning on April 19. While it is not possible to say how long Thomassin might have spent visiting Paris, it seems credible that his visit would not have lasted more than a month. Thus, since he leaves at the end of April, any mention of him would more than likely occur within that same month. An additional reason for attributing this diary excerpt to the month of April is that apart from two sheets from January, one from sometime after Grandville's July wedding, and one from December, the nine others belonging to the 1833 diary fall within the April 19 to May 6 sequence. Especially given the probable mention of Thomassin, chances are that this sheet as well is chronologically related to this sequence, that is, toward its beginning, which would be April.

Both the original lower edge and the worn, dog-eared lower right-hand corner indicate that the verso of the present sheet was originally its recto and at the bottom of a page where it constituted the last of the three entries on that page. However, the compiler of the Missouri Album apparently found the street scene drawn on the verso of the sheet more interesting and glued it to the album so that it, and not the theater box sketch on the recto, would be visible.

Grandville's interest in the theater was not limited to stage productions at the official institutions of the Comédie-Française, the Opéra-Comique, and the Odéon. He also frequented theaters along the

Fig. 60. *At the Theater,* circa 1833, drawing. Paris, Bibliothèque nationale de France.

Fig. 61. ***Un soir à l'opéra*** **(A night at the opera) page 100 from** ***Petites misères de la vie humaine,*** **1843, wood engraving. Collection Rebeyrat.**

boulevards, such as the Théâtre de la Porte-Saint-Martin (cat. no. 23), and, judging from the actor in contemporary dress here, vaudeville houses. Given the minuscule size of the figure onstage, it seems that Grandville had purchased an inexpensive seat at the back of a small and crowded box in the second tier if not up in the *paradis,* or peanut gallery. He understandably complains of his cramped quarters from which, as the accompanying drawing illustrates, he can scarcely see the action on the stage, which is mostly hidden from view by the silhouettes of the two women seated in front of him. His claustrophobic response to the unpleasant situation ("I'm ill at ease") causes him to reflect on the sad fate of captive animals, such as the tiger and bear drawn on January 3 (cat. no. 12) and the caged leopard, which he will sketch on April 20 (cat. no. 16) at the Jardin des Plantes. While it is not possible to identify the play (let alone the theater in which it was performed), the actor dressed in top hat and frock coat indicates that the presentation is probably typical vaudeville fare and not a production from the classic repertoire.

More than likely this was not the first nor the last time that Grandville's view of the stage was half obscured by those seated in front of him. He records the same situation in a related, more finished drawing at the Bibliothèque nationale de France where actors dressed in contemporary costume appear to perform in another vaudeville production (fig. 60) and again in a wash drawing at the Musée Lorrain.[15] Typically, Grandville incorporates this all-too-common experience into his satirical program. The result is an illustration to the chapter "Un soir à l'opéra" (A night at the opera) in *Petites misères de la vie humaine* a decade later (fig. 61), which is strikingly similar to both the sketch in the diary and figure 60.

It is easy to commiserate with Grandville, since most readers have probably found themselves in similar situations. But he must have been doubly chagrined, given the privileged access he had previously enjoyed at the Odéon thanks to Lemétheyer. He has learned his lesson, however. For when he attends a performance of *l'Auberge des Adrets* at the Théâtre de la Porte-Saint-Martin on April 27 (cat. no. 23), he will purchase a front-row seat in a stage-side box that will allow him a close-up and unobscured view of the play.

Neither a reading of, nor an explanation for the crossed-out passage in this diary fragment can be given.

13/1 recto

[promenade]
avec Thom et / Thom
reflexions morales, plaisanteries—
farceur d'accumuler—vantardise
le premier elan est le seul possible
quantum delicioso!!
([walk]
with Thom and / Thom
moral reflections, jokes—
joker for accumulating—bluffs
the first impulse is the only one possible
how delicious!!)

April(?), 1833
92 × 103
Pen and brown ink

Although it is impossible to read the word sliced by the upper edge of the sheet, what appears to be an initial letter "p" suggests that the word is "promenade" since the rest of the diary fragment does in fact refer to the conversation that Grandville had with a friend while out walking. The friend in question is "Thom et / Thom," more than likely an abbreviated reference to Thomassin, a visitor from the provinces whose departure, we have already seen in the discussion of the sheet's verso, is recorded in the entry for April 28, 1833 (cat. no. 24). The mention of "moral reflections" may refer to Grandville's penchant for discussing "profound and philosophical subjects" (cat. no. 19). But it appears that Thomassin is something of a buffoon, and the conversation turns to lighter fare that includes joking and farcical bluffing. Grandville enthusiastically joins in, trying to best Thomassin at his own game, and remarks "the first impulse is the only one possible." He concludes the entry with his assessment of the entertaining outing in a somewhat dubious Latin: "quantum delicioso!!" (how delicious!!).

The accompanying drawing at the bottom of the page, undoubtedly a scene witnessed during the walk, is equally lighthearted. As he approaches what appears to be the Pont-Neuf in his walk along the quays of the Seine, he finds himself behind a portly gentleman whose wide girth virtually blocks the way for other pedestrians who attempt to pass him on the narrow sidewalk.

16. 8/1 recto

entre pour rien .. .. excitation
doigts .. caressants — la rose mousseuse
fraiche et douce ——————— tu le tates
toi—ton oui petite Fleur
encore toi toujours toi

20 Samedi. ste. Hildegonde. 110–255.
Visite de phil...Menut et
fors.....qui lui m'a remet 150 francs
de chez madame Aubert
carreaux lavés —— une derniere fois
rue des petits Augustins!
Daumier vient nous allons ensemble
au Jardin des plantes causerie de peinture
Soleil du printems
aspect du peuple
De ces côtes la
tristesse

de retour les idées d'autrefois me reprennent
Chagrin—Crainte. philippon vient me prendre
nous allons a l'imprimerie—logement de rouvel (revel)
Joli...qui m'irait..[refections] reflections de nouveau
sur ce moment. . . . peine nouvelle—a l'imprimre
lithographic degout de ce que Je fais—
Craintes . . . . (Je retombe———
Sept cents francs une biblioteque (le bois) et
moi qui ait tant de peine a me decider
a me mettre en menage et qui ne depenserai
pas davantage!!

21 Dimanche. s. Anselme. 111–254.
(enter for free .. .. excitation
caressing .. fingers — the moss rose
cool and soft—————— you touch it
you - your yes little flower
you again always you

20 Saturday. St. Hildegund. 110–255.
Visit from Phil[ipon] Menut and
For[est] who hands over to me 150 francs
from Madame Aubert's
windows washed —— one last time
rue des Petits-Augustins!
Daumier stops by together we go
to the Jardin des Plantes talk about painting
springtime sun
appearance of the people
on their part
sadness

upon returning ideas from before seize hold of me again
Chagrin - Fear. Philipon stops by to pick me up
We go to the printing-house—lodgings of Rouvel [Revel]
Pretty...would be all right for me..[refections] reflections once more
on this moment... fresh pain — at the lithographic
printing-house disgust with what I do
Fears .... [I think back ———
Seven hundred francs for a bookcase [wood] and

I who am having so much trouble deciding
to enter into wedlock and who would not spend
any more money!!
21 Sunday. St. Anselm. 111–254.)

April 19–21, 1833
139 × 110
Pen and brown ink

This diary fragment begins an almost unbroken sequence of entries for eighteen days, from Friday, April 19 until Monday, May 6, 1833. The drawings from this section of the diary are especially dark and mysterious. Figures with exceptionally thick, heavy outlines appear against tenebrous backgrounds. Equally unusual is the extensive use of interior modeling and ink wash, which along with delicately penned diagonal hatching and crosshatching provides shading. The dark silhouettes of figures often blend in with the shadowy backgrounds, giving them the appearance of being engulfed by the surrounding atmosphere that, like a leaden fog, presses in from all sides. A de Chiricoesque foreboding seems to lurk in the shadows; an existential presentiment of fatalistic entrapment permeates the air. The darkly brooding quality of these extremely sensitive drawings seems to reflect Grandville's anxious or depressed state of mind at the time.

This sheet, approximately half of an entire page from the 1833 diary, is perhaps the most remarkable one in the entire Missouri Album. The drawings, accomplished on-the-spot sketches, deftly alternate with and enhance the entries, which are at times surprisingly intimate. When examining these latter, the reader at times has the uncanny sensation of peering over the artist's shoulder as he secretly recounts his private life or bares his soul.

The first entry, apparently from the evening of Friday, April 19, records in an intimate and poetic fashion a gallant adventure at a bordello to which he has been given free access. Given this and other evidence (Nancy, 172 and cat. no. 139), it seems that before his marriage Grandville regularly frequented houses of prostitution, particularly numerous in and around the Palais-Royal. The description of his arousal and caressing foreplay, his poetic reference to the female sex, the reference to former visits with the same partner ("you again always you") all indicate a certain amount of experience in the act of making love. The lady in question may or may not be "la Esmeralde," whom we will encounter in the diary entry from May 6 where there is again mention of prostitutes and sexual arousal (cat. no. 32). At the end of the entry Grandville has sketched a comely young woman carrying a large basket who suggestively leans against a phallic-shaped guard-stone. Highly finished drawings of prostitutes and brothel scenes from 1829 and 1830 further attest to Grandville's libidinous pursuits during his bachelor years (see Nancy, cat. nos. 138–41).

In the entry for Saturday, April 20, Grandville sees Philipon, Menut, and Forest, the last giving him money from Madame Aubert, makes preparations for leaving his garret apartment in the rue des Petits-Augustins, goes with Daumier to the Jardin des Plantes, accompanies Philipon to the printer, reveals his real attitude toward his career as a political caricaturist, and expresses certain reservations about his impending marriage. All-in-all, a very full day.

The first few lines for April 20 record the visit of Philipon, the tireless editor of *La Caricature, Le Charivari,* and the *Association mensuelle,* who lived nearby, in the company of two of Grandville's artistic collaborators on these publications, Menut and Forest.[16] Although Grandville worked only infrequently with Menut, previously encountered in cat. no. 11, he depended regularly on the help of Forest who, we will recall, also lived in the rue des Petits-Augustins. At the time of the visit, Forest was in the midst of interpreting a new series of Grandville's signature animal-headed human hybrids à la *Les Métamorphoses du jour,* which appeared in *Le Charivari* between February and June 1833. However, their most important project of the moment was a series of three double-plate lithographs entitled *Règne animal. Cabinet d'Histoire naturelle* for the April 18, May 9, and May 23, 1833, issues of *La Caricature* (figs. 73–75). It is safe to assume that they had also started work on the April 1833 plate of the *Association mensuelle, Contredanse monarchique* (Monarchic quadrille), published toward the end of that month.[17] The cause for the visit was apparently twofold. First and foremost, Philipon needed to make a rendezvous with Grandville for later on in the day so that the two of them could go to the printing house, probably Becquet's in the rue de Fürstenberg, in order to oversee the printing of a lithograph.[18]

Fig. 62. *Elle prétend qu'elle n'est pas prostituée* (She claims that she is not a prostitute), *Le Charivari,* April 23, 1833, lithograph. Paris, Bibliothèque nationale de France.

The work in question would most likely have been *Elle prétend qu'elle n'est pas prostituée* (She claims that she is not a prostitute; fig. 62), a caricature done in collaboration with Bernard-Romain Julien (1802–71) aimed at the conservative newspaper, *Le Constitutionel,* and published three days later in the April 23, 1833, issue of *Le Charivari.*[19] The second reason for the visit was for Grandville to receive via Forest 150 francs from his publisher, possibly payment for the first double-plate lithograph of *Règne animal,* published two days earlier in *La Caricature.*[20] Again, as on the verso of cat. no. 8, Grandville reports the money as coming from Madame Aubert, Philipon's half sister, who apparently managed the financial end of La Maison Aubert, which published and distributed *La Caricature* and *Le Charivari* in addition to publishing and selling prints.[21]

The next two lines have to do with basic housekeeping chores: he washes one last time the windows in his garret apartment at 10, rue des Petits-Augustins, which he will soon be leaving, for he will need larger quarters after marrying his first cousin, Henriette Fischer, in Nancy on July 22. The young couple will first install themselves in an entresol in the nearby rue Guénégaud. That apartment, however, proved to be too small, and they quickly found more spacious accommodations a short distance away at 1, rue des Grands-Augustins where they remained for approximately the next nine years. Located on the third floor overlooking the quai des Grands-Augustins and the Seine, the apartment provided plenty of northern light by which Grandville was able to work.

After the washing of the windows, Daumier arrives and the two artists go to the zoo at the Jardin des Plantes. They talk about painting. Grandville remarks about the spring sunshine and the aspect of people who, in general, appear to be sad. This passage is particularly important because it helps to document the relationship between Grandville and Daumier, two provincials who became the most important political caricaturists in France between the years 1830 and 1835.

Born in 1808, Daumier was five years younger than Grandville. He and his family arrived in Paris from Marseilles in 1816. When he started working for *La Caricature* in 1830, he was still unknown to the general public. Grandville by all accounts apparently arrived in Paris from Nancy in 1825 and established his credentials as a satirist several years later with the immensely successful *Les Métamorphoses du jour* of 1828–29. His celebrity continued to grow with each succeeding lithograph published in *La Caricature.* Proclaimed the "King of Caricature" by the paper in April 1832, Grandville inaugurated two more Philipon publications, the *Association mensuelle* and *Le Charivari* in August and December of that same year. When Daumier stopped by on April 20, 1833, Grandville was by far the most celebrated political caricaturist in France, if not in all of Europe, thanks to the international distribution of *La Caricature.* At first glance, the visit would appear to be that of a junior colleague to an established senior one.

Daumier, however, was rapidly becoming an important caricaturist in his own right. One year earlier, in the April 26, 1832, issue of *La Caricature,* Philipon had announced the "galerie de portraits des célébrités du Juste-Milieu" (portrait gallery of celebrities of the Middle-Course), a series of lithographic caricatures done from miniature clay busts that would appear in *La Caricature* and *Le Charivari* between 1832 and 1835 and would feature members of Louis-Philippe's self-proclaimed middle-of-the-road government. The author of the busts, which are now on permanent display in the Musée d'Orsay, was Daumier, who had begun working on them in 1832.[22] The evidence is very strong that these clay busts were used as models not only by Daumier, but also by Grandville, notably for his series of *Règne animal* lithographs, which he was then working on for *La Caricature.*[23] Seen in this light, Daumier's visit on April 20, 1833, was less that of a junior colleague than one of a close artistic collaborator.[24]

In addition, Daumier recently had grown in stature among opposition caricaturists as the result of a famous incident in the annals of political caricature: the *Gargantua* affair. In December 1831, Aubert published, as an independent print, Daumier's scatological lithograph representing Louis-Philippe as Rabelais's Gargantua (fig. 63).[25] Seated on his "throne," the pear-shaped giant ingests bag after bag of the people's money while simultaneously defecating favors snatched up by a crowd of courtiers. Daumier, along with the print's publisher, Aubert, and its printer, Delaporte, was brought to trial on February 23, 1832, and charged "with arousing hatred and contempt of the king's government, and with offences against the king's person."[26] The defendants were found guilty on all counts. Each was sentenced to a five-hundred-franc fine and a six-month jail term. Daumier served his time at the prison of Sainte-Pélagie in the rue de la Clef from August 31 until November 11, 1832, and at Dr. J. P. Casimir Pinel's sanatorium at 76, rue de Chaillot from November 11, 1832, until his release on February 14, 1833.[27] Thus, when he visited Grandville, he had been out of confinement for a little over two months. This circumstance was not lost on Grandville, and may in no small part account for the anxiety he expresses in the next passage of the diary entry.

While there were certainly other topics of conversation, Grandville specifically mentions that the two graphic artists talked about painting during their visit to the Jardin des Plantes. Painting as well as sculpture were very strong secondary interests of Daumier. However, Grandville's career as a painter is less well known. Grandville had mixed feelings about painting. We have seen in the biography that soon after his arrival in Paris, he experienced a very short, unsatisfactory stint in the studio of Hippolyte Lecomte. According to his friend and biographer, Clogenson, the reason for Grandville's brief stay

Fig. 63. Honoré Daumier, *Gargantua,* 1831, lithograph. Paris, Bibliothèque nationale de France.

in Lecomte's studio was because he grew impatient with the time-consuming process of mixing oil paints. Two other sources attribute his short career as an art student to Grandville's chafing at a newcomer's traditional subordinate role of working solely for or under the direction of the studio master, that is, Lecomte.[28] In either case, Grandville decided that the life of an academic painter was not for him. And yet, Grandville continued from time to time to try his hand at oil paints, "seized by an irresistible desire to return to painting."[29] In fact, one year after this conversation with Daumier, Grandville surprised his Lorrain compatriots by sending a small oil painting described as a "soldat de l'armée de la foi" (soldier of the army of the faith) to the 1834 Salon de la Société des Amis des Arts (Salon of the society of the friends of the arts) in his native city of Nancy. And several truly remarkable oil paintings by Grandville have survived.[30]

After mentioning the artistic conversation he had with Daumier, Grandville comments on the spring sunshine and on the general demeanor of the populace, which he finds to be sad. It is difficult to gauge the validity of this latter observation. Judging from the next passage in his diary, Grandville is going through a major crisis at this time, and it is entirely possible that he is projecting his own depressed mood onto the world at large. On the other hand, we do know that during the early years of Louis-Philippe's reign the king's authority and the legitimacy of his rule were frequently questioned both in the press and in the street. In which case Grandville's description of a general malaise could be accurate: three years later, the French population continues to brood over a second attempt at a republican revolution, which, like the first in 1789, ultimately ended in the return of a monarchy.

In addition to his own, Grandville observes other species, both plant and animal, at the Jardin des Plantes. This undoubtedly was the reason why he and Daumier decided to go there in the first place. He records some of the more exotic specimens in his diary. In the upper part of the sheet, in between and around two previously written entries, he squeezes in sketches of a date palm, a detail of a cluster of dates, and the head of a monkey. The monkey, in particular, has captured his attention, and he draws it two more times on the blank back of the page printed with the list of eclipses for 1833 (cat. no. 17 [recto]). At this point, he must have regretted not having brought a sketchbook along with him, and decided to sacrifice over half of the remaining space for Saturday the 20th to other scenes from the zoo: a stork, an elephant, a woman with a small boy, and a leopard. The figures tend to be drawn as large as possible within the space allowed with the result that they are not always in scale with one another (e.g., the stork and the elephant). As an afterthought, Grandville realized that he could not possibly leave the Jardin des Plantes without recording Mohammed Ali Pasha's giraffe, but he had already used all of the allotted space. His solution was both ingenious and elegant. By squeezing her in at the far left of the space remaining, he nicely set up a diagonal progression of images from lower left to upper right, passing through and emphasizing the head of the elephant in the middle and linking up with the diagonal of the fence in the top drawing.[31] He has thus simultaneously documented the giraffe and created a unifying page design while still leaving space for recording the rest of the day's activities. Unfortunately, it was scarcely enough, with the result that the last entry for April 20 was written in a cramped style.

We can only wonder what other thoughts Grandville would have confided to his diary if he had had more space in which to write. As it is, the confession contained in this entry constitutes the most important revelation to be found in the Missouri Album. Upon his return from the Jardin des Plantes, the anticipated arrival of Philipon and the visit to the lithographic presses elicit in Grandville recurrent second thoughts about his career as a political caricaturist: feelings of chagrin and fear run through him. Philipon arrives to pick up Grandville, and together they go to the printing house—again, probably Becquet's, which was located around the corner and just one block away in the rue de Fürstenberg. On the way, they see a certain Revel's lodgings that Grandville finds attractive, concluding that they would do for himself (and, presumably, his future wife). As they approach the lithographic printing house, Grandville again reflects on the moment at hand, which once more induces pangs of pain. Upon their arrival, Grandville experiences a loathing for what he is doing. Fear once more seizes him. Parenthetically, he notes that his mind has returned to another subject, seven hundred francs for a wooden bookcase, emphatically adding, "and I who am having so much trouble deciding to enter into wedlock and who would not spend any more money!"

This entry belies the general perception of Grandville as an irrepressible caricaturist who took special delight in hurling barbs at Louis-Philippe and his government. It lends credence to Clogenson's observation that Grandville was very equivocal about his career as a political caricaturist: "Ce n'était pourtant qu'au milieu de perpétuelles hésitations qu'il travaillait; il ne voulait pas aller si loin—mais le flot l'entraînait" (It was, however, only in the middle of perpetual hesitations that he worked; he did not want to go so far—but the flood carried him along).[32] Clogenson uses the general and noncommital term "flood," but it is possible to be more precise in pinpointing the who or what that goaded Grandville into producing his acerbic political commentary. All we need to do is listen to his friend and colleague, Daumier: "If Philipon had not been behind me to prod me unceasingly like one does to an ox with a plow, I would never have done anything."[33] We might have guessed. Who is it, after all, that arrives first thing on Saturday to make sure that Grandville will be free later on in the day, and then at the appointed hour drags him to the lithographic presses despite the artist's recurring pangs of fear and loathing for his profession? It is obvious from this entry that Daumier was not the only one in Philipon's stable of artists who needed prodding. In addition, it gives a very concrete example of how Philipon manipulated the artists under his command.[34]

The reasons for Grandville's very severe reservations about his career as a political caricaturist are not hard to find. Starting with the repressive ministry of Casimir Périer March 13, 1831, Louis-Philippe's police and courts of law were particularly avid in keeping track of and prosecuting those opposition journalists and caricaturists who were perceived as constituting an especially dangerous threat to the July Monarchy. Grandville knew of numerous examples close to home. Between March 1831 and the passage of the infamous "Laws of September" in 1835, *La Caricature* was subject to twenty-eight seizures, most of them before September 1832. From these resulted nine prosecutions; in six of them Philipon, as the journal's editor, was held personally responsible. All six trials involved offensive caricatures. Philipon was acquitted four times and convicted twice. Both convictions, which occurred on November 14, 1831, and March 7, 1832, carried a fine of two thousand francs and a jail term of six months. On June 8, 1832, Philipon received an additional fine of two hundred francs and a monthlong jail sentence for failing to pay a security deposit required of political newspapers (his defense that *La Caricature* was a satirical journal without any political agenda did not hold up in court). As a result, Philipon served thirteen consecutive months of confinement in 1832 and early 1833, first at the prison of Sainte-Pélagie and then at Dr. Pinel's sanatorium from which he was released on February 4, 1833.[35] During the last few months of his sentence he had the company of Daumier who, we will recall, also found himself at Dr. Pinel's between November 11, 1832, and February 14, 1833. Thus when Philipon and Daumier visited Grandville on April 20, 1833, both men had been released from confinement for only a very short period of time. Grandville must have wondered if he would be the next to visit Sainte-Pélagie and Dr. Pinel's *maison de santé.* For surely if someone as relatively obscure as Daumier, described as an "inconnu" (unknown) by the court that convicted him,[36] could receive a jail sentence for producing an offensive political caricature, what about the best-known opposition caricaturist of the day—himself? Given this context, the repeated mention of fear in the diary entry is understandable. It dramatically demonstrates the stress experienced by Grandville as a result of his heightened state of anxiety, if not paranoia.

Paranoia, it turns out, would have been justified, for Grandville already had had his own brush with the authorities. In late September 1831, Aubert published in quick succession two lithographs by Grandville and Forest that dealt with events surrounding Poland's own Revolution of 1830. The first, *L'ordre règne à Varsovie* (Order reigns in Warsaw), depicted the barbaric slaughter of Polish patriots at the hands of cossacks when the Polish insurrection ended with the fall of Warsaw to the Russians a few weeks earlier on September 8. The second, *L'ordre public règne aussi à Paris* (Public order also reigns in Paris), portrayed the bloody suppression by police of the ensuing riots in the streets of the French capital. The two prints were registered with the dépôt légal on September 20 and 24, 1831. Incensed by the sadistic manner in which they were represented in the latter composition, a squad of policemen showed up on Grandville's doorstep two weeks later on Thursday, October 6 with the intention of teaching the caricaturist a lesson. Fortunately, Grandville's friend and neighbor, the law student Gabriel Falampin, intervened. With a law book in one hand and two pistols in the other, he succeeded in convincing the intruders that they did not have the right either to take justice into their own hands or to violate a private domicile.[37]

Philipon immediately publicized the incident by giving a detailed account of it in the October 13, 1831, issue of *La Caricature,* and, in an apparent effort to protect Grandville from any further reprisals, attempted to shift the responsibility for the inflammatory print from the artist to the person who had signed its proofs, that is, himself.[38] Included in his report were the tactics employed by the police in order to intimidate Grandville: attempts to provoke the artist into a duel and threats of lying in wait to assassinate him on some street corner. He noted that the harassed artist filed a formal complaint with the chief of police.

Grandville documented this close call with Louis-Philippe's police in a third lithograph, *Oh! les vilaines mouches!!* (Oh! those nasty flies!!; fig. 64), which was signed with the pseudonym, "Victor L'aragné," and registered with the dépôt légal October 21, 1831.[39] Although he did not suffer any physical harm, other members of the opposition who were victims of the police apparently were not so lucky. On a preliminary study for the print, Grandville gave a particularly caustic description of the vindictive extralegal and illegal activities indulged in by the forces of order: "Cette espèce viole les domiciles, ne marche qu'en troupe, affectionne l'illégalité, le guet-apens, les provocations, etc., cruelle et indicative dans les émeutes; armé d'un aiguillon venimeux dont il se sert volontiers, s'acharne sur les soi-disant républicains" (This species illegally enters homes, walks around only in gangs, delights

Fig. 64. ***Oh! les vilaines mouches!!*** **(Oh! those nasty flies!!), 1831, lithograph. Paris, Bibliothèque nationale de France.**

in unlawful acts, ambushes, provocations, etc., cruel and informed by spies in riots; armed with a venomous sting that it readily uses, it sets upon so-called republicans).[40]

Soon after this incident, the repressive tactics of the Périer government resulted first in the conviction of Philipon on November 14, 1831, and then in the conviction of Aubert, Delaporte, and Daumier on February 23, 1832, for this last's *Gargantua.* Philipon's second conviction occurred on March 7, 1832. The fact that Grandville could have been seen in the company of these two political convicts on April 20, 1833, shortly after their release from confinement, would have confirmed his reputation as a suspicious character. Whether or not Grandville was kept under police surveillance is not known. However, two weeks later he did record in his diary a "Visit from policemen" (cat. no. 31) after previously making reference to the services of a lawyer (cat. nos. 20 and 28). The type of visit Grandville received is open to conjecture.

The mention of this visit, presumably to his home, makes us wonder if there were other places where Grandville may have played an unwilling host to Louis-Philippe's guardians of public order. The anxiety attack he experiences just before Philipon stops by to take him to the printing house gives us a clue. The mention of "fear" or "fears" both before going to and while at the printing house seem to indicate an aversion to it, one that may have been grounded in some earlier traumatic experience he had undergone there. Had he witnessed a brutal manifestation of the police similar to the one he portrayed seven months later in the November 1833 plate of the *Association mensuelle: Descente dans les ateliers de la liberté de la presse* (Raid on the workrooms of the liberty of the press; fig. 65)? Although we cannot be certain, between Grandville's diary entry and this very convincingly portrayed scene,

Fig. 65. ***Descente dans les ateliers de la liberté de la presse.*** **(Raid on the workrooms of the liberty of the press.), plate 16 of the *Association mensuelle,* November 1833, lithograph. Paris, Bibliothèque nationale de France.**

Fig. 66. ***1834. Soirée républicaine donnée dans les salons de la liberté de la presse.*** **(1834. Republican soirée given in the salons of the liberty of the press.), plate 8 of the *Association mensuelle,* April 1833, lithograph. Private collection.**

which Philipon described as being able to pass for a "history painting" in his commentary in *La Caricature* on December 5, 1833, the circumstantial evidence is compelling.

The sentences of Philipon and Daumier as well as his own all too familiar acquaintance with the police must have taken their toll. Evidence of a depressed state of mind can be found not only in the secret confessions to his diary, but also in a contemporaneous portrait from plate 8 of the *Association mensuelle: 1834. Soirée républicaine donnée dans les salons de la liberté de la presse* (1834. Republican soirée given in the salons of the liberty of the press; fig. 66). The lithograph was originally scheduled for the end of March, but, as Philipon notes in his commentary in *La Caricature* on April 18, 1833, printing difficulties postponed its publication until April (the print was registered with the dépôt légal on April 16, just four days before Grandville unburdened himself to his diary). The work optimistically predicts the establishment of a republican regime in the following year of 1834. At the far right of the composition, Jules David (1808–92), his collaborator on the print, has portrayed a particularly melancholic Grandville, whose head is bent forward with bearded chin resting on his chest (fig. 67).[41] A similar melancholy mood can be found in an especially somber self-portrait from around this same time where a haggard, gaunt-faced Grandville stares out somewhat defensively yet defiantly at the viewer (fig. 68).[42]

Fig. 67. Detail of *Soirée républicaine*. Private collection.

Fig. 68. *Self-Portrait,* circa 1833, drawing. Collection of Mrs. Noah L. Butkin.

The harassment of Grandville and his *La Caricature* colleagues was intimidating in and of itself. But almost exactly one year later Grandville would have the opportunity to meditate upon something far more insidious: the massacre of fourteen old men, women, and children at the hands of government troops at five o'clock in the morning on April 14, 1834, in an apartment house on a street in the working-class district, the rue Transnonain. This slaughter occurred in the aftermath of a Parisian popular uprising, inspired in part by the famous insurrection of workers at Lyon started five days earlier on April 9, and was immortalized by Daumier in the final plate for the *Association mensuelle,* which was simply yet eloquently entitled *Rue Transnonain, le 15 Avril 1834* (Rue Transnonain, April 15, 1834; fig. 69).[43]

Fig. 69. Honoré Daumier, *Rue Transnonain, le 15 avril 1834* (Rue Transnonain, April 15, 1834), plate 24 of the *Association mensuelle,* August and September 1834, lithograph. Paris, Bibliothèque nationale de France.

Grandville's growing sense of paranoia must have culminated in 1835 with the reestablishment of censorship as a result of the so-called "Laws of September," which, it should be emphasized, included a provision specifically targeting caricatures. Philipon, among others, accurately saw this provision as a direct attack against his two illustrated opposition newspapers, *La Caricature* and *Le Charivari.*[44] As Philipon's (and France's) leading political caricaturist, Grandville could only conclude that the new law was aimed directly at him. That he abandoned political caricature for the innocuous career of a book illustrator soon after the enactment of the September 1835 press laws should therefore come as no surprise.

The reasons for Grandville's anxiety on April 20, 1833, however, were not confined to concerns over what was becoming an alarmingly dangerous profession. He was also preoccupied with a major change that was about to take place in his private life: in precisely three months and two days, on July 22, he would be married. Grandville was not immune to the customary premarital jitters and, as might be expected from his centime-counting frugality, was particularly concerned about the additional expense of supporting a wife: "and I who am having so much trouble deciding to enter into wedlock and who would not spend any more money!!" In addition to the apprehension about the adjustment to married life, his marriage entailed still other concerns that could not be ignored. He had every reason to worry whether a court process or worse, a jail sentence, would cause him to be absent from his own wedding. And once a husband, he would have not only his own welfare, but also that of his wife and eventual family to protect from unsolicited visits by the police and possible acts of violence. Decidedly, Grandville was passing through a particularly stressful phase in his professional as well as private life.

17. 1/4 verso

ECLIPSES

Le 6 janvier, éclipse de Lune, en partie visible à Paris.
Commencement à 6h. 52m. du matin.
Milieu à 8h. 2 minutes.
Fin à 9h. 13 minutes.
Le 20 janvier, éclipse de Soleil, invisible à Paris.
Le 1 et le 2 juillet, éclipse de Soleil, visible à Paris.
Commencement à 11h. 10 minutes du soir.
Milieu à 0h. 49 minutes du matin.
Fin à 2h. 27 minutes.
Le 27 juillet, éclipse de Soleil, visible à Paris.
Commencement à 4h. 54 minutes du matin.
Milieu à 5h. 46 minutes.
Fin à 6h. 38 minutes.
Le 26 décembre, éclipse totale de Lune, visible à Paris.
Commencement à 7h. 52 minutes du soir.
Milieu à 9h. 40 minutes.
Fin à 11h. 29 minutes.

ÈRES OU PRINCIPALES ÉPOQUES EN 1833.

	An.s		Ans.
Commencement du monde.	**5833**	**De l'invention de la boussole.**	**573**
Depuis le déluge universel.	**4177**	**De l'inv. des moulins à vent.**	**538**
la naissance de Jésus-Chr.	**1833**	**De l'inv. de la poudre à can.**	**452**
mort et résurrection.	**1800**	**De l'inv. des canons et mous-quets.....................**	**495**
[fon]dation de Rome...	**2586**	**De l'invent. de l'imprimerie.**	**593**
[mon]archie française..	**1424**	**De la déc. du Nouv. Monde.**	**341**
[ ]orr. du calend. gr.	**249**	**De l'indépend. américaine.**	**59**
[monarch]ie actuelle....	**4**	**De l'invention du télégraphe.**	**39**
moulins à eau.	**1045**		

(ECLIPSES

January 6, eclipse of the moon, partially visible at Paris.
Beginning at 6:52 in the morning.
Middle at 8:02.
End at 9:13.
January 20, eclipse of the sun, invisible at Paris.
July 1 and 2, eclipse of the sun, visible at Paris.
Beginning at 11:10 in the evening.
Middle at 0:49 in the morning.
End at 2:27.
July 27, eclipse of the sun, visible at Paris.
Beginning at 4:54 in the morning.
Middle at 5:46.

End at 6:38.
December 26, total eclipse of the moon, visible at Paris.
Beginning at 7:52 in the evening.
Middle at 9:40.
End at 11:29.

ERAS OR PRINCIPAL EPOCHS IN 1833.

	Yr.s		Yrs.	
Beginning of the world.	5833	The invention of the compass.	573	
Since the universal flood.	4177	The inv. of windmills.	538	
the birth of Jesus-Chr.	1833	The inv. of cannon powder.	452	
death and ressurection.	1800	The inv. of cannons and mus-		
[foun]dation of Rome...	2586	kets......................		495
French [mon]archy..	1424	The inv. of the printing press.	593	
[ ]*orr.* of the Greg. calend.	249	The disc. of the New World.	341	
present [monarc]hy....	4	American independence.	59	
watermills.	1045	The inv. of the telegraph.	39)	

90 × 95

While at the zoo of the Jardin des Plantes on April 20, Grandville discovered that he did not have enough room to sketch the monkey whose head appears squeezed between the lines of the entry for that day. He paged through his diary looking for more space. He found it on the blank back of a page that was printed with a list of the eclipses for 1833. As usual, the compiler of the Missouri Album glued the "uninteresting" front of the sheet facedown so that the sketches on the back could be seen.

1/4 recto

April 20, 1833
90 × 95
Pen and brown ink

Although observed at a slightly different angle, this is the same monkey portrayed in the April 20 entry (cat. no. 16). The attitude of the head is the same and the graphic style is identical, particularly the manner in which hatching has been used to model the top of the monkey's head.

As is evidenced by this drawing, monkeys continued to attract Grandville's attention one year after the 1832 publication of *Singeries morales, politiques, etc.* discussed in cat. no. 10. Even though his impulse to sketch animals at the menagerie during his visit to the Jardin des Plantes with Daumier on May 20 seems to have been serendipitous, once he started sketching the monkey he must have realized that he could use it in one of the next plates of the *Règne animal* series. This is probably the reason why he found a place in his diary where he could draw its head in more detail and block out the rest of the body. Indeed, the monkey appears to be the initial study for the Siamese-twin monkeys of the "Jumeaux Doctrinaires" (Twin doctrinaires) found in plate 3 of the *Règne animal* (fig. 75): the crouched position with head thrust forward is the same, as is the profile of the head. The main difference is the angle of vision. Grandville apparently was only able to study the monkey in a three-quarter view, while the twins in the print are seen in strict profile. Monkeys will continue to inspire Grandville, reappearing in such later publications as *Scènes de la vie privée et publique des animaux* in 1842 and *Un autre monde* in 1844.

18. 14 recto

promenade
avec [Th]om/
[crossed-out word]
et Dat.

promenade
[avec]
[Mme] [crossed-out word]
[crossed-out word]
(walk
with Thom/
[ ]
and Dat.

walk
with
Madame [ ]
[ ])

April 21, 1833
114 × 112
Pen and brown ink, stump

Circumstantial evidence suggests that this undated diary fragment is the missing entry for Sunday, April 21, whose date is printed at the bottom of cat. no. 16. That it originally appeared at the bottom of a page as the entry for April 21, 1833, would have is attested to by the length of the sheet, its undisturbed lower edge, and the dog-eared lower right-hand corner, which is worn and soiled from repeated page turnings. Most decisively, indications of the branches of the orange tree cropped at the top of the upper drawing in this fragment are to be found precisely where they might have been, just below the printed word "Dimanche" at the bottom of cat. no. 16. (The right vertical edge of these fragments, which in both cases is the right edge of a diary page, has been left undisturbed. Eighty millimeters from that edge below the printed word "Dimanche" in cat. no. 16 are pen strokes similar to those of the orange tree's upper branches, which are eighty millimeters from the corresponding edge in the present drawing.) The fact that the contours of the cut edges at the top of this fragment and at the bottom of cat. no. 14 do not match indicate that one or both of the diary fragments was/were trimmed after the initial cut.

After a somewhat trying Saturday, Grandville relaxes on Sunday by taking two walks. He mentions that the one is with "Thom/," again probably an abbreviation for Thomassin (see cat. nos. 15 [recto] and 24), and "Dat," certainly another abbreviated name of an unidentified individual. The names of his companions on his second walk have been, for whatever reason, crossed out. It is interesting to note that Grandville's penmanship in these annotations is particularly crabbed, possibly reflecting a certain nervousness.

The accompanying drawings depicting scenes observed on his walks, however, are nothing less than spectacular. With a sure hand, he has produced two of the most beautiful works in his tenebroso style: as in a painting by Caravaggio, figures emerge from and disappear into an all-enveloping shadowy darkness, which lends to these works a distinctively mysterious, even disquieting air. The drawing at the top appears to represent one of the tree-lined allées, or walks, in the Tuileries Gardens, which Grandville frequented on a fairly regular basis (see cat. nos. 26 and 31 as well as Nancy, cat. no. 137). The mixed crowd depicted would have been typical for a Sunday when the rigid social segregation, observed by the more privileged classes during the week, disappeared with the influx of shopkeepers and working-class types on their day off.[45] From left to right, we see a boy playing in the gravel, a husky bull of a man who appears to be temporarily absent from his butcher's shop, a Romantic in form-fitting frock coat and tall, cone-shaped, broad-brimmed hat, the back of a fashionably dressed woman, a comically contrasting couple (short slender man in a long coat and high stovepipe hat and a tall, portly woman in equally exaggerated stylish gigot-sleeved dress and beribboned chapeau), in the distance a nanny in her distinctive high toque who carries a baby next to a top-hatted dandy, and at the right a couple seated against a planter. Farther to the right Grandville has redrawn from above the cone-shaped, broad-brimmed hat affected by the Romantic.

In the lower drawing, Grandville has captured the titillating view of a woman's shapely turned ankle as she steps into a dark passageway. As in the upper drawing, he has skillfully blended the image into the page support by stumping it around the edges, thereby providing a soft, atmospheric zone of transition between the dark shadows of the drawing and the white of the paper.

19. 8/1 verso

23 Mardi. s. Georges, martyr.*isé* **113–252.**

Mr forest pere
Se sciant Mr petitpoisson
promenade avec Guichard—
Dissertation sur differents sujets

profonds et philosophiques
douleur des Genoux—

24 Mercredi. ste. Beuve. 114–251.
(23 Tuesday. St. George, martyr.ed 113–252.

Mr. Forest senior
boring Mr. Petitpoisson
walk with Guichard—
dissertation on various
profound and philosophical subjects
pain in the knees—

24 Wednesday. St. Beuve. 114–251.)

April 23–24, 1833
139 × 110
Pen and brown ink

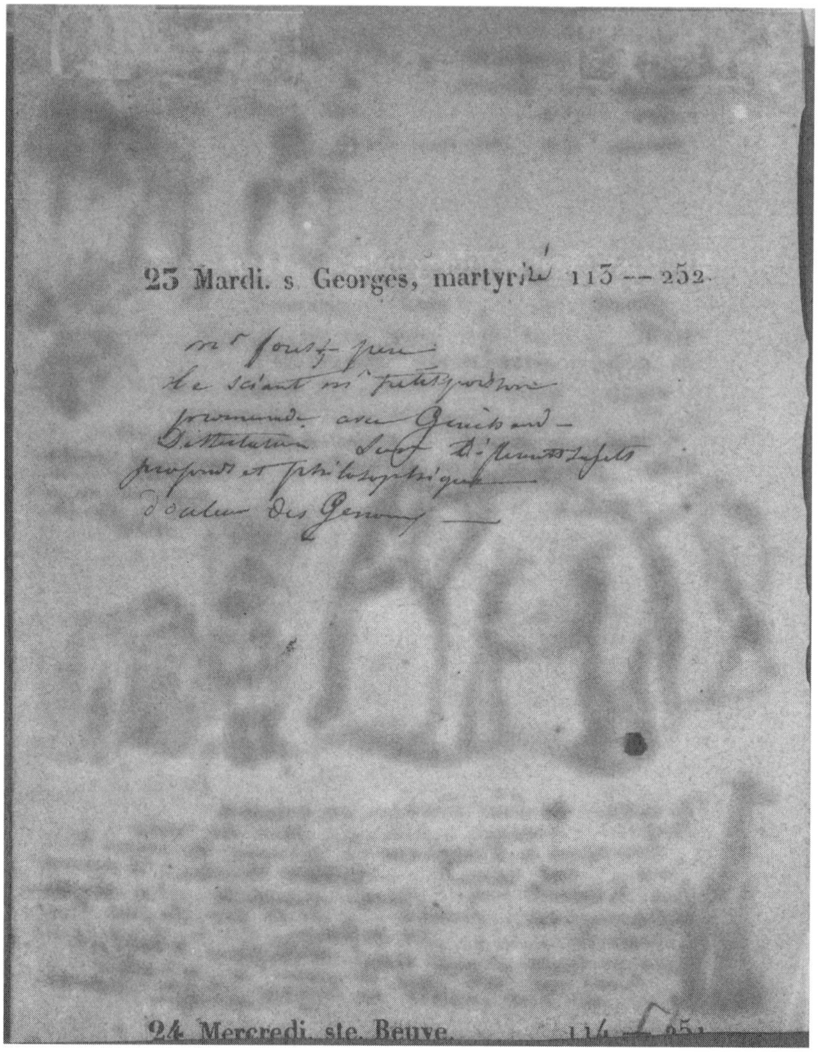

The ghost image from the opposite side of the sheet (cat. no. 16) is particularly visible.

Grandville playfully completes the abbreviation after St. George. He witnesses the father of Eugène Forest boring a certain Mr. Petitpoisson with his conversation. He then takes a walk with the painter Guichard first encountered in cat. no. 14. Their conversation revolves around various profound and philosophical subjects. Grandville complains of pain in his knees.

The reference to "dissertation on various profound and philosophical subjects" documents yet another, more serious side of Grandville's personality. Grandville was a poor student and never finished high school. But he possessed a naturally inquisitive mind. Thus, while he had no patience for formal philosophy, he nevertheless liked to philosophize about life and art. It was probably Charton who observed, "Étranger aux doctrines philosophiques, et même affectant de les dédaigner, il était cependant tourmenté du besoin d'en posséder une, de rattacher ses idées éparses à un principe général, de se faire une théorie de la vie, d'en déduire une théorie de l'art, et, à son insu, il était entraîné vers une sorte de vague panthéisme" (Stranger to philosophical doctrines, and even pretending to disdain them, he nevertheless was tormented by the need to possess one, to link his scattered thoughts to a general principle, to fashion for himself a theory of life, from which to deduce a theory of art, and, without knowing it, he was drawn to a type of vague pantheism)[46] After having kept vigil at Grandville's bedside during his final days, Charton wrote in his friend's obituary:

> Toute sa vie, il avait aimé et recherché les entretiens sérieux. Pendant ses derniers jours de raison, il nous fit appeler plusieurs fois près de lui pour nous interroger sur nos espérances, sur notre foi. Il embrassait avec ardeur les solutions les plus nobles, les plus consolantes de la philosophie. Ceux qui n'ont pu l'apprécier que par ses oeuvres, ne sauront jamais tout ce qu'il y avait dans cette intelligence distinguée, dans ce coeur excellent, de fortes reflexions, de dignes et hautes pensées, d'ardentes aspirations vers la vérité. Il appartenait par son caractère à cette famille d'écrivains, auteurs comiques ou chansonniers, que l'on se représente volontiers couvrant d'un masque riant leur figure grave et pensive.
>
> [Throughout his life, he had liked and sought out serious discussions. During his last days of lucidity, he called us several times to his side in order to ask us about our hopes, about our faith. He eagerly embraced the most noble and most comforting solutions of philosophy. Those who were only able to appreciate him through his work will never know all that there was of strong reflections, dignified and high-minded thoughts, fervent longing for the truth in that refined intelligence, in that excellent heart. By his character, he belonged to that family of writers, humorous authors or song-writers that one easily imagines hiding beneath a laughing mask their sober and pensive features.][47]

And Alexandre Dumas recalls the conversations he had with Grandville when visiting the artist's garret apartment in the rue des Petits-Augustins, "Que de bonnes et longues causeries! que de fins aperçus!" (Such good long talks! such astute insights!).[48]

Together with this entry from his diary, these accounts attest to the fact that Grandville was prone to pondering philosophical questions throughout his adult life. And during his bachelor years in Paris the opportunity apparently could present itself at almost any time: when conversing with Dumas in his apartment or, as is the case here, when out walking with friends. Given their shared interest in representing dreams (figs. 29, 34, 35, and 59), Grandville and Guichard may have talked about the mysterious and at times irrational operation of the human mind, a typically Romantic concern that anticipated Freud (see Nancy, cat. no. 110).

20. 14 verso

le dessin du Journal des enfans
Visite de missions [crossed-out word] toujours les

memes p[leurs bas niais] [crossed-out words]
Longue [crossed-out word] [leurs changement] de situation
n'a rien operé chez eux [Guiaud] le petit
Guiaud vient...beau tems soleil—:
[epusion {épucion?} de sentiment]...[illegible word]
[crossed-out words] Visite de
magister ploctius—
note [portée] a Mme Aubert
dessins - rapportés—

(the drawing for the *Journal des enfans*
Visit of the missions [ ] always the
same stupid low crying [ ]
Long [ ] their change in situation
has not changed anything with them Guiaud junior
Guiaud stops by...beautiful weather sun—:
[cleansing/clearing?] of mind...[ ]
[ ] Visit from
master Ploctius—
bill delivered to Mme Aubert
drawings - carried back—)

April 24, 1833
114 × 112
Pencil, pen and brown ink

The ghost image from the opposite side of the sheet (cat. no. 18) is again particularly visible.

At the same time that he expressed dissatisfaction with his career as a political caricaturist, Grandville started to explore the possibilities of another, less dangerous profession, that of a book illustrator, during which he would create drawings for wood engravings instead of lithographs. His first two wood-engraved illustrations were produced for an opposition pamphlet by Louis Benoit, *Physiologie de la poire* (Physiology of the pear; Librairies de la place de la Bourse et du Palais-Royal, 1832), that continued the same political satire as his lithographs for *La Caricature, Le Charivari,* and the *Association mensuelle.* However, his next four wood engravings appeared in the first volume (July 1832–June 1833) of the monthly publication *Journal des enfans* (Children's journal), and mark a departure from his political caricature program. Instead of being attacks on the government of Louis-Philippe, they are harmless illustrations for children's stories: *Portrait de J. P. Choppart* (Portrait of J. P. Choppart; October 1832, p. 121), *Les deux pâtres* (The two shepherds; February 1833, p. 231), *Les Aventures de J. P. Choppart* (The adventures of J. P. Choppart; April 1833, p. 313), and *Les Pages de l'Empereur* (The pages of the emperor; May 1833, p. 335).

The importance of both the medium and the content of these illustrations in establishing a precedent for Grandville's subsequent career cannot be overly emphasized. As a result of the reestablishment of press censorship with the so-called September Laws a little more than two years later, Grandville terminated his life as a political caricaturist and all but abandoned lithography. He spent the rest of his life collaborating with wood engravers in order to produce illustrations for books and periodicals, many of which were aimed wholly or in part at a juvenile public: *Musée des familles* (The family museum), *Le Livre des enfants* (The children's book), *Fables de La Fontaine, Voyages de Gulliver dans les contrées lointaines, Gazette des enfans* (Children's gazette), *Heures de l'enfance* (The hours of childhood; Delloye, 1839), *Aventures de Robinson Crusoë, Fables de Lavalette, Fables de Florian.* It is no wonder that certain of his contemporaries considered him to be "un dessinateur pour enfants" (a draftsman for children).[49] That Grandville should have produced so many works with children in mind may be traced to his genuine respect for them, as can be seen in a series of drawings done around 1830 on the eve of his career as an opposition political caricaturist (Nancy, 62 and cat. nos. 30–33). One is almost tempted to say that his political caricature career constituted a temporary interruption in a more fundamental interest: producing works for and about children.

The drawing for the *Journal des enfans* mentioned here is surely *Les Pages de l'Empereur* (fig. 70), which appeared as an illustration to the short story of the same title by James Rousseau in the publication's May 1833 issue, which, as usual, appeared on the twenty-fifth day of the month. This is probably the same drawing that Grandville mentions transferring to a wood engraving block on May 1 (cat. no. 27). It appears that Grandville has used his drafting pencil (the same one employed in the drawing?) to write the first line of this diary entry and to sketch the hand with pointing index finger.

He next records the visit of missionaries soliciting donations, and somewhat cynically comments on the usual strategies employed to gain sympathy for their cause. Guiaud stops by; Grandville refers to him as "Guiaud junior" in order to distinguish him from his father, with whom he was also acquainted (see cat no. 33). Although it is not mentioned specifically, the two artists probably go out for a walk, judging from Grandville's next remark about the beautiful sunny weather. The visit of his good friend Guiaud, the presumed walk in the open air, or both apparently had the salubrious effect of clearing his head. (Epusion appears to be an invented word by Grandville derived from *épucer* [to clean of fleas]; the connotation seems to be that Guiaud's visit helped to clean or clear his mind, possibly of troubling thoughts regarding his career as an opposition caricaturist or some legal matter.) He next mentions the visit of a certain master Ploctius. Just as he will do one week later when recording the visit of a master Paulus on May 2 (cat. no. 28), Grandville apparently has used his knowledge of Roman history in

Fig. 70. ***Les Pages de l'Empereur*** **(The pages of the emperor),** ***Journal des enfans,*** **May 25, 1833, wood engraving. Paris, Bibliothèque nationale de France.**

order to make a veiled reference to another, or perhaps the same, lawyer. "Ploctius" appears to be the misspelling of Lucius Plotius, a famous Roman rhetorician born in Gaul around 100 BCE, and would therefore refer to an attorney noted for his oratorial skills in court. Coupled with the reference to a visit from policemen on May 5 (cat. no. 31), it would seem that he has had a run-in with the law, causing him to seek legal counsel at the end of April and the beginning of May 1833. Unfortunately, the nature of these legal problems for the moment cannot be identified.

The last two lines of this diary entry testify once more to Madame Aubert's management of La Maison Aubert's finances and give us some insight into its business transactions with Grandville. He specifically mentions that it is to Madame Aubert that he has hand-delivered a bill, which more than likely listed his fee for a recently published print or prints such as *Elle prétend qu'elle n'est pas prostituée,* published the day before, April 23, in *Le Charivari* and whose printing he had probably overseen on Saturday, April 20 (cat. no. 16). He also reports that drawings were returned to him. Again, the assumption is that these would have been the finished studies for recently published work such as *Elle prétend qu'elle n'est pas prostituée* (other possible candidates would be drawings for the March 1833 plate of the *Association mensuelle, Soirée républicaine,* registered with the dépôt légal April 16 and the first plate of *Règne animal,* registered with the dépôt légal April 17 and published in *La Caricature* the following day, April 18).

As previously mentioned in the introduction to the 1833 diary, this entry, along with those in cat. nos. 11 and 16, allows us to piece together the procedure Grandville seems to have followed in order to have one of his drawings published as a lithograph by La Maison Aubert: in cat. no. 11 we learned that after finishing a drawing, he took it to one of his lithographic interpreters and blocked out the composition on the stone; he left the drawing and verbal instructions with his collaborator, who then finished the transfer; in cat. no. 16 we saw a very reluctant Grandville go to the printing house in the company of Philipon in order to oversee the printing of the lithograph; and here we discover that, once a print was published, he submitted his bill to Madame Aubert, who in exchange would return the drawing; he subsequently was paid by Madame Aubert. There probably were additional steps in this process, such as Grandville's correcting and giving his final approval of the transferred composition and the affixing of signatures (did each artist sign separately or did Grandville's collaborator sign for both of them?). And he may have waited to submit his bill until after the publication of several prints, thereby receiving in return more than one drawing as this diary entry mentions. Nevertheless, a clearer picture of how Grandville's drawings became published caricatures starts to emerge.

21. 11/1 recto

Avril.

25 Jeudi. s. Marc, *abst.* *inence* **115–250.**

(April.

25 Thursday. St. Mark, abst.inence 115–250.)

April 25, 1833
92 × 109
Pen and brown ink

Fig. 71. Masthead, *Le Charivari,* January 20, 1834, lithograph. Private collection.

Grandville has again completed the abbreviation after the name of the saint, which designates here a day of abstinence. This time his playfulness is accompanied by calculated irony as the drawing of a convivial group seated around a table set with plates, silverware, and a carafe provides a visual contrast to any notion of abstaining from physical appetites. The location of this festive gathering more than likely is Grandville's own one-room garret apartment. Despite his many worries, this drawing demonstrates that Grandville's life was not completely bleak during the spring of 1833.

The boon companions portrayed corroborate what we already know about Grandville's circle of friends at this time: they were generally young members of the artistic community, and, more specifically, were often his caricatural comrades-in-arms. Although the long-haired, goateed individual seated in profile at the far left has not been positively identified (as we will see later, circumstantial evidence suggests that he may be Menut), we recognize, proceeding to the right, Eugène Forest, Alexandre Dumas, and Louis Desnoyers, editor of *Le Charivari.* The lost profile of the bushy-haired person seated with his back turned toward the viewer appears to be a self-portrait of Grandville himself.

Forest may be identified thanks to a labeled portrait of him by Grandville in the masthead of the January 19–20, 1834, issues of *Le Charivari* where his same unmistakable features appear: long, narrow face, aquiline nose, pointed chin, distinctive vertical tuft of hair, and iron-rimmed glasses (fig. 71).[50] Grandville was soon to depict him again in the second plate of *Règne animal* (fig. 74), which would be published in *La Caricature* on May 9. But this time Forest will also sport a bushy moustache just as he does in the diary and in a slightly later August 1833 caricatured bust by Jean-Pierre Dantan (1800–69), known as Dantan jeune (fig. 72).[51] The resemblance between Grandville's portrait of Forest in the diary and that in *Règne animal,* however, does not stop there. A comparison of the former with the one of Forest in the preparatory study for plate 2 of *Règne animal* (fig. 76), demonstrates that Grandville has taken the head of Forest from the diary and reproduced it exactly in the caricature at precisely the same angle. As a result, two things become apparent. When he had dinner with his friends on April 25, Grandville was still working on the second plate of *Règne animal* and had not yet completed the figure of Forest, who is represented in the process of pinning the Benjamin Delessert bat to the wall of

Fig. 72. Dantan jeune [Jean-Pierre Dantan], *Eugène Forest,* 1833, plaster. Paris, Musée Carnavalet.

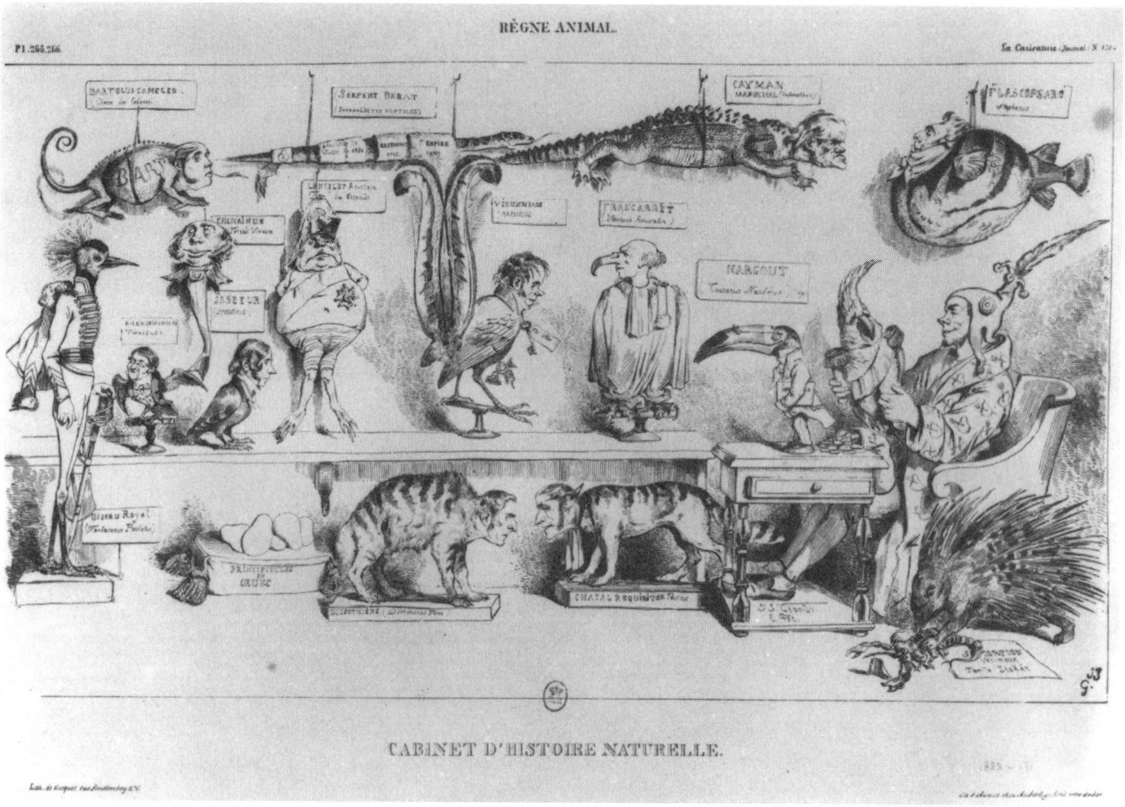

Fig. 73. *Règne animal. Cabinet d'Histoire naturelle* (Animal kingdom. Natural history collection; plate 1), plates 265 and 266 of *La Caricature,* April 18, 1833, lithograph. Paris, Bibliothèque nationale de France.

the *Cabinet d'Histoire naturelle,*[52] and his diary has once more served as a working sketchbook for a published print.

Grandville and Forest were particularly close at the time that they collaborated on the three *Règne animal* double-plate lithographs (figs. 73–75). This is evidenced not only by the portrait of Forest in Grandville's diary, but also by the clasped hands that accompany the two artists' signatures in the last two plates of the series (figs. 74 and 75). That a shared mutual trust and respect should have developed between them is not surprising, for they had worked hand in hand for nearly two years, since August 1831. Scarcely a project had been undertaken by Grandville that did not include the participation of Forest, whether caricatures for *La Caricature* and *Le Charivari* or separately published lithographic suites for Aubert. However, there appears to have been a falling-out between the two friends shortly after the last plate of the *Règne animal* series was published in *La Caricature* on the May 23, 1833. They worked together on two more lithographs for *Le Charivari, Inspection générale avec armes à feu et autres des deux gardes nationaux bien pensants des 12 légions de la garde nationale de Paris, dont un pour la banlieue.* (General inspection with fire- and other arms of two right-thinking national guardsmen from the 12 legions of the national guard of Paris, including one for the suburbs) and *Ceci, mesdames, vous représente l'un des plus grands hommes de l'époque* (This, my ladies, shows you one of the greatest men of the age),[53] which appeared in the issues of May 27 and June 6, 1833, respec-

Fig. 74. *Règne animal (suite) Cabinet d'Histoire naturelle. (suite)* (Animal kingdom [continued]. Natural history collection [continued]; plate 2), plates 271 and 272 of *La Caricature,* May 9, 1833, lithograph. Paris, Bibliothèque nationale de France.

tively. But after they produced *Le Jeu de bague nuptial,* published in *La Caricature* on June 20, 1833, there is an abrupt halt in their artistic partnership. In the months following, Grandville experimented with different collaborators, Julien, Traviès, and Desperet, before settling on this last as Forest's replacement. Grandville and Forest subsequently will work together only on very rare occasions during the remaining two years of *La Caricature*'s existence. For the moment, no explanation can be given for the deterioration in their relationship. Suffice it to say that this diary drawing is a close to final manifestation of a long and trusted friendship that was soon to be interrupted. By the time that *La Caricature* was resurrected as *La Caricature provisoire* on November 4, 1838, the rift between Forest and Grandville appears to have been mended. Forest regained his status as Grandville's regular lithographic collaborator, interpreting nine of the latter's twelve lithographs for the revived journal. Desperet, who in the meantime had become Grandville's indispensable assistant in the production of wood-engraved book illustrations (see Nancy, 362), executed the three remaining lithographs, double-plate caricatures of the *Grande course au clocher académique* (Great academic steeplechase; fig. 79 reproduces the third plate in this series).

Judging from a contemporary lithographic portrait (fig. 77), the person seated next to Forest in the middle of the composition and gesturing with his right hand as he leads the conversation is the garrulous Alexandre Dumas. Dumas knew Grandville during the artist's early bachelor years in Paris and seems to have visited him frequently at his rue des Petits-Augustins garret apartment. In his *Mémoires,*

Fig. 75. ***Règne animal (suite) Cabinet d'Histoire naturelle*** **(Animal kingdom [continued] Natural history collection; plate 3), plates 275 and 276 of *La Caricature,* May 23, 1833, lithograph. Paris, Bibliothèque nationale de France.**

Fig. 76. Study for plate 2 of *Règne animal. Cabinet d'Histoire naturelle* (Animal kingdom. Natural history collection.), 1833, drawing. Nancy, Bibliothèque municipale.

Fig. 77. Cacilie Brand, *Alexander Dumas,* 1833, lithograph. Paris, Bibliothèque nationale de France.

Dumas painted a particularly warm portrait of Grandville at this time, and describes his visits to the artist's aerie:

> Sourire fin et moqueur, yeux pétillants d'esprit, bouche railleuse, petite taille, grand coeur, mélancolie charmante répandue sur tout cela;—c'est vous, cher Granville [*sic*]! . . .
>
> Vous rappelez-vous, cher Granville [*sic*], le temps où j'allais vous voir dans votre mansarde de la rue des Petits-Augustins, mansarde d'où je ne sortais jamais sans emporter de merveilleux croquis?
>
> [Slight mocking smile, eyes sparkling with wit, bantering mouth, small stature, big heart, charming melancholy spread over all that;—that's you, dear Grandville! . . .
>
> Do you remember, dear Grandville, the time when I used to go see you in your garret of the rue des Petits-Augustins, garret from which I never left without taking away wonderful sketches?][54]

The camaraderie between Grandville and Dumas was still very much alive at the time of this diary entry. For when Dumas held his famous costume ball approximately one month earlier on March 30, 1833,[55] Grandville was among those artist friends called upon to decorate the four rooms of an empty apartment at 40, rue Saint-Lazare where the ball was to take place (according to Dumas the others were Delacroix, Louis and Clément Boulanger, Alfred and Tony Johannot, Decamps, Louis-Godefroy Jadin, Antoine-Louis Barye, Nanteuil; to these should be added Forest and Alfred-André Geniole).[56] Dumas describes Grandville's contribution in the following terms:

> Granville [*sic*], notre bon et excellent Granville [*sic*], charmant peintre des hommes bêtes et des animaux spirituels, se mit le premier à l'oeuvre.
>
> C'est lui qui, en effet, avait la plus rude besogne sur les bras . . . [il] prit un panneau de douze pieds de long sur huit de large, où il s'engagea à reproduire toutes nos charges dans un tableau représentant un orchestre de trente ou quarante musiciens, les uns froissant des cymbales, les autres secouant des chapeaux chinois, ceux-ci soufflant dans des cors et des bassons, ceux-là raclant des violons et des basses. En outre, il devait faire des danses d'animaux au-dessus de chaque porte.
>
> [Grandville, our good and excellent Grandville, charming painter of human beasts and of witty animals, was the first to set to work.
>
> It was he, in fact, who had the hardest job on his hands...[he] took a panel twelve feet long and eight feet high where he undertook to reproduce all our caricatures in a painting representing an orchestra with thirty or forty musicians, some clashing cymbals, others shaking Chinese pavilions, these blowing into horns and bassoons, those scraping away on violins and bass fiddles. In addition, he had to depict dancing animals above each door.][57]

Dumas observes that "l'atelier du peintre était un lieu de réunion et de causerie" (the painter's studio was a place for getting together and talking).[58] And indeed, as Clogenson relates, Grandville's attic apartment was particularly well adapted to receiving company.

> Il avait au cinquième étage, dans une maison située en face du palais des Beaux-Arts, une mansarde spacieuse, dont son esprit inventif savait tirer un rare parti. Outre le lit, la table et les six chaises qui composaient son ameublement, ses amis se rappellent un vaste rideau vert qui servait à partager en deux son appartement. Une partie, non éclairée, était sa chambre à coucher; l'autre, ornée d'une fenêtre en tabatière, par laquelle le soleil envoyait libéralement ses rayons, constituait l'atelier. Quand les visiteurs étaient nombreux, on enlevait le rideau, et le tout formait un vaste salon.
>
> [He had on the fifth floor [counted as the sixth floor in English], of a house located opposite the palace of Fine Arts, a spacious garret of which his inventive mind knew how to make exceptional use. Beside the bed, the table and six chairs which comprised its furnishings, his friends recall a huge green curtain which served to divide his apartment in two. One part, unlit, was his bedroom; the other embellished with a hinged skylight through which the sun liberally sent its rays, constituted the studio. When visitors were numerous, you drew back the curtain and the whole formed an enormous room.][59]

Of these gatherings, Dumas adds:

> Les jours où l'on était riche, on buvait de la bière; les autres jours, on se contentait de fumer, de crier, de déclamer, de rire.
>
> Granville [*sic*] riait peu, déclamait peu, criait peu, fumait peu, buvait peu. Il demeurait assis à une table, une feuille de papier devant lui, une plume ou un crayon à la main, souriant parfois, dessinant toujours.
>
> [The days when you were rich, you drank beer; the other days you contented yourself with smoking, shouting, haranguing, laughing.
>
> Grandville laughed little, harangued little, shouted little, smoked little, drank little. He remained seated at a table, a sheet of paper in front of him, a pen or pencil in his hand, smiling sometimes, drawing always.][60]

Dumas's account could very well be describing the scene here. For its intimacy suggests that it takes place not in a public restaurant but rather in someone's home, probably Grandville's own garret apartment with him and his guests gathered around the table that Clogenson mentions and seated on five of the six chairs. And typically, instead of taking part in the conversation, the host quietly records the scene in his diary. That Dumas found himself having supper in Grandville's apartment on April 25, 1833, is not surprising: the latter was merely repaying in kind the former for the supper served during the course of Dumas's costume ball several weeks earlier.

The portly figure at the far right of the composition appears to be Louis Desnoyers (1802–68) whom Grandville will depict two years later on the first page of *Le Charivari Monstre* (figs. 24 and 78) and again in the third and final plate of the *Grande course au clocher académique* from 1840 (figs. 79 and 80).[61] Desnoyers's chubby features, curly head of hair, cravat-swaddled neck, luxurious dressing gown, and smoking cigar are repeated with only slight modifications from one print to the next. In the diary drawing as well as in both prints and a somewhat later photographic portrait by Nadar (fig. 81), his curly hair sweeps upward into what might be described as a moderate coiffure à la girafe.

Fig. 78. Detail, column 2 of *Le Charivari Monstre,* July 31, 1835. Paris, Bibliothèque nationale de France.

Fig. 79. ***Grande course au clocher académique*** **(Great academic steeplechase; plate 3),** ***La Caricature,*** **February 16, 1840, lithograph. Paris, Bibliothèque nationale de France.**

Desnoyers and Grandville shared a number of common features. Both were provincials (Desnoyers was born in the village of Replonges, Ain) and belonged to the same generation. Like Grandville, Desnoyers was attracted to the theater. Soon after his arrival in Paris in 1828, he authored several vaudeville plays in collaboration with Varin (1798–1869), Étienne Arago (1802–92), and Desvergers. Several of these were signed with his nom de plume, Derville. Both men were republicans (in cat. no. 35 [verso] Grandville describes himself as a republican), and expressed their political convictions in the opposition press. In 1829, Desnoyers founded a republican political and literary journal, variously titled *Le Sylphe, Le Lutin,* and *Trilby,*[62] and in the following year signed, along with other Parisian journalists, a protest against Charles X's infamous ordinances of July 1830. After the Revolution of 1830, Desnoyers joined forces with Philipon. His first article for *La Caricature,* "Recette pour faire des rois constitutionnels" (Recipe for making constitutional monarchs) appeared in the journal on August 25, 1831, and was signed "L. Derville." Starting with the issue published on May 10, 1832, Desnoyers was *La Caricature*'s editor; he continued to serve in that function until the journal's forced demise at the end of August 1835.[63] In 1832 he also became one of the two principal charter shareholders of *Le Charivari* (the other was Philipon),[64] and served without interruption as that journal's editor from its inception in December 1832 until March 1834. It was probably as a result of his close association with

Fig. 80. Detail, plate 3 of *Grande course au clocher académique.* Paris, Bibliothèque nationale de France.

Fig. 81. Nadar, *Louis Desnoyers,* undated, photograph. Paris, Bibliothèque nationale de France.

La Caricature and his outspoken opposition to Louis-Philippe that Desnoyers went into hiding with the passage of the September Laws in 1835. Upon resurfacing, he founded *Le Siècle* with Armand Dutacq in 1836.[65]

A last shared point of interest was the production of works for children. Desnoyers was a founder of the *Journal des enfans,* which was a monthly publication of approximately thirty pages of readings especially written for children, mainly short stories containing edifying moral lessons. Published on the 25th of each month, the *Journal des enfans* first appeared July 25, 1832. Desnoyers was on the staff of the *Journal des enfans* from August 1832 until July 1833, which coincided wholly or in part with his editorship of *La Caricature* and *Le Charivari.* It surely is no mere coincidence that during this same twelve-month period the *Journal des enfans* published the original serialized version of Desnoyers's enormously popular "Les Aventures de Jean-Paul Choppart" (The adventures of Jean-Paul Choppart) for which, it should be noted, Grandville provided the two original illustrations. The story underwent numerous subsequent revisions until the definitive text appeared in Hetzel's 1865 edition, which carried the slightly different title of *Les Mésaventures de Jean-Paul Choppart* (The misadventures of Jean-Paul Choppart).[66] Desnoyers's equally successful *Les Aventures de Robert-Robert* (The adventures of

Robert-Robert), published as a book by Hortet et Ozane in 1839, also first appeared as a serialized feature in the *Journal des enfans* from October 1834 to January 1837 under the title of "Les Aventures amphibies de Robert-Robert et de son fidèle compagnon Toussaint Lavenette" (The amphibious adventures of Robert-Robert and his faithful companion Toussaint Lavenette). Both "Les Aventures de Jean-Paul Choppart" and "Les Aventures amphibies de Robert-Robert" appeared in the *Journal des enfans* when Grandville was concurrently producing for the publication some of his earliest wood-engraved illustrations.

Desnoyers's other activities included the founding of the Société des gens de lettres (Society of people of letters) in 1837 and writing a book of social commentary, *Esquisses contemporaines: La grande famille de ce monsieur Tartuffe* (Contemporary sketches: The great family of this mister Tartuffe), which was completed in 1840. It was certainly as a result of his multiple literary endeavors that he was depicted along with the likes of Hugo and Dumas as a contender for membership in the Académie française in Grandville's *Grande course au clocher académique.*[67]

Desnoyers's presence at a supper in Grandville's apartment on April 25, 1833, would have been perfectly natural. At the time, Grandville was working under his editorship on both *La Caricature* and *Le Charivari* and collaborating with him for the *Journal des enfans.* As we have seen in cat. no. 16, the artistic team of Forest and Grandville was creating lithographs for *Le Charivari* on a fairly regular basis between February and June 1833. And Grandville had recently completed the drawing for the second of his two wood-engraved illustrations to Desnoyers's "Les Aventures de Jean-Paul Choppart," different chapters of which, it will be recalled, appeared in the *Journal des enfans* between July 1832 and August 1833. Published on page 313 of the April 1833 issue of the *Journal des enfans,* this wood engraving was entitled appropriately enough *Les Aventures de J. P. Choppart* (The adventures of J. P. Choppart); his earlier *Portrait de J. P. Choppart* (Portrait of J. P. Choppart) had appeared on page 121 of the *Journal*'s October 1832 issue. Grandville and Desnoyers would also undoubtedly have been working closely together on the *Règne animal* commentaries, the first of which had appeared one week earlier in *La Caricature* on April 18, 1833.[68]

The identification of the figure seen from the back as a self-portrait is substantiated by more than Grandville's bushy head of hair and lost profile. Just as he has used the portrait of Forest for the second plate of *Règne animal,* Grandville appears to have been inspired by his own for the third and final plate of the series where he depicts himself in the process of sketching the stuffed animals on display (fig. 75).[69] It is not a direct copy as in the case of Forest. Nevertheless, the general attitude of being viewed three-quarters from the back is very similar. Grandville often included himself in scenes where he was present. For instance, he portrayed himself with his Lorrain compatriots in the circa 1829–30 drawing cited previously (Diary of 1830, note 11) and again circa 1830–31 when sketching in the street (Nancy, cat. no. 23).

As for the person seated at the far left, we can assume that he, like the others, was a friend of Grandville, and that everyone present knew everyone else. Grandville and Forest, for example, worked with Desnoyers on *La Caricature* and *Le Charivari,* and both had provided decorations for Dumas's famous ball a few weeks earlier on March 30. And even though Desnoyers is not mentioned in Dumas's *Mémoires,* there is every reason to believe that the two literary figures knew one another.

The identity of this unknown guest may be guessed from the probable reason for this particular group of men getting together in the middle of the week on Thursday, April 25: to celebrate the successful completion of the latest issue of a publication with which they would all at one point be connected, the *Journal des enfans,* which, as has already been noted, appeared on the 25th day of each month. In the April 1833 issue, Desnoyers published the seventh chapter of "Les Aventures de Jean-Paul Choppart" complete with the wood-engraved illustration by Grandville mentioned above. Another wood-engraved illustration for "Le Cerisier de Latenville" (The cherry tree of Latenville), a short story by Miss Maria

Fitz-Clarentz, was provided by Menut. This fact leads to the speculation that the figure at the far left may very well be Menut who would have been known to Forest and Desnoyers as a result of his work for Philipon and who had attended Dumas's costume ball "en page de Charles VII" (as a page of Charles VII).[70] (Should this be Menut, it then is surely no coincidence that the figure's nearly shoulder-length hair does in fact resemble that traditionally worn by fifteenth-century page boys during the reign of Charles VII from 1422 to 1461.)

Even as the celebrants toasted the newly published April issue of the *Journal des enfans,* they undoubtedly discussed plans for its future. For the journal's following May issue Grandville would provide the illustration for "Les Pages de l'Empereur" (fig. 70) discussed in cat. no. 20, and Forest an illustration for "Chroniques de France, ou Arthur de Bretagne" (Annals of France, or Arthur of Brittany) by André Delrieu. Dumas had not yet contributed to the *Journal des enfans,* but he would do so a little over one year later when his short story "Jacques Ier et Jacques II" (James I and James II) appeared in the June and July 1834 issues. It is entirely possible that during the commemorative soirée depicted here Dumas, forever in need of money, decided that he and his facile pen might also participate in the publication.

It is interesting to note that the closely knit group gathered around Grandville's table on April 25, 1833, helped to produce more than one child-oriented periodical. Desnoyers, Dumas, Forest, Grandville, and Menut would all be associated with the *Musée des familles,* the first issue of which appeared some five months later on October 3, 1833.[71] The evening's conversation may therefore have revolved around not just the *Journal des enfans,* but also the projected *Musée des familles.* Surely it was as a result of their experience with these two earlier children's publications that Desnoyers, Dumas, Grandville, and Menut four years later helped to launch yet a third, the *Gazette des enfans,* which made its first appearance January 1, 1837.[72]

22. 23/1 recto

26 Vendredi. s. Clet, pape. 116–249.

Geniti manu
Datif manu
accusatif manu
Voc. ô manu
ablatif manu
(neutre)
format
de Mme. R.
promenade
le long des
quais -
Mme de
Prew -
fait les
frais de
la
Conversation
halte la.
Autre Chose
Je ne
dis
pas -

(26 Friday. St. Cletus, pope. 116–249.

Geniti[ve] manu
Dative manu
accusative manu
Voc[ative] o manu
ablative manu
[neuter]
format
of Mme R.
walk
along the
quays -
Mme de
Prew -
is the
topic
of
conversation
stop there.
Something else
I
won't
say -)

April 26, 1833
100 × 111
Pen and brown ink

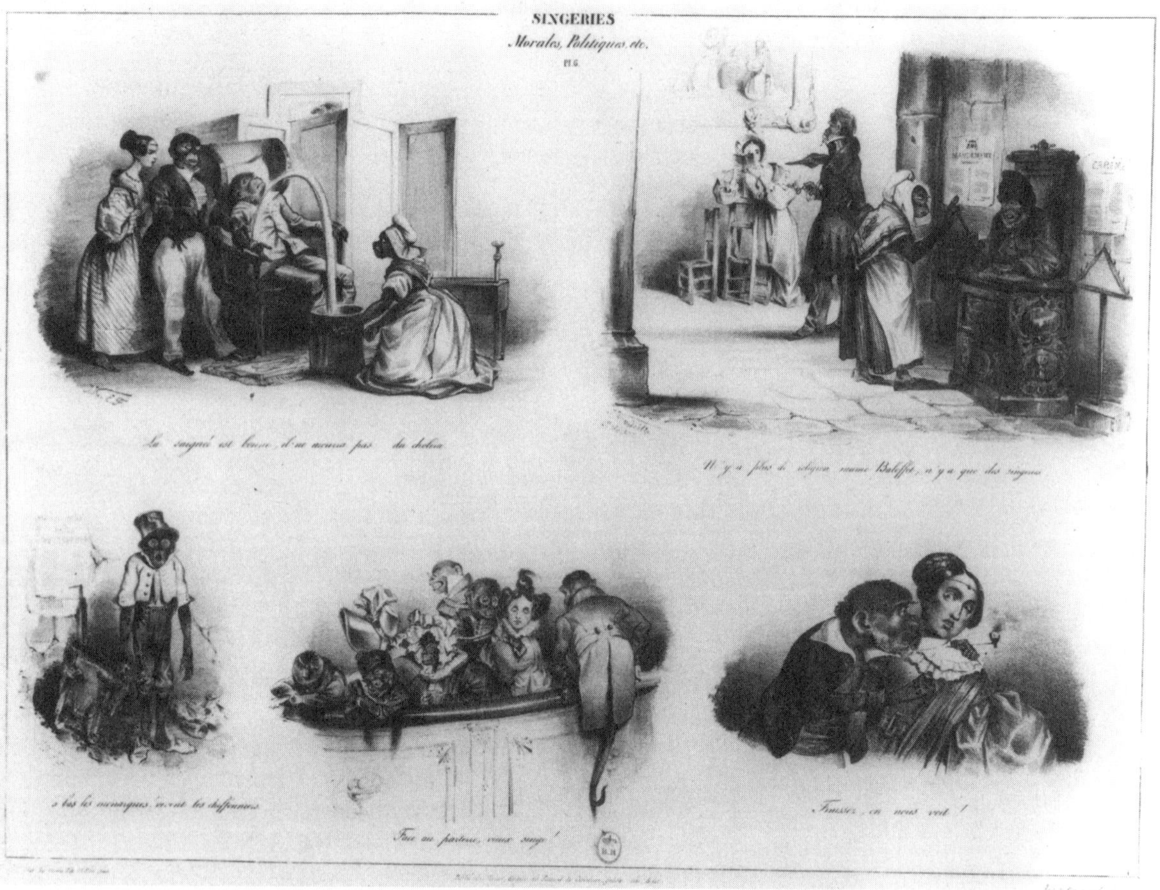

Fig. 82. ***Singeries Morales, Politiques, etc.*** **(Moral, political, etc. monkeyshines; plate 6), 1832, lithograph. Paris, Bibliothèque nationale de France.**

Both the drawing and the annotations of this diary fragment once more refer to Grandville's active interest in the fair sex. In the drawing, a young woman, dressed in the latest fashions of the day, half kneels on a chair in a church while an equally elegant dandy in top hat standing to the right stares at her. The theme is one that Grandville had treated one year earlier in plate 6 of the *Singeries Morales, Politiques, etc.*: "*N'y a plus de religion mame Baloffet, n'y a que des singeries*" (There's no religion any more missus Baloffet, there's only monkeyshines; figs. 82 and 83). This gallant scene is accompanied by what at first appears to be the incongruous declension of the Latin word for hand, *manus,* at the far right. However, it appears that Grandville has indulged himself in some suggestive wordplay. The declension does not start, as it should, with the nominative case, but with the genitive. The key to the pun is to be found in what appears this time to be Grandville's purposeful misspelling of *génitif* (genitive) as "Geniti," which may be read as the fanciful Latin plural of the prefix *génito* (genito, or genital). The matching of "Geniti" with "manu," or of genitals and hand, invites any number of possible interpretations. Suffice it to say that the connotation is probably similar to the genital/hand reference of "rose mousseuse" and "doigts caressants" in cat. no. 16. Grandville masks his double entendre

Fig. 83. Detail, plate 6 of *Singeries Morales, Politiques, etc.: N'y a plus de religion mame Baloffet, n'y a que des singeries* (Moral, political, etc. monkeyshines: There's no religion any more missus Baloffet, there's only monkeyshines). Paris, Bibliothèque nationale de France.

by presenting the rest of the declension. His erroneous designation that *manus* belongs to the neuter gender (it actually is feminine) again can be given a suggestive interpretation. The hand is indeed a neutral appendage that may be put to use by either sex.

"Mme. R.," who has provided Grandville with the format of his Latin declension, appears to be his companion as he takes a walk along the quays of the Seine River. A clue to her identity may be found in their topic of conversation, Madame de Prew, who is probably the keeper of a brothel: as we have already seen in cat. no. 10 (verso), it was very fashionable during the Romantic period for madams to use the particle "de" as part of their nom de guerre. Should Madame R. be a prostitute, the "something else" that Grandville declines to mention following their conversation may be easily guessed.

Given the above interpretation of Grandville's annotations, it may be assumed that the erotically tinged scene depicted in the accompanying drawing also features a prostitute: while she pretends to be attending to her religious devotions, she coyly attracts the attention of a potential client.

The contour of the cut at the bottom of this sheet exactly matches that at the top of the following diary fragment. Nothing therefore has been lost between the entries of April 26 and April 27, 1833.

23. 9/2 recto

27 Samedi. s. Polycarpe. **117–248.**
(27 Saturday. St. Polycarp. 117–248.)

April 27, 1833
60 × 112
Pen and brown ink

L'Auberge des Adrets (The sunny-side inn) by Messrs. Benjamin (Benjamin Antier), Saint-Amand, (Jean-Armand Lacoste) and Paulyanthe (Alexandre Chapponier) was probably the most popular French melodrama of the Romantic period if not of the entire nineteenth century. First performed at the Théâtre de l'Ambigu-Comique on July 2, 1823, it was revived at the Théâtre de la Porte-Saint-Martin on January 28, 1832, and again on April 25, 1833. It was still being presented on the Parisian stage in 1889 when it appeared once more at the Théâtre de la Porte-Saint-Martin. Grandville viewed the play on the third night of its 1833 revival, possibly encouraged by the glowing review that it had received the previous day in the Friday, April 26 issue of the *Figaro.* Judging from the elevated perspective and angle of vision in the scene at the center, he has studied the action from a box to the right of the stage.

As might be expected, Grandville has depicted the play's two principals, Frédérick Lemaître and Serres, in their starring roles of those "divins escrocs" (sublime crooks), Robert Macaire and his sidekick, Bertrand. The center drawing represents act 1, scene 10. Macaire and Bertrand are easily recognized by their distinctive costumes, the former in "son chapeau sans fond sur le côté, son habit vert rejeté en arrière, son pantalon rouge tout rapiécé, son bandeau noir sur l'oeil, son jabot de dentelle et ses souliers de bal" (his hat with a hole in the side, green coat shoved back, heavily patched red pants, black bandage over one eye, lace jabot and pumps; fig. 84), the latter "avec sa houppelande grise, aux poches démesurément longues" (with his grey greatcoat with overly long pockets).[73] The action takes

Fig. 84. Anonymous, *Frédérick Lemaitre* [*sic*] *(Auberge des Adrets),* undated, photolithograph after Carjat. Paris, Bibliothèque nationale de France.

place in the courtyard of the Auberge des Adrets, located "sur la route de Grenoble à Chambéry" (at Chambéry on the road to Grenoble). Grandville has faithfully reproduced the scenery at the front of the stage as described in the playbook: "au premier plan . . . des arbres sous lesquels sont placés des tables" (in the foreground . . . trees under which are placed tables). At one of the tables, Pierre, the waiter, has served Macaire and Bertrand a meal as they take a respite in their dusty flight from the prison at Lyon. Their repast is interrupted by the arrival of village peasants who start to dance in celebration of the arrival of Clémentine, the fiancée of Charles, the innkeeper's adopted son, who is to be married the following day. As fate would have it, Charles is the natural son of the n'er-do-well Macaire who had abandoned him before he was ever born. With an elegance matched only by his duplicity and sangfroid, Macaire joins the festivities and invites one of the young peasant women to dance a waltz with him, which Grandville represents on the right. Toward the left, Bertrand gallantly has risen from the table in order to present the rose from the buttonhole of his lapel to Macaire's comely partner. In the background may be glimpsed assorted village musicians and dancers.

The drawing at the far right depicts act 2, scene 4. In the first scene of the second act Macaire and Bertrand return to their room after having stabbed Clémentine's father, Mr. Germeuil, while he was sleeping and stolen the 12,000 francs that were to have served as Clémentine's dowry. In scene 2, Marie, a destitute woman whom Mr. Germeuil has befriended and who turns out to be the long-lost mother of Charles and wife of Macaire, attempts to leave the inn in the early morning hours only to be discovered in scene 3 by Pierre who questions her suspicious conduct. In scene 4, Macaire and Bertrand leave their room in order to investigate what the commotion is all about. While Macaire appears in a dressing gown, Bertrand wears a camisole and cotton bonnet ("en camisole et en bonnet de coton") just as Grandville has portrayed him here. By the end of the second act, the gendarmes have caught up with the escaped convicts and apprehended them. In the play's original third and final act, Marie, suspected of the attempt on Germeuil's life, is vindicated and the real perpetrators of the crime, Macaire and Bertrand, are under lock and key. The play ends as Charles, who has learned that Macaire is his father, helps him to flee. However, Bertrand, on whom Macaire has placed all the blame for the wrongdoing, fatally shoots him before he can make good his escape.

Dissatisfied with this original ending, Lemaître eliminated the third act for the revival and substituted at the end of the second a more sinister denouement with antigovernment overtones. Instead of remaining captive, Macaire and Bertrand break free from their guards by jumping into the orchestra and stage-boxes. As the gendarmes give pursuit, Macaire kills one of them, throws him onto the stage, and declaims:

> Tuer les mouchards et les gendarmes,
> Ça n'empêche pas les sentiments.
>
> [To kill informers and gendarmes,
> that doesn't prevent one from having feelings.][74]

This shorter and infinitely more subversive version of *l'Auberge des Adrets* became exceedingly popular, and it was the one that Grandville saw on April 27, 1833. The revised melodrama's popularity, however, proved its undoing. Brought to the attention of the government, it was ultimately banned.[75]

Outlawed from the stage, *l'Auberge des Adrets* continued to live on in literature and caricature. Grandville took the lead in the latter when, with the help of Desperet, he produced as the February 18, 1834, issue of *Le Charivari* a lithograph entitled simply *l'Auberge des Adrets* (fig. 85). Both the circumstances of the caricature's production and its content bear witness to the intensified efforts by the

Fig. 85. ***L'Auberge des Adrets, Le Charivari,*** **February 18, 1834, lithograph. Private collection.**

July Monarchy to silence the opposition press. For failure to pay a third fine leveled against it, *Le Charivari* saw its February 18, 1834, issue seized. In order to compensate subscribers for the missed issue, Philipon had Grandville produce his own version of *l'Auberge des Adrets,* which was to be distributed during the week of March 2. The print depicts Louis-Philippe as a club-wielding Macaire who addresses his minister of the interior, the long-nosed and bespectacled comte d'Argout disguised as Bertrand leaning on his own club, and other caricatured members of his government: the caption reads, "Eh bien camarades! comment supportez vous l'existence?" (And so comrades! how's life treating you?). Graffiti on the wall behind Louis-Philippe feature a pear (in French, pear has the added connotation of "fathead"), the famous attribute of the king invented by Philipon. Out of the back pocket of d'Argout protrudes a bulging bag of money labeled "fines." Directly behind him stands the uniformed Marshal Soult, minister of war. Lying prostrate in the background and seen between the king and d'Argout is a comely young woman who personifies the popular press, which at the time was being virulently attacked. Next to her right arm and hand, which are draped over a lithographic stone, is a sheet of paper with the words "Presse populaire" (popular press) and in her left hand is another sheet labeled "Bon Sens" (Common sense), a reference to the working-class newspaper of that name. (Founded in 1832, the same year as *Le Charivari, Le Bon Sens* was the organ of one of France's leading socialists, Louis Blanc [1811–82]; like both *La Caricature* and *Le Charivari,* it was subject to seizures, such as that of one of its supplements, reported in *Le Charivari* on August 10, 1833.) As part of its stepped-up campaign to curtail the influence of the popular press, the government was in the process of enacting additional legal restrictions. For example, on February 8, 1834, the Chamber of Deputies had recently voted for a law that severely curtailed public criers both from practicing their noisy profession in the streets and from selling or distributing broadsides, a main source of information for the proletarian masses whose periodic uprisings presented a very real and constant threat to the regime. The print, in short, likens the July Monarchy to a band of street thugs, led by Macaire/Louis-Philippe, who have bludgeoned the young and winsome popular press. *L'Auberge des Adrets* is typical of the political caricatures focusing on current issues of press freedom that Philipon regularly had his artists produce. However, that which is atypical is Grandville's use in February 1834 of those "sublime crooks," Macaire and Bertrand, as the vehicle for his political satire.

Earlier, on the eve of the Revolution of 1830, Grandville had played a central role in developing the definitive appearance of the hunchback Mayeux, the cartoon character subsequently associated with his colleague on the staff of *La Caricature,* Traviès (see Nancy, 187–93). A similar phenomenon occurred with Robert Macaire and Daumier. Grandville's caricatured use of Macaire predates Daumier's by some eight months. It was only with lithographs produced for *La Caricature* in November 1834 that Daumier started to explore the caricatural potential of Robert Macaire and, like Grandville, he began by representing Louis-Philippe in the guise of the notorious stage character.[76] But unlike his senior colleague, Daumier would continue to exploit Robert Macaire for social satire, first in his one-hundred-print series *Caricaturana* of 1836 and then in the twenty-print series *Les Robert-Macaire* of 1840–41 to the extent that Daumier and Robert Macaire became nearly synonymous.

24. 11/1 verso

Avril.

28 Dimanche. s. Vital, martyr. 118–247.

Depart de thomassin
Visite de St Pierre et de sa mere
envie - de sa position - en efffet
quelle plus belle pouvoir vivre en
son pays - en etre le premier pei[n]t[re]
pouvoir Venir a paris.. se mettre
au courant de la bonne peinture..
....nous verrons... a quel epoque
nos deux existences se rapprocherons.
a la tombe dirait Chardard!
diner chez Zen— lettre ecrite
promenade solitaire avec mon
Costu[me].. ho - torreador!
a plusieurs reprises.. toujours toujours
le même

(April

28 Sunday, St. Vitalis, martyr. 118–247.

Departure of Thomassin
Visit from Saint-Pierre and his mother

envy - of his position - indeed
what could be better than to be able to live in
your native region - to be its leading painter
to be able to come to Paris.. to keep
up-to-date with fine painting..
....we'll see... at what point
our two lives will be comparable.
not until the grave Chardard would say!
dinner at the home of Zen— letter written
solitary walk in my
suit.. ho -toreador!
repeated several times.. always always
the same)

April 28, 1833
92 × 109
Pen and brown ink

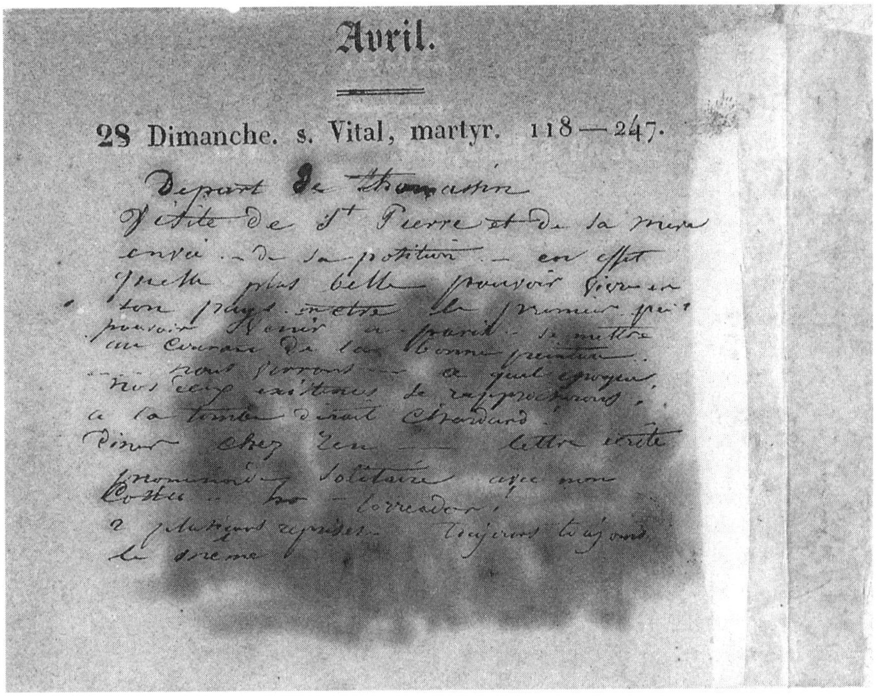
Avril.

28 Dimanche. s. Vital, martyr. 118—247.

The ghost image of the festive supper depicted on the opposite side of the sheet (cat. no. 21) is particularly apparent.

Grandville records in this diary entry the departure of Thomassin who presumably had been visiting Paris. Although we do not know his identity, it is possible that he may have been a friend from Nancy. For, according to Bénézit, there was a painter of religious subjects by the name of François Thomassin who was active in Nancy around 1620. The Thomassin mentioned here could have been one of his descendants.

Grandville also expresses his envy of the happy situation in which a visiting provincial painter, a certain Saint-Pierre, finds himself: being able to live in his native region where he is recognized as the leading painter while at the same time having the opportunity to visit the capital in order to keep abreast of the latest developments in painting. Reflecting on whether or not he will ever enjoy the same existence as Saint-Pierre, he provides the predictable response of his friend, Chardard, "not until the grave!" Grandville's envy of Saint-Pierre is real as he struggles to establish a place for himself in the Parisian art world, far from his beloved family and friends in Nancy.[77]

Grandville mentions having dinner at the home of a certain "Zen—." Given his active interest in the opposite sex, it can be assumed that "Zen—" is one of those ladies of easy virtue whose company he sought before his marriage. "Zen—" would then be the first three letters of a picturesque nom de guerre such as Zénobie, very much in vogue with the more elegant prostitutes during the Romantic period (see for example Zoraima and Zoé portrayed in Nancy, cat. no. 140).

After dinner, Grandville writes a letter and then rewards himself with one of his customary promenades. This time, he goes out walking alone, and, it being Sunday, he wears his suit, whose style is left to the reader's imagination. But it apparently had a certain theatrical flair, possibly a short cape, which elicited, as Grandville notes, uninvited calls of "ho—toreador!" This, it seems, is not the first time that the suit has provoked public ridicule, for he observes with some disgust "always always the same."

Grandville was by no means alone in presenting on occasion an unconventional appearance to passersby. As was alluded to in cat. no. 3, distinctive dress was indispensable for members of the Romantic generation in order to distinguish themselves from the common herd, and specifically from those hidebound conservatives, the classicists, a phenomenon Grandville recorded in his analysis of various types from around 1830 (see in particular the contrast between "a young Romantic student and a young Classicist" and "father and son Roman-tics" in Nancy, cat. nos. 63 and 87). Other Romantics who indulged themselves in Lavaterian exercises of sartorial differentiation included Eugène Devéria who liked to dress as a Spanish grandee in his Velázquez cloak and Théophile Gautier who, as we have already seen, wore a red velvet doublet to the first performance of *Hernani.* The caricatural sculptor, Dantan jeune, whose relationship with Grandville is explored in cat. no. 32, was also known for his careful yet slightly eccentric attire.[78] Undeterred by the prospect of additional public raillery, Grandville persists in his outward Romantic display. Two days later, on April 30, he once more will wear his suit on a promenade, this time in the Tuileries Gardens (cat. no. 26).

This entry for Sunday, April 28 is one of the few that appears to be complete. Had Grandville been a practicing Catholic, we might have expected his mentioning going to mass. But, as we have seen in the discussion of his spiritual life in cat. no. 19, Grandville was not religious in the traditional sense of the term. This is scarcely surprising for someone with republican convictions who undoubtedly equated the Church with its ally, the monarchical state, and with reactionary forces of repression in general. His caricatures are unfailingly anticlerical in nature, and, like many opposition caricaturists, he never tired of rendering the silhouettes of ecclesiastics as candle snuffers in a symbolic reference to their censorious attitude toward freedom of expression (see Nancy, cat. no. 173). Although, as Clogenson suggests, he tempered certain of his political convictions as he grew older (273), Grandville to the very end of his life kept his distance from the Church and tended to make light of Church institutions. This skepticism can be seen, for instance, in a letter to his Nancy relatives dated July 14, 1842 where he recounts the baptism of his newborn son, Georges, four days earlier on July 10. The ceremony took place at the parish church of Saint-Thomas-Acquin, eliciting from Grandville an irreverent pun at the expense of the church's patron saint who is referred to as "Thomas taquin" or "teasing Thomas." And while complimenting his son on a model comportment, he disparages the ritual involved: "il n'a pas du tout crié contre les salaisons et les graissages du culte; à Sa place j'aurais bien guelé—moi contre toutes ces farces là" (he didn't cry out at all against the religious saltings and oilings; in his place, me, I would have really bawled against all those farces).

25. 23/1 verso

29 Lundi. s. Robert, abbe. **119–246.**

forest vient Je commence le
dessin de pere hautain
Vexation—

(29 Monday. St. Robert, abbot. 119–246.

Forest stops by I begin the
drawing of father haughty
Vexation—)

April 29, 1833
100 × 111
Pen and brown ink

Forest arrives, probably in order to confer with Grandville about the last two sections of the *Règne animal* suite on which they were then collaborating (figs. 74 and 75). Grandville begins work on the drawing of duc Étienne Pasquier, president of the Court of Peers, who appears in the third and last of the large-format plates in the series. Appropriately enough, he will depict Pasquier with the head of a *grand duc* owl ("grand duke," great horned, or European eagle owl), a symbolic reference to both his noble title and his benighted politics.[79] In the lithograph, Pasquier appears at the far left with a label designating him as a "Grand duc. . . . Ct. 1 (Pairs, in pères)" (Grand duke [peers, in fathers]; the English translation does not do justice to the French homophone pun of *pairs* and *pères*). Grandville's designation of him in the diary as the "pere hautain," or "father haughty," may refer to his proud demeanor. This third plate of the *Règne animal* was registered with the dépôt légal on May 22, 1833, and published in *La Caricature* the following day, May 23.

Grandville's "vexation" noted at the end of this diary entry is particularly intriguing. It appears to result from one of two causes: dissatisfaction with his first attempt at depicting Pasquier or annoyance with Forest. Since he has not elaborated, it is impossible to say. However, given the apparent falling out between Grandville and Forest approximately two months later, it may indicate the beginning of some friction between Grandville and his longtime artistic collaborator.

26. 9/2 verso

30 Mardi. s. Eutrope. **120–245.**

dessin de perrotin achevé

promenade aux Thuileries
en costume

(30 Tuesday. St. Eutropius. 120–245.

drawing of Perrotin finished

walk in the Tuileries
wearing [my] suit)

April 30, 1833
60 × 112
Pen and brown ink

The contour of the cut at the top of this sheet matches that at the bottom of the sheet in cat. no. 25. As a result, nothing has been lost between the diary entries of April 29 and April 30, 1833. Ghost images of scenes from *l'Auberge des Adrets* on the opposite side of the sheet (cat. no. 23) show through the paper.

Grandville finishes the drawing of a certain Perrotin and goes for a walk in the Tuileries Gardens where he sketches in his diary strollers and children enjoying the open air. The finished drawing to which Grandville refers may very well have been a portrait of the book publisher Perrotin who, in collaboration with Fournier, will publish Grandville's first three illustrated books: *Oeuvres complètes de P. J. Béranger, Fables de La Fontaine,* and *Voyages de Gulliver dans les contrées lointaines.* If this is, in fact, the case, then two things become apparent. Grandville's skills as a portraitist, learned in the studio of his miniaturist father, were recognized, and he was called upon from time to time to draw portraits of his Parisian friends and acquaintances (examples of his considerable gifts as a portraitist may be found in Nancy, cat. nos. 45–55). Second, and more important, at the same time that he was producing illustrations for the *Journal des enfans* (cat. no. 20), he had begun to cultivate relationships with prospective book editors such as Perrotin: further evidence that in 1833 he was already contemplating the career of a book illustrator as an alternative to his unhappy one as a political caricaturist.

Grandville once more goes out for a walk in his suit. But remembering the unpleasant experience of two days earlier, he decides this time to go to a place where his sartorial splendor might be appreciated instead of ridiculed. He joins the beau monde at the Tuileries. Situated in front of the Tuileries Palace, official residence of France's monarchs, the Tuileries Gardens constituted the most elegant Parisian promenade for the better part of the nineteenth century. It was one of Grandville's favorite destinations when he went out walking, and he would go there again a few days later on May 5 (cat.

no. 31).[80] A visit to the Tuileries involved more than simply taking the air. It was an opportunity for members of the leisure class to be on display, or as Montigny in his guide for provincials puts it, "on s'y observe, tout en observant" (one is observed while observing).[81] The best time to make an appearance was immediately after the two hours traditionally set aside for lunch, that is, between two and three o'clock in the afternoon, preferably on a weekday when the hoi polloi would be working (the promenade tended to lose a certain amount of its bon ton on Sundays when it was invaded by the masses on their day off). Moreover, a visitor did not go just anywhere upon arriving. Instead, one went to that part of the gardens where others of one's social class tended to congregate. With this convention in mind, Montigny cautions his readers that the promenade "has its St.-Antoine district, its *Chaussée-d'Antin,* and especially its *faubourg St.-Germain.*"[82] He also observes that the Tuileries Gardens attracted not only the authentically rich but also "ceux qui veulent le paraître" (those who wish to appear to be so), adding "et dans Paris la différence n'est pas toujours visible au premier coup d'oeil" (and in Paris the distinction is not always apparent at first glance).[83]

Grandville definitely would have been one of those visitors who pretended to be more well-off than he actually was. He has taken his walk on a socially acceptable Tuesday around midday, judging from the shadows. However, not wishing to make a faux pas, he has avoided the more socially select parts of the gardens and chosen the broad promenade between the two basin ponds, which, like the Orangerie, was "abandonnée aux marmots et aux Bonnes" (left to children and maidservants).[84] Indeed, in the foreground of the drawing several children, accompanied here not by nannies but by their fashionably dressed parents, have gathered at the edge of one of the large basins in order to observe a little girl who appears to be recovering a toy sailboat with a stick, much as children still do today. A couple of elderly rentier types make an appearance at the right. And two grenadiers of the omnipresent National Guard wearing their distinctive, tall shakos have ambled over to have a look; one of them has placed his foot on the edge of the basin. On the receding diagonal at the left, stylish ambulators stroll arm in arm along the tree-lined alley.

The fact that Grandville decided to go the Tuileries Gardens on April 30 is not without significance. Perhaps he was in a festive mood, anticipating the *fête du Roi* (name day of the king) which would occur the following day, and would be announced by salvos of artillery at seven o'clock later on that same evening. Perhaps also he realized that the genteel atmosphere of the gardens would be broken on the morrow when they would overflow with holiday crowds.

27. 10/1 recto

Je fais le dessin sur Bois de mr Coste.
sortie avec mr R..., Jolie personne
au restaurant ... idée a ce sujet
les proletaires endimanchés
non pas sur le fauteuil
a la Francaise.

Mai.

1 Mercredi. s. LOUIS PHILIPPE. 121–244.

2 Jeudi. s. Athanase. 122–243.
(I do the drawing on wood of Mr. Coste
go out with Mr. R..., pretty woman

at the restaurant . . . idea on this subject
the proletarians dressed in their Sunday best
not in the easy-chair
in the French manner

May

1 Wednesday. St. Louis Philip. 121–244.

2 Thursday. St. Athanasius. 122–243.)

May 1–2, 1833
133 × 109
Pen and brown ink, brown wash, watercolor

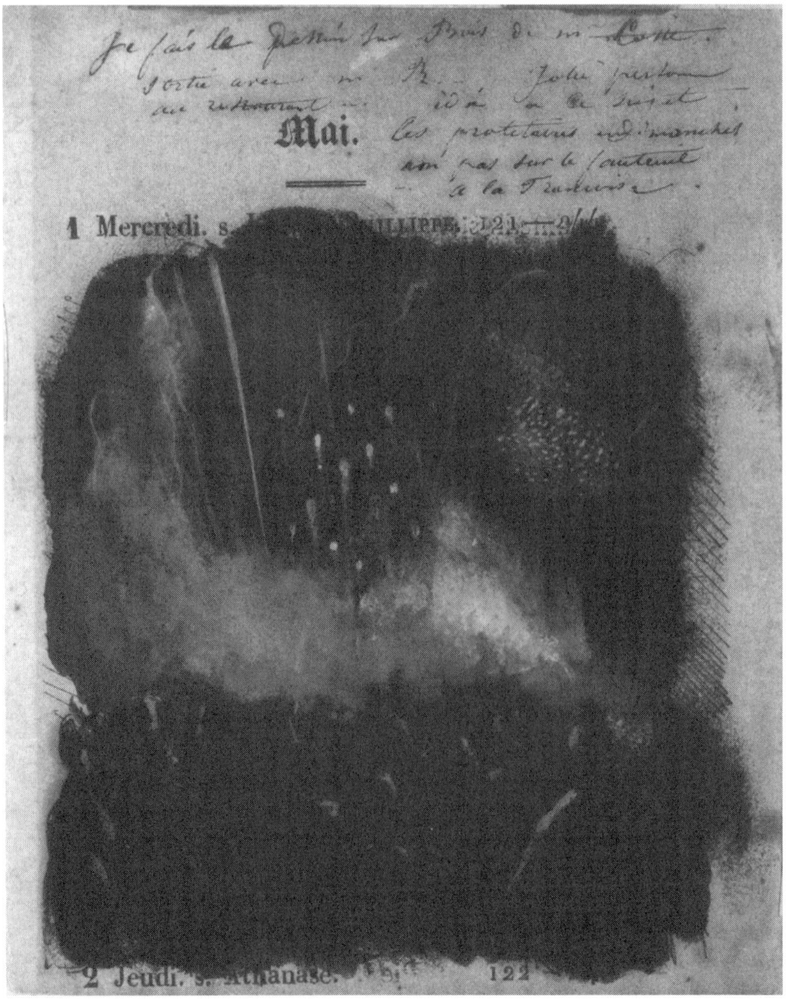

The saint for May 1, 1833, was the one after whom the king was named, St. Louis Philip. As a result, it was the king's name day, or the fête du Roi, a national holiday. Grandville has devoted the entire space for the day's entry to the delightful wash and watercolor drawing of the fireworks held in the king's honor. The rest of the day's events were recorded in the top margin of the page. Together with the previous diary entry, this one gives us some idea of his usual schedule, which seems not to have been unduly interrupted by the holiday: work on drawings in the morning, break for a walk around noon, lunch in a restaurant, entertainment in the evening.

In the first line, he notes that he has transferred a drawing onto wood in preparation for the engraving process. The wood engraving in question is undoubtedly *Les Pages de l'Empereur* (fig. 70), which appeared as an illustration to the short story of the same title by James Rousseau in the May 1833 issue of the *Journal des enfans.* The artist who engraved this vignette was Lacoste aîné whose name Grandville has shortened to "Coste." Lacoste aîné would appear to refer to the father of the father-and-son team of engravers who will later assist in the engraving of several of Grandville's illustrations to the *Fables de La Fontaine.*

He goes out with a certain Mr. R . . . with whom he again will go walking two days later (cat. no. 29). Afterward while at a restaurant, a pretty woman who has caught his eye gives him an idea for a composition. This bit of information confirms what we already know about Grandville: that he found artistic inspiration in his observations of everyday life and current events, and that he was, even in his most fantastic work, fundamentally a recorder of and commentator on his time and place.

As an official holiday, the fête du Roi gave the working class a rare day off in the middle of the week. Grandville, whose sympathies, like those of other republicans, lay with the oppressed poor, comments on "the proletarians" being up and about dressed in their Sunday best. He contrasts their vitality with the indolence of their social betters who would spend a holiday such as this by taking their ease in an armchair in the customary French fashion. It may at first appear to be contradictory that Grandville would pretend to be part of the beau monde in the Tuileries Gardens one day and express admiration for the working class on the next. But personal ambition and humanitarianism are not mutually exclusive among social reformers, either today or in the nineteenth century. Grandville at the time was struggling to make a success of himself and attain a certain level of social respectability so that he could marry and support a family, middle-class goals totally in keeping with his provincial petit-bourgeois background. Simultaneously, he recognized the existence of social injustice and was an advocate of the less fortunate.

In keeping with its role as the official government newspaper, *Le Moniteur universel* gave a glowing account of the fête du Roi the following day, May 2. Public games had been organized at either extremity of the capital, the Champs-Elysées and around the place du Trône (Throne Square; today place de la Nation, or Nation Square), undoubtedly in an effort to keep the unpredictable masses divided, occupied, and at a safe distance from the royal family. Crowds, presumably of a more bourgeois nature, thronged around the Tuileries Palace (including the gardens) and greeted the king whenever he made an appearance at his balcony with repeated shouts of "long live the King! long live the royal family!" The festivites culminated with illuminations and fireworks:

> Le soir, une très-riche illumination s'est développée sur toutes les lignes des Champs-Elysées, et offrait le coup d'oeil le plus pittoresque. Les danses étaient très-animées; le feu d'artifice, placé sur le quai d'Orsay, a été magnifique. Tous les édifices publics et la plupart des maisons particulières étaient illuminées.
>
> [In the evening, a very splendid illumination extended all along the edges of the Champs-Elysées, and offered the most picturesque sight. The dancing was very lively; the fireworks, located on the quai d'Orsay, were magnificent. All of the public buildings and most of the private homes were lit up.][85]

Grandville has recorded the "magnificent" fireworks along the quai d'Orsay in an equally magnificent wash and watercolor drawing. Spectators crowd the foreground as they and the artist view the display from the opposite bank of the Seine River. The blue, white, and red of the French tricolor patriotically light the sky in the exuberance of what appears to be the *bouquet,* or grand finale.[86]

28. 11/2 verso

nouvell lettres ecrite a ma Cousine—Il -
Visite de messire paulus - encore un
a sortir dit on d'affaire - il le fera
Certes bien — C'est assez de protection Comme cela
Cest assez preter ses epaules pour aider aux autres
a monter dessus ——
promenade avec Gomien rencontre de
Julien et de sa dame. ainsi.. que lui
bientot Ca furtivement le soir — en vraie
Chauve Souris — nous nous promenons avec
ma petite futê - mr depressoir
...mauvaise composition.. ...Seulement
la Jambinelle..tachée. - oh! iha!..
Voyez comme dit pigal plus se.. plus B.
(another letter written to my cousin - It -
Visit from Master Paulus - yet another
to get, as they say, out of trouble - he will
certainly do it well - That's enough protection like that
That's enough of lending his shoulders to help others
climb up ——-
walk with Gomien encounter
Julien and his lady. like him
soon That [walking about] furtively in the night - like
real bats - we walk with
my sly little minx - Mr. Depressoir
...bad composition.. ...Only
the leg..blotted.—oh! yikes!
See, as Pigal says, the more *se..* the more *B.*)

May 2, 1833
53 × 108
Pen and brown ink

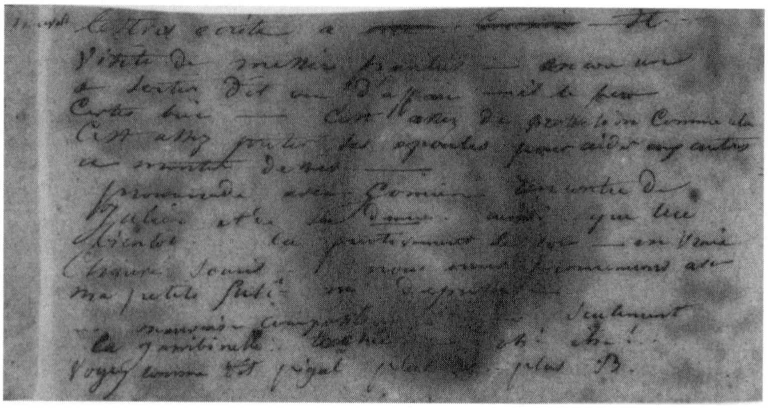

The contour of the cut at the top of this undated fragment matches perfectly the contour of the cut along the bottom of the previous drawing, cat. no. 27. Consequently, there is no doubt that it is the first part of the diary entry for May 2, 1833. The ghost image of the drawing from the May 5 diary entry on the verse of the sheet (cat. no. 31) is very evident.

Although the last half of the first line has been crossed out, it is still legible, and we learn that Grandville has written another letter to "ma Cousine." The female cousin in question is more than likely his future wife, Henriette Fischer (it will be recalled that Henriette's mother, née Marguerite Viot, and Grandville's mother, née Catherine Viot, were sisters). Indeed, it would be perfectly normal for the young couple to be engaged in an active correspondence during the months immediately prior to their wedding. Apparently in an effort to keep track of the letter, Grandville carefully notes having mailed it on the following day, May 3 (cat. no. 29).

The next five lines concern a legal process in which Grandville was then engaged. When the lawyer handling the case had visited him one week earlier, he referred to him as "master Ploctius" (cat. no. 20). As a precautionary measure and again in a display of his knowledge of Roman history, he here obliquely refers to the same or another attorney as "master Paulus" (Julius Paulus was a renowned second-century Roman judicial counselor). It appears that the lawyer, who has stopped by in order to confer with him, is experienced in cases such as Grandville's, and Grandville expresses confidence in his abilities. But for two full lines he complains about being dependent upon others for help and repeats, "that's enough." This fiercely independent stance belies Grandville's reputation for being a timid soul, and gives some indication of the drive and will to succeed on his own that propelled him to the top of the caricatural profession. It is probably in reference to the same court case that some policemen pay him a visit three days later on May 5 (cat. no. 31).

Grandville takes what presumably is an evening walk with one of the Gomien brothers, either Paul (1799–1846) or Charles (1808 or 1811–76), Lorrain compatriots born at Villers-lès-Nancy whose artistic careers in Paris paralleled his own.[87] They encounter the lithographer and Grandville's occasional collaborator, Julien, in the company of his wife. Grandville observes that he will soon find himself in a similar married state, and impishly fantasizes that, like Julien, he will furtively prowl about at night as though he were a bat in the company of his "petite futê" [*sic*] (*petite futée,* or "sly little minx"). The image he conjures up of a nocturnal couple flitting about mysteriously in the darkness like creatures of the night is a stereotypically Romantic one and invites comparison with one of his drawings from around 1829–30, *Espèces toutes romantiques en promenade dans les foyers et corridors sombres* (Completely romantic types walking in dark foyers and corridors; Nancy, cat. no. 108).

It is difficult to determine whether the unidentified Mr. Depressoir is an acquaintance or the subject of a drawing. The rest of the entry has to do with a composition Grandville was working on and with which he was dissatisfied. Apparently its only redeeming feature was the titillating view of a leg ("la Jambinelle"), and that was blotted (compare with Nancy, cat. no. 65 where Grandville notes "This drawing was done for the leg"). After a couple of exclamations, he quotes a saying by his fellow lithographer and caricaturist, Pigal, which is too abbreviated to decipher. Grandville would have come into contact with the slightly older artist while working for *La Caricature* and *Le Charivari.* The December 9, 1830, issue of *La Caricature* included Pigal's *Soirée du peuple* (The people's soiree), and in 1833 *Le Charivari* published four of his lithographs dealing with "scènes de moeurs populaires" (scenes of popular customs).[88] Unfortunately, it is not possible from this brief reference to determine when Grandville first made Pigal's acquaintance or the extent of their relationship. However, the two artists would have shared a common bond in their sympathetic portrayals of the working class.

29. 12/1 recto

3 Vendredi. Invention ste. Croix. 123–242.

nous allons forest Guiaud
et moi au Jardin
des plantes

Lettre
mise a
la poste

pantalon
d'été

promenade
avec Mr
R et S.D.

coucher de
bonne heur

(3 Friday. Invention Holy Cross. 123–242.

we go, Forest, Guiaud
and I, to the Jardin
des plantes

Letter
mailed

summer
pants

walk
with Mr.
R and S.D.

early
to bed)

May 3, 1833
117 × 113
Pencil, pen and brown ink

Grandville goes with Forest and Guiaud to the Jardin des Plantes where he sketches in his diary three exotic birds: a marabou, an ostrich, and a peacock, this latter drawn in pencil. At the children's zoo, he records a maid with two small children, one of whom appears to be feeding a goat; behind them stands a bespectacled rentier type.

Upon his return to his garret apartment in the rue des Petits-Augustins, he looked out the window only to find a woman in a gigot-sleeved dress across the way doing the same thing. As he sketches her, she stares at him while leaning on the window guardrail. Three years earlier, he had recorded the same view in the Carnavalet Sketchbook where another woman in a frilly bonnet leans out the same window and looks down into the street below (fig. 86). He probably had this particular image from his bachelor years in mind when he created *Frétillon* for the *Oeuvres complètes de P.-J. de Béranger* published in 1836 (fig. 87). Other views from windows provided Grandville with additional artistic inspiration. Along with the just cited drawing in the Carnavalet Sketchbook, Grandville produced an entire series

of street scenes around 1830 that were observed from upper-story windows, including, presumably, his own (see Nancy, cat. no. 27). These bird's-eye views anticipate the plunging perspectives in the chapter "À vol et à vue d'oiseau" (With the flight and view of a bird) in *Un autre monde.*

The rest of the day was spent in fairly mundane activities. He records mailing the letter that he had written to Henriette the day before. The warming weather causes him to mention a pair of summer pants. He takes a walk with two unidentified individuals, a Mr. R, mentioned two days earlier in cat. no. 27, and a certain S.D. He ends the day by going to bed early.

30. 10/1 verso

Mai.

4 Samedi. ste. Monique. 124–241.

Guiaud vient achever sa pierre
de la Jossomiel -
Suite Discution sur l'achat d'une robe
de Chambre d'autrefois —...
Dessin courageusement esquissé
femur et endé...Coutumance

Fig. 86. *Woman Leaning Out of Window,* page 43 verso from the Carnavalet Sketchbook, circa 1830, drawing. Paris, Musée Carnavalet.

[Pencil sketch of the mask, which appears in the May 5 entry (cat. no. 31)]

5 Dimanche. s. Pie V. 125–240.
(May

4 Saturday, St. Monica. 124–241.
Guiaud stops by to finish his stone
of *la Jossomiel*—
Continuation of discussion about the purchase of an
old-fashioned dressing gown—...
Drawing pluckily sketched
femur and *endé...Coutumance*

5 Sunday. St. Pius V. 125–240.]

May 4–5, 1833
133 × 109
Pencil, pen and brown ink

Fig. 87. *Frétillon.* from *Oeuvres complètes de P.-J. de Béranger,* 1836, wood engraving. Private collection.

Unfortunately, it was not possible to photograph this verso.

On May 4, Guiaud stops by to finish drawing an unidentified subject, "la Jossomiel," on his lithographic stone. It is doubtful that it was a composition on which Guiaud and Grandville were collaborating, for Guiaud appears to have left the field of political caricature shortly after working with Grandville on a series of lithographs in the latter half of 1830 and the beginning of 1831, which commented on the fall of Charles X. He afterward seems to have concentrated his efforts on being accepted at the Salon where he debuted in 1831 and continued to exhibit until 1876. Judging from the diary, Guiaud saw Grandville regularly during 1833: we know that he remained one of his close friends for the rest of Grandville's life. The purpose of Guiaud's visit is probably simply to allow the two friends to spend a Saturday working in one another's company.

This supposition provides a credible context for the rest of the diary entry. Guiaud and Grandville continue a discussion they had started earlier on the question of buying "an old-fashioned dressing gown." During the Romantic period, stylish young men considered a silk or velvet dressing gown, similar to those worn by eighteenth-century aristocrats, an indispensable part of their wardrobe. Besides being a practical extra layer of clothing in the days before central heating, it and the requisite matching bonnet were perfect for making the proper impression when entertaining women in their chambers.[89] Dantan jeune, for example, would play host during the 1830s "dressed in his long, thick *robe de chambre* and with a Greek bonnet on his head."[90] And Philipon wears an elaborately patterned dressing gown in his stylish portrait from around 1831 by Devéria (fig. 19) as does Desnoyers in Grandville's caricatured portrait of him for *Le Charivari Monstre* (fig. 78). The problem for marginally solvent individuals such as our two struggling artists was that such an accessory could be just as much a luxury item as the cashmere shawl, deemed equally essential for elegant young women of the time.[91] One can easily imagine the debate that ensued as the two young men, neither of whom could really afford such a prodigality, weighed the pros and cons of obtaining the coveted object tantalizingly beyond their means. The fact that members of Grandville's circle of friends such as Dantan jeune, Philipon, and Desnoyers either already owned a dressing gown or were about to buy one only would have served to intensify the discussion. It appears to have been a classic example of keeping up with the Joneses.

The topic of a dressing gown was still very much on Grandville's mind nine months later when he and Desperet produced for the February 2, 1834, issue of *Le Charivari* the lithograph reproduced in figure 88: *Hein! quand t'auras une pelure comme ça sus l'casaquin?—ah ben oui! n'y a que des feignans qui s'habillent avec.* (Hey! when are you going to wear a coat like that over your coveralls?—oh yeah! only loafers dress like that.). It is entirely possible that, as the accompanying text contends, Grandville was inspired by a conversation he had overheard between two workers standing in front of a fashionable clothing store window. In the lithograph, one of the men points to the two luxurious robes de chambre and a fancy, tassled bonnet on display. For good measure, Grandville adds a gender and class contrast in the two stylishly dressed women, one wearing a cashmere shawl, who peer into another display window nearby. Depending on either of two suppositions, there are very different ways to explain Grandville's motivation for producing this work. If he never purchased a dressing gown, the disdain expressed by the two workers portrayed could very well be his own as he simultaneously vents his frustration at not being able to afford the luxury item and attempts to purge himself of his desire to obtain it. However, if he finally purchased a robe de chambre (and the sketch in cat. no. 35 suggests that he did, along with a tasseled velvet bonnet), then he is poking fun both at himself and at working-class assumptions about the more well-to-do. In either case, the lithograph remains a study in contrasting class attitudes and values.

Either during or after the dressing-gown discussion, Grandville "pluckily" sketched a drawing. The mention of his pluck no doubt refers to his determination to continue working despite his reservations about his career as a political caricaturist and despite the legal problems he apparently was then facing. Such determination in the face of adversity seems to have been one of Grandville's character traits. He evinced a similar resoluteness and steely discipline in 1841 after the death of his second son, Henri, and again in 1842, after the death of his wife, Henriette: in both instances he refused to fall behind in his work despite his profound grief (see Nancy, 411–12).

In the last line of this entry, Grandville attempts to name two of the leg bones (*fémur,* or femur, and *péroné*[?], or fibula) and links them with the invented word "Coutumance," apparently derived from *coutume* (custom or habit). He seems to be saying that he has grown accustomed to the pain in his legs, which may be related to the pain in his knees he had complained about earlier (cat. no. 19). He possibly had been doing too much walking.

The pencil sketch that appears immediately below the writing seems to be a repetition of the mask that figures in the middle entry on the page (cat. no. 31).

Fig. 88. ***Hein! quand t'auras une pelure comme ça sus l'casaquin?—ah ben oui! n'y a que des feignans qui s'habillent avec.*** **(Hey! when are you going to wear a coat like that over your coveralls?—oh sure! only loafers dress like that.),** ***Le Charivari,*** **February 2, 1834, lithograph. Paris, Bibliothèque nationale de France.**

31. 11/2 recto

	du matin
	relative
	au Changeme[nt]
	de logis
	lettres
	ecrites
	a Chardin
	a Eulalie
Visite	*promenade*
de Gens	*au thuilies*
de police	———
	diner
	[Chez {?}]

(in the morning
relative
to change
of dwelling
letters
written
to Chardin
to Eulalie
walk
in the Tuileries
——————-
dinner
at the home of [?])

Visit
from
policemen

May 5, 1833
53 × 108
Pen and brown ink

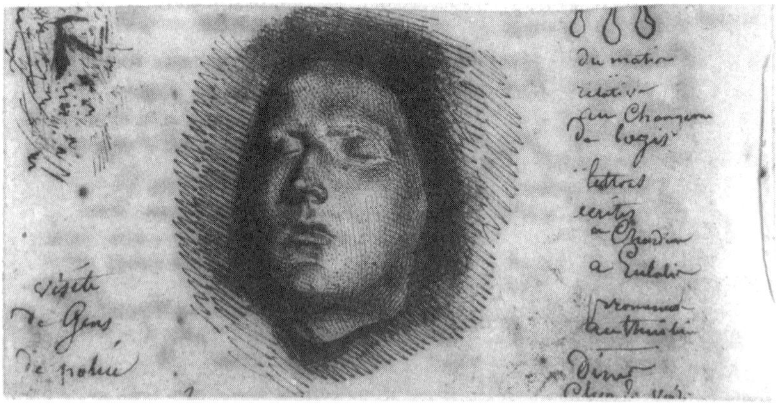

In the evening of what so far had been a fairly ordinary Sunday, Grandville draws in his diary by the light of a candle a plaster mask hanging on his wall. As Dumas observes in his *Mémoires,* plaster casts commonly adorned the studios of even the poorest artists during the Romantic period: "un atelier d'artiste, si pauvre qu'il soit, a toujours quelque chose de plus qu'une chambre d'employé; un croquis, une statuette, un plâtre, un vieux casque sans visière . . ." (a studio of an artist, no matter how poor he may be, always has something more than the room of a wage-earner; a sketch, a statuette, a plaster, an old helmet without its visor . . .).[92] And since, according to Grandville's neighbor, Clogenson, plaster casts hung on the walls of the room that Grandville used as a studio in his apartment at 26, rue des Saints-Pères near the end of his life,[93] we can safely assume that they had also earlier graced the walls of his apartment at 10, rue des Petits-Augustins. That masks were among these popular plaster decorations is confirmed by a contemporary lithograph by Menut published in *L'Artiste,* which depicts a studio still life where plaster masks hang on the wall alongside a painting by Murillo (fig. 89). The mask decorating Grandville's apartment appears not to be a cast of an antique statue. Nor is it the plaster of

Fig. 89. Menut [Marie-Alexandre Alophe], *Un Tableau de Murillo* (A painting by Murillo), *L'Artiste,* 1833, lithograph. Paris, Bibliothèque nationale de France.

Voltaire's grinning face, complete with hook for hanging on the wall, which figures in his 1836 painted still life (reproduced in Renonciat, 267). Instead, it may be the life mask of a person who remains to be identified. His sketch of it emerging out of the surrounding darkness constitutes a particularly sensitive study of chiaroscuro. Both the volume of the face and its complex topography, such as the swelling of the lips, the projection of the nose, and the bulging of the eyes, are defined with remarkable finesse. As a result, it possesses a delicate poetry that contrasts with the more summarily sketched carnival mask in cat. no. 11. To the left of the drawing are the markings left by the artist as he tested his pen to make sure that it was properly loaded with ink in order to execute the finely hatched lines and pinpoint dots used in the modeling of the mask.

In the space remaining on the right, he lists the events of the day before retiring for the night. The three drops of water that seem to drip from the upper right edge of the diary fragment are apparently

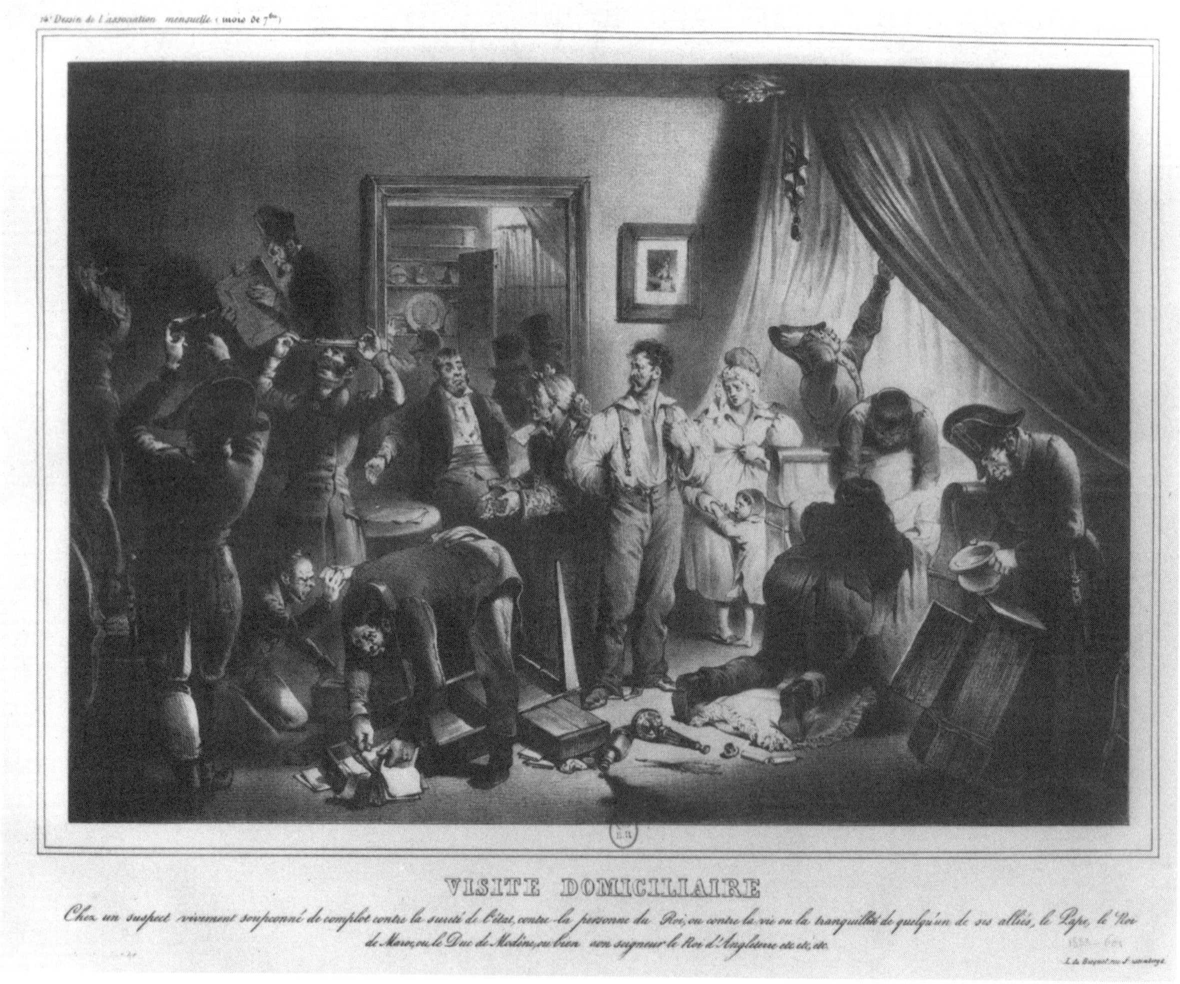

Fig. 90. ***Visite domiciliaire*** **(House call), plate 14 of the** ***Association mensuelle,*** **September 1833, lithograph. Paris, Bibliothèque nationale de France.**

the tears (literal or figurative? genuine or crocodile?) he had shed that morning at the thought of moving out of the garret apartment where he had lived since 1828. He wrote letters to a certain Chardin and to his sister, Eulalie, back in Nancy. He went for a walk in the Tuileries Gardens and had dinner at the home of a friend. Unfortunately, the remainder of his account has been cut off at the bottom.

It would appear that it was after drawing the mask and listing the day's activities that Grandville received the visit from the policemen that he records in the lower left-hand corner of the fragment. His commentary that followed unfortunately again has been cut off, and we are deprived of knowing the exact nature of the visit. It is doubtful that his apartment was ransacked like the one he depicted in *Visite domiciliaire* (House call) several months later for the September 1833 plate of the *Association mensuelle* (fig. 90). More likely the visit involved a relatively civilized interrogation about the case to which Grandville had obliquely referred twice earlier (cat. nos. 20 and 28).

32. 12/1 verso

6 Lundi. s. Jean Porte Latine. 126–239.

Guiaud, Forest nous allons
Voir un Logement ensemble
toujours beau Tems .. de la Chez Guichardet,
son ameublement Gentil.
puis chez Mme Aubert .. .. argent reçu
Diner avec la Esmeralde
promenade fort longue dans la même
direction que la veille. filles publiques
elegantes. Charges de Dantan.
fatigue. essai de license...
Juste et sage repression. la chaleur
a Certes de l'influence sur le phisique
(6 Monday. St. John before the Latin Gate. 126–239.

Guiaud, Forest we go
together to see an apartment
still fair weather .. from there to the home of Guichardet,
his nice furnishings.
then to Mme Aubert's .. .. money received
Dinner with the Esmeralde
very long walk in the same
direction as the day before. elegant
prostitutes. Caricatures by Dantan.
fatigue. licentious attempt...
Just and wise repression. the heat
certainly has an influence on the body)

May 6, 1833
117 × 113
Pen and brown ink

6 Lundi. s. Jean Porte Latine. 126—239.

The ink from the drawings of the May 3 diary entry on the recto of the sheet (cat. no. 29) has seeped through the paper, resulting in a very visible ghost image.

Having shed a tear at the thought of leaving his garret apartment at 10, rue des Petits-Augustins the day before, Grandville takes a look at new lodgings in the company of his inseparable companions, Guiaud and Forest. He takes advantage of the fine weather and proceeds to the home of a certain Guichardet whose furnishings he admires.[94] Then he goes to see Madame Aubert from whom he collects some money. He has dinner with "la Esmeralde," presumably a female acquaintance who has adopted for her own name a variation on that of Esméralda, the heroine from Victor Hugo's recently published best-selling novel, *Notre-Dame de Paris* (1831). He takes a long walk in the same direction as the day before. The reason for the repeated itinerary would appear to be the elegantly dressed prostitutes whom he encounters.

Judging from the next passage, the direction Grandville was walking appears to have been toward the rue Saint-Honoré and place de la Bourse. It was probably either in the shop window of the editor Neuhaus at 123, rue Saint-Honoré or in that of another editor, Susse, located on the corner of place de la Bourse and the passage des Panoramas, that he saw Dantan's caricatures. The Dantan in question is the sculptor Dantan jeune (Dantan the younger) previously encountered in cat. no. 21; his older brother, Antoine-Laurent Dantan, who, as we saw in the biography, was also a sculptor, was referred to as Dantan aîné (Dantan the elder).

Just as Grandville was the "Roi de la caricature" in two dimensions, Dantan jeune was the uncontested king of caricatures in three dimensions. In 1831, he began to produce miniature caricatural busts of contemporary celebrities, which quickly became very popular. By 1832, Susse apparently was selling them in his shop. Hoping to make his satirical sculptures known and available to a larger public, Dantan himself lithographed them in a series of installments published by Neuhaus that began to appear in January 1833 under the title of *Dantanorama*.[95] Like the somewhat later *Muséum Dantanorama* mentioned below, the title for the *Dantanorama* parodies the vogue for panoramas, which were housed in large rotundas, two of which flanked the extremity of the passage des Panoramas where Susse's shop was located, giving the passage its name. From Grandville's mention of "caricatures by Dantan," it is not possible to determine whether he saw Dantan's lithographs at Neuhaus's establishment or the actual caricatural busts at Susse's. Whichever the case, this diary entry proves that he was acquainted with Dantan's sculptural caricatures by May 6, 1833, at the very latest.[96] For apparently in the months that follow, Grandville started depicting them in a second series of lithographs, the *Muséum Dantanorama* (Dantanorama museum), the first eight of which were registered with the dépôt légal on December 16, 1833. Two other lithographers, Charles Ramelet (1805–51) and Lepeudry,[97] joined him in producing the twenty lithographs that comprised the series, published by Susse and Neuhaus in 1835 as an album. In addition to the initial eight lithographs, Grandville produced the last four and the album cover, which depicts the caricatural busts on display in Susse's showroom (fig. 91).[98]

Fig. 91. Cover from *Muséum Dantanorama* (Dantanorama museum), 1833, lithograph. Private collection.

The relationship between Grandville and the Dantan brothers remains to be clarified. While Dantan jeune did a caricatured bust of Forest (fig. 72), there is no evidence that he did one of Grandville, despite the fact that Grandville includes a bust of himself at the far left on the *Muséum Dantanorama*'s cover. Dantan aîné, on the other hand, accepted in May 1847 a commission from the Nancy municipal council to produce a marble bust of the city's recently deceased native son: although there is no proof that the marble bust of Grandville was ever started, let alone completed, two copies of the original plaster are to be found in Nancy, one in the Musée des Beaux-Arts (fig. 92) and the other at the Musée Lorrain.

Grandville's long walk apparently was a little too ambitious, for after he refers to Dantan's caricatures, he admits to being tired. This weariness, however, does not prevent him from making what he terms an "essai de license" (licentious attempt). It is difficult to determine who was the object of his libidinous attention. Was it "la Esmeralde" who may have accompanied him on his after-dinner walk? Or was it one of the elegant prostitutes he encountered during the promenade? In any case, he "justly" and "wisely" represses his urge, not so much as a result of moral strength as of physical fatigue. Unusually warm weather along with the long walk had taken its toll, leading him to conclude that "the heat certainly has an influence on the body."

33. 6/4 recto

Visite de Mr Guiaud pere
de fils d'Auguste—le mammifère
lettre d'eulalie et de duval
(Visit of Mr. Guiaud senior,
the son, Auguste—the mammal
letter[s] from Eulalie and Duval)

Late May-early July(?) 1833
43 × 111
Pen and brown ink

The cropped printed dates at the bottom of both sides of the sheet and the *tenebroso* style of the drawing on the recto establish that this fragment is from the 1833 diary. The entry's annotations suggest that it dates from sometime between late May and early July. The letter from his sister, Eulalie, may be in response to the one that Grandville sent to her on May 5 (cat. no. 31). Assuming this to be the case, one reason for the correspondence certainly would have been to plan Grandville's upcoming return to Nancy in order to marry his cousin Henriette on July 22. In addition, what is undoubtedly a reference

Fig. 92. Dantan aîné [Antoine-Laurent Dantan], *J. J. Grandville,* 1848, plaster. Nancy, Musée des Beaux-Arts.

to Auguste Desperet suggests that the entry was probably written at the time that Grandville was having his falling out with Forest and was actively looking for another artistic collaborator (see cat. no. 21).

Grandville records the visit of Guiaud and his father as well as of Auguste Desperet;[99] "the mammal" may refer to an unidentified work that he and Desperet were then working on. Interestingly enough, in diary entries from May 3 and May 6, 1833, Guiaud's name twice appears linked with that of Forest. That he is mentioned here along with Forest's ultimate replacement indicates that Desperet had become part of Grandville's closest circle of friends.

Grandville next mentions receiving letters from his sister, Eulalie, and his longtime supporter, the painter Pierre Duval Le Camus. It should be recalled that Duval Le Camus had encouraged Grandville to remain in Paris at a critical juncture by commissioning him to produce the lithographic suite *Les Dimanches d'un bourgeois de Paris* in 1828 and by even lending the disheartened young artist his own studio in which to work.

Grandville never tired of depicting contrasting types, a favorite subject of late eighteenth- and early nineteenth-century caricaturists (see Nancy, 88 and cat. nos. 71–82) that often incorporated the related topic of how clothing masks and transforms the human anatomy, already discussed in cat. no. 2 (recto). The drawing here of two men walking on what appears to be a sidewalk next to the embankment overlooking the Seine River exemplifies both these themes. Undoubtedly encountered on one of his promenades, the duo has caught Grandville's attention because of their divergent silhouettes. While the one stroller is clean-shaven and wears a fairly conventional top hat and cutaway, his companion in a frock coat has chosen a more picturesque Romantic look with his conically shaped broad-brimmed hat and pointed beard.

6/4 verso

pour Chercher
un individu
qui n'est pas
a paris

Seconde
promenade
[illegible
words]
place L. IXVI
boulevards
Station au
palais royal
Gateaux
retour.
bonsoir-

(in order to look for
an individual
who is not
in Paris

Second
walk
[ ]
[ ]
square Louis XVI
boulevards
Station at the
Palais-Royal
Cakes
return.
good night-)

Late May-early July(?) 1833
43 × 111
Pen and brown ink

Unfortunately, it is not possible to interpret the fragmented passage about looking for an individual "who is not in Paris." The other annotation, however, provides the itinerary for one of Grandville's extensive walks. Apparently his second promenade for the day, it presumably started at his apartment in the rue des Petits-Augustins and had as its initial destination square Louis XVI ("place L. IXVI [*sic*]"). From there he strolled along the boulevards and then proceeded on to a station (possibly either a bus stop or transport service center) at the Palais-Royal.[100] A pause is taken in order to sample some cakes or cookies, presumably purchased at a pastry shop. He then returns home where he describes the promenade in his diary, signing off with a "bonsoir" before going to bed. All in all, his ambulatory exercise continued on for some five or six kilometers. Should this distance be typical of Grandville's walks, which seem to have been taken daily and sometimes twice daily, it is no wonder that he occasionally complained of pain in his knees and legs (cat. nos. 19 and 30).

34. 8/2 verso

[10 M]ardi. ste. Valère. vierge. **344–21.**
([10 T]uesday. St. Valeria. virgin. 344–21.)

December 10, 1833
136 × 71

This diary fragment is blank except for the printed indications of the date and the ghost image of the eagle drawings on the opposite side of the sheet.

8/2 recto

13 Vendredi. ste Luce, vierge mart. **347**
(13 Friday. St. Lucy, virgin martyr 347)

December 13, 1833
136 × 71
Pen and brown ink

On December 13, 1833, Grandville seems once more to have visited the zoo at the Jardin des Plantes. The raptors attracted his attention and, as on previous occasions, he used his diary as a sketchbook. The result was these two studies of an eagle.

35. 13/2 recto

[words cut in half]
resultat de cette espece d indiscretion humeur
Cest toujours [des] le bon qui paye
Sagesse
([ ]
result of this type of indiscretion irritation
It's always [some] the good who pay
Restraint)

Circa August-December 1833
49 × 110
Pencil, pen and brown ink

Although this diary fragment carries no indications of a date, both the paper and the graphic style of the drawing suggest that it belongs to the diary of 1833.

The drawing appears to depict the recently married Grandville and his wife, Henriette, in their apartment at 1, rue des Grands-Augustins as they receive an inopportune visitor. Grandville pointedly ignores the intruder as he turns his back in order to work at his drafting table in front of a curtained window overlooking the quai des Grands-Augustins and the Seine River (what seems to be the same room, viewed in the opposite direction from his drafting table, is reproduced in Nancy, cat. no. 7). He wears what suspiciously looks like a long, flowing dressing gown, indicating that he finally succumbed and purchased the luxury item debated over by himself and Guiaud on May 4 (cat. no. 30). On his head is a bonnet similar to the one on display in fig. 88. It is possibly the same tasseled velvet bonnet worn in a contemporary self-portrait (Nancy, cat. no. 9).[101] Henriette sits at the left in front of what may be the wooden bookcase mentioned in cat. no. 16. She wears one of her typical voluminous gigot-sleeved dresses with pelerine. The ringlets that frame her long, oval face are identical to those in a somewhat later portrait (Nancy, cat. no. 10). The visitor, a dark profile seated in the foreground, stares into the fireplace at the far left.

The fragmented script for this setting appears above the drawing where Grandville comments on a certain type of indiscretion, which results in "humeur" (irritation), a word added in pencil. In a moralizing tone, he infers that it is always the good who pay for the indiscretions of others. He somewhat self-righteously concludes the entry with the word "Sagesse" (restraint), which seemingly refers to his difficult but successful control over the ill temper caused by the intrusion.

It is not difficult to imagine what might have happened. One of Grandville's friends, who was always welcome when Grandville lived alone as a bachelor, is now an unwelcome intruder into the private domestic life of Grandville and his wife when he stops by without warning for a visit. Our diarist, in his typical satirical fashion, illustrates his opinion of the trespasser by providing him with a pickle-shaped head (in French, pickle has the figurative connotation of dope or jerk). One year earlier Grandville had depicted two pickle-headed men in a plate for *Carte vivante du restaurateur: Cornichon pour deux Volaille froide* (fig. 11).

Both the composition of the drawing and its moralizing tone can profitably be compared with "une femme sage" (a wise woman) from around 1830 in the collection of the Nancy Musée des Beaux-Arts (Nancy, cat. no. 146).

13/2 verso

faites du nouveau, de recherché
Allez bonjour! ——-

maitre Drul...le radical....
lutte d'opinions - plus royaliste que le
roi, plus ressemblant que la nature,
plus republicain - que nous! Cest fort!
...Consolation electrique suivant Th. -
bossussant pour l'etu[de] —-
quai [?]
(create something new, unusual
Go ahead good day! ——-

master Drul...the radical...
clash of opinions - more royalist than the
king, more resemblant than nature,
more republican—than us! That's too much!
...Electric consolation according to Th. -
plugging away on the stu[dy] —-
quay [ ])

Circa August-December 1833
49 × 110
Pen and brown ink

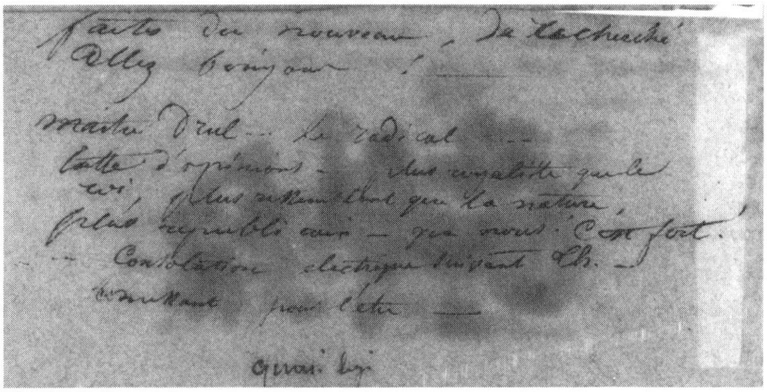

In the first two lines Grandville seems to be giving himself a pep talk as he starts another day of work. The emphasis on creating something new and unusual reflected the innovative spirit of the Romantic generation as a whole. However, for Grandville it became a veritable obsession, which is encapsulated in that statement he made toward the end of his life, previously cited in the biography: "I have imagined graceful monstrosities for the person who needs, above all, the new." Rightly or wrongly assuming what the public expected of him, "Du nouveau!" indeed became his artistic rallying cry, spurring him on to ever new heights of inventiveness. However, as we have seen, those images that he considered as being the most innovative, others disparaged as being overly bizarre. And it is not until the advent of those pertinacious nonconformists, the surrealists, that Grandville's unique achievement truly begins to be appreciated.

Grandville next records the visit of a certain radical "master Drul . . ." with whom he engages in a contest of opinions. The extremist views of this latter cause him in exasperation to exclaim: "more royalist than the king, more resemblant than nature, more republican—than us!" The last of these comparisons confirms what we already know of Grandville's political convictions.

Unfortunately, "master Drul . . ." cannot for the moment be identified. Should he be a lawyer as his title in French seems to indicate, he would once more demonstrate that Grandville was acquainted with a certain number of persons in the legal profession. Such acquaintances would scarcely be surprising given the frequent court cases brought against *La Caricature* and members of its staff.

The rest of this diary fragment remains somewhat abstruse. It is conceivable that the facetious comment from a certain Th. (more than likely an abbreviation for Grandville's witty friend Thomassin) about an "electric consolation" refers to the possibility that there might be someone more ardently republican than Grandville. The next line, in which Grandville has invented a new participial form of the verb "bosser" (to plug away, to keep one's nose to the grindstone), appears to record that he was hard at work on a study for a new composition. Unfortunately, the word after *quai* in the last line is illegible.

Notes

1. Vicaire, 2:52–53. The two works by Menut in *La Caricature* are plate 20, *Ménage parisien* (Parisian household) and plate 34, *Modes françaises* (French fashions), which appeared respectively in the issues of January 6, 1831 and February 24, 1831. The first is a mild social caricature and the second, as the title indicates, a plate of the latest French fashions.

2. Grandville was not shy when it came to giving explicit instructions to those who translated his carefully detailed drawings into another medium. For example, the Cabinet des estampes at the Bibliothèque nationale de France possesses an 1837 letter to the wood engraver Maurisset in which he explains for three long pages how to hatch shadows. We can safely assume that equally fastidious directions were given a few years earlier to his lithographers.

3. A gauge of their popularity may be found in an article that Balzac wrote for *La Silhouette,* "Etudes de philosophie morale sur les habitans du Jardin des Plantes," where he singles out the tiger and discusses at some length the bears (13th livraison [June 17, 1830]: 101–2).

4. "Les Promenades de Paris: Le Jardin des Plantes," *L'Illustration,* April 17, 1847, 107.

5. For example, in 1830 Grandville made a rough pencil sketch of people peering down into the bear pit on page 30 recto of the Carnavalet Sketchbook. A more finished pen and ink composition of this same scene from the same year is in the collection of the Stanford University Museum of Art. A reproduction of this later drawing may be found in Lorenz Eitner, Betsy G. Fryberger, and Carol M. Osborne, *Stanford University Museum of Art: The Drawing Collection* (Stanford, CA: Stanford University Museum of Art, 1993), 351.

6. For a particularly amusing and well-documented account of this journey, see Gabriel Dardaud, "L'extraordinaire aventure de la girafe du Pacha d'Egypte," *Revue des Conférences Françaises en Orient,* 15th year, no. 1 (January 1951): 13–21.

7. Grandville's acquaintance with and exploitation of the theories of Cuvier and Geoffroy Saint-Hilaire are discussed in Nancy, 14–19. See also Philippe Kaenel, "Le Buffon de l'humanité: La Zoologie politique de J.-J. Grandville (1803–1847)," *Revue de l'art,* no. 74 (1986): 21–28.

8. The publication consisted of ninety-one large-format tables or diagrams containing approximately five thousand figures. Each diagram illustrated in a clear and systematic fashion those animals belonging to a particular order. The pedagogic potential of these tables was recognized by the Royal Council on Public Instruction, which recommended in a ministerial memorandum dated August 27, 1832, that Comte's publication be used for the "study and teaching of natural history in university establishments."

9. Born in Grenoble just one year before Grandville, Joseph-Achille Comte (1802–66) was another provincial from the eastern part of France who succeeded in making his career in Paris. Interested in natural history from an early age, he eventually became a professor on the subject at the Collège Charlemagne. It is quite likely that the two men knew each other. Should this be the case, Comte would have been an authoritative source for Grandville's knowledge of natural history.

10. "J.-J. Grandville. Dessins inédits," *Magasin pittoresque* 23, no. 48 (December 1855): 382.

11. Dumas, 5:73.

12. Henry Dérieux, "Joseph Guichard, peintre lyonnais (1806–1880)," *Gazette des Beaux-Arts,* 5th ser., 5 (March 1922): 183. I wish to thank Valérie Durey, Chargée de la Documentation at the Lyon Musée des Beaux-Arts, for drawing my attention to this informative article on Guichard.

13. "Exposition au Louvre (Quatrième article) Histoire," *Journal des Artistes* 1, no. 12 (March 24, 1833): 198.

14. Dérieux, 183–84.

15. The tenebroso effects and distinctive diagonal hatching of the exceptional drawing in Paris indicate that it probably dates from the same year as the diary sketch, 1833. The donation number 8667, located in the lower right-hand corner of the drawing, indicates that it was one of the works given to the Bibliothèque nationale de France June 6, 1893, on behalf of Armand Grandville by his sole legatee, Albert Boidin.

16. Menut and Forest may have known each other before they became acquainted with Grandville. According to Bénézit, both were students of Camille Roqueplan. Menut was also a student of Paul Delaroche, one of the artists with whom Lemétheyer habitually surrounded himself at the Opéra-Comique where Grandville had made his acquaintance. As noted in the biography, Delaroche lived in the house next door to Grandville, and the two artists saw each other quite frequently during their younger days. Although we do not know how Grandville came into contact with his two artistic collaborators, it is possible that he met Menut through Delaroche and Forest through Menut. Or perhaps he met them through Aubert who had been publishing works by both men since before the Revolution of 1830.

17. It is difficult to give an exact date for *Contredanse monarchique,* which is not registered in the dépôt légal or mentioned in the *Bibliographie de la France.* But it was probably published during the week previous to May 2, 1833, when its description appeared in *La Caricature.*

18. Judging from the facts of publication on lithographs for the *Association mensuelle,* Becquet during the first part of 1833 had moved his establishment from 9, rue Childebert (today that portion of rue Bonaparte between rue Jacob and Saint-Germain-des-Près) to first number 9 and then to number 6 of the nearby rue de Fürstenberg. Grandville would have been intimately acquainted with the lithographic presses of Becquet, who had printed nearly all the plates for *La Caricature* since mid-March 1832, and many of those for the *Association mensuelle* since its inception in August of the same year. In addition to *Elle prétend qu'elle n'est pas prostituée,* Becquet printed all three plates of the *Règne animal* series (registered with the dépôt légal April 17, May 8 and May 22, 1833), which Grandville was working on at the time. As for the location of Becquet's printing house, it might be noted that in 1857, Delacroix established his residence and studio at 6, rue de Fürstenberg, where he remained until his death in 1863. The premises now house the musée Eugène Delacroix.

19. A native of Bayonne who followed an artistic career in Paris, Julien appears to have been Grandville's backup collaborator. From at least August 1832, Julien helped Grandville produce plates for *La Caricature* almost everytime that Forest did not. Their latest collaborative effort for the journal had been plate 258, *Messieurs, l'auteur de la pièce que nous avons eu l'honneur de jouer devant vous désire garder l'anonyme* (Gentlemen, the author of the play which we have had the honor of presenting to you desires to remain anonymous), which appeared in the March 21, 1833, issue. In addition, Julien had recently worked with Grandville on the February 1833 plate of the *Association mensuelle, Grenier d'abondance* (The granary of abundance); he would also assist Grandville with the *Association*'s September 1833 lithograph, *Visite domiciliaire* (House visit; fig. 90). Julien rarely collaborated with Grandville on work for *Le Charivari.* That it was he and not Forest who helped with *Elle prétend qu'elle n'est pas prostituée* was probably due to the fact that the latter was already occupied by the two major ongoing projects with Grandville previously mentioned: the series of animal-headed humans published in *Le Charivari* between February and June 1833 and the *Règne animal* series published in *La Caricature* between April 18 and May 23, 1833. Grandville mentions Julien in his May 2, 1833, diary entry (cat. no. 28).

20. It would be erroneous to assume from this single notation that 150 francs was the usual amount paid to Grandville for the equivalent of two single-plate lithographs published in *La Caricature.* Too many questions are left unanswered: Was the money in payment for one or more caricatural commissions? Was it in fact for work published in *La Caricature?* Did the

amount include Forest's share in the collaborative project(s)? On the other hand, 150 francs does not appear to be excessive remuneration for a double-plate print by France's most popular opposition caricaturist, especially when one considers that annual expenses of La Maison Aubert at the time were running in excess of 40,000 francs (Cuno, 23). It should be added that ten years later Daumier will agree to having his wages reduced to forty francs for each lithograph published in *Le Charivari* (Renonciat, 147).

21. Cuno, 23, 104–5. There is every indication that Aubert was not particularly adept when it came to financial matters. Cuno relates that it was as a result of "ruinous financial speculations" that Aubert had to sell his notaryship at Chalon-sur-Saône. At Philipon's suggestion, Aubert moved his family to Paris where his brother-in-law made him a business partner in the print shop venture that would become known as La Maison Aubert. However, Cuno also notes that Philipon's half sister, Marie, and Aubert "separated and formalized a division of property just before moving to Paris," and adds, "although Gabriel Aubert gave his name to the shop, all legal documents related to it were signed by . . . Marie Philipon, 'épouse separée quant-aux-biens de M. Gabriel Aubert,' and witnessed by Philipon." Thus, there were not just two but three business partners involved in the La Maison Aubert enterprise: Philipon, Aubert, and Marie Philipon Aubert. This amicable arrangement no doubt resulted from a universal recognition of Aubert's limited financial acumen. Judging from Grandville's diary entries, we may assume that there was also a mutual understanding that Marie supervise the monetary aspects of the operation. Much of the above information can also be found published in Cuno's article, "Charles Philipon, La Maison Aubert, and the Business of Caricature in Paris, 1829–41," *Art Journal* 43, no. 4 (Winter 1983): 347–54.

22. Pierre Cabanne, *Les Bustes des parlementaires par Honoré Daumier* (Lausanne: Edita, 1980), 10.

23. Nancy, 262–67.

24. The nature and extent of this artistic collaboration remain to be clarified. According to Delteil, the two artists worked together on only one lithograph for *La Caricature, Le médecin du Duc de Leuchtemberg,* plate 483 in the paper's April 16, 1835, issue (Delteil, 113). But they also appear to have collaborated on *Soufflez, soufflez, vous ne l'éteindrez jamais,* plate 375 for the issue of April 3, 1834.

25. The lithograph was registered with the dépôt légal on December 16, 1831 and not December 15 as Delteil would lead us to believe (Delteil, 34). Judging from rare impressions of its first state, which carries the inscription, "La Caricature (Journal)," the print originally was intended for that publication. However, according to a commentary by Philipon in the December 29, 1831, issue of *La Caricature,* the lithograph did not appear within the journal's pages because of its "faiblesse d'exécution," or weak execution ("16e, 17e et 18e saisies pratiquées chez M. Aubert"). This excuse was patently false and probably fooled no one familiar with Philipon. It seems more likely that the real reason for deciding at the last minute not to publish *Gargantua* in *La Caricature* was because Philipon knew the print would attract the attention of the authorities and did not want to risk yet another seizure of the paper.

26. Roger Passeron, *Daumier,* trans. Helga Harrison (Secaucus, NJ: Poplar Books, ca. 1981), 62. The quotation is from the official account of the trial, published in the February 23, 1832, issue of the *Gazette des Tribunaux,* which Passeron cites in full.

27. Louis Prouvost, "Chronologie: Autour de Daumier—1830–1835," in *Cahiers,* 106–7. The prison of Sainte-Pélagie took its name from the former convent for wayward women in which it was housed. Conditions within its humid walls were particularly insalubrious (Hillairet, 1:354–55). As Cuno notes on page 115, Pinel was a specialist in nerve and mental disorders who offered his progressive *maison de santé,* or sanatorium, to political prisoners at Sainte-Pélagie when their health became a critical problem. Advertisements for and descriptions of Pinel's sanatorium, which boasted extensive gardens reaching to the Champs-Elysées, appeared in *La Caricature* on January 24 and August 8, 1833, and in *Le Charivari* on July 23, 1833, and March 19, 1835.

28. Charton, 49; Nollet, 6–7.

29. Charton, 50.

30. The Musée Lorrain possesses the small (347 × 253 mm) oil of the soldier as well as a life-size (545 × 450 mm) self-portrait of the artist from around 1831 and a small (204 × 266 mm) landscape depicting a scene just outside Nancy along the Meurthe River, *Le pont de Malzéville et le Petit Jéricho* (The bridge at Malzéville and the Little Jericho), which has been given a date of around 1830. A large (880 mm × 1 m 10 mm) still life, signed and dated 1836, formerly in the collection of Pierre Parisot, belongs to the Nancy Musée des Beaux-Arts. This painting is probably the still life that was shown at the 1837 exhibition held by the Société des Amis des Arts in Nancy. Another large work (70 × 120 cm), which portrays a caricatured beau monde in the Tuileries Gardens and stylistically related to two caricatures of Parisian society published in the December 9 and 23, 1838, issues of *La Caricature provisoire,* is in a private collection in Paris. These paintings are reproduced in Renonciat, 121, 141, 143, 146, and 267.

31. The secondary role relegated to the giraffe in this group of drawings accurately reflects her fleeting popularity. Balzac had already observed in his 1830 *La Silhouette* article, "Etudes de philosophie morale sur les habitans du Jardin des Plantes," that only three years after her arrival at the Jardin des Plantes, the giraffe was no longer a novelty and had been reduced to

the status of a minor curiosity: "aujourd'hui on la dédaigne, on l'oublie; elle n'est plus visitée que par le provincial arriéré, la bonne d'enfans désoeuvrée, et le Jean-Jean simple et naïf" (today she is slighted, she is forgotten; she is no longer visited except by the backward provincial, the idle nanny, and the half-witted and naive simple Simon). But as this drawing testifies, the exotic animal could still inspire Grandville. Indeed, an entire chapter of *Scènes de la vie privée et publique des animaux*, "Tablettes de la girafe du Jardin des Plantes" (Tablets of the Giraffe of the Jardin des Plantes), will be dedicated to her. For this short story by Charles Nodier, Grandville produced a full-page illustration of the giraffe that carries the caption, "Lorsqu'on a vu l'homme d'un peu près, on est bien fière d'être Girafe" (Once you have seen man up close, you are quite proud to be a giraffe).

32. Clogenson, 273.

33. Robert Justin Goldstein, *Censorship of Political Caricature in Nineteenth-Century France* (Kent, OH: Kent State University Press, 1989), 125.

34. Cuno documents the control Philipon exercised over both his artists and his publications (120). In particular, he cites Thureau-Dangin's assessment of Philipon's overarching role:

> Par lui-même il dessinait peu, mais il savait grouper, lancer, échauffer les artistes qu'il employait, leur inoculait son fiel et son audace, leur fournissait des idées, des légendes, bravait les procès et les condamnations, et devenait ainsi, lui obscur, l'un des plus dangereux adversaires de la royauté nouvelle, l'empêchant d'acquérir ce prestige, cette "respectabilité", sans lesquels elle ne pouvait vraiment se fonder. (1:576)
>
> [He did little drawing himself, but he knew how to assemble, launch, fire up the artists whom he employed, he inoculated them with his venom and his boldness, he provided them with ideas, captions, he braved the lawsuits and the jail sentences, and thus he, obscure, became one of the most dangerous adversaries of the new royalty, preventing it from acquiring that prestige, that "respectability" without which it could not truly establish itself.]

35. Goldstein, 133; Cuno, 115.

36. Charles Ledré, *La Presse à l'assaut de la monarchie, 1815–1848* (Paris: Colin, 1960), 129.

37. Clogenson, 273.

38. Charles Philipon, "Grandville et les argousins de la police," *La Caricature*, October 13, 1831, 395–96.

39. I have given a more detailed account of this incident and the circumstances surrounding the production of *Oh! les vilaines mouches!!* in: "Grandville: Opposition Caricature and Political Harassment," *Print Collector's Newsletter* 14, no. 6 (January–February 1984): 197–201. Preliminary studies for the print may be found reproduced in Helena Domaszewska, "Zbiór Rysunków Grandville'a w Muzeum Narodowym w Warszawie" (The Drawings of Grandville in the National Museum of Warsaw), *Rocznik Muzeum Narodowego w Warszawie* 19 (1975), 561, and in Renonciat, 95.

40. The drawing is in a private collection.

41. Bechtel, plate 8 and commentary.

42. The drawing displays all the characteristics of the tenebroso style found in the drawings from the April-May 1833 diary: delicately penned lines, diagonal crosshatching, and the use of ink wash in parts of the background shading and around the figure's contours. This last gives the figure a distinctive halolike glow in its upper portion and causes the lower portion to blend into the shadowy background.

43. The date of April 15 in the lithograph's title is erroneous (see Prouvost in *Cahiers*, 108). A succinct account of the events leading up to the Rue Transnonain massacre is provided by Bechtel, 33–34.

44. Goldstein, 149, 154.

45. Louis-Gabriel Montigny, *Le Provincial à Paris, esquisses des moeurs parisiennes* (Paris: Chez Ladvocat, 1825), 1:86–88.

46. "J.-J. Grandville. Dessins inédits," *Magasin pittoresque* 23, no. 48 (December 1855): 382.

47. Charton, 50.

48. Dumas, 5:72.

49. Jean Adhémar and Jacques Lethève, *Inventaire du fonds français après 1800* (Paris: Bibliothèque nationale, 1955), 9:326.

50. This masthead, representing the staff of *Le Charivari*, first appeared in the issues from November 24–30, 1833, but without the accompanying labels. These were only added when the masthead made its brief reappearance in *Le Charivari* on January 19 and 20, 1834. In addition to Forest it depicts Julien, Michel Bouquet (1807–90), Aubert, Philipon, Daumier, Desperet, Traviès, and Grandville himself. Long attributed to Daumier, the masthead has proven to be by Grandville, thanks to a preparatory drawing in the collection of the Nancy Musée des Beaux-Arts (Nancy, cat. no. 202).

51. See Philippe Sorel, *Dantan jeune, caricatures et portraits de la société romantique* (Paris: Paris-Musée, 1989), 159. Grandville's relationship with Dantan jeune is explored in cat. no. 32.

52. For an iconographical analysis of this and the other plates in the *Règne animal* series, see Nancy, 262–65.

53. The full title of this pen lithograph is *Ceci, mesdames, vous représente l'un des plus grands hommes de l'époque, comme il vous est facultatif de s'en apercevoir, cet être me parait prédestiné à devenir un excellent mari, car il est du bois dont on les fait.—"Mais, me direz-vous, toi qui nous vantes ainsi ta marchandise, tu sais pourtant que nous n'aimons pas les gens de son pays, à cause de leur humeur belliqueuse, de leur esprit léger et de l'excessive amabilité de leur caractère"—A quoi je me permettrai de répondre: "Eh bien! raison de plus! vous pouvez prendre celui-là en toute assurance; je vous le donne à l'épreuve il n'a absolument rien de commun avec les autres naturels de sa contrée."* (This, my ladies, shows you one of the greatest men of the age, as you are granted the privilege of noticing, this creature appears to me predestined to become an excellent husband, for he is of the wood of which they are made.—"But, you will say to me, you who speak so highly to us of your merchandise, you know however that we don't like the people of his country because of their bellicose disposition, their frivolous spirit, and the excessive amiability of their character"—To which I will allow myself to reply: "Well! all the more reason! you can take that one there in full confidence; I give him to you as proof he has absolutely nothing in common with the other habitants of his country"). Even though the print is not signed and does not figure in any oeuvre catalog of the artist, it possesses the characteristic mannerisms of Grandville's style: meticulously detailed rendering of costumes, exaggerated facial expressions, and linear execution, including the diagonally crosshatched shadows characteristic of his work from 1833 (the treatment of the shadows is nearly identical with that in the *Règne animal* suite). That Forest was the lithographic interpreter is more difficult to demonstrate. Suffice it to say that the hard-edged crispness of the print's lines is identical to that found in *Contredanse monarchique,* the April 1833 plate of the *Association mensuelle* produced by Grandville and Forest around this same time. Moreover, Forest apparently continued to be Grandville's regular collaborator up until *Le Jeu de bague nuptial* (The wedding ring game) was published as plate 284 in the June 20 issue of *La Caricature.* The subject of both *Le Jeu de bague nuptial* and *Ceci, mesdames* revolves around the search for an appropriate spouse for Louis-Philippe's eldest son and heir to the throne, Ferdinand, duc d'Orléans. In the latter composition, Talleyrand, ambassador to England and key formulator of Louis-Philippe's foreign policy, is represented as a salesman hawking his dubious wares (the young duke in question) in front of assembled eligible young ladies.

54. Dumas, 5:72. Throughout his *Mémoires* Dumas consistently leaves out the "d" when spelling Grandville's name.

55. Dumas has led scholars to believe that his costume ball took place during carnival (5:54) in 1832 (5:76). However, documentary evidence points to the date of Saturday, March 30, 1833, or the day before Palm Sunday in the following year. As Josserand points out, there exists a lithographed invitation postmarked March 14, 1833, that asks guests to spend the evening of "samedi 30 mars" (Saturday, March 30) with "M. Alex. Dumas" (Mr. Alex. Dumas) and stipulates: "Le travestissement est de rigueur" (Disguise is obligatory; 5:71n1). Moreover, a description of the decorated rooms and the ball, itself, appeared in *L'Artiste* during the first week of April 1833 (see the note that follows).

56. "Bal costumé de M. Alexandre Dumas," *L'Artiste* 5, 10th livraison (April 1833): 119–21. On page 120 we read:

> A la seconde salle, la peinture comique, la caricature spirituelle: M. Granville [*sic*] a fait les bustes des principaux artistes à la manière de Dantan; M. Forez [*sic*], *la Danse de l'Ours et le Pacha;* M. Geniols [*sic*], *l'Auberge des Adrets;* M. Jadin, *un orchestre bouffon.*

> [In the second room, comic painting, witty caricature: Mr. Grandville executed busts of the principal artists in the manner of Dantan; Mr. Forest, *The dance of the bear and the pasha;* Mr. Geniole, *l'Auberge des Adrets* [see cat. no. 23 for this famous play that Grandville will attend on April 27]; Mr. Jadin, a buffoon orchestra.)

57. Dumas, 5:55, 59. Dumas's description of what Grandville painted contrasts with that found in *L'Artiste* (see previous note) where the "buffoon orchestra" is attributed to Jadin. Given Dumas's somewhat cavalier attitude toward history (consult "Défauts et valeur des Mémoires" in Dumas, 1:13ff.) and the fact that his account of the ball was written some twenty years after it had taken place, one is tempted to side with *L'Artiste* on the question of accuracy. But then the author of the *L'Artiste* article himself was not exactly a paragon of accurate reporting, especially when it came to the spelling of artists' names. Should the "buffoon orchestra" have been done by Grandville, it probably resembled his masthead for *Le Charivari,* which was first published eight months later on November 24, 1833 (fig. 71).

58. Ibid., 76.

59. Clogenson, 252.

60. Dumas, 5:76.

61. According to the key to *Le Charivari Monstre*'s iconography, which appeared in the August 15 issue of *Le Charivari,* the detail in figure 78 "représente, sous un double type, les traits les plus saillans de la littérature contemporaine" (depicts, by way of a double model, the most salient characteristics of contemporary literature). The "gros joufflu d'homme de génie" (big chubby man of genius) on the left "tient à la fois du Balzac, du Janin, du Sue et du Grand-Turc" (is based upon simul-

taneously Balzac, Janin, Sue and the emperor of the Turks). However, from all appearances the composite portrait also includes a large ingredient of *Le Charivari*'s one-time editor, Desnoyers. For a discussion of the fiery figure on the right, inspired in large part by Victor Hugo, see cat. no. 62. Plate 3 of *Grande course au clocher académique* was registered with the dépôt légal February 4, 1840, and published in the resurrected *La Caricature* on February 16, 1840 (plates 1 and 2 of the series, registered respectively with the dépôt légal on November 28 and December 18, 1839, appeared in the journal's December 15 and 29, 1839 issues). Modified versions of the three double-plate *Grande course au clocher académique* prints appeared in *Le Charivari* on February 19, 20, and 22, 1844: several of the heads, including that of Desnoyers, were replaced by those of other academic aspirants.

62. *Le Sylphe, journal des salons; Le Lutin, écho des salons;* and *Trilby, album des salons,* which first appeared on June 1, 2, and 3, 1829, were in reality "Un seul et même journal sous l'apparence de trois journaux différents, paraissant deux fois par semaine chacun, de façon à échapper au fisc" (One and the same journal in the guise of three different journals, each appearing twice a week, so as to deceive the Internal Revenue Service; Eugène Hatin, *Bibliographie historique et critique de la presse périodique française* [Paris: Firmin-Didot frères, fils et cie, 1866], 368). Desnoyers cleverly indicated that they were related by having all three printed on distinctive pink octavo format paper.

63. It should be added that in 1835, the March 17, 20, 21, 27, and April 8 and 12 issues of *Le Charivari* contain advertisements for *La Caricature* which bill it as a "Journal politique, Dirigé par MM. Ch. Philipon, L. Desnoyers et Grandville" (Political Journal, Edited by Messrs. Charles Philipon, Louis Desnoyers and Grandville). To what extent this claim is truthful in the case of Grandville remains to be determined. The advertisements nevertheless indicate the personalities with whom the publication was most closely identified during its final year.

64. Cuno, 122.

65. A biographical outline of Desnoyers may be found in the *Dictionnaire de biographie française* (Paris: Librairie Letouzey et Ané, 1965), 10, cols. 1493–94. For more detailed accounts of his life and work, see Eugène de Mirecourt, *Louis Desnoyers* (Paris: G. Havard, 1855) and Dr. Georges Collet, *Le Bressan Louis Desnoyers* (Vincennes: Impr. Rosay, 1938).

66. Ségolène Le Men, "De Jean-Paul Choppart à Struwwelpeter: L'Invention de l'enfant terrible dans le livre illustré," *Revue des Sciences Humaines* 99, no. 225 (January–March 1992): 45–59.

67. In the detail of plate 3 reproduced in fig. 80 can be read inscribed on the tree trunks next to Desnoyers's head the names of other publications with which he was affiliated: *Le Fou, Journal des salons, Figaro, Le Corsaire, Le National, Journal du peuple, Paris révolutionnaire,* and *Béotiens de Paris.*

68. The commentary for this first plate of the *Règne animal* suite was signed "L. Derv." Although the commentaries for the subsequent two plates are unsigned, there is every reason to believe that they were also written by Desnoyers.

69. It should be pointed out that the portraits of Forest and Grandville in plates 2 and 3 of *Règne animal* complement the one of *La Caricature*'s fool in plate 1 (fig. 73).

70. Dumas, 5:86; "Bal costumé de M. Alexandre Dumas," *L'Artiste* (April 1833): 120.

71. Between 1835 and 1847, twenty of Grandville's drawings were reproduced as wood engravings in the *Musée des familles* (see Renonciat, 295, for their complete list). Forest is named as one of the journal's contributing artists in its index for the years 1834–53. Although he does not appear as a contributing artist in this same index, Menut nonetheless provided the portrait of Baron Taylor on page 184 of the publication's March 1843 issue. Both Desnoyers and Dumas are listed as members of the periodical's staff in its first issue even though nothing by Desnoyers was ever published within its pages. Dumas, on the other hand, contributed regularly to the *Musée des familles* beginning in 1834.

72. Beginning in July 1839, a drawing by Grandville, engraved on wood by Verdeil, was used in the title of the *Gazette des enfans.* In the magazine's prospectus, Menut is mentioned as being one of its contributing artists, and the names of Desnoyers and Dumas head the list labeled "Pour la rédaction littéraire" (Literary editorial staff).

73. Frédérick Lemaître, *Souvenirs de Frédérick Lemaître, publiés par son fils* (Paris: Paul Ollendorff, 1880), 85.

74. Thureau-Dangin, 1:381.

75. Ibid., 1:382.

76. Delteil 95 and 97. The two lithographs were *Nous sommes tous d'honnêtes gens, embrassons-nous et que ça finisse* (We are all honest people, let's embrace and be done with it) and *Petits! petits! petits! . . . venez! venez! venez! . . . venez donc Dindons!* (Little ones! little ones! little ones! . . . come! come! come! . . . come then little turkeys!), plates 439 and 442 of *La Caricature,* which appeared in the November 13 and 27, 1834, issues.

77. There is a persistent tone of homesickness in the numerous letters Grandville writes to his family. He will even reproach family members if there occurs a lapse in their correspondence. In 1833, Nancy might just as well have been at the other end of the world. Before a railroad link was established between the Lorrain capital and Paris in 1849, travel between the two cities was unpleasant at best, requiring a journey over bumpy and dusty roads in a crowded and uncomfortable

public stagecoach. Grandville appropriately enough illustrates a journey with the Nancy diligence in *Petites misères de la vie humaine* on page 137.

78. Janet Seligman, *Figures of Fun: The Caricature-Statuettes of Jean-Pierre Dantan* (London: Oxford University Press, 1957), 41–42.

79. Playing on its titled name, Grandville used the "grand duke" owl as a stock symbol of reactionary aristocratic royalists in his caricature program. It appears twice in *Les Métamorphoses du jour:* a "grand duke" and his bat/wife are shown in front of their medieval château in the second state of plate 12, *Les lumières leur font mal* (Lights bother them) and Louis-Philippe's eldest son, Ferdinand, duc de Chartres (future duc d'Orléans), is represented as another "grand duke" in the process of an amorous conquest in plate 42, *Monseigneur je vous offre mes hommages ainsi que ma fille*" (Your Grace, I offer you my respects as well as my daughter; for a full description of this *métamorphose,* see Blanc, 284). Grandville will again use it in *Scènes de la vie privée et publique des animaux.* A "grand duke" adorned with royal fleurs-de-lis appears in the first volume at the bottom of page 136 as an illustration to P.-J. Stahl's short story, "Les Aventures d'un Papillon" (The adventures of a butterfly). And a grand ducal couple, once more covered with fleurs-de-lis, appears in the full page plate, *Madame la Duchesse chante un nocturne avec Monsieur le Duc, et dans ces moments-là, elle n'entend pas qu'on la dérange* (Madam the duchess sings a nocturne with mister the duke, and in moments like these she does not wish to be disturbed; the finished drawing for this wood engraving is reproduced in Nancy, cat. no. 261), which illustrates another short story by P.-J. Stahl in the same volume, "Souvenirs d'une vieille Corneille" (Memories of an old crow). P.-J. Stahl was the nom de plume of the book's publisher, Pierre-Jules Hetzel.

80. See also the drawing in Nancy, cat. no. 137. Grandville will dedicate two full-page illustrations to the Tuileries Gardens in *Scènes de la vie privée et publique des animaux: Le beau monde aux Tuileries* (The beau monde at the Tuileries) for P.-J. Stahl's short story, "Histoire d'un Lièvre" (Story of a hare; the finished drawing for this wood engraving is reproduced in Nancy, cat. no. 256) and *Vive, s'écriaient-elles, le jardin des Tuileries* (Long live the Tuileries gardens, they cried) for "Pérégrination mémorable du doyen des Crapauds" (Memorable peregrination of the oldest toad) by L'Héritier de l'Ain. However, perhaps his most remarkable evocation of the Tuileries promenade is to be found in an unfinished oil painting from a private Parisian collection (reproduced in Renonciat, 146). Although its content is pure Grandvillian social satire, its composition of the Parisian beau monde seated under the trees of a summer's afternoon uncannily anticipates Manet's *Music in the Tuileries* of 1862 (London, National Gallery).

81. Montigny, 1:89.

82. Ibid., 87. Named after the main arteries running through them, these Parisian districts reflect the three main stratifications of nineteenth-century French society: the St.-Antoine quarter was largely inhabited by the working class, the Chaussée-d'Antin by bourgeois nouveaux riches, and the faubourg St.-Germain by the aristocracy.

83. Ibid., 85.

84. Ibid., 89.

85. "Partie non officielle, Intérieur," *Le Moniteur universel,* May 2, 1833, 1220.

86. This drawing might profitably be compared with *Le Bouquet,* plate 56 of *La Caricature,* published two years earlier on May 12, 1831. The composition of a crowd in the foreground admiring fireworks is similar. However, in the lithograph the fireworks are in the middle ground as opposed to the background and brightly illuminate the spectators.

87. Like Grandville, Paul became a student of Mansion, but unlike him continued to pursue a career as a miniaturist, exhibiting portraits at the Salon between 1824 and 1846, and obtaining medals in 1833 and 1846. A portrait painter as well as a miniaturist, Charles entered the École des Beaux-Arts in 1828, and studied under Hersent and Delaroche. He exhibited mostly portraits at the Salon between 1831 and 1875, earning a third-class medal in 1840 and a second-class medal in 1844. For these and other details on the Gomien brothers, see Bénézit, 5:100.

88. The four lithographs and the dates of their appearance are *Scènes familières: Ma destitution* (Domestic scenes: My dismissal; July 5), *Scènes familières: On n'est pas plus aimabe* [*sic*] (Domestic scenes: There isn't anyone more pleasant; August 5), *Monsieur d' la Rocambole, mon honorable ami* (Mister of the Spanish garlic, my honorable friend; September 9), *Prolétaire* (Proletarian; September 16).

89. Fashion plates attest to the popularity of dressing gowns for men during the early 1830s. See for example "15 9bre 1832 Costumes Parisiens (3031)" in the Maciat collection (Maciet 214, vol. 12, Modes 1832) at the Bibliothèque des arts décoratifs in Paris. The description of the dressing gown and bonnet portrayed reads, "Robe de chambre en velours doublée de satin—Toque de velours" (Velvet dressing gown lined in satin—Velvet bonnet).

90. Seligman, 42.

91. According to Françoise Tetart-Vittu, a research assistant at the Musée de la Mode et du Costume, prices for dressing gowns and cashmere shawls varied widely. Nevertheless, an idea of just how expensive a cashmere shawl could be can be

found in the listing of prizes for the Monville lottery, published in the January 20, 1846, issue of *Le Corsaire-Satan:* "Une écharpe en cachemire. 500 fr." (A cashmere shawl. 500 francs). It will be recalled that in 1840 the annual expenses for an average skilled worker's entire family in Paris was only approximately twice this amount, or 950 francs.

92. Dumas, 5:76.

93. Clogenson, 275.

94. The Guichardet in question is most likely Jean-Francis Guichardet (1804?–61). A fixture of the Bohemian literary set, he would play an important editorial role in the publication of Curmer's *Français peints par eux-mêmes* and *Le Prisme* (The Prism), which Grandville helped to illustrate at the beginning of the 1840s.

95. For this and other information on Dantan jeune, see Janet Seligman, *Figures of Fun: The Caricature-Statuettes of Jean-Pierre Dantan* (London: Oxford University Press, 1957) and Philippe Sorel, *Dantan jeune, caricatures et portraits de la société romantique* (Paris: Paris-Musée, 1989).

96. Given Grandville's close ties with the Parisian caricatural world, it seems more than likely that he would have been acquainted with Dantan jeune's sculptural caricatures when they first made their appearance. The date of May 6, 1833 merely establishes a documented terminus ad quem. That this is indeed the case is indicated by the previously cited April 1833 *L'Artiste* article, according to which Grandville was inspired by Dantan's work when producing his decorations for Dumas's famous ball of March 30, 1833, some five weeks earlier: "Mr. Grandville executed busts of the principal artists in the manner of Dantan."

97. Ramelet was part of Philipon's stable of lithographers. For example, he translated into lithographs a series of drawings done by Daumier while the latter was in prison. Published as a series entitled *L'imagination* (The imagination), they began to appear in *Le Charivari* on January 14, 1833. A painter of landscapes and genre scenes, Ramelet exhibited at the Salon from 1834 to 1847.

98. On the cover, Grandville has represented a bust of himself at the far left opposite Dantan jeune's pockmarked self-portrait to which he has added a crown of miniature portrait busts. The album appeared in two installments, both of which included the cover. Each sheet of the album contained two numbered lithographs. The first installment consisted of twelve lithographs on six sheets. Grandville contributed No. 1 Paganini, No. 2 Collinet, No. 3 Dantan jeune, No. 4 Bertini, No. 5 Levasseur, No. 6 Nourrit, No. 7 Martin, and No. 8 Ponchard (these were the eight registered with the dépôt légal December 16, 1833); Lepeudry contributed No. 9 V. Hugo, No. 10 A. Dumas, No. 11 Lablache, and No. 12 Santini. The second installment consisted of eight lithographs on four sheets. Ramelet contributed No. 13 Rossini, No. 14 Hitz, No. 15 Ciceri, and No. 16 Horace Vernet; Grandville contributed No. 17 Nathan Rothschild, No. 18 Lord Sefton, No. 19 Wellington, and No. 20 Lord Brougham. I wish to thank Sam Clapp for his help in identifying the subjects in the second installment.

99. At first glance, one might suppose that Grandville has recorded the visit "de Mr Guiaud pere" and "de fils d'Auguste" (of the son of Auguste). However, given his often less than perfect syntax, it is more likely that he has recorded the visit "de Mr Guiaud pere," "de [Guiaud] fils" and "d'Auguste." In the letter that served as a preface to the bound drawings for the *Fables de La Fontaine* at the Nancy Bibliothèque municipale, Grandville refers to Desperet as "Auguste Desp," which seems to indicate a preference for calling his collaborator by his first name.

100. Several transport services, or *messageries,* were to be found in the vicinity of the Palais-Royal: the messageries Vincent et Caillard in the rue du Bouloi, the Messageries générales in the rue Grenelle-Saint-Honoré (today, rue Jean-Jacques Rousseau), and the Messageries royales in the rue Notre-Dame-des-Victoires (Hillairet 1:227, 674–75; 2:189).

101. That Grandville did, indeed, wear a "bonnet de velours" while working is documented on page 356 of the November 1855 *Magasin pittoresque* article, "J.-J. Grandville: Dessins inédits."

Diary of 1834

Documentation for the existence of fragments from the 1834 diary is meager. Only one, 1/2, carries a date of 1834 and that has been written, as though after the fact, in pencil on a sheet of pen and ink drawings. One other fragment appears to be related stylistically to it. Both display the tenebroso effects found in the drawings from the 1833 diary, but the penmanship seems to be somewhat more delicate, and Grandville's relationship to the images more detached. Apart from these slight differences, they could just as well date from 1833. That these two small fragments were indeed originally part of the 1834 diary remains a matter of conjecture.

36. 1/2 recto

1834

1834
34 × 82
Pencil, pen and brown ink

The subject of the drawing to the left is similar to that from 1833 found in cat. no. 22. A fashionably dressed woman half kneels on a tilted chair used as a prie-dieu as she reads from a prayer book in a church. This time, however, she is alone and observed from a distance. Like the praying women in cat. no. 2 (recto), she has been drawn in strict profile with the result that her silhouette is almost solely that of her garments, her face being hidden by the brim of her hat. Even though depersonalized and abstracted, she presents a more convincing image of genuine piety than the coquettish young woman from the year before.

The drawing to the right depicts a woman in her apron seated at a kitchen table next to a bowl. Above her head is a shelf on which are displayed plates and what are presumably other kitchen utensils. If the drawing is indeed from 1834, as the penciled date would have us believe, the woman may be the Grandville household's maid, Mlle Rosalie ("Rose") Méline, frequently mentioned in Grandville's correspondence with his family after his marriage.

1/2 verso

. . . *Blanhisseur*
(...launderer)

1834
34 × 82
Pen and brown ink

The only annotation on the verso of this fragment is an incomplete and incorrectly spelled reference to a launderer.

37. 5/3 recto

1834(?)
21 × 33
Pen and black ink

The drawing on this postage-stamp-sized fragment depicts two horsemen whose profile silhouettes present a contrast. While the one sits erect on a white horse, the other leans forward on the back of a black horse. Instead of brown ink, Grandville has uncustomarily used black ink for the execution of this tiny vignette.

5/3 verso

[fragment of writing]

1834(?)
21 × 33
Pen and brown ink

1836 Sketchbook

The Missouri Album contains seven sheets of the same dimensions (105 × 175–77 mm) and same weight that appear to have belonged at one point to the same sketchbook. Most of the drawings on the sheets are projects for children's publications: a whimsical alphabet and illustrations for the legend of Saint Nicholas and "Little Red Riding Hood." Four of the seven studies for "Little Red Riding Hood" are directly related to the wood-engraved illustrations for Perrault's fairy tale found in the initial 1836 installment of *Le Livre des enfants* by Elise Voïart and Amable Tastu, which was first announced in the December 3, 1836, issue of the *Bibliographie de la France* (subsequent installments of *Le Livre des enfants* contained Grandville's illustrations to three other Perrault fairy tales, "Tom Thumb," "Puss in Boots," and "Bluebeard").[1] As a result, it is reasonable to assume that these studies and the other drawings on the seven same-sized sheets all date from around 1836 and were once part of a sketchbook from that year.

The 1836 Sketchbook provides further evidence that after his unhappy career as a political caricaturist, and in the wake of the 1835 September Laws, Grandville decided to explore the possibility of becoming an illustrator of works for children (we have already seen in cat. nos. 20 and 21 that he provided the original images of Desnoyers's Jean-Paul Choppart for the *Journal des enfans* in 1832 and 1833). This decision would have been influenced not only by his natural affection and respect for children, but also by the burgeoning commerce in children's books.

Literacy increased dramatically among the French populace during the Romantic era. As a result, there was an equally dramatic increase in demand for literature aimed specifically at children, the "nouveaux lecteurs," or "new readers."[2] Aubert quickly grasped the business potential of this phenomenon.[3] In fact, the first publication of La Maison Aubert was the *Abécédaire en action* (Primer in action), which was registered with the dépôt légal on December 26, 1829, only eleven days after the founding of the print shop December 15, 1829.[4] However, just as Grandville's interest in children faded with the political upheavals of the Revolution of 1830, so did that of La Maison Aubert. Both the artist and his future publisher dedicated their energies to political caricature. After the reestablishment of press censorship with the September Laws of 1835, Grandville and Aubert were forced to focus their attention elsewhere. Aubert switched to social caricature and to the lucrative trade in children's literature. Grandville, who had begun his career as a social commentator (e.g., *Les Métamorphoses du jour*) and had already provided illustrations for the *Journal des enfans* in 1832 and 1833, naturally followed suit.

The number of works that La Maison Aubert created solely for children was significant. As Ségolène Le Men mentions in her important study on abecedaries, or primers, Aubert quickly developed an important catalog of works for children.[5] And it comes as no surprise that the artists who he depended on for these publications rich in images were the very same ones who, like Grandville, only shortly before had been producing scathing caricatures against the regime of Louis-Philippe.

Aubert's primers were particularly popular. In his *avis de l'éditeur* (publisher's note) for the *Alphabet illustré par E. Forest* (Illustrated alphabet by E. Forest) of 1838, he expresses pride in their success and lists the artists who produced them:

> Lorsque j'eus l'idée d'employer le talent des plus habiles lithographes à l'exécution des Alphabets, il n'existait encore dans le commerce de la lithographie que des Abécédaires en bandes, mal imprimés, très

mal dessinés, et coloriés plus mal encore. Les miens, dus au crayon de MM. Bouchot, Daumier, Desperet, Forest, Lassalle et Traviès, obtinrent un succès inoui. Tout le monde connaît à présent ces piquants personnages grotesques, ces costumes, ces sujets militaires, et autres, qui réussissent si bien à fixer dans la mémoire des enfants le souvenir des lettres et des mots. J'ai donc amené une petite révolution dans ce genre d'ouvrages.

[When I had the idea of employing the most skillful lithographic talent for the production of alphabets, there still existed in the lithographic trade only primers in strips which were poorly printed, very poorly drawn, and even more poorly colored. Mine, issued from the pencil of Messrs. Bouchot, Daumier, Desperet, Forest, Lassalle, and Traviès, achieved an unprecedented success. Everyone is now familiar with those lively grotesque figures, those costumes, those military and other subjects that succeed so well in fixing in children's memory the recollection of letters and words. I thus brought about a little revolution in this type of work.][6]

Grandville thus was not alone in redirecting his caricatural skills, as the mention of his former colleagues on the staff of *La Caricature,* Daumier, Desperet, Forest, and Traviès demonstrates. But why is he not listed among those contributing to Aubert's series of primers?

One answer to this somewhat embarrassing question may be that although he was interested in children's publications, Grandville's particular satirical turn of mind remained uninspired when it came to producing primers, as the incomplete whimsical alphabet in cat. nos. 38 and 39 would seem to demonstrate. Another possible answer is that the artist, now married and with a family to support, found that providing illustrations for books was a more lucrative use of his time.

This is not to say that Grandville did not participate in producing the various types of children's literature that La Maison Aubert never ceased to turn out: primers, albums, macédoines (combinations of images from various sources), alphabet strips, and book albums.[7] He did, but in a very secondary fashion. Most if not all of the images by Grandville in Aubert's "children's bookstore" are *réemplois,* or reused ones, either from existing woodblocks or from previously published lithographs transferred onto woodblocks. For instance, the images in A. de Savigny's *Historiettes et images* (Short stories and images; 1840) are reimpressions of the woodblocks originally produced for *La Chronique de Paris* (The Paris review; Aubert had earlier reemployed some of these same woodblocks for *Le Musée parisien* [The parisian museum] of 1835).[8] All three of Grandville's contributions to *Le Grand Abécédaire en action* (The large primer in action; 1844) are recycled images as well. Once more, two of them are reimpressions of woodblocks: the one on page 31 is a reprint of *Vieux habits, vieux galons* (Old clothing, old braid) from the first volume of the *Oeuvres complètes de P. J. de Béranger* of 1836 and that on page 78 is a reprint of the title illustration for the *Gazette des enfans* from 1839. The third *réemploi,* however, provides an example of a lithograph, in this case Grandville and Forest's *Commerce anglais* (English commerce) from the May 10, 1840, issue of *La Caricature,* which was transferred to a woodblock and in the process miniaturized: what originally had been a 18.5 cm square lithograph was reduced to a 7 cm square wood engraving by Pierre Verdeil (1812–?) so that it would be on the same scale as other images in the primer.[9] Other children's publications edited by Aubert, which included the participation of Grandville's images if not directly of Grandville himself, include the *Vocabulaire des enfants* (Word-book for children; 1839) and the *Nouvel Abécédaire illustré par MM. Daumier, Forest, Grandville et autres artistes du musée Philipon* (New primer illustrated by Messrs. Daumier, Forest, Grandville and other artists of the Philipon museum; 1845).[10]

It should be emphasized that Aubert was by no means either the only publisher of children's books or the only one to reuse existing images. Hetzel, for instance, published a series of children's books entitled *Le Nouveau magazin des enfants d'Hetzel* (Hetzel's new magazine for children) in which appeared

Le Livre des petits enfants, nouvel alphabet (The book for little children, new alphabet; 1843). The image by Grandville on page 107 for "Le Renard et le chien" (The fox and the dog) is a reimpression of the head of the dog in *Mon ravisseur était un des laquais du roi* (My abductor was a footman of the king), an illustration for "Histoire d'un Lièvre" from the first volume of *Scènes de la vie privée et publique des animaux.*[11]

38. 15

A B C D E
F G H
I J K L
M N

1836
105 × 177
Pencil and watercolor

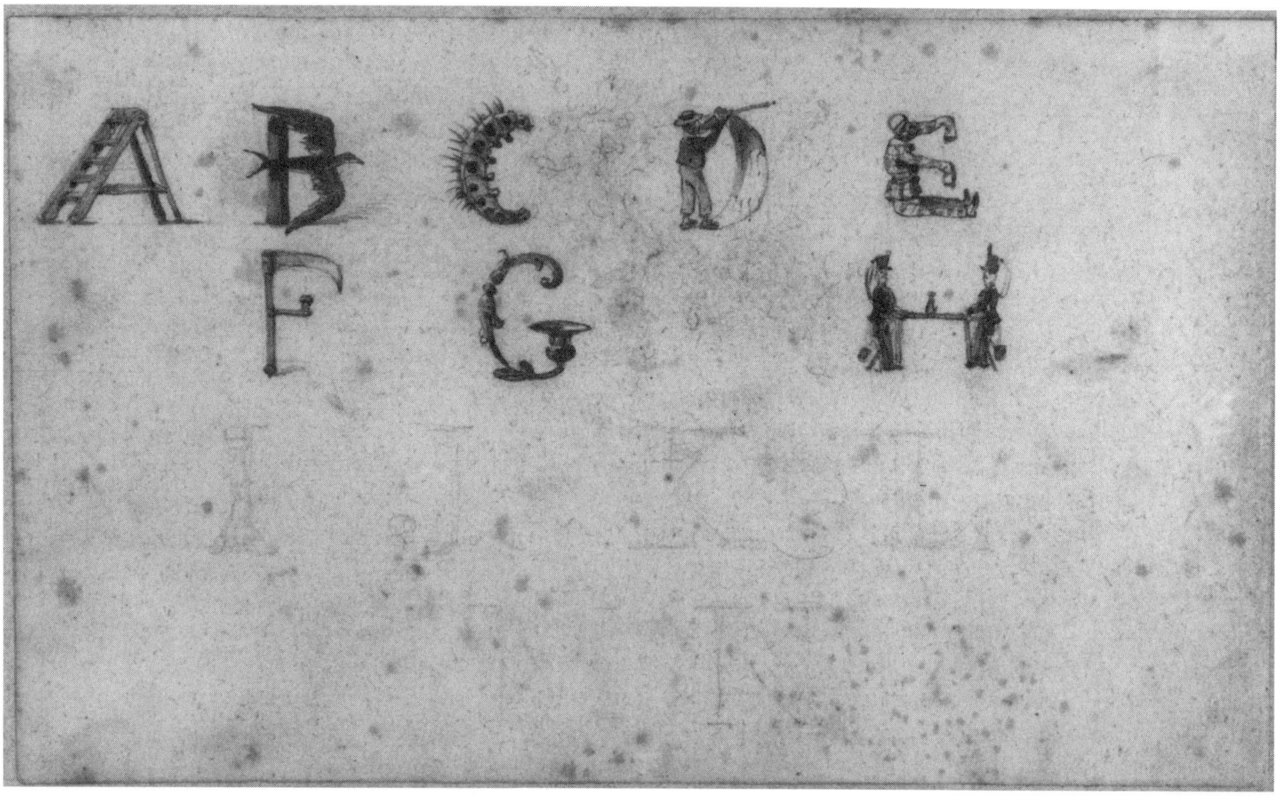

Alphabets de fantaisie (whimsical alphabets) naturally proliferated during the Romantic period, which was itself characterized by artistic inventiveness and flights of the imagination.[12] As might be expected, Grandville helped to contribute to this widespread phenomenon by producing his share of fanciful lettering. And yet, despite their curious configurations, they often follow well-established artistic precedents.

Fig. 93. Title of *Le Charivari Monstre,* July 31, 1835. Paris, Bibliothèque nationale de France.

For instance, the anthropomorphic letters found in the title of *Le Charivari Monstre* from July 1835 (fig. 93) follow a modern tradition dating back to the Renaissance and recall the anthropomorphic alphabet that Daumier produced for Aubert during the same year.[13] In 1837, Grandville produced animal-shaped letters (fig. 94) for the *Fables de La Fontaine* of 1838 that may be compared to those in an undated nineteenth-century French *Alphabet d'Animaux.*[14] Other examples of Grandville's talent for fanciful lettering include animal-shaped letters of a more whimsical nature in *Scènes de la vie privée et publique des animaux,* where insects, snails, and snakes twist, curl, and slither while spelling out the book's title; a madcap script forming the words JOCO SERIA in *Petites misères de la vie humaine;* letters constructed as though from blocks of stone for the heading of the tables to *Un autre monde;* and a poetically floral and ribboned orthography in the frontispiece to *Les Fleurs animées.*[15]

Although Grandville actively participated in the Romantic fad for picturesque and fanciful lettering, he never published a complete *alphabet de fantaisie.* But as this and the following catalog entry demonstrate, at one point he apparently considered doing so. Chronologically situated between the anthropomorphic lettering for *Le Charivari Monstre* and the animal-shaped letters for the *Fables de La Fontaine,* this alphabet is very much in the spirit of Victor Adam's *Nouvel abécédaire en énigmes* (New primer in riddles) published by Rittner et Goupil in 1833 (fig. 95) and by another contemporaneous anonymous *Alphabet grotesque* (Grotesque alphabet) produced around 1836.[16] The *chenille* (caterpillar)-shaped "C" and the *faux* (scythe)-shaped "F" here indicate that Grandville at times would form a letter from the animal or object whose name began with that same letter. Again, this is not a new idea as the scythe-shaped "F" from Adam's *Nouvel abécédaire en énigmes* demonstrates (fig. 96). Other whimsically shaped letters include "A" in the shape of a ladder; "B" as a flying bird; "D" as a sailor looking through a telescope in front of a billowing sail; "E" as a clown; "G" as a rococo sconce; and "H" as two grenadiers at a table. These first eight letters of Grandville's *alphabet de fantaisie,* which are delicately tinted with watercolor, appear to be finished. The rest of the letters on the page, however, are only lightly sketched in pencil and retain their standard appearance.

There is every reason to believe that Grandville started work on the alphabet at Aubert's behest, and that it was to form part of yet another *abécédaire* published by La Maison Aubert. An explanation for

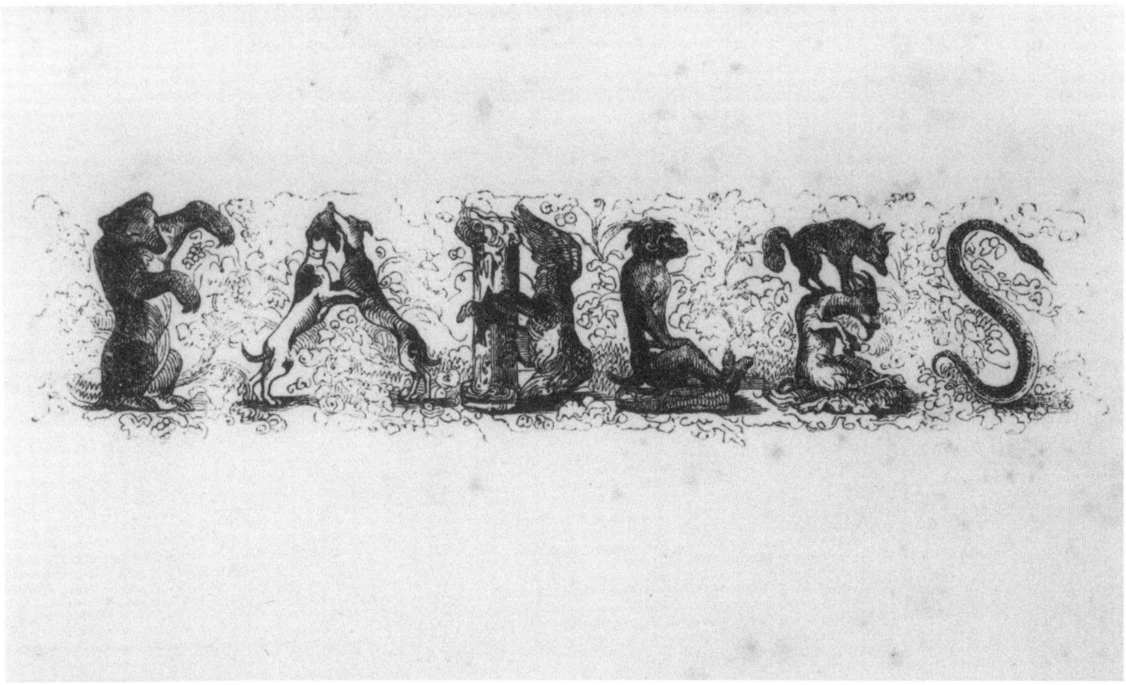

Fig. 94. Title from *Fables de La Fontaine,* 1838, wood engraving. Private collection.

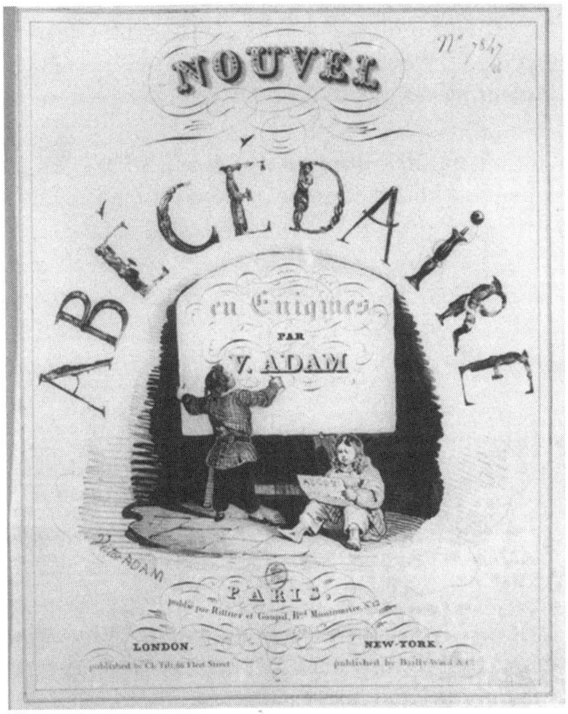

Fig. 95. Victor Adam, title from *Nouvel abécédaire en enigmes,* (*New Primer in Riddles*), 1833, lithograph. Paris, Bibliothèque nationale de France.

Fig. 96. Victor Adam, detail of "*F*" from *Nouvel abécédaire en énigmes,* 1833, lithograph. Paris, Bibliothèque nationale de France.

its incomplete state may be found on the opposite side of another sheet where Grandville has blocked out the letters for the remainder of the alphabet (cat. no. 39): his work was interrupted by a commission to illustrate "Little Red Riding Hood" for the first volume of *Le Livre des enfants,* which, as we have seen, was initially announced December 3, 1836, in the *Bibliographie de la France.* The alphabet may have been permanently abandoned when Grandville received the even more important commission to illustrate the *Fables de La Fontaine,* whose first installment was registered in the *Bibliographie de la France* on January 28, 1837.

It should be added that Grandville indulged his whimsy by creating fanciful numbers as well as letters. A famous example may be found in the insect-inspired house number painted on the wall surrounding his summer residence at Chatou in 1846 (fig. 107).

39. 16 verso

O P Q R S
T U V
X Y
Z

1836
105 × 177
Pencil

Judging from the uneven cuts along the side of this sheet and that in the previous catalog number, the two pages that contain the studies for the uncompleted alphabet were originally opposite each other in the open sketchbook, thereby enabling Grandville to see the entire alphabet that he was working on at

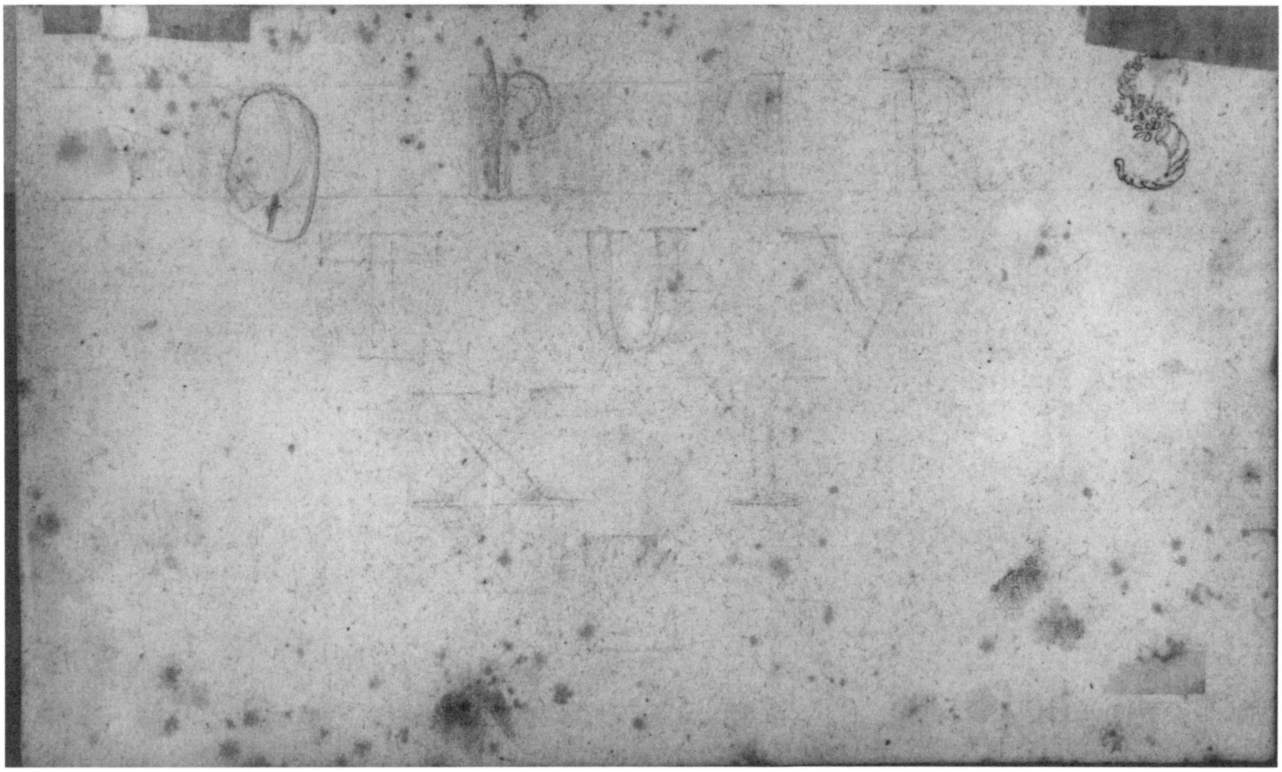

once (in the previous catalog number, the cut that separated the sheet from the sketchbook is along the right edge; the corresponding cut of the present sheet, when viewing its verso, is along the left edge). Thus the drawing on page 15 of the Missouri Album (cat. no. 38) was originally on the verso of a sketchbook page, and what is now the verso of the drawing attached to page 16 was originally on the recto of the sketchbook's following page.

This drawing represents the second half of the alphabet begun in the previous catalog entry. However, it includes two anomalies: there is no "W" and the "Q" is drawn as a lower case "q." Only the letter "S" has undergone metamorphosis, being transformed into a cornucopia out of which spill flowers. All the other letters, lightly sketched in pencil, retain their conventional shapes. It should be added that the letters "O" and "P" appear to have been at one point traced over by a child.

16 recto

Two studies for "Little Red Riding Hood":
"Va voir comment se porte ta mère-grand . . . porte lui une galette et ce petit pot de beurre." (Go see how your grandmother is feeling . . . carry a pancake and this small pot of butter to her.)
"Le Loup lui demanda où elle allait." (The Wolf asked her where she was going.)

1836
105 × 177
Pencil and watercolor

As was discussed earlier in cat. nos. 20 and 21, Grandville made his debut as an illustrator of children's stories in 1832 and 1833 when he produced, among others, the first depictions of Louis Desnoyers's Jean-Paul Choppart for the *Journal des enfans.* His next venture in the field consisted of illustrations to four children's stories by Perrault published in *Le Livre des enfants* in 1836 and 1837: "Little Red Riding Hood," "Tom Thumb," "Puss in Boots," and "Bluebeard." The seven watercolor-tinted pencil drawings in this and the next two catalog entries are preparatory studies for "Little Red Riding Hood."[17]

The idea of illustrating Perrault apparently had occurred to Grandville as a young man while he was still in Nancy, for pages from a circa 1821 sketchbook in the Musée Carnavalet contain drawings carefully labeled "La Barbe bleue" (Bluebeard; D.6423 [18]) and "la belle au bois dormant" (Sleeping Beauty; D.6423 [19]). But it was his illustrations to "Little Red Riding Hood" for *Le Livre des enfants* that first saw publication. From all appearances, Grandville was the first French artist to depict multiple scenes of a Perrault fairy tale in the same publication.[18]

The seven pencil and watercolor studies in the Missouri Album appear to be early working studies for "Little Red Riding Hood." Of these, only four were eventually published, and then only after undergoing significant modifications worked out in at least one set of intermediary drawings (see the two drawings from the Nancy Musée des Beaux-Arts reproduced in figures 98 and 100). The reason why only certain scenes were chosen for publication is probably the result of standard editorial practice: Grandville was asked to submit a series of drawings from which, it was understood, four would be selected. Reading from left to right, the seven scenes appear in proper narrative sequence. As he had done while working on the alphabet, Grandville started on the left page of a double page spread with the result that the first five scenes could be seen together. (This procedure can again be determined by the uneven cuts along those edges where the sheets would have been attached to the sketchbook. In the present sheet of drawings, the cut is along the right edge, indicating that it was executed on the verso of one of the sketchbook's pages; the corresponding cut in the sheet of drawings that follows is along the left edge, indicating that it was on the front of a sketchbook page.)

The first of the two drawings on the first sheet corresponds to the beginning of the story where Little Red Riding Hood listens to her mother's instructions, "Va voir comment se porte ta mère-grand'; car on m'a dit qu'elle était malade: porte-lui une galette et ce petit pot de beurre." (Go see how your grandmother is feeling; for she told me that she was sick: carry a pancake and this small pot of butter to her.). While offering to her small daughter the pot of butter and the pancake held in her right hand, the mother raises her left with the index finger extended in a standard admonitory gesture. On tiptoe, Little Red Riding Hood reaches expectantly toward the food she is to carry to her grandmother. On her head she wears her distinctive *chaperon,* a "small stylish cap worn by women of the aristocracy and middle classes in the 16th and 17th centuries."[19] *Chaperons* were usually brightly colored and often red like the one that gave Little Red Riding Hood her name, which in French is *le petit Chaperon rouge,* literally "little red cap." This initial scene of the series was never published.

The second vignette on the sheet, however, did see publication, but only after substantial changes were made. It represents a key moment in the narrative, when Little Red Riding Hood first encounters the Wolf: "En passant dans un bois, elle rencontra compère le Loup, qui eut bien envie de la manger; mais il n'osa, à cause de quelques bûcherons qui étaient dans la forêt. Il lui demanda où elle allait." (While passing through a wood, she encountered father Wolf who very much wanted to eat her; but he did not dare because some woodcutters were in the forest. He asked her where she was going.). In this early, wide-angled version of the scene, Little Red Riding Hood wears the same two-pocketed white apron over a long-sleeved striped dress as in the scene with her mother. She carefully carries the pot of butter in the crook of her right arm while she steadies the pancake on the top of the pot with her left hand. Viewed slightly from above, she tilts her head with the result that her red cap is plainly visible. To the right, the Wolf appears in full profile, and on the far right looms a large gnarled oak tree. In the final, published version (fig. 97) the scene has been greatly condensed, focusing directly on the two protagonists. Seen slightly from below, the Wolf and Little Red Riding Hood stand on diverging

Fig. 97. ***Le Loup lui demanda où elle allait.*** **(The Wolf asked her where she was going.) from** ***Le Livre des enfants,*** **1836, wood engraving. Paris, Bibliothèque nationale de France.**

diagonals leading into the background. Also Little Red Riding Hood now wears a light-colored shift that falls unevenly over a dark dress with short puffed sleeves. More importantly, she hugs the pot of butter and the pancake to her chest as though she were protecting them from the jaws of the hungry Wolf. Because of the angle of perspective, only the rim of her cap can be seen. Located on an opposite receding diagonal, the Wolf appears in three-quarter view instead of in profile and has taken on a more wily air. His foreshortened body points to the most significant change between the early sketch and the published wood engraving: the addition of one of the all-important woodcutters without whose presence, the narrative emphasizes, the Wolf would have devoured Little Red Riding Hood on the spot. Last, the forest is no longer represented by the towering oak tree, but by a background of densely grouped truncated tree trunks.

40. 17 recto

Three studies for "Little Red Riding Hood":
"Le Loup se mit à courir . . . La petite Fille s'amusait à cueillir des noisettes et à faire des bouquets." (The Wolf began to run . . . The little girl amused herself by gathering hazelnuts and making bouquets.)
"Il heurte, toc, toc." (He knocks at the door, knock, knock.)
"Il se jeta sur la bonne femme, et la dévora en moins de rien." (He threw himself upon the old woman and devoured her in nothing flat.)

1836
105 × 177
Pencil and watercolor

Of the three studies on the recto of this sheet, just the one on the left saw publication, and then only after undergoing considerable modification (fig. 99). The full text for the scene reads:

> Le Loup se mit à courir de toute sa force par le chemin qui était le plus court, et la petite fille s'en alla par le chemin le plus long, s'amusant à cueillir des noisettes, à courir après des papillons, et à faire des bouquets des petites fleurs qu'elle rencontrait.
>
> [The Wolf began to run with all his might on the path that was the shortest, and the little girl departed on the longest path, amusing herself by gathering hazelnuts, running after butterflies, and making bouquets of little flowers she found along the way.]

In the sketchbook study here, Little Red Riding Hood faces the viewer as she runs after butterflies. However, in the wood engraving her back is turned as she kneels down beside and clings to a bush with both hands in order to get a closer look at the lepidoptera fluttering nearby. A highly finished preparatory drawing for the wood engraving in the Nancy Musée des Beaux-Arts (fig. 98) indicates that Grandville had originally conceived of the kneeling child as clutching the bush with only one hand

Fig. 98. Study for *Le Loup se mit à courir . . . La petite Fille s'amusait à cueillir des noisettes et à faire des bouquets.* (The Wolf began to run . . . The little girl amused herself by gathering hazelnuts and making bouquets.), 1836, drawing. Nancy, Musée des Beaux-Arts (Inv. 877.766).

Fig. 99. *Le Loup se mit à courir . . . La petite Fille s'amusait à cueillir des noisettes et à faire des bouquets.* (The Wolf began to run . . . The little girl amused herself by gathering hazelnuts and making bouquets.) from *Le Livre des enfants,* 1836, wood engraving. Paris, Bibliothèque nationale de France.

while with the other she prepares to catch a butterfly resting on a branch. In the wood engraving the resting butterfly has been replaced by leaves, and the upward reaching hand clasps a branch that has been added in order to justify the arm's extended gesture. Grandville has also added the mill in the background, which indicates the direction in which the grandmother's house is located. The other main difference between these three versions of the scene is Little Red Riding Hood's attire. In the sketchbook study she again wears an apron over her long-sleeved striped dress, in the drawing from Nancy she wears just the dark dress with puffed sleeves, and in the final wood engraving a light-colored shift has been added to the dark dress. The only element that remains basically unchanged in all three renditions is the running Wolf in the background.

The other two drawings on the sheet were never published. The middle one portrays the Wolf on hind legs knocking at the grandmother's door. The one on the right represents the gruesome scene in which the Wolf devours the bedridden woman. That it is not the subsequent scene where the Wolf crawls into bed after closing the door is indicated by the pronounced bulge of the grandmother's body under the blankets.

17 verso

Two studies for "Little Red Riding Hood":
"Le petit Chaperon rouge se déshabille." (Little Red Riding Hood gets undressed.)
"Ma mère grand', que vous avez de grandes dents." (Grandmother, what big teeth you have.)

1836
105 × 177
Pencil and watercolor

Fig. 100. Study for *Le petit Chaperon rouge se déshabille.* (Little Red Riding Hood gets undressed.), 1836, drawing. Nancy, Musée des Beaux-Arts (Inv. 877.767).

Fig. 101. *Le petit Chaperon rouge se déshabille.* (Little Red Riding Hood gets undressed.) from *Le Livre des enfants,* 1836, wood engraving. Paris, Bibliothèque nationale de France.

Both the scenes depicted on the verso of this sheet saw publication in *Le Livre des enfants,* but, as usual, only after being extensively altered. In the one on the left, Little Red Riding Hood gets undressed after the Wolf, in the guise of the grandmother, says to her, "Mets la galette et le petit pot de beurre sur la huche, et viens te coucher avec moi." (Place the pancake and the small pot of butter on the chest and come to bed with me.). The little girl obediently follows the Wolf's instructions. She has placed the pancake and the pot of butter as well as her red cap on the chest to the right and is in the process of undressing before climbing into bed. With her back modestly turned to the Wolf, who greedily stares at her, she unfastens her undergarment after having let her striped dress fall to the floor. Wearing the grandmother's large bonnet on his head, the Wolf lies under the covers in a simple four-poster bed. Above the bed hangs what appears to be a print, probably of a religious nature. In the published wood engraving (fig. 101), this scene is both greatly condensed and elaborated upon. Most of these changes may be found in a highly finished intermediary drawing at the Nancy Musée des Beaux-Arts (fig. 100). The space in which the action takes place has been contracted. Little Red Riding Hood stands next to the bed with the result that her head is now on the same level as that of the Wolf, thereby providing a more direct visual contrast between evil and innocence symbolized by the two protagonists. The chest, which along with the side of the bed originally helped to define a triangular space at the apex of which was Little Red Riding Hood's head, takes on a less prominent role and is discretely placed against the wall beneath the window in the background; the fallen dress has disappeared. At the same time, descriptive detail proliferates in the later drawing. The bed now boasts a canopy with curtains and is richly carved. Under the bed appear a chamber pot and the sleeve of a garment, the latter, of course, belonging to the robe of the devoured grandmother. Next to the bed stands a chair. The window, through which the mill may be glimpsed, displays a more elaborate pattern of glass panes. Little Red Riding Hood wears a headband and what appear to be slippers. One last detail, the print above the bed has been replaced by a cross of which only the bottom part may be seen. Minor changes take place between the Nancy drawing and the published wood engraving. The bed canopy is only hinted at and the sleeve of the grandmother's robe is now patterned. The cross has become completely visible and is adorned with a sprig of flowers. Instead of a headband, Little Red Riding Hood wears a skullcap, which is fastened under her chin. A leafy tree rather than the mill is seen through the window, whose panes are arranged in a simple lozenge pattern. The formerly plain chest has been decorated with scrollwork.

The scene on the right is the immediate sequel to that on the left and depicts the tale's famous ending: "Le petit Chaperon rouge . . . va se mettre dans le lit, où elle fut bien étonnée de voir comment sa mère-grand' était faite en son déshabillé." (Little Red Riding Hood . . . climbs into bed where she is very surprised to see how her grandmother looked undressed.). Little Red Riding Hood wears a nightcap tied to her head and with one hand points toward the curious features of the Wolf's head. Her other hand reaches out over the blankets. It is not possible to determine which surprised observation Little Red Riding Hood is making to the Wolf, but judging from her upward gaze into the Wolf's face and her pointing finger, it could very well be "Ma mère-grand', que vous avez de grands yeux!" (Grandmother, what big eyes you have!). The fact that the Wolf wears a large bonnet that covers the entire back part of his head would seem to eliminate the possibility of her remarking about the Wolf's large ears. In anticipation of his devouring the little girl, the Wolf reaches toward her with one hairy paw. In the wood engraving (fig. 102), which is entitled *Ma mère grand', que vous avez de grandes dents.* (Grandmother, what big teeth you have), Little Red Riding Hood's nightcap is no longer tied to her head, and both her arms are under the covers. The pointing hand has been slightly lowered, allowing the nose of the Wolf to approach even more closely that of his victim. The Wolf's bonnet has been replaced by a head covering that does not hide his ears. The reaching paw has been eliminated, but the Wolf's intent may be easily read in the same bulging eye and snarling mouth that are depicted in the sketchbook drawing.

Fig. 102. ***Ma mère grand', que vous avez de grandes dents.*** **(Grandmother, what big teeth you have.) from** ***Le Livre des enfants,*** **1836, wood engraving. Paris, Bibliothèque nationale de France.**

41. 18 recto

The legend of Saint Nicholas and two playing children

1836 or after 1842
105 × 177
Pencil and watercolor

In the same sketchbook where he depicts the tale of Little Red Riding Hood, Grandville illustrates with a watercolor-tinted pencil drawing the famous legend of the patron saint of his native Lorraine, Saint Nicholas. A fourth-century bishop of Myra in what is present-day Turkey, Nicholas was widely known for his piety. In 1087, his remains were spirited out of Turkey to Bari by merchants from that southern Italian city. During the reign of the Holy Roman Emperor Henry IV (1056–1106), a certain Aubert from the small Lorrain village of Port along the banks of the Meurthe River made a pilgrimage to Bari in order to visit the recently transferred body of the saint. Much to his surprise, he discovered that the person in charge of guarding the saint's remains was a Lorrain compatriot, who according to certain versions of the story was even a relative. Thus it was fairly easy for him to obtain a knucklebone from the saint's skeleton and secretly carry it back to the village of Port. No sooner did the holy relic arrive in Lorraine than miracles started to take place. A first church to house the relic and accommodate the influx of pilgrims was soon constructed. The decision to erect the present Flamboyant Gothic basilica of Saint-Nicolas-de-Port was formally made in 1481 by René II, duke of Lorraine, in gratitude for his decisive victory over the Burgundian duke, Charles the Bold, at the Battle of Nancy in 1477. However, the first stone was not laid until around 1492.[20]

Grandville has depicted the most famous episode from the life of Saint Nicholas and the one particularly appealing to children. According to the legend, as recounted in Gérard de Nerval's 1842 version of a song some four centuries old, three children were gleaning in the fields one day when they came upon the house of a butcher who invited them inside. No sooner had they entered the door than the butcher killed the children, cut them up into little pieces, and placed their remains in a salting tub. Seven years later, Saint Nicholas crossed the same fields and came upon the house of the butcher. Offering the saint his hospitality, the butcher prepared to serve him a meal. Refusing both the ham and the veal offered him, Saint Nicholas requested, "De ce salé, je veux avoir, Qu'y a sept ans qu'est dans l' saloir." (Of that salted meat, I want to have, that for seven years has been in the salting tub.). At these words, the butcher fled out the door while Saint Nicholas called after him to repent and beg God's forgiveness. He then went over to the salting tub and laid three fingers on its rim. Upon spreading them, the three children were resurrected:

> Le premier dit: "J'ai bien dormi";
> Le second dit: "Et moi aussi";
> Et le troisième répondit:
> "Je croyais être en Paradis!"
>
> [The first one said: "I slept well";
> The second one said: "And me too";
> And the third one responded:
> "I thought I was in Paradise!"][21]

The scene from the story that artists traditionally depict is where the three children rise together out of the tub upon their resurrection. Grandville, however, has chosen to represent their grisly massacre. One child is already in the salting tub, another kicks and screams while in the clutches of the murderous butcher, and the third cowers piteously as he kneels in prayer. Just as certain scenes in his illustrations to "Little Red Riding Hood" are unprecedented so this one appears to be. In order to situate the narrative in the ancient Near East, Grandville includes some Oriental details of dubious historical accuracy: the butcher wears a fezlike cap and the salting tub next to the one in which the children are being placed is decorated with a typical Eastern blue on white floral design accented by orange.

The dating of this drawing is problematic. Since it appears on one of the pages from the 1836 Sketchbook, the initial assumption is that, like the studies for "Little Red Riding Hood," it also dates from 1836. But the circumstantial evidence that it may have been added to the sketchbook after 1842, specifically in 1846, is compelling. Gérard de Nerval (1808–55), credited with the revived interest in French folk songs during the Romantic period, first published "Saint Nicolas et les trois petits enfants" (Saint Nicholas and the three little children) along with other traditional folk songs in the July 9, 1842, issue of *La Sylphide.*[22] Nerval's version of the legend of Saint Nicholas differs from that found in an earlier version published by Hernault in 1582 where, as Marrou informs us, "il n'est pas question de trois enfants, mais de trois clercs, trois écoliers du saint" (it is not a question of three children, but of three clerks, three of the saint's schoolboys).[23] It seems that oral tradition gradually transformed the three schoolboy clerks into three little children. We do not know which version of the legend Grandville might have learned as he was growing up in Nancy. However, we do know that as late as 1904 the three clerks version of the song was still to be found in Lorraine.[24] In any event, it was Nerval who popularized the three little children version of the song when he published his *Vieilles ballades françaises* in *La Sylphide* in 1842. The fact that Grandville illustrated this particular version seems more than coincidental. Another clue that argues for dating this drawing after 1842 may be found in the upper right-hand corner of the sheet where Grandville sketched two children at play who bear a striking resemblance to his two sons, Georges and Armand, as they appeared in 1846 (see fig. 119). The boy rolling a hoop could very well be the four-year-old Georges, and the infant lying on his stomach could just as well be the one-year-old Armand who either has not yet learned how to walk or has taken a tumble while attempting to do so. Assuming that these two children are in fact Grandville's sons and that they were sketched around the same time as the illustration for the legend of Saint Nicholas, their presence would substantiate a date of 1846 for the latter. Should this be the case, Grandville would have added the drawing to the 1836 Sketchbook ten years later than the illustrations for "Little Red Riding Hood." While admittedly hypothetical, there is a credible explanation for why Grandville might have kept illustrations to children's stories together in one album: after having used the 1836 Sketchbook for an early set of drawings illustrating Perrault's fairy tale, Grandville continued to add to it other drawings for the amusement of his children. As a result, the sketchbook evolved into a type of illustrated children's book for use within the intimacy of his own family. This would have been in keeping with what is known about Grandville's habit of producing toys for his children (see cat. no. 48); figure 103, in fact, reproduces what appears to be a shadow theater puppet of the same large-nosed, fez-capped evil butcher with a screaming child in his hands as the one portrayed in the present legend of Saint Nicholas drawing.

Fig. 103. ***Butcher from the Legend of Saint Nicholas*, circa 1836–46, cut paper. Present location unknown.**

42. 19 recto

Whimsical landscape

1836?
105 × 177
Pencil and watercolor

This watercolor-tinted pencil drawing of a whimsical landscape, populated in part by humanoid insects, is a classic example of Grandville's inventive artistic program. A duck and a frog confront one another from opposite banks of a stream. The foreground features a long-legged spider on the left and to the right a squirming worm that appears to be following an anthropomorphized mother ant with a child ant in tow. The mother ant wears an apron and carries a baguette of bread under her left arm while with her right hand she holds onto her child who in turn holds a windmill-shaped pinwheel. Above the ants, Grandville illustrates a pun with the dragonflies daintily carrying parasols as though they were fashionable young women out for a stroll: the word for dragonfly in French is the same as that for a young lady, demoiselle. In the middle distance, two people cross the stream in a boat. Above them in the background stands a stork. In the upper left-hand corner appears a peasant family. The father leads a donkey. The mother carries one child in her left arm while with her right hand she holds onto another child who walks beside her. Judging from the mother's distinctive Norman headdress, Grandville has depicted a corner of the Normandy countryside.[25]

The animals found in this fantastic landscape are typical of those Grandville was fond of drawing throughout his career. Indeed, many of them are related to scientifically accurate studies reproduced in the Nancy catalog: the wild duck may be compared to those in cat. nos. 214–16, the frog to those in cat. nos. 248–50, the spider to that in cat. no. 306, the ants to those in cat. no. 233, and the elegant demoiselles to the exceptionally beautiful ones in cat. no. 238.

However, like the animals in the Nancy catalog, the whimsically animated ones here are difficult to date. If they were done in the same year as the studies for "Little Red Riding Hood," it is tempting to see them as anticipating or being contemporary with similarly anthropmorphized animals done for the *Fables de La Fontaine,* the first installment of which, as previously noted, was announced in the *Bibliographie de la France.* on January 28, 1837. The interaction of the animals in the foreground of the present work recalls similar compositions for the *Fables.* One might, for example, compare the ants to the one in "La Cigale et la Fourmi" (The Ant and the Grasshopper), or the frog to the ones in "Les deux Taureaux et la Grenouille" (The Two Bulls and the Frog); the squirming worm calls to mind the curled serpent in "Le Serpent et la Lime" (The File and the Serpent). Although interesting, these parallels with the *Fables de La Fontaine* do not incontrovertibly prove that the drawing dates from 1836. Like the illustration to the legend of Saint Nicholas in the previous entry, it could just as well have been a later addition to the 1836 Sketchbook.

43. 20 recto

Right profile of a sheep; front view of a dog

1836
105 × 177
Pencil and brown wash

Grandville appears to be imitating the illustrations for a natural history text as he draws this sheep and dog either in strict profile or a full-frontal pose. Whether or not he observed them, as well as the pig and goat in the following entry, while vacationing in Normandy or during some other excursion into the countryside cannot be determined. Equally moot is the year from which they date. However, the relatively robust draftsmanship is more characteristic of the 1830s than the 1840s when Grandville employed a more delicate line. Thus it is possible that these drawings date from 1836 and may be related to animal studies for the *Fables de La Fontaine.* The sheep, for instance, may be profitably compared to those portrayed in "Le Berger et son Troupeau" (The Shepherd and His Flock) and the dog to the one in "L'Ane et le Chien" (The Donkey and the Dog).

44. 21 recto

Right profile of a pig; left profile of a goat

1836
105 × 177
Pencil and green wash

The ink drawings done by a child on the opposite side of the sheet (cat. no. 86) show through the paper.
Stylistically, this pig and goat are directly related to the sheep and dog in the previous entry. The strict profile poses in imitation of natural history illustrations and the use of the pencil and wash are iden-

tical. This time a stone and a bit of vegetation accompany the animals, giving the impression that they were observed while grazing in a pasture. Parallels again may be drawn between these animals and those found in Grandville's illustrations for the *Fables de La Fontaine,* such as the goat that appears in "La Génisse, la Chèvre et la Brebis en société avec le Lion" (The Heifer, the Goat, and the Ewe in Company with the Lion) and the pig who figures in "Le Cochon, la Chèvre et le Mouton" (The Pig, the Goat, and the Sheep).

Notes

1. *Le Livre des enfants* was published by Paulin in six volumes between 1836 and 1838. Although the *Bibliographie de la France* announced the publication for the first time on December 3, 1836, it was not until January 14, 1837, that it listed the completed first volume that contained the five illustrations for "Little Red Riding Hood" (2, 3, 5, and 6) along with the six illustrations for "Tom Thumb" (132, 134, 139, 141, 144, 147). The third volume, registered in the *Bibliographie de la France* on March 4, 1837, contained the seven illustrations for "Puss in Boots" (74, 76, 77, 78, 80, 82, 83) and the fifth volume, registered in the *Bibliographie de la France* along with the sixth volume on December 23, 1837, contained the nine illustrations for "Bluebeard" (71, 72, 76, 77, 79, 80, 82, 83).

2. Ségolène Le Men, "Quel est donc le livre qui peut les captiver ainsi?" in *Livres d'enfants, livres d'images* (Paris: Editions de la Réunion des musées nationaux, 1989), 5.

3. Ségolène Le Men discusses at length Aubert's considerable contribution to the publishing of children's books during the July Monarchy in her article, "De l'image au livre: L'Editeur Aubert et l'abécédaire en estampe," *Nouvelles de l'estampe,* no. 90 (December 1986): 17–30.

4. Cuno, 105–6.

5. Ségolène Le Men, *Les Abécédaires français illustrés du XIXe siècle* (Paris: Promodis, 1984), 54.

6. Ibid., 52.

7. Le Men describes in detail these different types of children's publications in her previously cited article, "De l'image au livre."

8. Le Men, "De l'image au livre," 26–27; Renonciat, 289, 295.

9. Grandville was only one of many artists whose images were reissued by Aubert in children's publications. Lemen describes *Le Grand Abécédaire en action,* which carried the subtitle of *dessins par MM. Daumier, Gavarni, Johannot et autres artistes,* as "l'aboutissement extrême de la doctrine du réemploi" (the ultimate end result of the reuse doctrine; "De l'image au livre," 27).

10. Le Men, "De l'image au livre," 26, 28. A comprehensive list of Aubert's publications for children, which featured reemployed images by Grandville, remains to be compiled.

11. Four other images in *Le Livre des petits enfants* have been attributed to Grandville: *La Cigale et la fourmi; Le Renard et le corbeau; La Mère, l'enfant et les sarigues;* and *Le Loup et l'agneau.* Of these, the last two are *réemplois* from *Le Livre des enfants,* 5:68 and 84.

12. Ségolène Le Men, "De l'image au livre," 24. According to Le Men, the vogue for whimsical alphabets was as much due to a renewed interest in lithography and the nascent phenomenon of modern advertising as to Romanticism.

13. Robert Massin, *La Lettre et l'image, la figuration dans l'alphabet latin du huitième siècle à nos jours* (Paris: Gallimard, 1970), 67; Le Men, "De l'image au livre," 21. The complete alphabet is reproduced in Massin, 75.

14. Joseph Balthazard Silvestre, *Alphabet-album: Collection de soixante feuilles d'alphabets historiés et fleuronnés tirés des principales bibliothèques de l'Europe, ou composés par Silvestre* (Paris: J. Techener, 1843), plate 4.

15. Reproduced in Massin, 144, 145, 149.

16. The title page for the anonymous *Alphabet grotesque* is reproduced in Massin, 77, plate 220. Grandville may have been personally acquainted with Victor Adam (1801–66) since both men were affiliated with *La Caricature* and *Le Charivari.* Between November 18, 1830 and March 17, 1831, four of Adam's lithographs appeared in *La Caricature* (Vicaire, 2:51–53). And in 1834 he had three lithographs published in *Le Charivari: La Baleine.* (The whale; August 2); *Ecole royale de natation* (Royal swimming school; August 3); and a plate from *Grand voyage dans les Indes* (Long journey in the Indies; September 5).

17. Grandville's preliminary studies usually consist of pencil sketches, which are often gone over in pen and ink. However, he occasionally also used watercolor. For instance, a series of large format pen and watercolor studies exists for *Les Métamorphoses du jour* and apparently for *Singeries morales, politiques, etc.* as well (see Helena Domaszewska, "Zbiór

Rysunków Grandville'a w Muzeum Narodowym w Warszawie," *Rocznik Museum Narodowego w Warszawie* 19 [1975]: 542–46). In addition, an extensive and remarkable series of pencil and watercolor floral studies was done in preparation for *Les Fleurs animées* (see Nancy, cat. nos. 290–314).

18. Ever since the original edition of the *Contes de Perrault* in 1697, there traditionally appeared only one illustration for each fairy tale. Research at the Bibliothèque nationale de France and the Bibliothèque de l'heure joyeuse in Paris failed to uncover any French publication in which were illustrated multiple scenes from a single story before those done by Grandville for "Little Red Riding Hood" and published in *Le Livre des enfants* in 1836.

19. Jack Zipes, *The Trials and Tribulations of Little Red Riding Hood: Versions of the Tale in Sociocultural Context* (South Hadley, MA: Bergin & Garvey, 1983), 54.

20. For this and other information on Saint Nicholas and the basilica of Saint-Nicolas-de-Port, see *La Basilique de saint Nicolas en Lorraine* (Saint-Nicolas-de-Port: Connaissance et Renaissance de la basilique de Saint-Nicolas-de-Port, 1979).

21. Henri Davenson [Henri Irénée Marrou], *Le Livre des chansons*, 3rd ed. (Neuchâtel: Editions de la Baconnière, 1946), 263–65.

22. Ibid., 11. They were published under the title of *Vieilles ballades françaises* (Old French ballads), the first version of Nerval's *Chansons et légendes du Valois* (Songs and legends of the Valois).

23. Ibid., 265–66.

24. Ibid., 266.

25. According to Clogenson, Grandville and his family spent six weeks during the late summer and early fall of 1845 at the hamlet of Engreville near Gaillon in Upper Normandy (275). It is entirely possible that Grandville had earlier vacationed in Normandy. Should this be the case, this drawing may indicate that he visited there in 1836.

Diary of 1846

The excerpts from the 1846 diary are especially valuable because they provide a firsthand narrative of the last full year of Grandville's life. From all appearances, it was one of his happiest. And contrary to posthumous biographical accounts, there is no evidence of Grandville leading a circumscribed, hermetic existence. Nor is there any indication of a febrile mind. Sketches, along with the few annotations that survive, reveal both a busy social life and a witty individual in full possession of his faculties.

In 1846 Grandville was a forty-three-year-old man in his prime. He was firmly established in his career as a book illustrator. Constantly solicited by editors, he did not lack for work.[1] Consequently, monetary matters were no longer a problem. As seen in the biography, by 1843 he had amassed a personal fortune of over 53,000 francs at a time when the annual living expenses for the family of an average skilled worker in Paris were 950 francs.[2] He had attained a certain level of affluence. His household still included Rose, the maid encountered in cat. no. 36, and he could afford a comfortable fourth-floor apartment at 26, rue des Saints-Pères, a very respectable street on the edge of the aristocratic faubourg Saint-Germain.[3] After the heart-rending loss of his first two children and his first wife in the space of four years, he had succeeded in establishing a second family whose members consisted of the last remaining son from his first marriage, Georges, his second wife, Céline, and their son, Armand. He freely abandoned himself to his newfound happiness.

However, as we saw in the biography, no sooner was the year over than tragedy struck yet again. Toward the middle of January 1847, Georges died from a sudden illness. Annihilated, Grandville apparently lost the will to live, and died himself of complications from what seems to have been either a throat angina or a severe case of tonsillitis two months later on March 17. In a letter dated February 6, 1847, to his uncle and father-in-law, Antoine Fischer, Grandville somewhat pathetically recalls the idyllic existence he had only recently enjoyed:

> pour la première fois peutêtre de ma vie que je me laissais aller à l'insouciance de l'avenir, aux éspérances que j'avais le droit d'en attendre (en retour de tant de peines passées), pour la premiere fois que je me lais-

> sais vivre heureux dans le présent en jouissant de cette bonne vie de famille d'interieur, sans songer à la question pécuniaire, voila, que le destin (je ne nommerai pas la providence par respect pour vous et pour elle) vient me frapper une quatrieme fois dans la même plaie—à peine cicatrisée.
>
> [[it was] for perhaps the first time in my life that I gave way to unconcern for the future, to hopes that I had the right to expect (in return for so many past sufferings), for the first time that I let myself live happily in the present by enjoying that good interior family life, without giving a thought to financial matters, [when] behold, fate (I will not say providence out of respect for you and for it) comes to strike me a fourth time in the same wound—scarcely healed.]

His reference to "that good interior family life" would at first seem to confirm the account, most probably penned by Charton and previously cited in the biography, that "From the crack of dawn, he was seated at his desk, pencil in hand; he never went out, allowed himself no walks, no visits, no recreation whatsoever." Charton adds in the artist's obituary that during his final years Grandville was one of those individuals who "étrangers aux agitations et aux plaisirs du monde, sans aucune activité extérieure, voués à un travail sédentaire, enfermés dans le silence de l'atelier, ne peuvent et ne veulent demander de distractions, d'encouragements, d'éléments de bonheur qu'aux affections et aux espérances de la vie domestique" (strangers to the agitations and pleasures of the world, without any outside activity, dedicated to a sedentary occupation, closed up in the silence of the studio, cannot and will not ask for diversions, encouragements, fundamentals of happiness other than the affections and assurances of domestic life).[4]

It is quite understandable that after so many recent personal tragedies, Grandville would have especially appreciated the reassuring tranquillity of a quiet and well-regulated domestic existence. But contrary to what Charton would have us believe, Grandville was anything but a recluse cut off from the rest of the world. Even without the 1846 diary, which records frequent diversions, our suspicions are aroused when it is flatly stated that Grandville, the inveterate walker of the early 1830s, never went out for a stroll. If the thirty-five fragments from the 1846 diary that survive are a representative sampling (and there is no reason to believe that they are not) they eloquently attest to a fairly active life outside the home during the final year of his life. As might be expected, certain outings were specifically meant for or included the children, such as a shadow theater performance. And while Grandville was no social lion, he nevertheless was an active participant during the busy winter social season: two Saturdays in a row he goes to first a "soirée Bixi" and then a "Soirée de l'Odéon" (cat. nos. 46 and 47). Two weeks later he once again finds himself on the social circuit attending a performance of Corneille's *Cinna* and what is probably another elegant soirée (cat. no. 52); his continued interest in the theater comes as no surprise. And when he moved to Chatou in March for a prolonged summer stay, he and the rest of his family enthusiastically joined in the local sport of fishing to the extent that it competed with his work schedule (see appendix). So much for the myth of the hermetic artist, virtually glued to his work table, who allowed himself "no recreation whatsoever." While not mentioned in what remains of the 1846 diary, there may have also been excursions away from Paris and its environs during the course of the year similar to the six-week stay in Normandy in the late summer and early fall of 1845 or trips to Nancy to visit members of Grandville's and Céline's families in the Lorrain capital.

Clogenson's account of Grandville's final years contrasts with that provided by Charton. Grandville's neighbor at 26, rue des Saints-Pères, he enjoyed a privileged access to the artist and his family, joining Grandville when he caught flies for his pet frog in the courtyard or visiting the family after dinner. He appears to have been accepted almost as an additional member of the household who shared in their domestic existence on virtually a daily basis. As a result, his account rings more true. Since it provides the context for the events recorded in the 1846 diary, it is quoted at length:

C'est en octobre 1845 que je l'ai connu. Il arrivait de Normandie, où il avait été passer six semaines au hameau d'Engreville près de Gaillon, avec sa femme et ses deux enfants,—Georges qui avait alors quatre ans, et Armand qui venait de naître. "Le séjour de la campagne, le repos, *le bon pain,* l'avaient, disait-il, ragaillardi." Quoiqu'on remarquât toujours en lui une disposition naturelle à la mélancolie, il était d'une gaieté douce; il ne riait pas, mais il souriait.

Il demeurait alors rue des Saints-Pères, 26, et j'habitais la même maison. Il y avait une cour avec quelques grands arbres; à onze heures, après son déjeuner, si le temps était beau, je le voyais descendre enveloppé d'une casaque verte, et s'approchant d'un mur où donnait le soleil, il attrapait des mouches pour une petite grenouille, sa favorite, qu'il avait constamment près de lui sur sa table. Je descendais alors, et la chasse terminée nous remontions dans son atelier.

Son atelier était une chambre de son appartement dont quelques siéges [*sic*] sculptés, deux bahuts et une grande table en vieux chêne, sur laquelle il travaillait, formaient l'ameublement. Aux murailles, on voyait appendus des plâtres, quelques dessins ou peintures d'artistes qu'il avait connus, et au-dessus de sa table, derrière lui quand il dessinait, la grande et si remarquable gravure de Kaulbach, *la Maison des fous.*

Grandville était petit, maigre, d'apparence presque chétive;—il avait les yeux d'une nuance assez difficile à dire—comme bruns,—le nez gros, la bouche moyenne, les lèvres fines et recouvertes d'une épaisse moustache. Sa physionomie, où se peignait [*sic,* peindrait] d'ordinaire une sorte de somnolence, ne savait rien cacher de ce qu'il éprouvait;—elle s'animait d'un feu soudain devant ce qui était beau, ou quand il regardait ses enfants. A l'époque dont je parle, quoiqu'il n'eût guère que quarante ans, ses cheveux grisonnaient; on voyait que d'irréparables malheurs l'avaient frappé. Il aimait à penser à ceux qu'il avait aimés, —bien qu'il n'en parlât que rarement,—et pour que leur souvenir ne le quittât jamais, il avait placé sur la cheminée de sa chambre les bustes des deux enfants qu'il avait perdus.

Georges leur frère,—qui ne devait pas leur survivre longtemps,—était toujours à ses côtés. Bien des fois, en entrant, je l'ai trouvé assis sur la table où travaillait l'artiste, au milieu de ses crayons, le regardant dessiner. Je n'ai jamais vu d'enfant dont les traits m'aient paru plus charmants et plus expressifs. Je me le rappelle encore avec ses cheveux blonds et ses yeux bleus, les bras autour du cou du pauvre artiste! Le père et l'enfant ne causaient entre eux qu'à voix basse,—souvent même un regard leur suffisait pour s'entendre. Bien des fois je suis resté auprès d'eux, feuilletant quelque album, sans qu'un mot, dans l'espace d'une heure, ait été prononcé.

La sympathie et l'admiration que j'éprouvais pour Grandville, ne lui avaient pas échappé,—il m'en avait une sorte de reconnaissance, aussi j'étais reçu chez lui presque à toute heure. Quelquefois le soir, après son dîner, je venais le voir; je trouvais toute la famille réunie dans l'atelier, l'artiste dessinait à la lueur de sa lampe, Mme Grandville s'occupait à quelque ouvrage d'aiguille, Armand, son plus jeune fils, dormait dans son berceau, et Georges, assis près de son frère, le regardait dormant. A huit heures Grandville disait: *Il faut coucher l'enfant,*—et la mère emportait le berceau et se retirait emmenant Georges par la main. Resté seul avec Grandville, nous entamions quelque grande discussion à propos de ses *Fleurs animées,* dont il me montrait les croquis. Un jour que j'admirais l'originalité charmante de ses compositions: "J'ai imaginé quoi, me dit-il, des monstruosités gracieuses, pour l'homme auquel il faut à tout prix du nouveau,—mais je n'invente pas,—je ne fais qu'associer des éléments disparates, et enter les unes sur les autres des formes antipathiques ou hétérogènes." D'autres fois nous nous laissons aller à quelque causerie sans objet, en prenant le thé; Grandville avait alors des mots charmants, toujours attentif aux moindres désirs de sa femme, il l'appelait *celle qui fait vouloir le bon Dieu,*—et c'était charmant de le voir n'avoir pas d'autre volonté que la sienne.

[It's in October 1845 that I made his acquaintance. He was coming back from Normandy where he had spent six weeks in the hamlet of Engreville near Gaillon with his wife and two children—Georges who was then four years old and Armand who had just been born. "The stay in the country, the rest, *the good bread* had cheered him up," he said. Although you always noticed in him a natural tendency toward melancholy, he possessed a quiet cheerfulness; he didn't laugh, but he smiled. [Compare this description of Grandville with the remarkably similar one by Dumas in cat. no. 21.]

At the time, he was living at 26, rue des Saints-Pères, and I lived in the same house. There was a courtyard with some large trees; if the weather was nice, at eleven o'clock, after his lunch, I would see him go down wrapped in a green jacket and, approaching a wall lit by the sun, he caught flies for his small pet frog which he constantly kept close by him on his work table. Then I would go down and, once the hunt was over, we would go back up into his studio.

His studio was a room in his apartment furnished with some carved chairs, two hutches, and a large old oak table at which he worked. You would see hanging on the walls plaster casts, some drawings and paintings by artists he had known, and, above his table, behind him when he drew, the large and so remarkable engraving by Kaulbach, *The Madhouse.*

Grandville was small in stature, thin, almost puny in appearance;—he possessed eyes of a color difficult to describe—brownish,—a large nose, an average mouth, thin lips covered with a thick moustache. His features, where there normally appeared a type of sleepiness, didn't know how to hide anything that he felt;—they would light up with a sudden fire in front of something beautiful or when he looked at his children. At the time about which I am talking, even though he was scarcely forty years old, his hair was turning gray; you could see that he had been struck by irreparable misfortunes. He liked to think of those he had loved,—even though he talked about them only rarely,—and in order that their memory should never leave him, he had placed busts of the two children he had lost on the mantel of the fireplace in his bedroom.

Their brother Georges,—who would not survive them for very long,—was always at his side. Many times, upon entering, I found him seated on the table where the artist was working in the middle of his pencils, watching him draw. I have never seen a child whose features appeared to me more charming and expressive. I remember him still with his blond hair and blue eyes, the arms around the neck of the poor artist! Father and child only talked to each other in a whisper,—often only a glance was all they needed to communicate. Many times I remained next to them, leafing through some album, without a single word being uttered in the space of an hour.

The sympathy and admiration I felt for Grandville had not gone by unnoticed,—he showed me a type of gratitude, such that I was welcome in his home at any hour. Sometimes in the evening, after dinner, I stopped by to see him; I would find the whole family gathered together in the studio, the artist drawing by the light of his lamp, Mme Grandville occupied with some needlework, Armand, his younger son, sleeping in his cradle, and Georges, seated next to his brother, watching him sleep. At eight o'clock Grandville would say: *Time to put the child to bed,*—and the mother would carry away the cradle and leave the room, leading Georges by the hand. Remaining alone with Grandville, we would open some long discussion concerning his *Fleurs animées,* sketches of which he showed me. One day when I was admiring the delightful originality of his compositions: "I have imagined," he told me, "graceful monstrosities for the person who needs, above all, the new—but I do not invent—all I do is bring together incompatible elements and graft incongruous and heterogeneous forms onto one another." Other times we let ourselves go on chatting about nothing in particular while drinking tea; Grandville would then have delightful things to say, always attentive to the least desires of his wife, he would refer to her as *she who determines the good Lord's will*—and it was charming to see him have no other will than hers.][5]

Clogenson's description of the room in which the artist worked matches perfectly the floor plan Grandville drew of the rue des Saints-Pères fourth-floor (in French, third-floor) apartment on which he even indicated the arrangement of the furniture (fig. 104). The oak work table is located by the the room's single window, which looks out onto the tree-shaded courtyard mentioned by Clogenson. The light entering from Grandville's right would seem to indicate that he was left-handed.[6] Behind the chair, on the wall next to the fireplace, would have hung Kaulbach's *Madhouse* (fig. 105).[7] One of the *bahuts,* or hutches, flanked by two of the carved chairs, is located on the wall opposite the fireplace, the other on the wall opposite the window.[8] In addition to the "Atelier" (studio) and the "Chambre à Coucher" (bedroom) are a "Salon" (living room), a "Salle à manger" (dining room), a "Cuisine" (kitchen), and a "Couloir" (hallway) leading to a discreetly placed "lieux" (privy). In the bedroom can be seen the

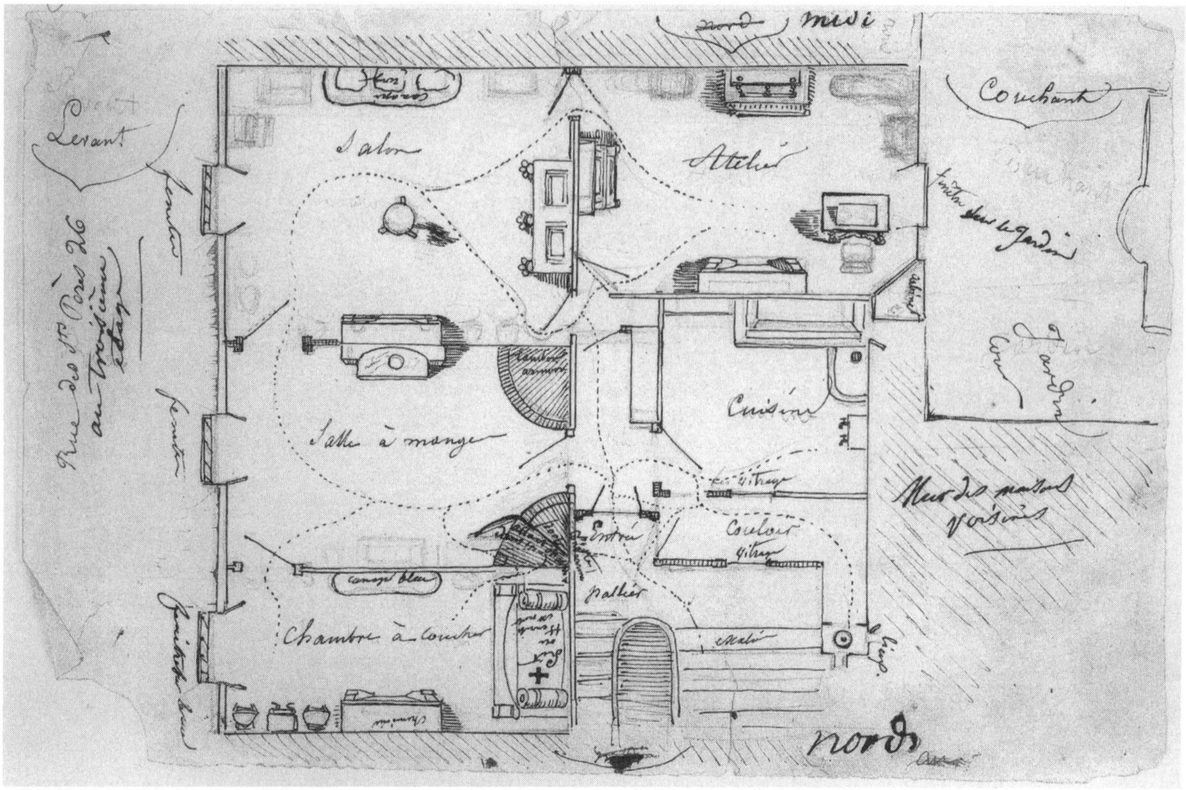

Fig. 104. ***Rue des Sts Pères 26 au troisième étage*** **(Third floor of 26, rue des Saints-Pères), circa 1843–46, drawing. Private collection (reproduction forbidden).**

fireplace mantle on which stood the plaster busts of his deceased sons Ferdinand and Henri, which are still in the family. The bed, as Grandville has carefully noted, is the same one in which his first wife, Henriette, died. This comfortably furnished apartment tangibly demonstrates that Grandville's successful career had established him firmly within the middle class.

While Grandville spent the winter months of January and February at the apartment in Paris, by March he appears to have already moved with his family to their summer residence in Chatou, a modest yet commodious house located at 48, rue de Saint-Germain (today, 48, avenue Foch; fig. 106).[9] In a whimsical fashion typical of his style, he at one point during the summer of 1846 transformed insects into the number 48 of his street address and painted them on one of the pilasters of the wall surrounding the property (fig. 107).[10] The Grandville family remained in Chatou until late October, or for approximately eight months. Thus it is not surprising that most of the 1846 diary fragments date from their extended stay there.

Chatou was located on the first passenger rail line in France, which was inaugurated on August 24, 1837, and linked Paris with the small western suburb of Le Pecq. As a result of its newly facilitated access, Chatou quickly became popular as a summer retreat for Parisians seeking relief from the heat and dust of the capital. Artists in particular were attracted to the picturesque right-bank village and the bucolic île de Chatou, or isle of Chatou, located in the middle of the Seine River. Chatou consequently

Fig. 105. Heinrich Merz after Wilhelm Kaulbach, *Narrenhaus* (Madhouse), undated, steel engraving. Paris, Bibliothèque nationale de France.

developed into something of an artists' colony, remaining a center of artistic activity up until the First World War.[11]

Just as he had in Paris, Grandville became friends with one of his neighbors at Chatou, a middle-aged bachelor and fellow artist by the name of Charles Duval who lived directly across the street at 37, rue de Saint-Germain (today 81, avenue Foch). According to the Chatou municipal archives, Duval was a "peintre sur verre," or painter on glass, who on May 9, 1841, purchased a parcel of land on which he had constructed a house in the picturesque chalet style.[12] Both Grandville's house and Duval's were almost adjacent to the now vanished forest of Vésinet where Duval undoubtedly found the birds that he from time to time carried across the street, presumably to serve as models for his more famous artistic neighbor. The unmarried Duval seems to have adopted Grandville's family as his own and, like Clogenson, apparently stopped by frequently for visits: he is referred to three times in what remains of the Chatou section of the 1846 diary and depicted once (cat. no. 54).

By far the most frequent references in the 1846 diary are to the weather, which Grandville habitually recorded at the beginning of each entry along with the day of the week and its date. As a result,

Fig. 106. Marguerite Cordier, *48 rue St Germain—Chatou: Maison où habita J. J. Grandville à la fin de sa vie* (48, rue de Saint-Germain—Chatou: House where J. J. Grandville lived at the end of his life), undated, drawing. Private collection (reproduction forbidden).

we can trace, for example, the relentless progression of a tropical heat wave during one of the hottest summers on record. In fact, the entire year of 1846 was warmer than usual, which undoubtedly accounts for the Grandvilles' extended summer season at Chatou.

Despite his crowded social calendar, visits from neighbors, the summer's heat, and the ever-present temptation of fishing when at Chatou, Grandville in 1846 completed one major project, *Les Fleurs animées,* and started another, *L'Ingénieux Chevalier Don Quichotte de la Manche.* He finished the former in October (cat. no. 75), by which time he had also completed all the illustrations to the first part of the latter. Work on the second part of *Don Quixote* was cut short by the artist's death on March 17, 1847.

Grandville appears to have kept his 1846 diary in a fairly ordinary notebook. The pages are printed with brown horizontal lines 7.5–8.5 mm apart. Left margins are designated by two vertical brown lines 7.5–8.5 mm apart and right margins by another pair of brown lines the same distance apart with a third

Fig. 107. Anonymous after Grandville, *Numéro fantastique peint par Grandville sur le pilastre d'une maison de campagne à Chatou* (Fantastic number painted by Grandville on the pilaster of a country house at Chatou), *L'Illustration,* October 7, 1848, wood engraving. Paris, Bibliothèque nationale de France.

brown line 16.5–17 mm to their left. Judging from one of the larger fragments (cat. no. 52), there were at least four diary entries per page, with each entry occupying on the average four or five lines. In the upper left-hand corner of each page Grandville wrote the year 1846. Grandville began each diary entry by noting in the left margin the day of the week with its date written between the two vertical lines. Below the day of the week would appear a brief description of climatic conditions and then a postage-stamp-sized drawing depicting one of the day's main events. For the most part, the left edges of the fragments containing the drawings coincide with the left edge of a page, leading to the conclusion that the drawing rectos were originally part of the back of a diary's page. To the right of the two vertical lines were written the four or five lines of the main body of the diary entry, fragments of which often appear along the right edge of a drawing, overlapping the second vertical line.

Like the one from 1830, the 1846 diary doubled as an account book. The word "Dépense," or expenditure, appears at the top of the versos of those drawings that have the year 1846 written at their top. It would thus seem that while Grandville recorded daily events on the left pages of his diary, he listed each day's expenses on the opposite, right page. Assuming this to have been the case, the lists of numbers and calculations on the versos of the diary fragments would be remnants of account keeping done several days earlier. Again, just as in the 1830 diary, Grandville apparently kept track of every centime spent, a true testament to his well-known frugality: "Il était économe et sobre. Il n'avait aucun vice, aucune manie dispendieuse, pas même celle du cigare." (He was thrifty and temperate. He had no vice, no expensive craving, not even that for cigars.).[13]

As usual, the compiler of the Missouri Album saved only the drawings from the 1846 diary. Unlike the 1830 and 1833 diaries, Grandville seems not to have used the 1846 diary as a supplementary sketchbook. For the most part, the drawings record in a summary but witty fashion the most memorable of various days' activities, which are sometimes identified by brief captions: a social gathering, a fishing expedition, the passing of animals on their dusty way to Parisian slaughterhouses. On less eventful days, he sketched a still life or redrew a model he had been examining in preparation for an illustration to *Les Fleurs animées.* While the latter were probably done from life, most of the drawings in the 1846 diary appear to have been done from memory.

45. 3/1 recto

Samedi *17*
Pluie
RAYON DE SOLEIL!..

la nourice va ax Tuileries

Dimanche *18*
(Saturday 17
Rain
Ray of sunshine!..

the wet nurse goes to the Tuileries

Sunday 18)

January 17–18, 1846
40 × 37
Pen and brown ink over pencil

In 1846, the 17th and 18th fell on Saturday and Sunday during the months of January and October. Since October 18 is accounted for elsewhere (cat. no. 73), Sunday the 18th here consequently belongs to the month of January. Further evidence for a January dating of this diary fragment can be found in the wet nurse. Armand, the only child to have resulted from Grandville's second marriage, was born on June 2, 1845. In January 1846 he would have been seven months old and still very much in need of a wet nurse; this would not have automatically been the case in October when he had reached the age of sixteen months.

As he often does in the diary of 1846, Grandville begins his entry for Saturday, January 17 by recording the climatic conditions: rain followed by a ray of sunshine, the latter cleverly portrayed in a sketch of the sun peeping from behind a cloud. Armand's wet nurse, wearing her distinctive bonnet and holding the seven-month-old infant in her arms, takes advantage of the break in the weather and goes for a walk in the Tuileries Gardens. The sun, wet nurse, Armand, and the trees are all represented in a schematic, comic-book style that, like the pencil underdrawing, is not seen in later drawings from the 1846 diary. These are two more reasons for situating this diary fragment at the beginning of the year.

3/1 verso

[fragment of a list of numbers]

January 1846
40 × 37
Pen and brown ink

46. 6/5 recto

Auguste vient
prendre le dessin
du chien et le berger.

SOIRÉE *24.*
BIXI.

Samedi *24*
(Auguste stops by
to take the drawing
of the dog and the shepherd.

Soirée 24.
Bixi.

Saturday 24)

January 24(?), 1846
47 × 36
Pen and brown ink

During the year 1846, the 24th fell on a Saturday during the months of January and October. The soirée depicted here would seem to be part of the winter social season, situating this diary fragment in January. The mention of Auguste as well argues for the earlier month. As in cat. no. 33, the Auguste in question is no doubt Auguste Desperet, Grandville's artistic collaborator since the latter part of 1833 (see cat. no. 21). However, for whatever reason, Desperet appears not to have assisted Grandville with *Les Fleurs animées,* the first installment of which was registered in the *Bibliographie de la France* on April 25, 1846.[14] It therefore seems more likely that Desperet would have stopped by to pick up one of the artist's drawings in January rather than in October.

The drawing "of the dog and the shepherd" presumably refers to an illustration for Lavalette's fable, "Le Berger et son Chien" (The Shepherd and His Dog). Several years earlier, Grandville had in fact illustrated the *Fables de Lavalette* (Hetzel et Paulin, 1841), but there was no plate representing "The

Shepherd and His Dog." It is possible that the drawing taken by Desperet was one produced for the book, but had remained unpublished. Why Desperet should have been interested in this particular drawing in 1846 remains a mystery.

The drawing in the diary appears to depict the "Soirée Bixi." "Bixi" may well be the somewhat abbreviated spelling of Bixio. If this is indeed the case, the reference then surely is to Jacques-Alexandre Bixio (1808–65), an ardent liberal and polymath who, although a doctor, never practiced medicine and pursued instead the twin careers of journalist and publisher. Among his many accomplishments were the founding of the *Revue des Deux Mondes* with François Buloz (1803–77) and the publishing of important books on agriculture.

There would have been numerous opportunities for Grandville to make Bixio's acquaintance. Both fought during the Revolution of 1830 and became leading members of the opposition with the establishment of the July Monarchy: Grandville's identification with Philipon and *La Caricature* was matched by Bixio's affiliation with Armand Carrel and *Le National.* Among friends the two men held in common were Jules Taschereau, at one point an associate of Carrel on the staff of *Le National,* and the mime artist, Alexandre Vattemare, encountered in cat. no. 4. Perhaps most significantly, they were both closely linked to Pierre-Jules Hetzel. The publisher of Grandville's *Scènes de la vie privée et publique des animaux* had a long-standing relationship with Bixio who lent him money when he found himself in financial difficulties. Interestingly enough, one such occasion was in 1846.[15]

A natural leader who, as we have just seen, possessed a generous disposition, Bixio was well-known in the upper echelons of the French business and political worlds. Auguste Villemot describes his character and the gatherings of accomplished individuals, which he liked to organize:

> C'était un grand coeur, un grand esprit, et, ce qui est infiniment plus rare, un caractère . . . Sa parole pouvait s'élever jusqu'à cette éloquence captivante des choses bien comprises et bien dites, et il savait mêler, aux matières les plus arides, tous les agréments d'un esprit orné, aimable, séduisant, inépuisable en ressources imprévues et ingénieuses. Dans toutes les réunions d'hommes, et je parle des hommes les plus éminents, il exerçait une domination incontestée, qu'il ne recherchait pas, et qui venait à lui par l'ascendant de son caractère, la fermeté de sa parole, l'autorité et la compétence de ses appréciations sur toutes choses. Pendant trente ans, il a rassemblé, dans son salon, les hommes les plus considérables de son temps; quelques-uns le dépassaient dans leur spécialité; aucun n'aurait pu diriger, dans son ensemble, ce concert des plus hautes capacités. Chez lui et ailleurs, Bixio semblait de président né de toutes les réunions . . . A ses débuts dans le monde, il avait trouvé la vie difficile; il était fils de ses oeuvres, et il était fier de l'effort qu'il avait dû faire pour conquérir sa place dans la Société. Il y a plus de vingt-cinq ans, il avait fondé le *dîner des parvenus* qui, tous les mois, réunissait à la même table, des hommes occupant les premiers postes dans l'Etat, dans les arts et dans la littérature. La condition sine quâ non de l'admission était de justifier qu'on était entré dans le monde sans patrimoine, et qu'on ne devait sa fortune qu'à ses talents et à son industrie.

> [He was a good-hearted man, a great mind, and, what is infinitely rarer, a personality . . . His speech could elevate itself to that captivating eloquence of things well-understood and well-spoken, and he knew how to add to the most dry subjects all the embellishments of a cultivated, amiable, alluring intellect unlimited in unexpected and ingenious resources. In all the assemblies of men, and I am talking about the most eminent men, he exercised an undisputed dominion that he did not seek out and that came to him by the superiority of his character, the firmness of his speech, the authority and competence in his appreciation for all things. For thirty years he assembled together in his salon the most notable men of his time; some of them surpassed him in their specialty; none would have been able to manage in the whole that union of the highest capacities. In his home and elsewhere, Bixio seemed the born leader of all assemblies . . . When he started out in the world, he found life difficult; he was the product of his work, and he was proud of the effort he had had to put forth in order to gain a place in society. Over twenty-five years ago he founded the *dinner of parvenus* that every month brought together at the same table men occupying the highest positions in the State, the

> arts, and literature. The sine qua non condition of admission was to prove that you had entered into the world without inheritance and that you owed your fortune only to your abilities and your industriousness.[16]

The sketch seems to represent Bixio presiding at one of his parvenu dinners. Dressed in formal evening attire, he stands at the left in front of a table on which are what appear to be large albums, perhaps containing Grandville's own work, which would have constituted his artistic contribution to the evening. As a former leader of opposition political caricature, celebrated book illustrator, and self-made man, Grandville would have been eminently qualified to participate in one of Bixio's gatherings.

6/5 verso

[fragment of a list of numbers]

January(?) 1846
47 × 36
Pen and brown ink

47. 4/2 recto

Couvert..
boue....
Soirée de l'Odèon

tems se maintient
(Cloudy..
mud....
Odéon soirée

weather unchanged)

January 31, 1846
36 × 34
Pen and brown ink

Even though this diary fragment is not dated, there is every reason to believe that the soirée at the Odéon theater depicted here took place on January 31, 1846.

By the end of December 1845, the 1846 winter social season had already begun, and balls were being held in "guinguettes, des grands restaurants, et des salles d'hiver" (road houses, large restaurants, and assembly halls),[17] as well as in Parisian theaters that were transformed into large open dance halls thanks to temporary floors constructed over the orchestra at the same level as the stage. For instance, in its December 28, 1845, issue, *L'Artiste* relates, "Les fêtes de l'hiver ont commencé de toutes parts. Tout le monde est revenu; les salons se rouvrent; la jeunesse rentre en danse.—Ce soir, il y a bal à l'Opéra, et Musard fils n'attend que le 1er janvier pour donner le branle à l'Opéra-Comique." (Everywhere the winter festivities have begun. Everyone has come back; the salons are reopening; young people return dancing.—Tonight there is a ball at the Opera, and Musard junior is only waiting for the first of January to get going at the Opéra-Comique.)[18] So numerous, in fact, were the balls in 1846 that the chief of police, Gabriel Delessert (1786–1858), was moved to report in a bulletin dated February 15, "Une quantité extraordinaire de bals publics et privés a eu lieu cet hiver, à aucune époque la population n'a été plus en train de s'amuser." (An extraordinary number of public and private balls have taken place this winter, at no other time has the population ever been more in the midst of amusing itself.).[19] Grandville joined in the festivities.

Judging from the very proper formal evening attire worn by the sedate couple in the background, the Odéon soirée depicted here is not the traditional (and traditionally unruly) carnival masquerade ball of students and their grisettes, which Grandville had earlier portrayed in 1828 (Nancy, cat. no. 39).[20] Instead, it appears to represent the elegant benefit ball held January 31, 1846, by the newly formed Association des artistes peintres, sculpteurs, graveurs, architectes et dessinateurs (Association of professional painters, sculptors, engravers, architects and draftsmen), one of the numerous mutual aid societies that, in the absence of unions and state-supported social programs, proliferated in France during the nineteenth century.[21] The Association des artistes, as it was commonly called, was founded by the famous promoter of the arts, Baron Taylor (1789–1879). Having earlier established the highly successful Association des artistes dramatiques (Association of professional dramatists) and Association des artistes musiciens (Association of professional musicians), Taylor outlined to a group of well-known painters on December 7, 1844, his plan for a third artistic association. One week later, the *Journal des Artistes* published the statutes of the new organization, which were based directly on those of the two preceding ones. The first two articles of the association's charter defined its raison d'être:

> ART. 1er. Une Association est établie par les présents Statuts entre tous les Artistes Peintres d'histoire ou de genre, Sculpteurs, Graveurs, Architectes et Dessinateurs.
> ART. 2. Le but de cette Association est la création d'une caisse de secours dans l'intérêt des Artistes faisant partie de l'Association.
>
> (Article 1. The present statutes establish an association among all professional history or genre painters, sculptors, engravers, architects, and draftsmen.
> Article 2. The goal of this association is the creation of a relief fund for artists belonging to the association.)[22]

Grandville and a number of his friends and artistic collaborators, including Duval Le Camus, Falampin, Forest, Guiaud, and Menut, were among the association's founding members. Several of them even took on positions of responsibility during the organization's early years. For instance, Duval Le Camus, who had been decorated with the Legion of Honor in 1837, served as one of the governing committee's vice presidents from the association's inception through 1848 and was president of the commissions responsible for organizing the benefit balls of 1846 and 1847. Guiaud was a member of the governing committee from 1845 through 1847. Falampin, one of the original secretaries for the association, was also a member of the governing committee in 1846.[23]

Like its two sister organizations, the Association des artistes met with almost instant success. One year after its inception, two major fund-raising events were organized: an exhibition and a benefit ball. The exhibition, which featured the work of David, Prudhon, Ingres, Delacroix, Delaroche, Horace Vernet, and Ary Scheffer among others, opened at the Galerie des Beaux-Arts, boulevard Bonne-Nouvelle during the first week of January 1846.[24] The ball, organized by a special commission headed by Duval Le Camus, was held later that same month on January 31 in the freshly renovated Odéon theater, where its new director, the celebrated actor of the Romantic stage, Bocage (1799–1862), had recently instituted a small museum of contemporary art.[25] The February 4, 1846, issue of the official government newspaper, *Le Moniteur universel,* gives a concise account of the festive occasion:

> Le bal des artistes peintres, sculpteurs, architectes, graveurs, dessinateurs, qui a eu lieu avant-hier à l'Odéon, a été d'une magnificence digne de la nouvelle association. Seize à dix-sept cents voitures ont déposé au péristyle de l'édifice, de neuf heures du soir à une heure du matin, les quatre mille personnes qui, de tous les

points de Paris, se rendaient à l'Odéon. Le péristyle, les escaliers, le foyer, la salle étaient spendidement éclairés. Dans la salle, de grand banderoles qui descendaient le long des parois portaient les noms des artistes les plus célèbres des écoles italienne, française, flamande, hollandaise, espagnole, etc., et les noms des plus illustres protecteurs de l'art. Une belle figure, debout dans un char traîné par quatre chevaux, représentait la France entourée de tous les attributs des arts. Les lustres et les fleurs étaient répandus de tous côtés avec une prodigalité grandiose. On a dansé depuis dix heures du soir jusqu'à cinq heures du matin, et l'on n'a eu à déplorer aucun accident.

[The ball of professional artists, sculptors, architects, engravers, draftsmen, which took place the day before yesterday [*sic*] at the Odéon was of a magnificence worthy of the new association. From nine o'clock at night until one o'clock in the morning, sixteen to seventeen hundred carriages dropped off at the building's peristyle the four thousand people who from all over Paris made their way to the Odéon. The peristyle, the staircases, the lobby, the auditorium were splendidly lit. In the auditorium, long banderoles which ran down along the walls bore the names of the most famous artists of the Italian, French, Flemish, Dutch, Spanish, etc. schools, and the names of the most illustrious art patrons. A beautiful figure, standing in a chariot drawn by four horses, depicted France surrounded by all the attributes of the arts. Chandeliers and flowers were scattered everywhere with a majestic lavishness. They danced from ten o'clock at night until five o'clock in the morning, and there was not a single mishap to regret.]

A lithograph by Guiaud of the second benefit ball held at the Odéon on February 20, 1847, gives an idea of what the flower-bedecked theater must have looked like during the original ball of 1846 (fig. 108). In its more detailed account of the evening, the *Journal des Artistes* notes that although members of the artistic community composed the vast majority of those in attendance, other segments of French society were present as well: "la politique et la noblesse, la magistrature et la finance, l'administration et l'armée, avaient voulu s'unir de coeur aux bienfaisantes vues de l'association et payer aussi de leur personne dans cette brillante solennité" (the body politic and the nobility, the magistrature and the world of finance, the administration and the army wished to unite their hearts with the benevolent aims of the association and also to contribute to this brilliant celebration by their presence).[26]

As a charter member of the Association des artistes, Grandville naturally would have wanted to attend its first annual benefit ball on the evening of Saturday, January 31, 1846. In his small sketch of the occasion, he represents part of the elegant crowd in the background. The two Arabs in the foreground are more than likely members of the Moroccan ambassadorial mission, which was then visiting Paris.[27] The figure closest to the viewer may be the Moroccan ambassador, himself, Ben-Achache, dressed in a formal white burnoose like the one he would wear on February 13 when presenting to Louis-Philippe in the Cour du Carrousel of the Tuileries Palace the six Arab horses sent as a gift by the emperor of Morocco.[28]

The cloudy weather and the muddy conditions reported by Grandville would have been typical for January 1846, during which there were "neuf jours de beau temps, treize jours de temps couvert, deux jours de brouillards, sept jours de pluie" (nine days of fair weather, thirteen days of cloudy weather, two days of fog, seven days of rain).[29]

4/2 verso

[fragment of a list of numbers]

January 1846
36 × 34
Pen and brown ink

Fig. 108. Jacques Guiaud, *Foyer de l'Odéon: Bal de l'Association des Artistes Peintres &a.* (Foyer of the Odéon: Ball of the Association of professional painters etc.), *Journal des Artistes,* February 28, 1847, lithograph. Paris, Bibliothèque nationale de France.

48. 4/4 recto

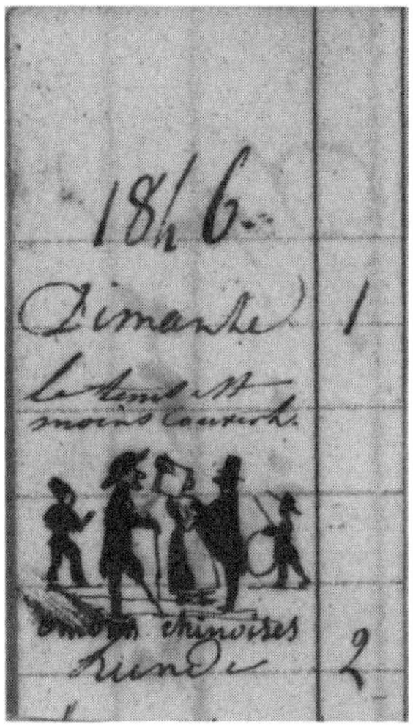

1846
Dimanche *1*
le tems est
moins couvert.

ombres chinoises
Lundi *2*
(1846
Sunday 1
the weather is
less overcast.

shadow-show
Monday 2)

February 1–2(?), 1846
67 × 37
Pen and brown ink

This and the next four diary excerpts all carry dates that could have fallen in any of three months: February, March, or November 1846. However, the dismal climatic conditions that predominate—"weather more and more cold," "cloudy weather," "fog"—would seem to indicate the wintry month of February and the continuation of the same type of weather that had prevailed during the preceding month of January.

On what is presumably Sunday, February 1, the sky is less overcast. Having spent the previous evening with Céline socializing at the Odéon, Grandville may have decided that it was Georges's turn to go out on the town, and treats him to a shadow-show whose silhouetted figures he sketches in the diary. Their destination more than likely would have been the Palais-Royal where at nos. 119 and 120 in the galerie de Valois François Dominique Séraphin had established his famous *théâtre d'Ombres chinoises et de Marionnettes* (Shadow-show and puppet theater) in 1784. The Palais-Royal would remain its home until 1860 when the theater was transferred to the boulevard Montmartre.[30]

Grandville appears to have had an ongoing fascination with *ombres chinoises* (literally, "Chinese shadows" in reference to their supposed oriental origins), which bear a direct relationship to his own early satirical *ombres portées,* or "cast shadows" (see Nancy, cat. nos. 112, 173–77). For example, the black silhouetted figures produced for the last chapter of *Petites misères de la vie humaine* of 1843 directly imitate *ombres chinoises* as does the world-turned-upside-down image of *Les Ombres françaises* (The French shadows) created around the same time for the "La Jeune Chine" (The young China) chapter of *Un autre monde,* which parodied the La Jeune-France designation of French Romantics (fig. 109). And judging from the cutout paper doll–like figure of the evil butcher clutching a terrified child from the legend of Saint Nicholas seen in cat. no. 41 (fig. 103), he may have improvised his own shadow-show performances as home entertainment for the children.[31] Like the puppets used in *ombres chinoises,* it presents a strong, somewhat exaggerated silhouette and has small cutout openings for the eye and mouth. That Grandville did in fact produce paper cutout figures for domestic recreation is documented in an article entitled "Découpures, ou ombres éclairées" (Cutouts, or illuminated shadows) published in the *Magasin pittoresque* shortly before his death. It describes his experiments with paper cutouts and the "shadows of a truly curious effect" that he was able to obtain, some examples of which were represented in his own accompanying illustrations (fig. 110).[32]

Fig. 109. ***Les Ombres françaises*** **(The French shadows.) from** ***Un autre monde,*** **1844, wood engraving. Private collection.**

4/4 verso

Dépense
(Expenditure)
[fragment of a list of numbers]

February(?) 1846
67 × 37
Pen and brown ink

49. 4/6 recto

Jeudi *5*
tems plus, en
plus froid

[*Vendredi* *6*]
(Thursday 5
weather more and
more cold

[Friday 6])

Fig. 110. *Découpures, ou ombres éclairées* (Cutouts, or illuminated shadows), *Magasin pittoresque*, February 1847, wood engraving. Paris, Bibliothèque nationale de France.

February 5–6(?), 1846
45 × 36
Pen and brown ink

As the temperature dropped, Grandville probably contented himself with staying indoors, hence this still life of eggcups, glasses, bottle, and breadbasket, the quiet domesticity of which calls to mind Chardin. Even though he is not known as a practitioner of the genre, Grandville occasionally amused himself with still life compositions as is attested to by the remarkable oil painting from 1836, formerly in the collection of Pierre Parisot and now in the Nancy Musée des Beaux-Arts.

4/6 verso

[fragment of a list of numbers]

February(?) 1846
45 × 36
Pen and brown ink

50. 2/1 recto

1846
Samedi 7
tems couvert
Brouillard.
(1846

Saturday 7
cloudy weather
Fog.)

February 7(?), 1846
71 × 37
Pen and brown ink

Grandville probably did not have a great deal to report as he presumably continued to stay indoors, avoiding the inclement weather. Unwilling to leave his diary entry for the day devoid of any drawing, he sketched his desk lamp.

2/1 verso

Dépense
(Expenditure)
[fragment of a list of numbers]

February(?) 1846
71 × 37
Pen and brown ink

51. 3/6 recto

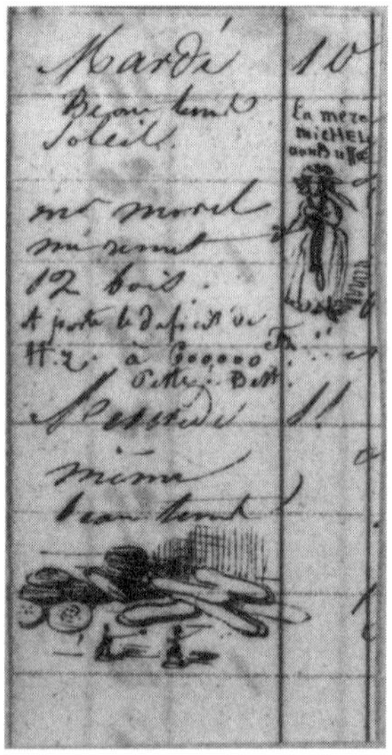

Mardi *10*
Beau tems *La mèzo*
Soleil *MiCHEL*
au Bullic [?]
Mr Morel
me remet
12 bois
A porte le deficit de
H.z. à 600,000
Peste! Best!
Mercredi *11*
méme
beau tems
(Tuesday 10
Fair weather The mezzo-soprano
Sun Michel[ ]
at the Bullic[ ]
Mr. Morel
returns to me
12 wood blocks
Carried forward the deficit of
H[et]z[el] to 600,000
Blast! Best!
Wednesday 11
same
fair weather)

February 10–11(?), 1846
72 × 36
Pen and brown ink

What is presumably February 10, 1846, turns out to be a beautiful, sunny day. A certain Mr. Morel returns twelve wood-engraving blocks, which supposedly brings the amount that "H.z." (surely a reference to the publisher Pierre-Jules Hetzel) owes Grandville to 600,000 francs, causing our artist to exclaim, "Peste! Best!"

The first publication that Grandville worked on for Hetzel after the unfortunate misunderstanding three years earlier concerning the genesis of Tony Johannot's *Voyage où il vous plaira* (Voyage to where it will please you; see Nancy, 341–42) was the *Almanach du jour de l'an* (New Year's Day almanac) recorded in the *Bibliographie de la France* on January 10, 1846.[33] Its conception was similar to the celebrated *Scènes de la vie privée et publique des animaux,* the last project on which Hetzel and Grandville had collaborated: a series of short articles or poems by eminent contemporary writers accompanied by illustrations provided by Grandville and several other equally distinguished artist-draftsmen. The authors, certain of whom had participated in the earlier publication, were Balzac, the marquis de Belloy, Alexandre Dumas fils, Henry Egmont, Théophile Gautier, Léon Gozlan, Arsène Houssaye, Laurent Jan, Émile de Labédollière, August Lireux, Alfred de Musset, and Hetzel himself, under his nom de plume, P.-J. Stahl. Besides Grandville, the artists included Bertall (1820–82) and Alcide Joseph Lorentz (1813–?).[34]

It seems probable that at least some of the wood-engraving blocks returned by Hetzel via Mr. Morel were for the *Almanach du jour de l'an.*[35] That Grandville's contribution to the publication brought the amount that Hetzel owed him to a total of 600,000 francs is clearly a facetious exaggeration. As seen in the inventory drawn up at the time of his second marriage, Grandville's total fortune in October 1843 came to 53,765.87 francs; 5,000 of that sum was owed to him by Hetzel and Paulin, presumably for the illustrations to the recently completed *Scènes de la vie privée et publique des animaux.* That the outstanding balance Hetzel owed Grandville should have increased one-hundred-twenty-fold during the intervening period of two years and four months strains the imagination. Nevertheless, the exaggeration seems to be in proportion to Grandville's frustration with the slowness with which the financially strapped editor liquidated his debt toward him (the 3,000 franc loan from Bixio to Hetzel mentioned in cat. no. 46 gives some indication of Hetzel's solvency problems in 1846). This frustration is amplified by the rhymed mild curse that follows in which Grandville equates "Peste!" (literally, "Plague!") with Best, the name of the wood engraver who often worked for Hetzel and who may have engraved the blocks being returned to the artist.

Squeezed into the right of this fragmented entry for Tuesday the 10th is a sketch of the mezzo-soprano whom Grandville heard sing later that evening. The name of the mezzo (Mlle Michel?) and the place of the performance (aux Bullic [*sic?*]) are possibly incomplete and remain unconfirmed.

On the following day Wednesday, the 11th, the same sunny weather prevailed. The still life of an impressive array of pastries, including what appear to be éclairs, takes on the appearance of a rocky landscape in front of which two toy lead soldiers wage combat.

3/6 verso

[fragment of a list of numbers]

72 × 36
February(?) 1846
Pen and brown ink

52. 4/1 recto

1846
Vendredi 13
Soleil mais tems
froid.

Samedi 14
même tems

Dimanche 15
Même tems,
Brouillard.

Lundi 16
(1846
Friday 13
Sun but cold
weather.

Saturday 14
same weather

Sunday 15
Same weather,
Fog.

Monday 16)

February 13–16, 1846
132 × 39
Pen and brown ink

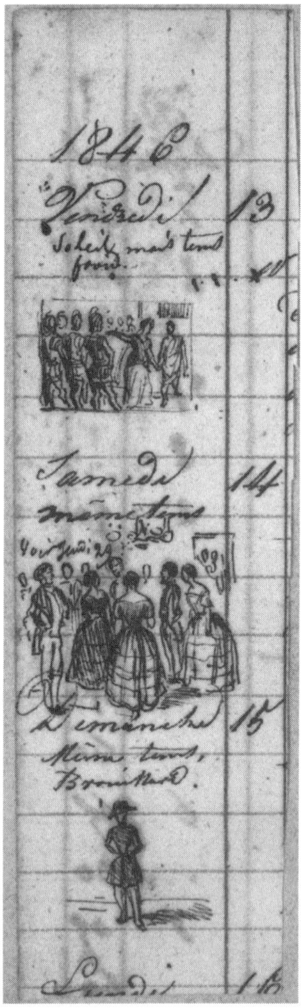

The scene from Corneille's classic 1641 tragedy, *Cinna,* depicted at the top of this diary fragment, situates it in the month of February. On Thursday, February 12, 1846, *Cinna* was presented by the Comédie-Française at the Théâtre-Français with two of the most famous actors of the day, Geffroy and Mlle Rachel in the starring roles of Cinna and Emilie.[36] In his sketch, presumably done on Friday the thirteenth, Grandville has recorded his souvenir of the previous evening's performance. Typically, he has represented the climax of the drama that occurs in act 5, scene 2 when Emilie announces to Augustus that it was she and not her lover, Cinna, who instigated the conspiracy against the emperor's life. Grandville appears to have viewed the performance from the left side of the orchestra with the result that members of the imperial guard have blocked from his view Augustus and the emperor's wife, Livia. He, however, had a clear view of the histrionics of Mlle Rachel who is shown interpreting the role of Emilie in the center of the composition. Geffroy, in the title role of Cinna, stands draped in a toga at the right.

This sketch is the only framed drawing in the Missouri Album. There is a precedent for this incongruity. Unlike all the other images in *Un autre monde* of 1843–44 that are vignettes, the illustrations for the satirical chapter on neoclassicism, "Une journée à Rheculanum" (A day at Rheculanum), are circumscribed by stark, single-lined rectangular frames in imitation of the neoclassic line engravings that they spoof. Grandville no doubt felt that given the Roman setting of Corneille's classic tragedy, his visual souvenir of it merited an appropriate Roman, that is, neoclassic frame. He may also have had in the back of his mind the notion of producing a parody of such stage-inspired neoclassic paintings as Guérin's famously histrionic *Phaedra and Hippolytus* of 1802 (Louvre), which depicts the climatic scene from the tragedy *Phèdre* by Corneille's rival, Racine.

Two days later, Grandville continued his busy social life and attended an unidentified elegant gathering—probably another soirée—which is depicted under the entry for Saturday the fourteenth.

The figure at the bottom of the sheet dressed in what appears to be the uniform of the École Polytechnique may be the noted chemist, Edmond Frémy (1814–94). In 1840 he started out as an assistant lecturer in chemistry at the elite École Polytechnique; in January 1846 he was promoted to the rank of professor.[37] Beginning in 1842 he was also chosen to teach the chemistry courses at the Muséum d'histoire naturelle by Gay-Lussac whose chair at the Muséum he occupied upon the latter's death in 1850. Grandville could have known Edmond through his older brother, Arnould Frémy (1809–?), who, along with three other associates of *Le Charivari,* recently had written the text to *Cent proverbes* of 1845.[38] The sketch may very well commemorate Edmond's newly elevated position at the École Polytechnique, even though as a civilian professor he would not have worn a uniform. Grandville's likely acquaintance with Edmond Frémy in 1846 would help to explain the existence of a series of drawings at the Nancy Musée des Beaux-Arts (Inv. 877.1279—877.1288), depicting an animated chemistry of personified elements that the artist appears to have worked on during the last year of his life.

4/1 verso

Dépense
(Expenditure)
[fragment of a list of numbers]

February 1846
132 × 39
Pen and brown ink

53. 3/8 recto

15

March 15, 1846
56 × 28
Pen and brown ink

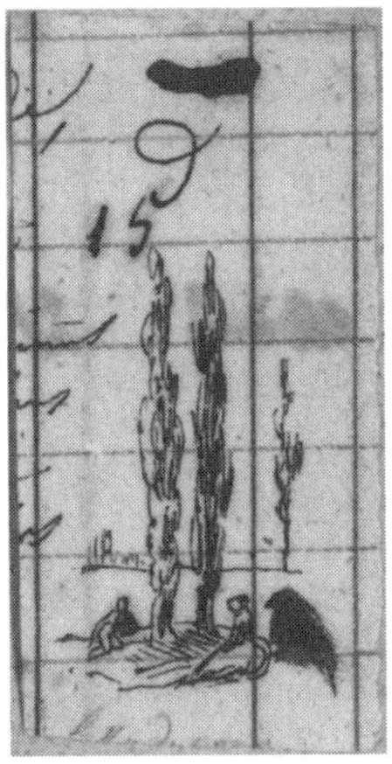

Given the date of March 21 on the back of this fragment, the "15" on the recto would appear to indicate the earlier date of March 15.

A wall like the one seen in this diary sketch encompassed the house and small park of Grandville's residence at 48, rue de Saint-Germain in Chatou. There is good reason to believe that the drawing represents Céline and Georges resting by the park wall next to some poplar trees, an omnipresent part of the Chatou landscape in the nineteenth century just as they still are today. If this is in fact the case, the sketch would seem to indicate that Grandville and his family had left their Paris apartment by March 15 for what would prove to be an extended stay at Chatou. Normally March weather would not encourage a move to a rural village residence and its accompanying outdoor lifestyle. However, according to repeated reports in *Le Moniteur universel,* the spring of 1846 was as unusually mild as the preceding winter had been.[39] The precocious warmth was a harbinger of what would be an exceptionally long and hot summer.

While the sketch more than likely documents the family's move to Chatou, it also demonstrates Grandville's irrepressible urge to transform the everyday world into an imaginary one of his own invention. In a typically whimsical fashion, he has drawn the shadow cast on the wall by Céline as the silhouette of a bird in imitation of his earlier caricatural *ombres portées.*

Unlike other excerpts from the 1846 diary, which carry fragments of writing along their right edge, this is the only one which shows fragmented words along the left, indicating that it was cut from the right margin of the page. If so, it demonstrates that Grandville would repeat the date along the right margin where he occasionally would also draw a sketch.

3/8 verso

Mars. 21
(March. 21)

March 21, 1846
56 × 28
Pen and brown ink

Only the date, handwritten in pen and ink, appears on the verso of this diary fragment.

54. 2/5 recto

pluie battante

Jeudi *19*
(driving rain

Thursday 19)

March 18–19, 1846
42 × 37
Pen and brown ink

In 1846, the 19th fell on a Thursday during the months of February, March, and November. Given the person portrayed, it is likely that this diary fragment dates from March when Grandville apparently was already at Chatou. Also, the reference to "driving rain" would seem to describe a typical springtime downpour known as a *giboulée de mars.*

Fig. 111. ***Vieux Garcon de 50a moins 3 mois . . . ah! les Beaux oiseaux maman, que duval apporte à mon Père*** **(Fifty-year-old-minus-three-months bachelor . . . oh! the pretty birds, mama, that Duval brings my father), 1846, drawing. Nancy, Musée des Beaux-Arts (Inv. 877.522).**

The caricatured portrait is that of Grandville's neighbor across the street, the painter on glass Charles Duval, who often stopped by with injured or orphaned birds for the animal-loving Grandville to adopt or sketch. It is identical to the head in a remarkable 196 × 65 mm full-length pencil drawing of Duval at the Nancy Musée des Beaux-Arts (fig. 111): annotations at the bottom record his age and bachelor status as well as Georges's exclamation upon seeing the birds, which he clutches in either hand, "ah! les Beaux oiseaux maman, que duval apporte à mon Père" (oh! the pretty birds, mama, that Duval brings my father).

2/5 verso

[fragment of a list of numbers]

March 1846
42 × 37
Pen and brown ink

55. 2/7 recto

Jeudi	*2*
	vin
	mis
averse	*en*
furieuse	*Boute[ille].*
(Thursday	2
	wine
raging	bottled
downpour)	

April 2, 1846
42 × 37
Pen and brown ink

In 1846, April 2 was the Thursday before Palm Sunday. Despite his ambivalent attitude toward Christianity, Grandville has drawn this tiny vignette of Christ's entry into Jerusalem, possibly in order to entertain Georges who, as Clogenson states, was constantly by the artist's side. He has followed the traditional iconography for this Palm Sunday subject: Christ rides through the streets seated on a donkey as crowds hail him, and place palm branches in his path. A figure with arm raised in salute stands at the right; what appears to be a palm branch is being waved at the left.

As he so often does in the 1846 diary, Grandville notes the climatic conditions, which in this case included a particularly heavy April shower. He also mentions the decanting of wine into bottles, possibly in preparation for a formal Palm Sunday meal.

2/7 verso

[fragment of a list of numbers]

April 1846
42 × 37
Pen and brown ink

56. 4/5 recto

Mardi *7*
pluie le matin
il se remeta beau

Mercredi *8*
(Tuesday 7

rain in the morning
it went back to being fair

Wednesday 8)

April 7–8, 1846
42 × 36
Pen with brown and black ink

The dates of Tuesday the 7th and Wednesday the 8th occurred during the months of April and July in 1846. The rain recorded by Grandville would have been more characteristic of weather conditions during April, hence the probable date from this month.

Judging from this diary fragment and that from September 1 (cat. no. 70), live ducks were acquired regularly by the Grandville household during their stay at Chatou. The periodic purchase of the fowl strongly suggests that they were kept less as backyard pets than as future main courses on the family dinner table. True, the little ducklings here might have served as an amusement for the children with the approach of Easter on April 12, but the fate ultimately reserved for them was probably of a culinary nature.

4/5 verso

[fragment of a list of numbers]

April 1846
42 × 36
Pen and brown ink

57. 7/2 recto

1ere Soirée
à la lumière
Ms armand
et Georges
pleinement
endormis

Vendredi 8
(first evening
by light
Messrs. Armand
and Georges
soundly
asleep

Friday 8)

May 7–8, 1846
58 × 39
Pen and brown ink

After mentioning that the lengthening daylight hours enabled passing the evening of May 7 without the need of artificial light, Grandville notes that his two sons are soundly asleep. He then draws the eleven-month-old Armand playing with a whip. Whips, it appears, were among the playthings regularly given to the Grandville children. In a humorous letter to his family dated September 21, 1836, where he recounts the harrowing stagecoach ride back to Paris from Nancy, Grandville notes that Ferdinand, his first son who was then almost two years of age, managed to throw three toy whips out of the diligence door window.

7/2 verso

[fragment of a list of numbers]

May 1846
58 × 39
Pen and brown ink

58. 2/3 recto

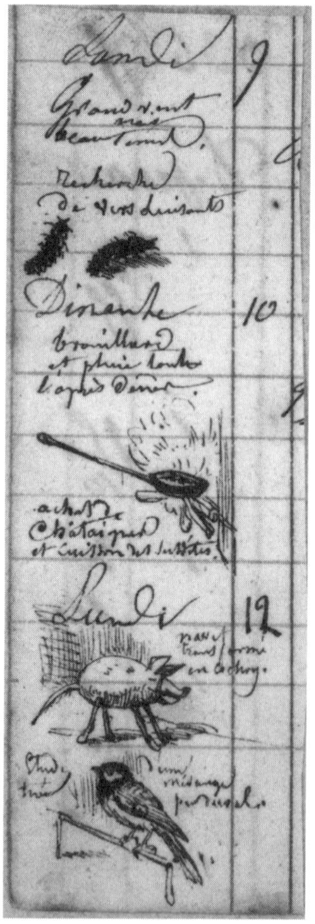

Sam[e]di 9
Grand vent
mais
Beau tems.

recherche
de vers Luisants

Diman[c]he 10
brouillard
et pluie toute
l'après dîner.

achat de
Châtaignes
et cuisson ressussites.

Lundi 12
navet
transformé
en cochon.

Etude d'un
mésange
tr[ou]vé par duval.
(Saturday 9
Strong wind
but
Fair weather.

search
for glowworms

Sunday 10
fog
and rain the entire
time after dinner.

purchase of
Chestnuts
and successful roasting.

Monday 12
turnip
transformed
into a pig.

Study of a
titmouse
found by Duval.)

May 9–11, 1846
115 × 39
Pen and brown ink

As with most people, the demands of family and work made for days that were more busy than others. This would have been especially true for someone working at home with two small children. From all appearances, the weekend of May 9–10 and the following Monday were particularly hectic. The staccatolike phrases of these diary entries as well as the incompletely spelled days of the week attest to the rapidity with which they were written. Moreover, a seemingly rushed Grandville has rashly changed the date of Monday from the 11th to the 12th. The apparent time constraints, however, have not kept him from producing delightfully amusing vignettes.

After commenting on the windy yet sunny weather conditions for Saturday, Grandville records the hunt for *vers luisants,* or glowworms. The glowworms in question were no doubt needed as models for the one carrying a lantern in the preparatory drawing for the *Pavot,* or "Poppy" plate of *Les Fleurs animées* (fig. 112), the publication on which he was then working. As the sketch in the diary demonstrates, once he returned home he studied the glowworms as they crawled over his work table. The large and exceptionally fine study of life-size glowworms at the Nancy Musée des Beaux-Arts (Nancy, cat. no. 232), which is closely related to the diary sketch, was undoubtedly done at this time. It would have been from such true-to-life studies that Grandville whimsically transformed one of his models into the humanoid glowworm that lights its way through the darkness as the rest of the insect world sleeps under the narcotic influence of the poppy seeds being scattered by the personified poppy flower above them.

On the following day, Sunday, the weather worsened with fog and rain lasting throughout the afternoon after the traditional Sunday dinner. The main event of the day was the purchase of chestnuts and successfully roasting them over a fire in the snug comfort of the Grandville home.

No indication of the climatic conditions is given for Monday. However, the rainy weather may have continued, in which case attempts would have been made to amuse the children who were kept from

Fig. 112. Study for *Pavot* (Poppy), 1846, wash drawing. Nancy, Bibliothèque municipale.

going outdoors. Such is the possible context for the turnip turned into a pig. The ever-friendly Duval at one point stopped by with a titmouse that he had found: Grandville sketched it on a perch.

2/3 verso

Dépense
(expenditure)
[fragment of a list of expenses]

May 1846
115 × 39
Pen and brown ink

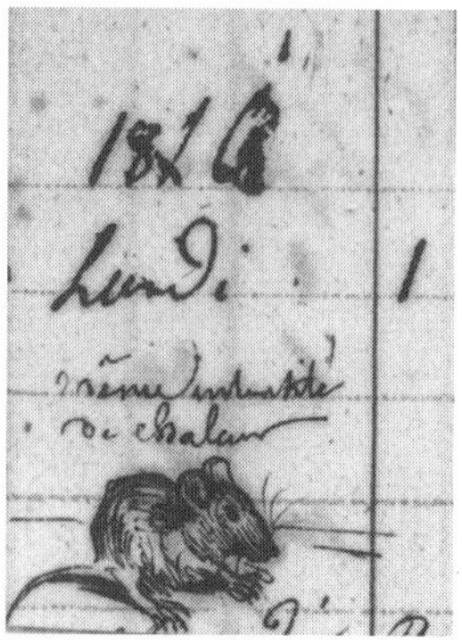

59. 3/5 recto

1846
Lundi 1
même intensité
de chaleur

(1846
Monday 1
same intense
heat)

June 1, 1846
54 × 36
Pen and brown ink

As has already been noted, the winter and spring of 1846 were unusually mild (cat. no. 53 recto). This unseasonable warmth was a harbinger of the exceedingly hot summer to come. Under the rubric "Hygiène," *Le Moniteur universel* noted in its August 14, 1846, issue, "L'an 1846 restera certainement, comme son correspondant du siècle dernier (1746), une année remarquable par la chaleur. Le thermomètre se soutient à un degré très-élevé pour notre climat" (The year 1846, like its correspondent from the last century [1746], will certainly remain noteworthy for the heat. The thermometer maintains a very elevated degree for our climate). According to this diary entry, the intense heat had already begun to make itself felt in late May. Repeated remarks about the abnormally hot weather appear in the diary throughout the summer of 1846.

Grandville's affection for animals extended beyond the keeping of a frog in a glass jar on his desk and the taking care of birds that his neighbor Duval brought to him. He also at one point made friends with a baby mouse who makes its appearance in this diary entry only to die one month later (cat. no. 62). There must have been times when Grandville's studio resembled a miniature animal shelter.

3/5 verso

Dépense
(Expenditure)
[fragment of a list of expenses]

May 1846
54 × 36
Pen and brown ink

60. 5/5 recto

Meme ciel pur
bleu, soleil ardent
chaleur égale...
au mardi

Jeudi *4*
(Same pure blue
sky, scorching sun
equal heat...
until Tuesday

Thursday 4)

June 3–4, 1846
51 × 37
Pen and brown ink

Although the prolonged, intense heat during the summer of 1846 must have been insufferable for humans, it was perfect cactus weather. In addition to the two compotes with spoons and a carafe, the table top still life here features two potted plants, including a phyllocactus in full bloom on the left. Whether or not plants like animals, were Grandville's constant companions is hard to say. But it is safe to assume that those sketched in the diary served more than a decorative purpose. The cactus appears to be the same three-blossomed phyllocactus studiously examined in a large format, watercolor-tinted pencil drawing at the Nancy Musée des Beaux-Arts (Nancy, cat. no. 303). Carefully preserving their proper botanical appearance, Grandville uses the orange-petaled flowers for the hat and sleeves of the personified cactus he was in the process of producing for *Les Fleurs animées* (fig. 113). Thus, like the glowworms in cat. no. 58, he has again recorded in the diary the model from which he was working at the time. Although the blossoms of the other potted plant are not as readily identifiable as those of the phyllocactus, they appear to be those of an amaryllis.

Fig. 113. Study for *Cactus* (Cactus), 1846, wash drawing. Nancy, Bibliothèque municipale.

5/5 verso

[fragment of a list of numbers]

June 1846
51 × 37
Pen and brown ink

61. 5/7 recto

Chaleur continue et augmente.

Vendredi 5

[Samedi 6]
(Heat continues and increases.

Friday 5

[Saturday 6])

June 4–6, 1846
58 × 36
Pen and brown ink

We know from a letter written on October 20, 1846, and transcribed in the appendix, that during his stay at Chatou Grandville reserved his Tuesdays for making trips into Paris where he no doubt conferred with his editors and engravers about works then in progress, *Les Fleurs animées* and *L'Ingénieux chevalier Don Quichotte de la Manche.* However, there must have been times when either he was obliged to remain in Paris for more than one day or he postponed his trip into the city until later in the week. Either or both of these circumstances may have occurred during the first week of June with the result that Grandville finds himself in Paris on Friday, June 5.

There is no letup in the tropical weather: the temperature continues to climb. On June 5, Grandville decides to seek relief from the heat in the time-honored fashion and goes for a swim. According to Mlle Blampin, archivist for the city of Chatou, there were no bathhouses at Chatou in 1846. Hence the sketch probably represents the interior of one of the Parisian bathing establishments found in boathouses along the Seine, such as the celebrated Bains de la Samaritaine, located by the Pont Neuf where the famous pump house once stood, or the nearby Bains Henri IV, moored along the north side of the western tip of the île de la Cité, which Grandville had depicted eleven years earlier in *Le Charivari Monstre* of 1835 (fig. 114).[40] Just as he had done in this comical vignette, Grandville draws one of the ladders leading down into the water. Despite its small size, the drawing admirably conveys the impression of men swimming about and otherwise disporting in the water. A drawing of male bathers at the Nancy Musée des Beaux-Arts documents a visit to the baths around 1837 (fig. 115). The bathers in the diary

Fig. 114. Detail, column 8 of *Le Charivari Monstre*, July 31, 1835. Private collection.

Fig. 115. *Four male bathers*, circa 1837, drawing. Nancy, Musée des Beaux-Arts (Inv. 877.1182).

sketch, *Le Charivari Monstre* vignette, and the Nancy drawing all wear bathing trunks as prescribed by police by-laws.[41]

5/7 verso

[fragment of a list of numbers]

June 1846
58 × 36
Pen and brown ink

62. 3/7 recto

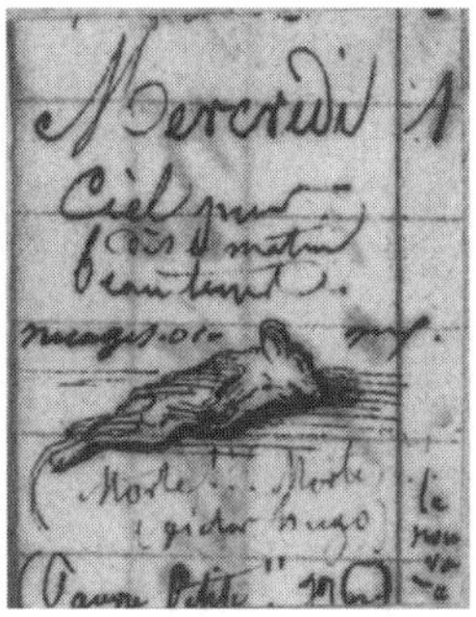

Mercredi 1
Ciel pur
dès le matin
beau tems.
nuages. orageux.

(Morte!!! Morte!!! *la*
(Victor Hugo) *nou*
(Pauvre petite!! JJGr.) *va*
à

(Wednesday 1
Clear sky
since morning
fair weather.
clouds. stormy.

[Dead!!! Dead!!! the
[Victor Hugo] *nou*
[Poor little thing!! JJGr.] goes
to)

July 1, 1846
41 × 32
Pen and brown ink

On the morning of Wednesday, July 1, the sky was perfectly clear. However, later on in the day threatening storm clouds moved in. The ominous change in the weather provided a fitting background for a tragedy: the young mouse encountered in cat. no. 59, and which Grandville had been keeping as a pet, died. Grandville pencils two sensitively detailed life-sized portraits of the recently deceased mouse in a large format drawing at the Nancy Musée des Beaux-Arts dated "1846 1er Juillet" (Nancy, cat. no. 227). The sketch in the diary is similar to the watercolor-tinted one on the left in the Nancy drawing. In order to give to the death its proper tragic dimension, he quotes a spurious passage from Victor Hugo's *Hernani,* "Dead!!! Dead!!!"[42] and then provides his own citation, "Poor little thing!!" which he signs with an abbreviation of his signature, J. J. Grandville. His tongue-in-cheek parody of heroic tragedy only partially conceals Grandville's genuine grief at the loss of his departed animal companion.

3/7 verso

[fragment of a list of numbers]

June 1846
41 × 32
Pen and brown ink

63. 3/3 recto

tems se remet
le soir

Jeudi *16*
(weather gets better
in the evening

Thursday 16)

July 16, 1846
40 × 35
Pen and brown ink

In 1846, the 16th fell on a Thursday during the months of April and July. Given the reference made to fishing during what is surely the month of July in cat. no. 65, it is likely that this diary fragments also dates from that month.

In the introduction to the 1846 diary, reference was made to an informative and entertaining article entitled "Les Loisirs de Chatou," which appeared in *L'Illustration* on October 7, 1848. The author of the article, a certain "F. M.," notes in his opening sentence, "Chatou . . . est un lieu cher aux artistes, mais surtout aux pêcheurs à la ligne, deux vocations qui ne s'excluent pas, au contraire." (Chatou is a spot dear to artists, but above all to anglers, two vocations which are not mutually exclusive, quite the contrary.). And, after proclaiming the former river port to be the fishing capital of the western Parisian suburbs, he proceeds to provide his own "physiology" of the indomitable Chatou fisherman:

> Chatou est le premier *port de pêche* qui soit de Paris jusqu'au Pecq. Il est aux pêcheurs à la ligne ce qu'Asnières est aux canotiers. C'est là et non ailleurs qu'il faut venir étudier sur nature les moeurs singulières de ces hommes intrépides et méconnus, de ces hommes de génie, puisque le génie c'est la patience, qui sous une enveloppe de glace poussent les passions volcaniques jusqu'à demeurer immobiles dix heures de suite, en équilibre sur une pierre mouvante, le corps plié, le bras tendu, la tête penchée, les pieds dans l'eau. A Chatou tout le monde est pêcheur, c'est de droit. Moi seul peut-être n'ai pas encore subi le baptême de la ligne, mais cela viendra forcément. En attendant, j'apprends la langue du métier, qui est fort riche, je vous jure, et parfaitement inintelligible aux profanes. C'est un *glossaire,* je ne voudrais pas dire un *argot,* des plus agréables. Quand on dit devant moi: "Je viens de *monter le coup.*—J'avais ma ligne *en bannière.*—Êtes-vous *sur crin* ou *sur racine?*—Je m'en vais *hécher* [*sic*] l'asticot," etc., je sais ce que parler veut dire; mais je ne vous le dirai pas; faites comme moi, venez à l'école.

> [Chatou is the most important *fishing port* that there is between Paris and Le Pecq. It is to anglers what Asnières is to boaters. It is there and at no other spot that one must come to study in their natural state the peculiar customs of these intrepid and misunderstood men, these men of genius, since genius is patience, who under a glacial exterior volcanic passions drive on to the point of remaining motionless for ten hours on end, balanced on a rocking stone, body bent, arm extended, head tilted, feet in the water. Everyone is an angler at Chatou, it is a right. I am perhaps the only one not to have as yet undergone the baptism of the fishing line, but that will inevitably come. While waiting, I learn the language of the trade which is, I swear to you, quite rich and perfectly unintelligible to the uninitiated. It is a *glossary,* I should not wish to say a *slang,* of the most agreeable kind. When someone says in front of me: "I just *landed one.*—My line was *hanging.* —Are you using *Florentine silkworm gut* or *English silkworm gut?*—I'm leaving *to bait the hook* with a worm," etc., I know what it means to speak; but I won't tell you; do as I do, come to school.]

Grandville may have inherited an interest in fishing from his father who is shown angling in an early drawing at the Musée Lorrain (fig. 116). Both his diary and his correspondence from 1846 reveal that he surely ranked among Chatou's more avid artist/fishermen. And like many anglers, Grandville had his own favorite fishing spot, the elongated and picturesque isle of Chatou, which is described in the

Fig. 116. ***Papa allons nous en, attends donc je viens d'avoir un coup*** **(Papa let's go, now wait I just had a bite), circa 1818, drawing. Nancy, Musée Lorrain.**

L'Illustration article as "île verdoyante, plantée de saules et de peupliers admirables, semée de mystérieux taillis, tapisée de prés luxuriants, [qui] est l'une des promenades favorites, l'une des joies et l'une des splendeurs de Chatou" (verdant isle, planted with admirable weeping willows and poplars, scattered with mysterious thickets, carpeted with luxuriant fields, [that] is one of the favorite promenades, one of the joys, and one of the splendors of Chatou). On October 20, near the end of his extended stay at Chatou, Grandville enthusiastically adds in the letter to his publisher, Fournier, which is transcribed in the appendix, "Cependant hier encore, je Suis allé faire mes adieux à l'ile de Chatou et par un Soleil magnifique. J ai encore pu tirer de leaux une Centaine de poissons dont huit à dix pesant un quarteron........et dans l'espace de trois heures Seulement" (Meanwhile yesterday I went once more to say goodbye to the isle of Chatou and under a magnificent sun. I was still able to pull out of the water around a hundred fish of which eight to ten weighing a quarter pound........and in the space of only three hours). No wonder Chatou was so popular with anglers! It comes as no surprise that fishing ranks second only to the weather as the topic most frequently found in those fragments that survive from the Chatou section of the 1846 diary.

The line of fishermen in the present sketch attests to the popularity of recreational fishing at Chatou. The view appears to be from the isle of Chatou overlooking the Rueil-Nanterre plain on the opposite bank of the Seine River. The two children in the foreground examining the contents of a bait bucket or tackle box are more than likely Georges and his toddler little half brother, Armand. For just as with his father, who in figure 116 is portrayed angling in the company of Grandville's sister, a somewhat bored Eulalie, Grandville's fishing expeditions were often family affairs. The still life of fish at the bottom presumably documents the day's catch.

3/3 verso

[fragment of a list of numbers]

July 1846
40 × 35
Pen and brown ink

64. 5/9 recto

[illegible fragmented words]
Ciel pur.
Soleil brûlant
mais Soirée déja
fraiche
Dur démon ahsi
(Clear sky.
Burning sun
but the evening already
cool
Cold-hearted devil, oh yes)

July(?) 1846
42 × 37
Pen and brown ink

This diary fragment carries no written indication of date. However, since reference is made to the burning sun, it more than likely belongs to either June, July, or August, those summer months during which the prolonged 1846 heat wave was most intense. Because of its subject matter, it has been grouped with other July fishing scenes. The lower left-hand corner of the sheet is the well-worn corner of the page.

During the day, the sun sent down its burning rays, unimpeded by any clouds in the sky. But the air quickly turned cooler as the sun sank below the horizon. It is probably toward evening that Grandville and his family have taken a stroll to the isle of Chatou in order to catch the fresh breeze blowing off

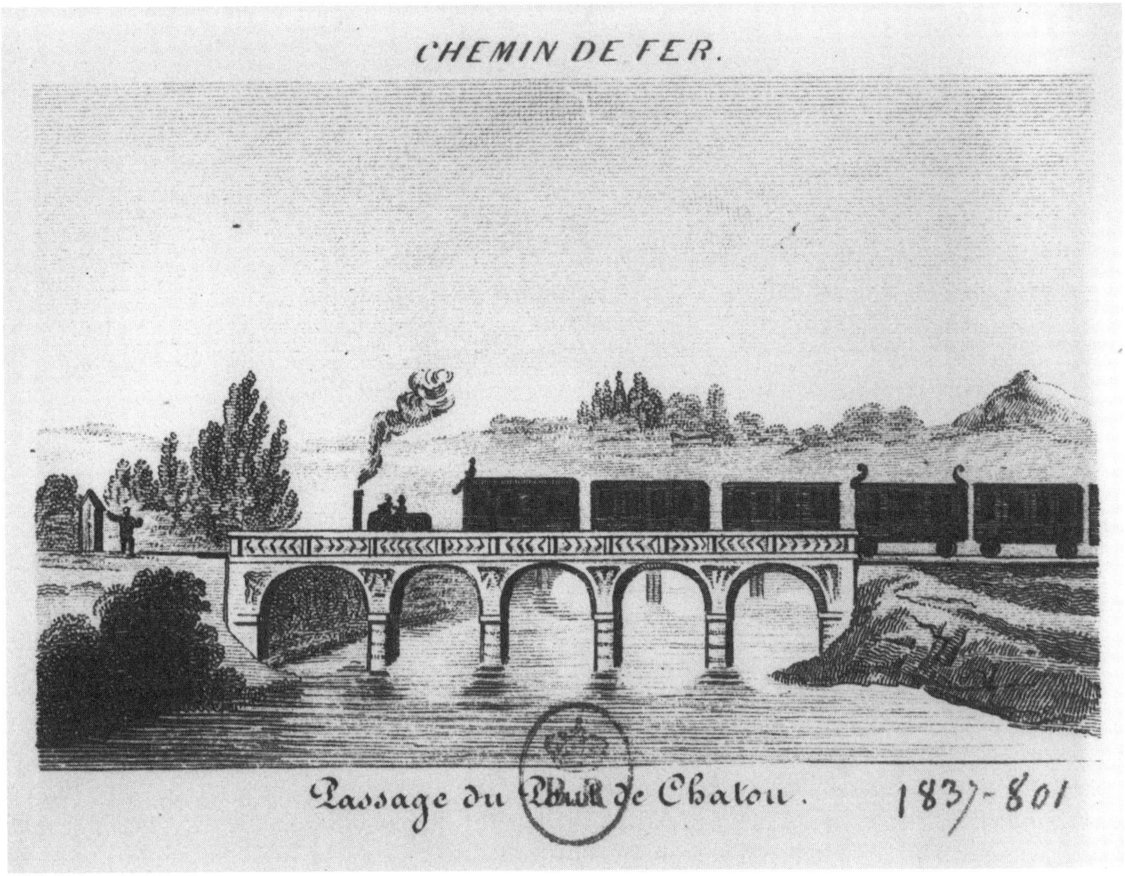

Fig. 117. Anonymous, *Chemin de fer: Passage du Pont de Chatou.* (Railroad: Crossing the bridge at Chatou), 1837, lithograph. Paris, Bibliothèque nationale de France.

the water and enjoy a little fishing. Grandville sketches Céline angling from the shore and Georges in his wide-brimmed straw hat observing the operation from the riverbank. Written directly above her head, the "cold-hearted devil" appears to be a facetious reference to Céline, whose iron-willed determination proved to be the undoing of more than one fish. In the background, a train on the Paris-Le Pecq line crosses the arched Pont de Chatou (fig. 117) in a blur. If the fishing location is the same as in the previous diary fragment, the section of the bridge portrayed would be that which linked the isle of Chatou and Rueil.

5/9 verso

[fragment of a list of numbers]

July(?) 1846
42 × 37
Pen and brown ink

65. 5/6 recto

Jeudi *23*
Ciel pur
chaleur très
forte. *rammodage*
des bottes

[illegible word] *revoyer à la péche* [?]
Vendredi 24
même tems
(Thursday 23
Clear sky
very intense
heat. mending [?]
of boots
[ ] to send back to fishing [?]
Friday 24
same weather)

July 23–24, 1846
50 × 35
Pen and brown ink

The intense heat continues. Grandville sketches a pair of boots that apparently have just been repaired (he once more has invented a new word, *rammodage,* which apparently is meant to be some form of the verb *ramender,* to mend). Whatever the case, their well-worn condition immediately calls to mind van Gogh's later portrait of battered work boots.

One major disadvantage of living at 48, rue de Saint-Germain was that it lay on the most direct route between the Poissy stockyards and Paris. Judging from this and the two following diary fragments, herds of sheep, pigs, and cattle were a regular sight as they made their dusty way during the evening hours to the slaughterhouses of the hungry capital. Grandville duly notes their passage. The cloud of dust sent up by the flock of sheep here must have been irksome, but is nothing compared to that raised by a herd of cattle one week later (cat. no. 67).

The enigmatic sketch of a man (Grandville?) examining what may be a gigantic creel (in order to accommodate his considerable catch?) and brandishing a fishing rod with an oversized hook and sinker at the bottom of the sheet surely refers in some way to that favorite Chatou pastime of fishing.

5/6 verso

[fragment of a list of numbers]

July 1846
50 × 35
Pen and brown ink

66. 3/4 recto

D surmer [?]

lourd

Lundi *27*

même
tems
nuages qui passent
et se fondent.
Mardi *28*
Ciel pur sans un
nuage. Sictmuth [?]
insupportable

de lundi
(*D surmer* [?]

sultry

Monday 27

same
weather
clouds which pass
and fade away.
Tuesday 28
Clear sky without a
cloud. *Sictmuth* [?]
unbearable

from Monday)

July 27–28, 1846
85 × 38
Pen and brown ink

Monday the 27th and Tuesday the 28th in this diary fragment could belong either to April or July. However, the leafy trees and the blooming water lily indicate the later month.

The word at the top of this diary fragment remains enigmatic. Equally mysterious is the sketch below the recording of the *lourd,* or "sultry," weather conditions. Although the arched structure has not been identified, it may represent the remains of the seventeenth-century Marly aqueduct, only a short distance from Chatou.

On Monday the 27th the same sweltering weather conditions prevail as clouds blowing in from the English Channel pass overhead and evaporate into the hot air. Like the glowworms in cat. no. 58 and the phyllocactus in cat. no. 60, the flowering water lily, probably a nenuphar, more than likely refers to studies from life for the particular *fleur animée* he may have been working on at the time, *Nénuphar*

Fig. 118. Study for *Nénuphar* (Nenuphar), 1846, watercolor. Nancy, Bibliothèque municipale.

(Nenuphar), a watercolor study of which is seen in figure 118. To the right of the water lily pad is a partially blotted-out pig that Grandville decided to draw along with its brethren under the entry for Tuesday the 28th.

Not having had enough room to draw Monday's passing herd of swine under the entry for the 27th, Grandville uses the space under the following day, Tuesday the 28th, and labels the sketch "from Monday." The unbearable stench (*sictmuth?*) of the pigs may still have been fresh in his mind twenty-four hours later.[43]

3/4 verso

[fragment of a list of numbers]

July 1846
85 × 38
Pen and brown ink

67. 4/3 recto

Même chaleur
Poussière à

etrangler
passage des Boeufs

Coup de pistolet
tiré vis
à vis
du Roi

Vendredi *31*
Chaleur
suffocante

Semblant
d'orage
(Same heat
Strangling
dust
passing of cattle

Pistol-shot
fired
towards
the King

Friday 31
Suffocating
heat

Semblance
of a storm)

July 30–31, 1846
82 × 37
Pen and brown ink

By the end of July, the unrelenting summer heat had become so intense that Grandville is moved to describe it as "suffocating." To make matters worse, the dust stirred up by passing livestock was becoming increasingly irritating. As might be expected, it was the larger animals that sent up the most dust, with cattle being the worst offenders. After enduring the stench of pigs a couple of days earlier, on July 30 the Grandville household suffered through a "strangling dust" caused by the notorious *troupeau féroce,* or "wild herd." The herd got its name because, as the previously cited article on Chatou explains, "il se compose de tous les boeufs méchants du marché de Poissy réunis en un convoi et menés nuitamment à Paris sous la garde de bouviers à cheval, véritables *picadores*" (it consists of all the bad-tempered cattle from the Poissy market herded together into a convoy and driven at night to Paris under the care of drovers on horseback, veritable *picadores*).[44] Adding to the general unpleasantness was the noise caused by the bellowing bovines and, one imagines, the shouts of the drovers.

Louis-Philippe's rule as the "King of the French" was anything but untroubled. Between the two revolutions that awarded and dispossessed him of the throne, he suffered through a number of popular uprisings and assassination attempts, these latter often occurring on the anniversary of the Trois

Glorieuses, July 27, 28, and 29, 1830. As we saw in the biography, the most infamous attempt on the king's life was Fieschi's on July 28, 1835, which served as the catalyst for the voting in of the equally infamous September Laws of that year. A less-tragic assassination attempt occurred almost to the day eleven years later on the evening of July 29, 1846. *Le Moniteur universel* gave the official account of the incident on the following day, July 30:

> Paris, le 29 juillet.
> Ce soir, à sept heures et demie, au moment où le Roi, accompagné de la Reine et de la famille royale, au milieu des acclamations de la population, s'est présenté au balcon des Tuileries pour entendre le concert, deux coups de pistolet ont été tirés sur S.M. Le Roi n'a pas été atteint. L'assassin a été immédiatement arrêté; il avoue son crime.

> [Paris, July 29.
> This evening at seven thirty, at the moment when the King, accompanied by the Queen and the royal family, presented himself to a cheering crowd on the balcony of the Tuileries Palace in order to listen to a concert, two pistol-shots were fired at His Majesty. The King was not hit. The assassin was immediately arrested; he confesses to his crime.]

On the same day, Grandville recorded in his diary the attempted assassination, cleverly illustrating it with a firing pistol. In its August 1 issue, *L'Illustration* provided the name of the assassin, Joseph Henry, and reported the results of the preliminary investigations: "Toutes les circonstances du crime démontrent que cet assassin est un homme atteint d'aliénation mentale" (All the circumstances of the crime demonstrate that the assassin is a man suffering from mental derangement).

It is difficult to gauge Grandville's attitude toward Louis-Philippe in his clever, yet brief and matter-of-fact recording of the assassination attempt. But there is no indication of any malice toward the king as one might expect from a republican and former leading opposition caricaturist. It is possible that, as Clogenson contends, Grandville moderated his political views as he grew older. We do know that both he and his first wife, Henriette, were genuinely saddened in July 1842 by the sudden death of the duc d'Orléans, which was referred to by Grandville in a letter to his Nancy relatives as "la mort fatale et cruelle du prince royal Duc d'orlèans" (the fatal and cruel death of the royal prince the duc d'Orléans).[45]

The last vignette under Thursday the 30th represents an elegantly clad, unidentified gentleman who bows as he holds his top hat in his hands. Despite the suffocating heat, Grandville goes fishing the following day, Friday the 31st. He proudly portrays his prize catch of the day.

4/3 verso

[fragment of a list of numbers]

July 1846
82 × 37
Pen and brown ink

68. 5/1 recto

1846
Samedi 15
le tems chaud

et beau le matin
Change vers 2hrs
nuages—vent

Dimanche 16
Tems lourd et
beau

Lundi 17
mème tems
Jeune Hirondelle
apportée par
duval.
[*Mardi 18*]
(1846
Saturday 15
hot and fair
weather in the morning
Change around 2 o'clock
clouds - wind

Sunday 16
Sultry and fair
weather

Monday 17
same weather
Young Swallow
brought by
duval.
[Tuesday 18])

August 15–18, 1846
148 × 36
Pen and brown ink

Festivities, probably in honor of the Feast of the Assumption, occur during the weekend of August 15–16, despite the hot and humid weather. The morning of the holiday proper, August 15, was filled with sunshine. However, by early afternoon a storm front had blown in. Grandville sketches Céline who has fallen asleep on a sofa. The two little figures at the right who appear to be floating through the air with their arms and legs spread apart remain a mystery. Later on in the day, a crowd of people gather around what looks like a giant puppet on a rise overlooking the Seine River. In the background, a train crosses what appears to be the recently inaugurated viaduct at Saint-Germain-en-Laye, which extended the Paris-Le Pecq railroad line. On the evening of Sunday the 16th, a fireworks display along the poplar-lined banks of the Seine is reflected in the river's waters.

The same sultry weather continues on into Monday. Duval arrives with yet another bird for Grandville who sketches it in his diary. This time it is a young swallow that may have fallen out of its nest.

5/1 verso

dépense
(expenditure)
[fragment of a list of numbers]

August 1846
148 × 36
Pen and brown ink

69. 5/4 recto

Mercredi *26*
beau tems

STATION
CHATOU
(Wednesday 26
fair weather

Chatou
Station)

August 26, 1846
54 × 36
Pen and brown ink

Grandville, Céline holding Armand in her arms, and Georges in his wide-brimmed straw hat stand safely behind a fence while watching the train that will carry Céline's mother to Paris roll into the Chatou station. As he had done earlier when summering at Saint-Mandé, Grandville played host to visiting relatives from Nancy at Chatou. We do not for the moment know when Madame L'hullier arrived to visit her daughter's family, but in a letter dated Sunday, August 23, 1846, and addressed to the book dealer A. Le Chevalier at 60, rue de Richelieu, Grandville announces her imminent departure three days later on Wednesday the 26th. After taking the train into Paris, she would have had to transfer to a stagecoach in order to proceed to Nancy (rail service to Nancy, it will be recalled, was not instituted until 1849). As his drawing of the stagecoach indicates, Grandville apparently accompanied his mother-in-law into Paris in order to see her safely embark on the final leg of her journey. While in town, Grandville intended to take up Le Chevalier's standing invitation to dinner. The purpose of the letter was to inquire whether or not Wednesday the 26th would suit his host. According to Grandville's meteorological annotation, our voyagers had a sunny day for their travels. Céline's mother would again visit her daughter's family some five months later, at the beginning of March 1847, during Grandville's fatal illness.

Despite their miniscule size, the sketches from the 1846 diary are remarkable for the precision of their execution. The foreshortening of the stagecoach horses here merits particular attention, and once more attests to Grandville's skills as a miniaturist.

5/4 verso

[fragment of a list of numbers]

54 × 36
August 1846
Pen and brown ink

70. 2/4 recto

1846
Mardi *1*
nuages..
un peu de
pluie...

achat de deux canards
vivants
(1846
Tuesday 1
clouds..
a little
rain...

purchase of two live
ducks)

September 1, 1846
76 × 37
Pen and brown ink

The incomplete dates on this and the two following diary fragments indicate that they are from either September or December 1846. However, circumstantial evidence suggests that all three excerpts belong to the month of September. For example, it is doubtful that Grandville would have kept two live ducks in his Paris apartment during the month of December. This supposition and the vegetation behind the ducks strongly hint that the cloudy and rainy Tuesday the 1st here dates from September.

The ducks are differentiated from one another by their plumage. They may be mallards, with the lighter female to the left and the darker male to the right. If this is the case, they could be the same mallards that figure in two remarkable, nearly life-size pencil and watercolor drawings at the Nancy Musée des Beaux-Arts (Nancy, cat. nos. 214 and 215).

2/4 verso

Dépense
(Expenditure)
[fragment of a list of numbers]

August 1846
76 × 37
Pen and brown ink

71. 5/8 recto

Lundi *7*

beau tems, orageux
orage à 11hrs du soir
(Monday 7

fair weather, stormy
storm at 11 o'clock at night)

September 7, 1846
34 × 38
Pen and brown ink

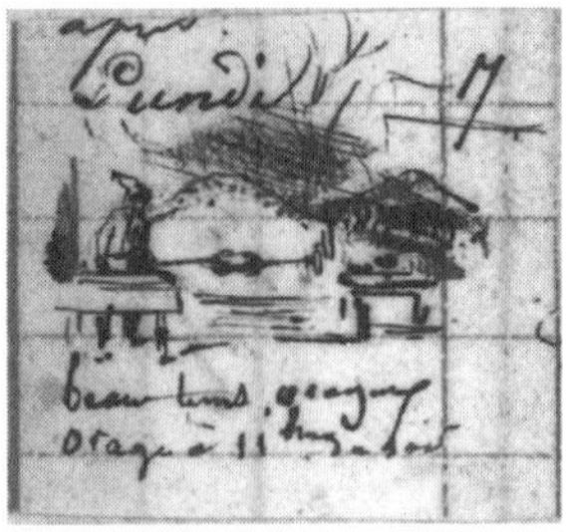

This diary fragment appears to depict a sequel to the purchase of the two ducks depicted in the preceding one, hence its date of September.

Was Grandville an amateur chef as well as an amateur fisherman? It appears that a week following their purchase, one of the ducks ended up on a spit in what may have been the large, open-hearth fireplace of the kitchen at 48, rue de Saint-Germain. The figure standing behind a table and wearing a toque could be the artist himself.

As usual, Grandville has recorded the day's weather conditions, which progressively got worse: sunshine gave way to stormy skies, and finally, at eleven o'clock at night, to a full-blown storm.

5/8 verso

[fragment of a list of numbers]

September 1846
34 × 38
Pen and brown ink

72. 2/6 recto

1846
Dimanche 27
il pluvotte

Lundi 28
(1846
Sunday 27
it rains

Monday 28)

September 27–28, 1846
64 × 38
Pen and brown ink

On a rainy Sunday the 27th, neither Grandville nor the rest of the family could indulge themselves in their favorite pastime of fishing on the isle of Chatou. In order to compensate for this disappointment, a substitute for the Seine River has been found in the form of a water-filled tub into which the children have cast their lines. Céline kneels on the floor and assists Armand whom she holds in her arms. The bare-legged Georges, dressed in a loose tunic, fishes on his own. His skimpy attire argues for this amusing scene taking place during September and not the wintry month of December.

2/6 verso

Dépense
(Expenditure)
[fragment of a list of numbers]

September 1846
64 × 38
Pen and brown ink

73. 4/7 recto

tems couvert
et doux

Dimanche 18
le tems se
remet.
(cloudy and mild
weather

Sunday 18
the weather
gets better.)

October 17–18, 1846
34 × 38
Pen and brown ink

The numbered days of the week on this and the following diary fragment could be from either January or October 1846. Both, however, assuredly date from the month of October. For example, the mild weather mentioned here certainly did not occur in January. On the contrary, it indicates that the same meteorological conditions that caused unusually hot temperatures during the summer resulted in a pleasantly warm fall. The still life of a salt shaker next to a steaming pot on a trivet conjures up the simple pleasures of a quiet domestic existence.

4/7 verso

[fragment of a list of numbers]

October 1846
34 × 38
Pen and brown ink

74. 4/8 recto

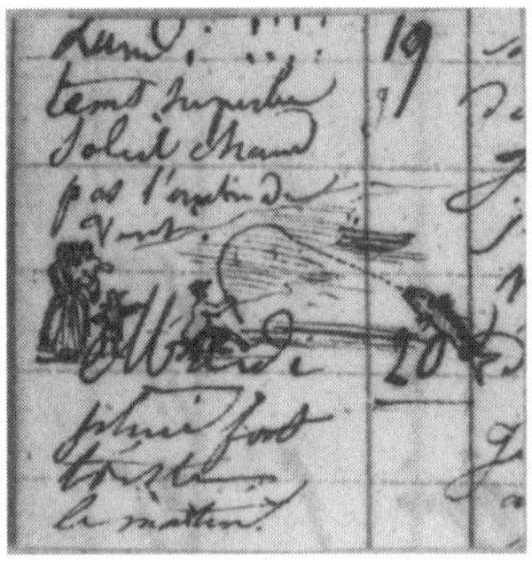

Lundi!!!! *19*
tems superbe
Soleil chaud
pas l' [illegible word] *de*
Vent.

Mardi *20*
pluie fort
triste
le matin.
(Monday!!!! 19
superb weather
warm Sun
not the [ ] of
Wind.

Tuesday 20
very dismal
rain
in the morning.)

October 19–20, 1846
41 × 39
Pen and brown ink

Grandville's October 20, 1846, letter to his former publisher Henri Fournier, transcribed in the appendix, corroborates that this diary fragment is from October (in 1846 Fournier was working for the publishing house of Mame in Tours). Monday the 19th was an exceptionally beautiful day, which well merited the four exclamation points given it by Grandville: both the "Soleil magnifique" (magnificent sun) in the letter and the "superb weather warm Sun" recorded in the diary attest to that. Grandville took advantage of the fine weather to make a farewell fishing expedition to the isle of Chatou before moving back to Paris with his family for the remainder of the autumn and winter. His enthusiasm is palpable as he relates his success to Fournier in the passage previously cited in cat. no. 63: "I was still able to pull out of the water around a hundred fish of which eight to ten weighing a quarter pound........and in the space of only three hours." And in his diary he sketches the hooking of one of the quarter-pounders, which, in keeping with standard fishing reportage, is somewhat exaggerated in size. The rest of the family witnesses the exploit. Both Armand, held in the arms of Céline, and Georges excitedly point at the prize catch. This image of radiant triumph provides an amusing contrast with the self-deprecatory satire of another drawing from around this same time where Armand and Georges observe with dismay as their father meets with less than complete success (fig. 119).[46] The idyllic tableau of Grandville's family rejoicing in his good luck is especially poignant when we realize that the fishing expedition on October 19 may very well have been the last before the artist's demise five months later.

By the following morning of, Tuesday, October 20, the weather had taken a decided turn for the worse: "le tems est si hideux" (the weather is so dreadful), he writes to Fournier, and later records in his diary, "very dismal rain in the morning." However, as we learn from the letter transcribed in the

Fig. 119. E. after Grandville, *Petites misères de la pêche à la ligne* (Little misfortunes of angling), 1846, drawing. Nancy, Musée Lorrain.

appendix, when a break in the clouds occurs, he dashes off for his weekly trip into Paris in order to deliver to Fournier's former foreman and contact person in Paris, Jules Claye, his most recent work for the second part of *Don Quixote:* a prepared woodblock destined for the wood engraver Chevauchet and the first of the drawings for the steel engravings being done by François Théodore Ruhierre (1808–84). The drawing, finished just two days earlier, depicts the encounter of the "hero of La Mancha" with "the lion cage" (fig. 124). As we will see in the next diary fragment, Grandville's embarking on the second series of drawings for *Don Quixote* occurred while he was simultaneously completing work on *Les Fleurs animées.*

4/8 verso
[fragment of a list of numbers]

October 1846
41 × 39
Pen and brown ink

75. 3/2 recto

1846 22
Mercredi 21
Vent considerable *la*
averses
consecutives.

fin des Dessins *23.*
des Fleurs
animees 23 22.
Jeudi
(1846 22
Wednesday 21
considerable Wind the
consecutive
downpours.

last of the Drawings 23.
for *Les Fleurs*
animées 23 22.
Thursday)

October 21–22, 1846
71 × 40
Pen and brown ink

Like many of us, Grandville occasionally got confused about the date of a particular day. Such is the case with this diary fragment, which documents the termination of his work on *Les Fleurs animées.* It appears that he accurately recorded the date of Wednesday the 21st only to change it to the 22nd. He then proceeded to date the following day, Thursday, as the 23rd. Discovering his error, he corrected himself by writing the date for Thursday in the double-sized numerals "22," which are underlined for additional emphasis. His confusion may have occurred when he continued his diary at the top of a new page, which he, as usual, labeled with the year 1846. When he determined the correct date, he underlined not only the 22nd but also "Tuesday 20," the date of the last entry on the previous page (cat. no. 74).

That the two days in question are indeed October 21 and October 22, 1846, may be determined by a process of elimination. If they were Wednesday the 22nd and Thursday the 23rd, these two days would have fallen in either April or July. The second and definitive version of the contract for *Les Fleurs animées* was signed on February 19, 1846 (Renonciat, 298); the book's first installment was reported in the *Bibliographie de la France* on April 25, 1846. It is highly unlikely that even an artist as prolific as Grandville would have finished a frontispiece, two *faux-lettres,* and fifty plates for *Les Fleurs animées* by April 22, or in a little over two months' time and before the appearance of the book's first installment. As for Thursday, the 23rd of July, it already has been accounted for in cat. no. 59. Wednesday the 21st and Thursday the 22nd occurred during the months of January and October in 1846. January is even more improbable than April as the month in which Grandville finished work on *Les Fleurs animées,* leaving October as the only possibility.

The completion of the last drawings for *Les Fleurs animées* on Wednesday, October 21, 1846, presumably would have allowed adequate time for their translation into steel engravings for the book's final weekly installments in December and January (the 83rd and last installment was reported along with the previous two in the *Bibliographie de la France* of January 16, 1847). Whether or not the *Giroflée* (Gillyflower) sketched here was in fact Grandville's last drawing for *Les Fleurs animées* remains a moot point. It does, however, figure among his last eight plates for the publication.

That Grandville had completed the drawings for the first part of *Don Quixote* and started on those for the second part while simultaneously finishing *Les Fleurs animées* demonstrates his ability to work on more than one project at a time.[47]

3/2 verso

Dépense
(Expenditure)
[fragment of a list of numbers]

October 1846
71 × 40
Pen and brown ink

76. 10/3

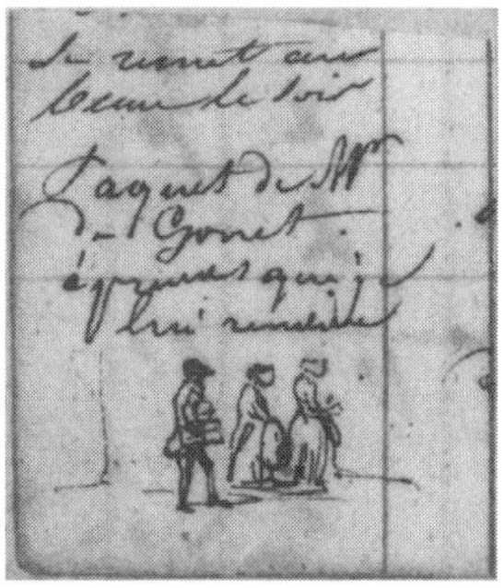

Se remet au
beau le soir

Paquet de Mr
de Gonet
épreuves que je
lui renvoie
(Returns to
being fair weather in the evening

Packet from Mr.
de Gonet
proofs that I
send back to him)

October(?) 1846
41 × 36
Pen and brown ink

Because of the reference to Gabriel de Gonet, the publisher of *Les Fleurs animées,* this undated diary fragment could date anytime from April until the end of 1846. However, it has been grouped with the previous diary fragment, which concerns this same publication. As in cat no. 64, the lower left-hand corner of the sheet is a worn corner of a diary page.

After recording that the weather had cleared up by evening, Grandville mentions that he had received a package from de Gonet, and that he in turn had sent back proofs to his publisher. The procedure described would appear to be a standard one. While receiving one package of proofs for his inspection and approval, Grandville returns another. The publication involved can only be *Les Fleurs animées.*

The sketch at the bottom of the sheet depicts two women and a man walking in file. That their profiled appearance is determined mainly by their apparel once more exemplifies Grandville's never-ending fascination with how clothing simultaneously masks the body and projects the particular image we wish to present to the world.

77. 5/2 recto

paris...
Ch[?] d'armand fait
Mardi 27
tems mis au
beau.
(Paris...
Ch [?] of Armand done
Tuesday 27
weather turned
fair.)

October 27, 1846
48 × 37
Pen and brown ink

Tuesday the 27th here surely dates from October and not from the other possible month, January. Having made a farewell visit to the isle of Chatou one week earlier (cat. no. 74), Grandville and his family move back to Paris. The artist sketches Georges in the process of observing a mover who is unloading household effects from a horse-drawn cart (for earlier, more detailed studies of horse-drawn carts, see Nancy, cat. nos. 34 and 35). The items would then have to be carried up to the Grandvilles' fourth-floor apartment at 26, rue des Saints-Pères. Fortunately, the weather cooperated.

5/2 verso

[fragment of numerical calculations]

October 1846
48 × 37
Pen and brown ink

78. 2/2 recto

tems pluvieux
toute la Journée
(rainy weather
the entire Day)

1846
51 × 37
Pen and brown ink

There are no clues that allow a more precise dating of this and the following diary fragment.

On a rainy day, Grandville amuses himself as best he can in his studio. Judging from his sketch of an easel and painter's palette, he may have worked on an oil painting as he occasionally was wont to do.

2/2 verso

[fragment of a list of numbers]

1846
51 × 37
Pen and brown ink

79. 7/4 recto

1846
id 1[5]

Deficit de 20
francs dans
(1846
idem 1[5]

Deficit of 20
francs in)

1846
56 × 34
Pen and brown ink

As we have seen, Grandville rigorously kept a detailed account of his expenditures. In the 1846 diary, this account-keeping usually occurred on the pages opposite the ones where the events of the day were written. However, the twenty-franc deficit noted here was important enough to figure in a regular diary entry. In contrast to this disappointing bit of information, Grandville sketches a perky little dog.

7/4 verso

Dépense
(Expenditure)
[fragment of a list of numbers]

1846
56 × 34
Pen and brown ink

Notes

1. "J.-J. Grandville: Dessins inédits," *Magasin pittoresque* 23, no. 48 (December 1855): 380.

2. The marriage contract between Grandville and Céline, dated October 24, 1843, states that at the time of his second wedding Grandville's personal fortune came to 53,765 francs and 87 centimes. This same document specifies that Céline

brought a 10,000-franc dowry to the marriage in addition to an undetermined amount from the estate of her deceased father, Jean Nicolas L'hullier, a retired captain and chevalier of the Legion of Honor. After Grandville's death, the family fortune will allow Céline to live in Nancy as a rentier, the designation ascribed to her by a posthumous *déclaration du comparant.* It is probable that Céline also eventually inherited a certain sum of money from her widowed mother, née Marie Anne Villeneuve, who also lived in Nancy as a rentier.

3. The substantial building in which the apartment was located still stands and today houses the École des Ponts et Chaussées (School of Bridges and Highways).

4. Charton, 49.

5. Clogenson, 275.

6. The light also entered from the right of his work table at Saint-Mandé (Nancy, cat. no. 11). In a circa 1831 self-portrait (Nancy, cat. no. 23), Grandville does appear to be sketching with his left hand.

7. Wilhelm Kaulbach (1805–74), one of the most celebrated German academic artists of his day, drew *Das Narrenhaus* (The Madhouse, or "Maison des fous") in 1835. Heinrich Merz (1806–75) translated the original pencil drawing into the large format engraving (518 x 680 mm) reproduced in fig. 105. There is every reason to believe that this is the same "large and so remarkable engraving" that hung in Grandville's studio. A clue to Grandville's interest in the work may be found in a smaller-scale lithographic version of *The Madhouse* (209 x 297 mm) published by Lemercier in 1838 (the lithograph is a reverse image of the engraving from which it may have been copied). With no reference to the original title in either French or German, it carries the legend, *Planches physiologiques: Système de Lavater. Pl. 4* (Physiological plates: Lavater's system. Pl. 4). The strongly expressive physiognomies of the deranged individuals do in fact seem to illustrate Lavater's theory on how outward physical appearance reflects the moral character of an individual, a concept that we know fascinated Grandville, who employed it in his own caricatural description and classification of different types. Grandville was not alone in appreciating Kaulbach's *Madhouse.* Baudelaire, for instance, refers to it twice, once in the "Salon de 1859" and again in "L'art philosophique" (Charles Baudelaire, *Oeuvres complètes* [Paris: Editions du Seuil, 1968], 401, 425). We do not know if Grandville was acquainted with any other work by Kaulbach or with Kaulbach himself. It is generally agreed, however, that the German artist was familiar with the work of Grandville, notably *Scènes de la vie privée et publique des animaux,* which directly influenced Kaulbach's illustrations to Goethe's *Rein*eke Fuchs (Reynard the Fox; Tübingen: J. G. Cotta, 1846). In fact, the similarity between Grandville's and Kaulbach's humanoid animals in these two works was so close that in 1864 they were combined together into a single publication, *Album des Bêtes à l'usage des gens d'esprit* (Album of animals intended for witty people), which included a text by Aurélien Scholl and Charles Joliet (Paris: Aux Bureaux de Nain jaune).

8. The furniture remained in the possession of relatives until fairly recently when, found to be too dark and heavy for modern tastes, it was sold (conversation with Dominique Courvoisier, July 1992).

9. According to Mlle Paulette Blampin, archivist for the city of Chatou, many of the houses at Chatou were rented to Parisians for the summer during the nineteenth century: this may well have been the case with the one at 48, rue de Saint-Germain. As late as 1952, the house and the wall surrounding both it and the small park behind it were still standing. Unfortunately, since then the house has been torn down to make way for a complex of apartment buildings that covers the entire site. Much of what appears to have been the wall at the back of the property, however, can still be seen.

10. The wood engraving reproduced in figure 107 originally illustrated an article dedicated to Chatou in the October 7, 1848, issue of *L'Illustration,* "Les Loisirs de Chatou" (The leisures of Chatou), 93–94. The article describes some of the village's more notable residents, including Grandville, and gives the following account of the picturesquely shaped number adorning the wall of his former residence:

> Ce fut l'un des derniers séjours de notre pauvre Grandville, ce merveilleux artiste enlevé si prématurément à ses travaux et à nos vives sympathies. Granville [*sic*] est mort le 17 mars 1847, et, dans l'été de 1846, sa main sans cesse préoccupée de chercher la forme vivante sous les objets inanimés, s'amusait, en une heure de caprice, à tracer ce fantastique numéro que reproduit notre gravure: c'était celui de la modeste maison qu'il habitait à Chatou, dans la rue dite de Saint-Germain, à quelques pas de la forêt de Vésinet. On le voit encore sur la muraille, et il faut espérer que le propriétaire aura le bon goût de conserver avec soin cette fantaisie presque suprême par sa date, où se retrouvent au reste tout le faire et le cachet du grand artiste. Après avoir donné la vie aux astres et aux planètes, démêlé la femme dans la fleur et l'homme dans l'insecte, il en était venu à animer les chiffres. Une sauterelle obliquant ses ailes de gaze et un scarabée arrondissant ses huit pattes lui avaient fourni en un clin-d'oeil un no 48 irréprochable de précision arithmétique. S'il eût vécu, nul doute que, nouvel Amphion, il eût animé les pierres.

> [This was one of the last sojourns of our poor Grandville, that wonderful artist taken away so prematurely from his work and from our heartfelt sympathies. Grandville died March 17, 1847, and in the summer of 1846 his hand, constantly preoccupied with searching living form beneath inanimate objects, in an hour of whimsy amused itself by drawing this fantastic number that our engraving reproduces: it was that of the modest house that he lived in at Chatou on the street called de Saint-Germain, a few steps away from the forest of Vésinet. You can still see it on the wall, and one must hope that the owner will have the good judgment to preserve carefully this, by its

date, almost last fantasy where are to be found moreover all the skill and distinctive style of the great artist. After having given life to stars and to planets, detected women in flowers and men in insects, he arrived at animating numbers. A grasshopper slanting its wings of gauze at an angle and a beetle [actually a spider; there is a beetle, but it forms a period] making its eight feet round provided him in the wink of an eye with a flawless number 48 of arithmetical precision. Had he lived, no one doubts that, like a new Amphion, he would have animated stones.]

11. The île de Chatou became so popular with the Impressionists that part of the island was renamed the "Ile des Impressionistes" in their honor. At the beginning of the twentieth century, Chatou became a center of Fauvism. Two of Matisse's close associates, André Derain, a native of Chatou, and Maurice Vlaminck, shared the same Chatou studio. Together with their followers, these two painters formed the Fauve "School of Chatou."

12. The description of Duval as a "peintre sur verre" suggests that he earned his living by producing reverse glass paintings, which at the time were used extensively to decorate store windows. Like Grandville's house, Duval's has given way to a modern apartment building.

13. *Magasin pittoresque* (December 1855): 380.

14. Grandville, himself, refers to Desperet's collaboration in the past tense when in 1846 he writes his famous preface letter to the bound drawings of the *Fables de La Fontaine.*

15. Odile and Henri-Jean Martin, "Le monde des éditeurs," in *Le temps des éditeurs: Du Romantisme à la Belle Époque,* vol. 3 of *Histoire de l'edition française,* eds. Henri-Jean Martin and Roger Chartier (Paris: Promodis, 1985), 174–75, 184. On page 184 is reproduced a note dated December 29, 1846, that accompanied a 3,000-franc loan from Bixio to Hetzel.

16. Luc Wetzel, *Alexandre Bixio* (Montbéliard: Imprimerie et lithographie de Henri Barbier, 1869), 8–9. This opuscule is a reprint of a May 1866 article that appeared in the *Mémoires de la Société d'Emulation de Montbéliard.* For additional information on Bixio, see the *Dictionnaire de biographie française.*

17. François Gasnault, *Guinguettes et lorettes: Bals publics et danse sociale à Paris entre 1830 et 1870* (Paris: Aubier, 1986), 159.

18. "Revue de la semaine," *L'Artiste,* 4th ser., 5, 9th livraison (December 28, 1845): 141. Established by the regent in 1716, the *bal de l'Opéra* (Opera ball) was the first ball open to the public. The public before the Revolution was, however, a very select one. And even under the July Monarchy, an entry ticket costing ten francs continued to guarantee its bon ton. Beginning in 1840, Philippe Musard (1793–1859), a veritable living legend, conducted the Opera balls. Nicknamed "the Napoléon of the quadrille," Musard was by far France's most famous orchestra leader and composer of dance music in his day. The *bal Musard,* or Musard ball, at the Salle Le Peletier, where the Opera was located between 1821 and 1873, quickly became an institution. It not only announced the carnival season: it was also considered as "le clou de l'année dansante" (the chief attraction of the dance year). In 1845, Louis Huart was able to write, "A notre époque, tout le carnaval parisien se résume à peu près dans le bal de l'Opéra" (In our time, the entire Parisian carnival season can be all but summed up in the Opera ball; *Paris au bal* [Paris: Aubert, 1845], 39). Alfred Musard (Musard fils) followed in his famous father's footsteps. However, the balls of the Opéra-Comique at the Salle Favart, place des Italiens (renamed place Boieldieu in 1852) could not match those of the Opera, which enjoyed a pan-European reputation. For this and other information on Musard and the Opera balls, see Gasnault, particularly pages 13, 66–67, 158–71.

19. Gasnault, 159.

20. For the notoriety of Odéon carnival balls, see Gasnault, 72–73.

21. Under the Second Empire, the government started in 1852 to regulate these independent associations and the Ministry of Interior began publishing its multivolumed *Rapports à l'empereur sur la situation des sociétés de secours mutuels par la Commission supérieure d'encouragement et de surveillance des sociétés de secours mutuel* (Reports to the emperor on the situation of mutual-aid societies by the high commission on the encouragement and surveillance of mutual-aid societies). Additional information on mutual aid societies may be found in the periodical dedicated to them, the *Bulletin des sociétés de secours mutuels,* which began publication in 1854.

22. "Association des artistes peintres d'histoire ou de genre, sculpteurs, graveurs, architectes et dessinateurs," *Journal des Artistes,* 2nd ser., 1, 38th livraison (December 15, 1844): 433.

23. This and other valuable information concerning the Association des artistes may be found in its yearbooks, preserved at the Fondation Taylor in Paris.

24. "Une exposition hors du Louvre," *L'Artiste,* 4th ser., 5, 12th livraison (January 18, 1846): 186–89; "Actualités.—Souvenirs," *Journal des Artistes,* 2nd ser., 3, 1st livraison (January 4, 1846): 8; "Exhibition de l'Association des artistes peintres, sculpteurs, architectes et graveurs," *Journal des Artistes,* 2nd ser., 3, 2nd livraison (January 11, 1846): 9–10. The exhibition was more successful than anyone had dared to hope. Part of its success no doubt resulted from the novelty of an art exhibition independent of the annual Salon shows at the Louvre, a phenomenon that was pointedly emphasized by the title of the review published in *L'Artiste.* It and the rotating exhibition of contemporary works at the Odéon theater (see following

note) represent early challenges to the Salon, which will multiply during the course of the nineteenth century, reducing the academic institution to second-rate status by the century's end.

25. "Actualités.—Souvenirs," *Journal des Artistes,* 2nd ser., 3, 46th livraison (November 9, 1845): 415–16. The description of this "new museum" reads in part: "[Bocage] a donc transformé une espèce de galerie, qui ne servait à rien, en un foyer où les artistes seront à tour de rôle conviés tous, sans distinction de genre ni d'école. Ceux-là que le jury académique aura frappés sans pitié pourront enfin appeler au public d'un arrêt inique." ([Bocage] has thus transformed a type of corridor which had no function into a vestibule where artists, by turns, will all be invited, without distinction as to genre or school. Those whom the academic jury will have struck down without mercy will finally be able to appeal an unfair decision with the public.). At the time of the ball, the Odéon museum featured works by two of Grandville's close friends, *Matelots* (Sailors) by Duval Le Camus and *Cirque de Gavarni* [*sic*] (Cirque at Gavarnie) by Guiaud.

26. "Fête de l'Odéon," 2nd ser., 3, 6th livraison (February 8, 1846): 44.

27. Parisian carnival balls had become part of the regular tourist circuit for visiting foreigners, including Muslims. In 1844, for instance, Arab leaders sent by Marshal Bugeaud, governor general of Algeria, attended the *bal de l'Opéra* (Gasnault, 164).

28. "Faits divers," *Le Moniteur universel,* February 14, 1846, 371.

29. Ibid., February 16, 1846, 397.

30. Hillairet, 2:224.

31. Grandville, we know, often produced other paper cutout figures as toys for his children (see "J.-J. Grandville: Dessins inédits," *Magasin pittoresque* 23, no. 45 [November 1855]: 358). Until recently, twelve of these still belonged to Grandville relatives. Four of them are reproduced in *Très Beaux Livres et manuscrits,* catalog no. 8 (Paris: Librairie Valette, n.d.).

32. "Découpures, ou ombres éclairées: Dessins par J.-J. Grandville," *Magasin pittoresque* 15, no. 8 (February 1847): 60–61.

33. As mentioned in the introduction to the 1836 Sketchbook, the illustrations attributed to Grandville in Hetzel's 1843 *Le Livre des petits enfants, nouvel alphabet* were reimpressions of existing woodblocks.

34. John Grand-Carteret, *Les Almanachs français* (Paris: J. Alisié et Cie, 1896), 563.

35. None of the illustrations in the *Almanach du jour de l'an* carry Grandville's signature. Only five appear to be attributable to him: those on pages 84, 86, and 99, and possibly those on pages 100 and 162.

36. "Programme des spectacles," *Le Corsaire-Satan,* February 12, 1846. Edmond-Aimé-Florentin Geffroy (1804–95), who first appeared at the Comédie-Française on June 17, 1829, as Orestes in Racine's *Andromaque,* played leading roles in both comedies and tragedies. Elisabeth Rachel Félix (1821–58), who adopted the stage name of Mlle Rachel, made her brilliant debut at the Comédie-Française on June 12, 1838, in the role of Camille in another classic tragedy by Corneille, *Horace* (Geffroy played the younger Horace). Four days later on June 16, she interpreted the same role as depicted here, that of Emilie in *Cinna.* During her entire career she remained, as the *Petit Robert* succinctly puts it, "l'interprète admirée des héroïnes de Corneille et des princesses de Racine" (the admired interpreter of the heroines of Corneille and the princesses of Racine). For additional information on Rachel, see Rachel M. Brownstein's *Tragic Muse: Rachel of the Comédie-Française* (New York: Alfred A. Knopf, 1993).

37. An ordinance of January 2, 1846, appointed Frémy professor of chemistry at the École Polytechnique; he assumed his professorial duties on January 6.

38. The other authors were Amédée Achard, Taxile Delord, and Émile Forgues. Additional information concerning *Cent proverbes* may be found in Nancy, 348.

39. See the paper's rubric "Partie non officielle: Intérieur." March 3, 10, and 13, 1846.

40. For the location of these boathouses, see *Deux siècles d'architecture sportive à Paris* (Paris: Mairie du XXe arrondissement, 1984), 32, 34.

41. Guillaume de Bertier de Sauvigny, *Nouvelle Histoire de Paris, La Restauration, 1815–1830* (Paris: Hachette, 1977), 182.

42. Grandville had earlier used the same "quotation" in a double *portrait-charge* of contemporary authors on page 1 of *Le Charivari Monstre,* dated July 31, 1835 (fig. 78). A systematic analysis of *Le Charivari Monstre,* published in the August 15, 1835, issue of *Le Charivari,* gives the following description of the fiery romantic playwright on the right:

> Ses cheveux sont hérissés, ses sourcils crispés, ses yeux écarquillés comme ceux d'un chat qui a bu du vinaigre. Sa main droite tient une longue plume de corbeau, sa gauche presse convulsivement un poignard du moyen-âge, et derrière lui pendille le long du mur sa bonne lame de Tolède. Ce type tient tout à la fois du Dumas, du Hugo, du Berthaud et du Pétrus Borel. C'est le drame, c'est la poésie satanique, frénétique, vitriolique, hyperbolique, hydrophobique, galvanique, amphigourique.

> [His hair stands on end, his eyebrows are knit, his eyes pop out of their sockets like those of a cat that has drunk vinegar. His right hand holds a long crow's quill, his left convulsively grips a medieval dagger, and along the wall behind him dangles his good Toledo blade. This type simultaneously smacks of Dumas, Hugo, Berthaud, and Pétrus Borel. It's drama, it's satanic, frenetic, vitriolic, hyperbolic, hydrophobic, galvanic, amphigoric poetry.]

But just as the figure on the left basically represents Louis Desnoyers (see cat. no. 21), the composite portrait to the right has been principally inspired by Victor Hugo. Like Shakespearean tragedies, Hugo's dramas often ended with a corpse-littered stage. Such is the case of *Hernani* where the three principal characters all die during the last ten lines of the play to the accompanying dialogue of "Mort! Mort! . . . Morte!" (Dead! Dead! . . . Dead!). It is probably in parody of this famous ending that Grandville represents Hugo in the throes of poetic inspiration as he wildly pens the lines:

> ....morte!....morte!!.......
> ....on ne peut pas plus morte!!!..
> (.........dead!....dead!!.......
> ....one cannot be more dead!!!..)

43. Grandville's spelling capabilities were at times limited; nevertheless, *sictmuth* has less of a French than a German quality to it. Indeed, it may be a word of Germanic origin belonging to some Lorrain patois.

44. "Les Loisirs de Chatou," *L'Illustration,* October 7, 1848, 94.

45. Ferdinand, duc d'Orléans, the eldest son of Louis-Philippe and heir to the throne, died a few hours after being involved in a freak carriage accident on July 13, 1842. Grandville's letter to his family was written the following day, July 14. His main reason for writing the letter was to give worried family members a detailed medical update on Henriette whose health had been undermined as a result of giving birth to the couple's third child, Georges, on or around July 9. It is significant that Grandville could express sympathy for the duc d'Orléans at the very moment when he was preoccupied with what was to be his wife's fatal illness. Henriette died of peritonitis less than two weeks later on July 27.

46. This drawing in the collection of the Musée Lorrain is a copy of an unlocated original by Grandville. In the lower left-hand corner appear Grandville's initials and the date "1846"; in the lower right-hand corner is presumably the initial of the copyist, "E." The water lily next to Grandville's signature is almost identical to the one that figures in cat. no. 66, and allows us to suppose that it was executed at Chatou during the summer of 1846. In addition, Georges wears the same wide-brimmed straw hat seen twice in the Chatou section of the 1846 diary (cat. nos. 64 and 69). An appropriate title for this unlabeled drawing would be "Petites misères de la pêche à la ligne" (Little misfortunes of angling): as Grandville fishes a long-handled frying pan out of the river, Georges accidentally kicks over the can of worms, and the day's catch spills out of a creel and back into the water. The vine growing around the artist's leg refers to the stoic immobility of the well-seasoned Chatou fisherman.

47. This is not the first instance of Grandville working on more than one important project simultaneously. For example, shortly after the death of his first wife, Henriette, Grandville wrote to his sister-in-law, Catherine "Minette" Fischer, on August 4, 1842, that he simply could not afford the time to visit her and the rest of the family in Nancy because of his work backlog on "deux entreprises capitales" (two major enterprises), which were the *Petites misères de la vie humaine* and *Scènes de la vie privée et publique des animaux.*

1846

The first three drawings that follow appear to document the last, happy year of Grandville's life and thus complement the excerpts from the 1846 diary presented in the previous section. Two of them exhibit the use of gray wash like the two studies for *Les Fleurs animées* found in figures 112 and 113. Together, these works exemplify Grandville's apparent preference in 1846 for gray wash as opposed to the brown wash that he habitually had used in earlier drawings, such as those in the 1833 diary. Because it also displays this distinctive use of gray wash, a fourth drawing, the caricatured portrait of a man, has been grouped with them.

80. 22/1

Mr Grandville Paris
(Mr. Grandville Paris)

1846
82 × 100
Pencil, gray wash, watercolor

Perhaps better than any other drawing in the Missouri Album, this charming, watercolor-tinted portrait of his family documents the contented domestic existence that Grandville enjoyed during the last full year of his life. Céline, followed by Georges, seems to have just gotten the day's mail and hands to Grandville a letter addressed to him. While reaching to receive the letter with his right hand, Grandville holds Armand in his left arm. The scene appears to take place in the room that served as Grandville's studio in the apartment at 26, rue des Saints-Pères: the oak desk where he worked is sketched in gray wash behind him. Everyone looks as though dressed for cooler weather, suggesting that the drawing was done either during the early part of 1846 or during late autumn, after the family's return to Paris following their extended summer stay at Chatou.

Even though the drawing appears to have been done fairly quickly, with little regard for a polished appearance, the various members of the family have been accurately portrayed. Wearing a plaid smock, Grandville, himself, is easily recognizable from the self-portrait done late in his life (frontispiece). He sports the same beard and thick moustache, here tinted a reddish brown just as in an earlier painted self-portrait at the Musée Lorrain, and his prominent forehead displays the same receding hairline.[1] Céline, surprisingly, looks almost exactly as she does in a photograph taken some twenty years later (fig. 120).[2] Although somewhat heavier, her facial features in the photograph are identical to those in the drawing: oval face, full puffy cheeks, deep-set eyes, small nose and mouth. She even wears her hair in the same fashion, parted in the middle and pulled back. The children may be compared to their portraits in the copy of the 1846 Grandville drawing reproduced in fig. 119. Armand appears to be wearing the same wide-brimmed straw hat worn by Georges in the fishing scene. And in both cases Georges wears a similar belted tunic that flares out at the bottom. In his right hand Georges holds a miniature drum major's baton as he playfully marches behind Céline, as though in a parade.

Fig. 120. Perin & Schahl, *Madame Grandville, née Catherine Marceline L'hullier,* circa 1862–67, photographic *carte de visite.* Private collection.

81. 22/2 recto

Lioness in a cage

1846
71 × 81
Gray wash

As we have already seen in diary fragments from that year, Grandville was a frequent visitor to the Jardin des Plantes in 1833. And we know that he continued to seek artistic inspiration there since more than one anthropomorphized or metamorphosed denizen of its menagerie, or zoo, populate *Scènes de la vie privée et publique des animaux* and *Un autre monde.*[3] Furthermore, there is every reason to believe that upon establishing a family after his marriage in 1833, Grandville would have wanted to share with his children his love of animals by taking them to the Jardin des Plantes. Such appears to be the case here. The child pointing to a lioness in her cage undoubtedly is the four-year-old Georges who once more wears a belted tunic and a straw hat. To the left, an equally attentive dog sits on the ledge of the barred cage staring in at the wild feline. The glowering, half-snarling expression on the lioness's face indicates that Grandville sympathized with the frustrated animal as she paced back and forth in her cage seeking to escape and calls to mind his observation in cat. no. 15 (verso), "Surely lions and bears must suffer horribly in their cages."

22/2 verso

[Fragment of a letter]

1846
71 × 81
Pen and brown ink

Judging from the writing on the verso of the drawing, it may have originally illustrated a letter, possibly to some family relative. The penmanship, however, does not belong to Grandville. A comparison with correspondence known to be written by her indicates that the author of the script was probably Céline.

82. 18 verso/2

Caricature of a man looking at a giant snail;
on the left, the light sketch of a woman

1846(?)
69 × 52
Pencil, pen and brown ink, watercolor

There is no reason to believe that this drawing, which is arbitrarily glued to the back of one of the pages from the 1836 Sketchbook, dates from that year. Quite the contrary, the presence of the crudely drawn snail and the thin-lined penmanship of the standing figure argue for a date of 1846. The manner in which it has been attached to the larger sheet unfortunately prevents an examination of the drawing's verso.

The drawing appears to be a collaborative effort on the part of Grandville and his son, Georges. Clogenson's account of their particularly close relationship, previously quoted in the introduction to the 1846 diary, bears repeating here:

> Many times, upon entering, I found him seated on the table where the artist was working in the middle of his pencils, watching him draw. I have never seen a child whose features appeared to me more charming and expressive. I remember him still with his blond hair and blue eyes, the arms around the neck of the poor artist! Father and child only talked to each other in a whisper,—often only a glance was all they needed to communicate. Many times I remained next to them, leafing through some album, without a single word being uttered in the space of an hour.

One can well imagine that Georges was not always content simply to sit on his father's work table and watch him draw. There surely must have been times when he wanted to imitate him by producing his own drawings, and that seems to be the case here.

According to expert opinion, the snail in the lower left-hand corner of the sheet could very well have been done by a four-year-old child under the guidance of a professional artist. However, the man standing next to the snail—with the exaggeratedly startled expression on his face, over-sized head, and accurately detailed stylish circa 1846 outfit—presents a classic example of Grandville's caricatural style (see Nancy, cat. nos. 77–105). The distinctively delicate, thin-lined penmanship used in the modeling of the figure is characteristic of the artist during his final years.

Given this information and Clogenson's account, the following plausible scenario presents itself. At some point during 1846, the four-year-old Georges amused himself by drawing a snail in pencil on a scrap of paper under the attentive eye of his indulgent parent. Grandville then added the expertly drawn, small-scale figure who stares in amazement at the gastropod's gigantic size. Both the spiral of the snail's shell and the figure were tinted with watercolor. The lightly penciled sketch of the woman to the left and the random marks on this irregularly cut sheet do, indeed, seem to indicate that it at one point had been a half-discarded scrap of paper similar to many that might have littered Grandville's drafting table.

83. 10/2

Head of a man

1846(?)
44 × 49
Pen and brown ink, gray wash

This mildly exaggerated portrait of a chubby-cheeked man typifies Grandville's gifts as a caricaturist and may be compared with a series of caricatured masculine heads in the collection of the Nancy Musée des Beaux-Arts (e.g., Nancy, cat. nos. 88–104). Like the previous drawing, its thin-lined penmanship is characteristic of Grandville's graphic style from around 1846.

Notes

1. Grandville did, indeed, have chestnut-colored hair. The late Pierre Parisot, a great-nephew of the artist, possessed a lock of Grandville's hair wrapped in a piece of paper that carried the annotation "Cheveux d'Adolphe Grandville Mors 17 Mars 1847 donné à moi Sa belle Soeur par Celine 7 Juin 1847" (Hair of Adolpe Grandville deceased March 17, 1847 given to me his sister-in-law by Céline June 7, 1847). Clipping and guarding a lock of hair from a departed loved one was a widespread nineteenth-century custom. In the case here, it was undoubtedly Céline who clipped the hair from the head of her deceased husband and then gave it to Pierre Parisot's grandmother, Madame Jules Parisot, née Louise Catherine Fischer (1814–1902), a sister of Grandville's first wife Henriette. After more than one hundred years, the wiry hair still retained its reddish brown color. For a color reproduction of the Musée Lorrain oil portrait, see Renonciat, 121.

2. This photograph, formerly in the Cournault collection at Malzéville, is inscribed on the back, "Mme Grandville Femme du peintre" (Madame Grandville Wife of the painter). I thank Christian Debize for his expert opinion on its date.

3. See Nancy, 292, and Philippe Kaenel, "Le Buffon de l'humanité: La Zoologie politique de J.-J. Grandville (1803–1847)," *Revue de l'art,* no. 74 (1986): 21–28.

Drawings Attributable to Grandville

The two small drawings that follow present no parallels with the various diary excerpts and offer no clues as to their dates. Judging from the fragment of writing on its verso, the first one of an Indian appears to have originally been part of a letter written by Grandville himself. Given the authorship of the letter, there is little reason to question the authorship of the drawing. Even smaller than the first, the second drawing of a double rainbow may also have illustrated a letter. However, due to the manner in which it has been attached to a page from the 1836 Sketchbook, it is not possible to determine if writing also appears on its verso. There are few if any indications to argue either for or against the drawing's authenticity.

84. 25/2 recto

"Indian" playing four drums

No date
53 × 71
Crayon noir and watercolor

Parisians first made their acquaintance with the original inhabitants of the New World when Jacques Cartier accompanied a legation of Indians to France in 1536. A number of other Native American delegations followed, particularly during the eighteenth century. It was, however, during the nineteenth century that Indians most frequently visited French shores, from the famous appearance of Osages in 1827 to that of the Iowas and Ojibways under the supervision of George Catlin (1796–1872) in 1845 and 1846; Buffalo Bill's Wild West Show, featuring the famous Sioux warrior, Sitting Bull, along with other Indians, rounded out the century with a European tour between 1888 and 1892.[1]

The six Osages who arrived in Paris from the banks of the Missouri in 1827 created a sensation. During their visit, they "were welcomed by Charles X at Saint-Cloud, dined with the Duke of Luxembourg, were entertained by high society and threw chamber pots down from the window of their hotel onto overly curious Parisians."[2] Just as they did with Mohammed Ali Pasha's giraffe in that same year, numerous lithographers recorded this equally novel and exotic presence in the French capital.[3] Grandville's own, somewhat belated response consisted of a caricature published in *La Silhouette* in January 1830 (fig. 121). Primarily a satire on current fashions, the work features two other stock caricatural themes of which he was particularly fond: the world turned upside down and the contrast. Entitled *La*

Fig. 121. ***La Revanche, ou les français au Missouri*** **(The retaliation, or the French in Missouri),** ***La Silhouette,*** **January 1830, lithograph. Paris, Bibliothèque nationale de France.**

Revanche, ou les français au Missouri (The retaliation, or the French in Missouri), the lithograph depicts a group of scantily clad aborigines in the wilds of Missouri gawking at a group of uniformed and modishly dressed French on display as though at a circus sideshow. As explained in the print's accompanying commentary, a "great warrior" (presumably Osage) recently returned from Europe draws the attention of his fellow tribesmen to the finer points of the "so grotesque costumes" worn by the extravagantly clothed foreigners.

Parisians once more were visited by Indians when a group of fourteen Iowas and then eleven Ojibways accompanied the tour of Catlin's "Indian Gallery" in 1845 and 1846. Catlin was fortunate to have the support of Louis-Philippe, who fondly recalled his three years of exile in the United States during the French Revolution. When Catlin's rental contract expired, the king allowed the artist's collection of Native American artifacts and paintings recording the fast-disappearing Indian way of life to be exhibited in the Salle des Séances (Conference Room) of the Louvre. He even ordered fifteen of the paintings copied for the museum of Versailles. Finally, he arranged for two private performances of Catlin's Indians, commissioning one of his favorite artists, Karl Girardet (1813–71), to commemorate the first one in a painting that was shown at the Salon of 1846, *Le roi Louis-Philippe, la reine Marie-Amélie et*

Fig. 122. Gavarni, *Sauvage de n'importe où et tambour de la Garde nationale* (Savage from anywhere and drummer from the National Guard) from *Musiciens comiques ou pittoresques* (Comic or picturesque musicians), 1844, lithograph. Private collection.

la duchesse d'Orléans assistant dans le Salon de la Paix aux Tuileries à une danse d'Indiens Iowas que leur présente le peintre George Catlin, le 21 avril 1845 (King Louis-Philippe, Queen Marie-Amélie, and the duchesse d'Orléans attending in the Room of Peace at the Tuileries Palace a dance by Iowa Indians that the painter George Catlin presents to them on April 21, 1845).[4]

Given this repeated exposure to the exotic costumes and dances of New World aborigines, it is not surprising that "Indians," complete with drums, became a fixture at carnival masquerades. Gavarni documents this phenomenon in an 1844 lithograph, *Sauvage de n'importe où et tambour de la Garde Nationale* (Savage from anywhere and drummer from the National Guard; fig. 122).[5] From all appearances, Grandville's Indian belongs to the same race of wildly drumming, fanciful impersonators. That his bare-chested and colorfully feathered drummer is not an authentic Indian manifests itself in the man's full and bushy growth of facial hair. As a result, there is every reason to believe that the drawing constitutes a souvenir from some carnival soirée. If so, it would once more attest to Grandville's active social life.

25/2 verso

Mon cher Mr Luh
quoique j'eusse besoin de que
avant la grande epoque (en

l'un [illegible words]
(My dear Mr. Luh[ ]
although I would have needed *que*[ ]
before summer time (in
the one [ ])

No date
53 × 71
Pen and brown ink

Written in Grandville's distinctive penmanship, the fragment of a letter on the verso of the drawing argues for its authenticity. Because of their incomplete state neither "Mr Luh[ ]" nor the topic of the letter can be identified.

85. 20 verso

A double rainbow

No date
42 × 50
Watercolor

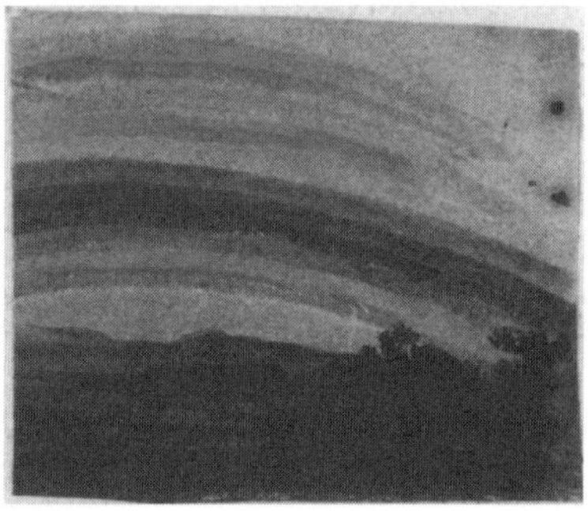

Similar in scale and execution to the previous watercolor, this poetic drawing of a rare natural phenomenon may also have been done by Grandville. The fact that it has been glued to the back of one of the pages from the 1836 Sketchbook does not necessarily mean that it dates from that year.

Notes

1. For this and other information concerning the interaction of Parisians with Indians, see Château de Blérancourt (Aisne), Musée national de la Coopération franco-américaine, *Sur le sentier de la découverte: Rencontres franco-indiennes du XVIe au XXe siècle* (Paris: Editions de la Réunion des musées nationaux, 1992).
2. Ibid., 146.
3. See the series Qb1, *Histoire de France* (1827) in the Cabinet des estampes at the Bibliothèque nationale de France.
4. *Sur le sentier de la découverte,* 23, 87. Girardet's painting, which is in the collection of the Musée national du Château at Versailles, is reproduced on page 23. Coincidentally, it is Girardet who will be called upon to provide the last of the illustrations to Mame's 1848 edition of *Don Quixote* when Grandville's work on the publication was cut short by his death (see appendix).
5. I thank Arsène Bonafous-Murat for bringing this print to my attention.

Children's Drawings

According to professionals in the field of art education, the five drawings that follow were produced by children ranging between approximately nine and sixteen years of age.[1] It is more than likely that these drawings, like the one in cat. no. 82, were done by one of Grandville's children. Given the age span, that would automatically be Armand, Grandville's only child from his second marriage and the only one of his four children who lived beyond his fifth birthday (fig. 123). Should these drawings indeed be by Armand, their presence in the Missouri Album would substantiate the supposition, explored in the epilogue, that he was the album's compiler. No attempt has been made to date the drawings. They have been arranged in a chronological sequence according to the probable age at which they were executed.

86. 21 verso

Child's drawings

105 × 177
Pen and brown ink

These drawings and the one in the following catalog entry were probably done by a child between the ages of nine and twelve. The likelihood that Grandville, himself, had transformed the 1836 Sketchbook into a type of illustrated children's book for his own children's amusement was explored in cat. no. 41. The fact that the drawing here was done directly on the back of one of the pages from the sketchbook would indicate that it had, indeed, been turned over to a child at a later date, after the sketchbook had served its professional purpose, and possibly even after the artist's death. It seems reasonable to assume that only one of Grandville's own children would have been allowed to draw on the back of one of his works. Such an assumption would strengthen the probability that Armand was the aspiring young draftsman.

87. 19 verso

Siege of a castle

88 × 179
Pencil

This drawing is glued to the back of one of the pages from the 1836 Sketchbook. Like those in the previous entry, it was probably done by a child between the ages of nine and twelve. Its more advanced treatment of a unified narrative subject, the siege of a castle, would place it toward the end of this particular age span.

88. 25/1 recto

Seven caricatured figures in a row

96 × 154
Pencil, brown ink stains

This and the next two drawings appear to have been done by an adolescent hand. The inept draftsmanship of the one here, notably in the physiognomies and in the haltingly contoured outlines of the figures' silhouettes, precludes its being done by Grandville. Nevertheless, the varied assortment of social types, aligned somewhat haphazardly as though they were drawn in the order in which they were encountered in the street, calls to mind very similar bas-relief compositions of social types depicted by Grandville around 1830 (cf., Nancy, cat. nos. 24, 28, 60, 65, 66). Even the cast of characters is the same—a National Guard drum major, a rentier type, a nanny carrying an infant, children, and a policeman—as is the satirical tone. Given these factors, there is good reason to believe that this drawing, as well as the following related one in cat. no. 89, are copies or tracings done after original Grandville compositions by someone in their early teens.

These works once more invite a certain amount of speculation regarding their author. What other teenager besides Armand would have had both direct access to Grandville's artworks and the motivation to simulate them? It is entirely possible that as part of an adolescent search for identity Armand would have experimented with imitating his father's caricatural talents in a drawing such as this.

25/1 verso

Lilies of the valley

96 × 154
Pencil

89. 23/2

Sapper

101 × 42
Pencil

Identical in style to the caricatured figures of the previous catalog number, this sapper may again have been done by Armand in imitation of his father.

90. 18 verso/1

Woman seated in front of a balustrade with a child on her lap

96 × 105
Pencil

This drawing, glued to the back of one of the pages from the 1836 Sketchbook, appears to have been done by someone in his midteens. And like the three previous ones, it more than likely was done by an adolescent Armand. This time, however, the aspiring young artist has not imitated one of his father's works. Instead, he has tried his hand at executing an original composition. Just as with many of Grandville's own adolescent drawings, this is probably the portrait of a family relative in Nancy. The full, crinoline dress with pelerine worn by the woman as well as the ringlets of hair that frame her face were fashionable during the Second Empire, when Armand would have been in his teens.

Note

1. For a detailed discussion of artwork done by children during various stages of their mental development, see Viktor Lowenfeld and W. Lambert Brittain, *Creative and Mental Growth,* 8th ed. (New York: Macmillan, 1987).

Epilogue

Concerning the Compiler of the Missouri Album

The Missouri Album contains a uniquely valuable collection of documents relating to the life of Grandville. But who compiled the album remains a mystery. Although the truth of the matter may never be known, circumstantial evidence strongly suggests that the person most likely to have owned the documents and to have possessed the motivation to edit them for posterity would have been the artist's son and sole surviving direct descendant, Armand (fig. 123).

Given the intimate nature of the contents of the Missouri Album, mainly fragments from Grandville's diaries and those parts of the 1836 Sketchbook that could have served as entertainment for his children, they probably remained in the family after the artist's death. Armand, we know, inherited many of the drawings from Grandville's studio: it is reasonable to assume that he also fell heir to those private family documents that form the basis of the contents of the Missouri Album.

Born June 2, 1845, to Grandville's second wife, Céline L'hullier, Armand was only twenty-one months old when his father died on March 17, 1847. Shortly after the artist's death, Céline moved back to Nancy in order to be with her relatives. It is in the Lorrain capital that Armand grew up and apparently remained for the rest of his short life. The little we know about Armand comes principally from speeches made during the 1893 inaugural ceremonies for the monument to his father, which Armand had provided for in his will (see Nancy, 416–17). After its unveiling, the mayor of Nancy, Mr. Maringer, gave a brief sketch of Armand's life, which, it turns out, was as ill-fated as those of his half brothers:

> Beau, intelligent, d'un caractère fier, de goûts aristocratiques, Armand Grandville fit de bonnes études au Lycée de Nancy d'abord, puis à la Faculté de Droit. Vers la vingtième année, une fièvre typhoïde compromit gravement sa santé pour tout le restant de sa courte vie. Obligé de renoncer à la chasse, aux longues marches, aux exercices de sport qu'il aimait et qui allaient bien à sa tenue élégante, il se confina dans son cabinet, modifia ses habitudes et s'absorba désormais dans des travaux purement intellectuels.
>
> Il suivit les cours des Facultés et devint l'un des membres assidus de cette regrettée Conférence Stanislas qui groupait alors nombre d'esprits curieux et alertes. Il y produisit quelques travaux distingués et empreints d'une véritable originalité. Ennemi de la phrase, dédaigneux des succès faciles, son esprit avait une rigueur toute scientifique et philosophique. Chez lui, nul pédantisme, nul désir de plaire, mais de solides convictions et un coeur droit. Avec ses livres, quelques amis et surtout la compagnie de sa mère, sa vie était remplie. C'est vous dire, Messieurs, quel coup terrible lui porta la mort de cette mère adorée, survenue en 1888. Son désespoir fut navrant. A dater de ce jour, ses forces s'épuisèrent rapidement, et, moins de deux ans après, le jour même de l'inauguration de la statue de Jeanne d'Arc, il mourait à l'âge de quarante-cinq ans.
>
> [Handsome, intelligent, possessing a proud character and aristocratic tastes, Armand Grandville did well first at the Nancy high school and then law school. Around the age of twenty, typhoid fever severely compromised his health for the entire rest of his short life. Compelled to give up hunting, long walks, the sporting activities that he liked and that were well suited to his elegant bearing, he confined himself to his study, changed his habits, and absorbed himself thereafter with purely intellectual work.

Fig. 123. Anonymous, *Jean-Baptiste Armand Grandville,* undated, photograph. Private collection (reproduction forbidden).

> He took university courses and became one of the regular members of that regretted Stanislas Conference which at the time gathered together a number of inquisitive and alert minds. There he produced several distinguished works stamped by a genuine originality. The enemy of pretentious language, disdainful of easy successes, his intellect possessed an absolutely scientific and philosophical rigor. With him, no pedantry, no desire to please, but solid convictions and an honest heart. With his books, some friends, and especially the company of his mother, his life was complete. This explains to you, gentlemen, what a terrible blow the death of this adored mother in 1888 delivered to him. His grief was heart-breaking. From that day forward, his strength rapidly declined and, less than two years later, the same day as the inauguration of the statue of Joan of Arc, he died at the age of forty-five.][1]

The inauguration of the statue of Joan of Arc in Nancy and the death of Armand Grandville occurred on June 28, 1890. What the mayor declines to mention, but what we know from relatives, is that Armand died of pulmonary tuberculosis. According to Émile Krantz, dean of the Faculty of Letters at the University of Nancy and one of Armand's close circle of friends, he appears to have already contracted the disease by 1888, the year in which his mother passed away.

That Armand died of consumption is a key factor when attempting to reconstruct the circumstances surrounding the genesis of the Missouri Album. Consumption is a slow death. Family lore has it that in order to communicate with the children of relatives without exposing them to his illness, Armand would write notes and slip them under the door to his room. The exchange of notes became a game the children delighted in playing. But Armand also had the time to attend to more serious matters, such as the drawing up of his will, dated May 2, 1890. More importantly for the present discussion is that he as well had the time to reflect on how best to deal with the considerable number of his father's drawings and personal documents in his possession. Deciding what to do with the drawings was fairly simple: he willed them to his close friend, fellow lawyer, Conseiller de préfecture à Nancy (counselor at the prefecture in Nancy), and sole legatee, Albert Boidin, who then distributed them to the Nancy Musée des Beaux-Arts, the Musée Lorrain, the Nancy Bibliothèque municipale, and the Bibliothèque nationale de France in Paris. Intimate family documents, however, were a more delicate matter.

Of particular concern to Armand was the extensive correspondence between his parents "concerning questions on art and personal psychology" and his father's biography, which his mother had been writing based on this same correspondence. Armand arranged that both be incinerated upon his death. They were. Krantz finds the motivation for the destruction of these invaluable documents in the character of Armand, whom he describes as "un délicat scrupuleux qui craignait le regard du public dans les choses intimes, et qui ne se croyait jamais assez défendu contre la curiosité indifférente qu'il exagérait peut-être" (a meticulously finicky person who dreaded the eye of the public in private matters and who never believed that he had done enough to defend against indifferent meddling which he perhaps exaggerated).[2]

Of an equally intimate and revelatory nature were Grandville's diaries. Given Armand's character and the probability that he possessed the diaries, it is easy to imagine that he would have wished to prevent them as well from falling under the indiscreet gaze of the public eye. But he would have been confronted with a dilemma: how to protect the family's privacy and yet preserve the witty and often beautiful examples of his father's draftsmanship that the diaries contained. He could not simply leave orders for the diaries to be burned wholesale like the correspondence and the biography. Filial piety and respect for his father's artistic legacy would have prevented that. Nor could he trust someone after his death to separate the drawings from the written entries in a manner that would have met with his approval. As a result, he probably concluded that if he wanted the job done properly, he would have to do it himself. And so, he cut the drawings out of the diaries and glued them onto the pages of a souvenir album. At the same time, he included pages from a beloved sketchbook in which his father had drawn illustrations to children's stories and which he fondly remembered viewing during his childhood. Last, in a poignant gesture symbolically reuniting son and long-lost father, Armand inserted some of his own drawings with those of his parent. The result was the Missouri Album.[3]

The above scenario is, of course, imaginary. But at the same time, given the contents of the album and Armand's fanatical protection of his family's privacy, it is a credible one. Should it be true, or merely close to the truth, two questions arise. What did Armand do with the mutilated remains of the diaries from 1830, 1832, 1833, and 1846 after the compilation of the Missouri Album? And what happened to the diaries presumably written during the other years between 1830 and 1846 and those before 1830? The answer to the first question seems self-evident: they would have been most certainly destroyed. The answer to the second is less apparent. Assuming that they were written, they may have suffered a fate similar to those represented in the Missouri Album and are to be found piecemeal somewhere in other albums. Or perhaps they have survived intact and await discovery. Or, as improbable as it may seem, they may never have existed.

Notes

1. Nancy, *Inauguration du monument de J. - J. Grandville* (Nancy: Imprimerie Coopérative de l'Est, 1893), 5–6.

2. Ibid., 16–17. As one of the two witnesses who signed Armand's death certificate, Émile Krantz must have been a particularly close friend. On page 12 of the *Inauguration,* he describes both the emotional state of the proud but disease-ridden Armand when reaching the decision to destroy his parents' correspondence and the execution of Armand's last wishes:

> Je dois dire ici pour ceux qui voudraient croire à l'existence d'une correspondance sur laquelle on pourrait compter pour entreprendre la biographie de Grandville, je dois dire que cette correspondance n'a existé que jusqu'au lendemain de la mort de son fils. Si Madame Grandville, sa veuve, n'avait pas été emportée par une maladie aussi soudaine, il était convenu entre elle et un ami de son fils que ces nombreuses lettres, presque toutes addressées à elle, et portant sur des questions d'art ou de psychologie intime, seraient dépouillées et publiées en grande partie dans une biographie du grand artiste. Mais Armand Grandville, déjà atteint par le mal cruel qui devait l'emporter, après avoir essayé tout seul, au lendemain de la mort de sa mère, ce dépouillement douloureux qui lui déchirait le coeur et lui arrachait à chaque page des sanglots, y renonça dans un dernier accès de faiblesse. Sa volonté suprême fut que le tout fut impitoyablement brûlé. Je vois encore dans un coin du salon le petit meuble de laque où l'exécuteur testamentaire dut, par la volonté du mort, prendre ce trésor d'informations, cette histoire d'une âme au suprême degré intéressante, curieuse d'elle-même et pathétique, pour en faire une cendre à jamais muette, tout ému et tout contristé de sa déplorable mission.
>
> [I must say here for those who would like to believe in the existence of a correspondence on which one would be able to depend for undertaking the biography of Grandville, I must say that this correspondence existed only up to the day after the death of his son. If Madame Grandville, his widow, had not been carried away by such a sudden illness, it was agreed between her and a friend of her son that these numerous letters, almost all addressed to her, and concerning questions on art and personal psychology, would be sifted through and in large part published in a biography of the great artist. But Armand Grandville, already suffering from the cruel disease that would carry him off, after having tried all by himself, after the death of his mother, this painful examination process which tore out his heart and at each page brought forth sobs, gave up in a last fit of weakness. His supreme wish was that all of it be mercilessly burned. I still see the little enameled piece of furniture in a corner of the room where the executor of the will, totally distraught and saddened by his lamentable duty, was obligated by the deceased's command to take this treasure of information, this history of a soul supremely interesting, curious and moving by itself, so that it be reduced to ever mute ashes.]

Later on in the same speech on page 17, Krantz states that Céline's biography of her husband, apparently well advanced at her death, met the same fate: "Armand Grandville, avec son tempérament si fier d'initié, ordonna que cette biographie qui avait survécu jusqu'à sa mort fut brûlée dès qu'il aurait fermé les yeux: elle le fut" (Armand Grandville, with his so self-righteous temperament of an initiate, ordered that this biography which had survived up until his death be burned as soon as he had closed his eyes: it was).

3. Should Armand have been the compiler of the Missouri Album, this circumstance would account for why select diary entries were left virtually intact. The most important example is that found in cat. no. 16 where Grandville confides his disgust with his career as a political caricaturist. Given what we know about him, it was probably very important for Armand, a lawyer and well-respected member of Nancy bourgeois society, to leave for posterity evidence that his father was not the wild-eyed revolutionary his political caricatures would lead the casual observer to believe: he wished to sanitize his father's leftist political reputation.

Appendix

The appendix consists of a letter written by Grandville at Chatou on Tuesday, October 20, 1846, and addressed to his editor, "Mr. H. Fournier, Chez Mr Mame, Tours."[1] Its transcription and translation are done in the same fashion as those for the diary fragments: the transcription appears in italics line by line following the original document, Grandville's orthographic and grammatical errors have been respected, and crossed-out words that are legible appear between brackets; the translation follows. The letter is important not only because it complements the Chatou section of the 1846 diary. It also provides valuable information on Grandville's continued working relationship with his longtime publisher, Henri Fournier, while producing the illustrations for what was to be his penultimate publication, *L'Ingénieux Chevalier Don Quichotte de la Manche* (The ingenious gentleman Don Quixote of La Mancha; Mame, 1848) and affords additional insight into his character.

The address on the letter confirms that in 1846 Fournier was no longer at the publishing house he had cofounded in 1824 with his friend and fellow native of Tours, Jules Taschereau. Under his direction, the press had published, in a steady stream, the majority of Grandville's illustrated books: *Oeuvres complètes de Béranger* (1836), *Fables de La Fontaine* (1838), *Voyages de Gulliver* (1838), *Aventures de Robinson Crusoë* (1840), *Petites misères de la vie humaine* (1843), *Un autre monde* (1844), and *Cent proverbes* (1845). However, Fournier had run into financial difficulties. By 1845 control of the press had been turned over to a company of shareholders, and he had accepted the invitation of another friend and native of Tours, Alfred Mame (1811–93), to head the typographical section of his family's substantial publishing firm in that city. The running of the press he had helped to found in Paris was entrusted to his steadfast foreman and friend, Jules Claye (1806–86), under whose iron-willed leadership it rebounded and flourished. Fournier became Mame's close collaborator.[2] With the illustrations to *Don Quixote,* Grandville continued to work for Fournier in his new position. And, judging from this letter, Fournier in turn continued to depend on Claye, in this case to act as the convenient liaison between himself, now in Tours, and the Paris-based Grandville.

The letter also reveals the human side of Grandville as it provides insights into his well-regulated work schedule while at Chatou (Tuesdays were reserved for weekly trips into Paris), his systematic frugality (he saved his drawings as carefully as he managed his money), the discipline he exercised in his work (he adhered to Fournier's schedule when producing the drawings for *Don Quixote*), his weakness for fishing (apparently the only activity that was allowed to interfere with his work), and his playful wit (his gentle teasing of Fournier and the pun played on Claye's name). The generally cheerful tone of the letter attests to the contentment Grandville savored during the last year of his life. The warmth of his humanity comes through in the expression of his great respect and friendship for Fournier. The last few lines of the letter where he writes how wonderfully everything is going with his family are especially poignant. It underscores once more how unexpected the death of Georges just three months later was going to be: a fatal shock that would convulse the unsuspecting artist and loving father to his very core.

Mon cher Mr Fournier,
Je ne sais trop comment je
vais vous faire passer ce 5me
dessin, 1er de la nouvelle serie
que j'ai (ici à Chatou), terminé
depuis deux jours. aujourdhui
mardi est mon jour de voyage
à Paris mais le tems est si hideux
que je ne sais si [je ne sais si]
j'aurai le courage de me mettre
en route.
revenons à ce nouveau dessin. il
est du nombre de ce ceux que
je ne consens pas à donner à Mr
Mame très Sérieusement parlant
veuillez vous charger de lui renouveller
l'intention bien formelle dans laquelle
je suis de rentrer en possession sinon
de ces trois dessins, au moins des
deux tiers - et ce sujet est un de
ceux que je n'abandonnerai comme
<u>Soult</u> qu'avec la vie.......
je ne l'ai pas signé non plus, à cause
de cela même et uniquement pour cela.
Je pense que vous serez satisfait de
me voir ainsi suivre vos indications
et ne pas jeter la perturbation dans
lordre de votre immuable programme.
Je tiens en ce moment le
sujet de la cage <u>aux lions</u>
et je ne vois plus, tant d'ennui
à traiter <u>pour l'acier</u> le sujet
des no<u>pces</u> de Camache.
de plus je viens d'entamer la Seconde
Serie des bois du texte. et j'en
ai un a remettre aujourdhui même
à Maitre Chevauchet - Ceux
de la 1ere partie sont tous en
mains. vous voyez de quel train
tout cela marche et que
vous n'avez qu'a commander pour
être obei...il est vrai dajouter
pourtant que le mauvais tems qui
m'interdit la pêche y est pour
beaucoup—priez donc dieu qu'il
[nous] envoie beaucoup d'eau sur
terre....et vous verrez [Se terminer
promptement les] pleuvoir aussi
les dessins et les bois et Se terminer
ainsi cette trop fameuse histoire

du Héros Manchois.
Cependant hier encore, je Suis allé
faire mes adieux à l'ile de Chatou
et par un Soleil magnifique
J ai encore pu [prendre] tirer de leaux une Centaine
de poissons dont huit à dix
pesant un quarteron........
et dans l'espace de trois heures Seulement.
Voici un rayon de Soleil, je vous
quitte vous et Chatou pour
aller remettre et ce mot
et ce dessin et ce bois
à paris entre les mains de
Mr Claye qui n'aura pas
j'espere pris celle des Champs
Surquoi je vous salue
cordialement et amicalement
et surtout Lestement

tout mon monde va à merveille
en est il ainsi du vôtre?
de votre famille?
réadieu
JI. Grandville

Chatou 20 Octobre
1846

Les indications et observations mises en
marge de ce dessin pourrait je pense
suffire à Mr Ruhierre dont
je n'ai encore rien vu......
rien pu louer..-

[My dear Mr. Fournier,

I don't quite know how I
am going to have delivered to you this fifth
drawing, first in the new series
that I completed (here at Chatou)
two days ago. Today
Tuesday is my traveling day
to Paris, but the weather is so dreadful
that I don't know if [I don't know if]
I will have the courage to start out
on the road.
Back to this new drawing. It
is among those that
I do not consent to be given to Mr.
Mame. Very seriously speaking,

Figure 124. ***L'animal ouvrit la gueule, fit un long bâillement, et tirant une langue de deux pieds, il s'en débarbouilla les yeux et toute la face*** **(The animal opened its mouth, yawned leisurely, and sticking out its two-foot-long tongue, cleaned its eyes and washed its entire face) from** ***L'Ingénieux Chevalier Don Quichotte de la Manche,*** **1848, steel engraving. Paris, Bibliothèque nationale de France.**

please take it upon yourself to restate
the very express desire that
I am to get back into my possession if not
these three drawings, at least
two-thirds of them—and this matter is one of
those that I will not abandon, like
Soult, except with my life[3].......
I haven't signed it either, precisely because
of that and only because of that.
I believe that you will be pleased to
see me thus follow your instructions
and not throw into disorder
the order of your immutable program.

At the moment I am working on the
subject of the lion cage [fig. 124]
and I no longer see that much trouble

tackling for the steel the subject
of Camacho's wedding.[4]
Plus I am just beginning to start in on the second
series of wood engravings for the text. And I
have one to give this very day
to master Chevauchet[5]—Those
from the first part are all in
his hands. You see with what speed
all of this proceeds and that
you only have to command in order
to be obeyed...it is true to add,
however, that the bad weather which
prohibits me from fishing has a great
deal to do with it—therefore pray to God so that He
sends [us] lots of water on
earth....and you will see [promptly
brought to a conclusion] also rain
drawings and wood blocks and
thus bring to a conclusion this too famous story
of the hero of La Mancha.
Meanwhile yesterday I went once more
to say goodbye to the isle of Chatou
and under a magnificent sun.
I was still able [to take] to pull out of the water
around a hundred
fish of which eight to ten
weighing a quarter pound........
and in the space of only three hours.
Behold a ray of sunshine, I
leave you and Chatou in order to
go deliver and this letter
and this drawing and this wood engraving block
in Paris into the hands of
Mr. Claye who will not have,
I hope, taken off.[6]
Upon which I salute you
cordially and amicably
and especially smartly.

All my people are doing wonderfully.
Is it the same with your's?
with your family?
Good-bye again
JI. Grandville

Chatou 20 October
1846

The instructions and observations placed in
the margins of this drawing should, I think,

be able to suffice for Mr. Ruhierre[7] from whom
I have not yet seen anything......
not been able to praise anything.]

Notes

1. The letter was previously in a private collection. Its present location is unknown.

2. For this and additional information on Claye, Fournier, and Mame, see Alphonse Alkan Ainé and Leprince, *Les Quatre Doyens de la typographie parisienne* (Angers: A. Burdin, 1889); Charles Noblet, *Jules Claye, imprimeur* (Paris: Pillet et Dumoulin, 1886); Albert Quantin, "M. Alfred Mame et la maison Mame," *Le Livre,* March 10, 1883, 65–72; and "M. Henri Fournier (1800–1888)," *Le Livre,* May 10, 1888, 133–39.

3. Without the contract for *Don Quixote,* it is not possible to determine what arrangements had been made with Mame concerning the ownership of Grandville's drawings for the two-volume work. But it would appear that the publisher had the right to a certain number of them. Grandville insists, however, that he is to retain possession of at least two of the three that he had recently completed. He emphasizes his determination on this point by evoking a legendary remark made by Marshal Soult (1769–1851), Louis-Philippe's minister of war from November 17, 1830, until July 18, 1834, whom he had included in his 1834 *l'Auberge des Adrets* caricature (fig. 85). Defending the marshal's salary that he continued to draw while simultaneously receiving that of a cabinet minister, in 1832 Soult made one of those characteristically gruff statements for which he had become famous: his salary as a marshal would be taken from him "qu'avec la vie" (only with his life, or over his dead body). This and other biographical information on Soult may be found in Adolphe Robert and Gaston Cougny, *Dictionnaire des parlementaires français* (Paris: Bourloton, 1889–91), 5:336–38.

4. The illustrations for *Don Quixote* consisted of twenty-four wood and eight steel engravings. None of them, however, feature Camacho's wedding. Perhaps Grandville's ambivalent attitude toward the subject caused it to be eliminated.

5. Chevauchet was a wood engraver regularly employed by Fournier. Grandville had worked with him for ten years, since his first book published by Fournier, *Oeuvres complètes de Béranger* of 1836. Chevauchet was one of at least four engravers who produced the wood engravings for *Don Quixote.*

6. The English translation "taken off" does not do justice to the pun that Grandville has played on Claye's name, pronounced like the French word for key, which is spelled either *clef* or *clé.* A literal translation of the last part of the sentence would read, "Mr. Claye who will not have, I hope, taken that of the fields." The pun turns on the French expression *prendre la clé des champs* (take the key to the open fields) which has the connotation of running off or slipping away. Grandville here only half-jokingly expresses the hope that the reliable but now busier-than-ever Claye will not be absent when he arrives to deliver the letter, drawing, and woodblock intended for Fournier.

7. As mentioned in cat. no. 74, François Théodore Ruhierre was the engraver who produced all eight steel engravings for *Don Quixote.*

Bibliography

Grandville's major works, along with other of his productions mentioned in the text, have been listed separately according to the terminal year of their publication; in the case of newspapers and periodicals, the inclusive dates of his participation have been given. Also listed separately in chronological order are those articles illustrated by Grandville in the *Magasin pittoresque,* which are referred to in the text. (For more comprehensive catalogs of Grandville's work, see Nancy and Renonciat.) Listings of other sources complete the bibliography.

Grandville Publications

1826

Costumes de théâtre. Paris: Engelmann.
Les Dimanches d'un bourgeois de Paris, ou les tribulations de la petite propriété. Paris: Langlumé.

1827

Chaque âge a ses plaisirs. Paris: Gihaut.
La Sibylle des salons. Paris: Engelmann.

1829

Les Métamorphoses du jour. Paris: Bulla.
La Silhouette, 1829–30.

1830

La Caricature, 1830–35.
Le diable boiteux; L'homme à dix visages, ou l'art de sortir de prison; Le paquebot, ou seul pour sept
Galerie mythologique. Paris: Bulla.
Principes de grammaire. Paris: Senefelder.
Voyage pour l'éternité. Paris: Bulla et Aubert.

1831

Album cosmopolite: Walter Scott (schériff) Lisant le Riot act à Alexandre-rassemblement. Paris: Adrien.
L'Ordre règne à Varsovie; L'Ordre public règne aussi à Paris; Oh! Les Vilaines Mouches!! Paris: Aubert.

1832

Association mensuelle, 1832–34.
Benoit, Louis. *Physiologie de la poire.* Paris: Libraries de la place de la Bourse et du Palais-Royal.
Carte vivante du restaurateur. Paris: Aubert.
Le Charivari, 1832–35.
Journal des enfans, 1832–33.
Petite Macédoine d'Aubert. Paris: Aubert.
Singeries morales, politiques, etc. Paris: Aubert.

1834

Les Breuvages de l'homme. Paris: Neuhaus.
La Chronique de Paris, 1834–35.
Magasin pittoresque, 1834–47.

1835

Musée des familles, 1835–47.
Le Musée parisien. Paris: Aubert.
Muséum Dantanorama. Paris: Susse and Neuhaus.
Les Parisiens pittoresques. Paris: Aubert.
Types modernes, observations critiques, le dedans de l'homme expliqué par le dehors. Paris: Neuhaus.

1836

Le Livre des enfants, 1836–38. Paris: Paulin.
Béranger, Pierre Jean de. *Oeuvres complètes de P. J. de Béranger.* 3 vols. Paris: Fournier aîné et Perrotin.

1838

La Fontaine, Jean de. *Fables de La Fontaine.* 2 vols. Paris: Fournier aîné et Perrotin.
Swift, Jonathan. *Voyages de Gulliver dans les contrées lointaines.* Paris: Fournier aîné et Perrotin.

1839

La Caricature provisoire, then *La Caricature,* 1839–43.
Gazette des enfans, 1839.
Grande course au clocher académique. Paris: Beauger.
Orsini, Virginie. *Heures de l'enfance.* Paris: Delloye.
Vocabulaire des enfants. Paris: Aubert.
Voyage moral et pittoresque du Prince Kamchaka. Paris: Aubert.

1840

Boileau, Nicolas. *Oeuvres de Boileau.* Paris: J. Desmalis.
De Foe, Daniel. *Aventures de Robinson Crusoë.* Paris: Fournier aîné.
La Fontaine, Jean de. *Fables de La Fontaine.* Vol. 3. Paris: Fournier aîné.
Savigny, A. de. *Historiettes et images.* Paris: Aubert.

1841

Le Prisme. Paris: Curmer. (Complementary volume to *Les Français peints par eux-mêmes* published by Curmer between 1840 and 1842.)
Soudille de Lavalette, Charles-Guillaume. *Fables de Lavalette.* Paris: Hetzel et Paulin.

1842

Boitard, Pierre. *Le Jardin des Plantes.* Paris: Dubochet.
Florian, Jean-Pierre Claris de. *Fables de Florian.* Paris: Dubochet.
Les Français peints par eux-mêmes. 8 vols. Paris: Curmer.
Scènes de la vie privée et publique des animaux. 2 vols. Paris: Hetzel et Paulin.

1843

L'Illustration, 1843–46.
Le Livre des petits enfants, nouvel alphabet. Paris: Hetzel.
Petites Misères de la vie humaine. Paris: Fournier.

1844

Le Grand Abécédaire en action. Paris: Aubert.
Un autre monde. Paris: Fournier.

1845

Cent proverbes. Paris: Fournier.
La Bruyère, Jean de. *Les Caractères ou les moeurs de ce siècle.* Paris: Belin-Leprieur.
Nouvel Abécédaire illustré par MM. Daumier, Forest, Grandville et autres artistes du musée Philipon. Paris: Aubert.

1846

Almanach du jour de l'an. Paris: Hetael.
Reybaud, Louis. *Jérôme Paturot à la recherche d'une position sociale.* Paris: Dubochet, Le Chevalier et Cie.

1847

Les Fleurs animées. Paris: de Gonet.

1848

Cervantes, Miguel de. *L'Ingénieux Chevalier Don Quichotte de la Manche.* Tours: Ad. Mame et Cie.

1849

Les Étoiles. Paris: de Gonet.

Magasin pittoresque

"Découpures, ou ombres éclairées. Dessins par J.-J. Grandville," 15, no. 8 (February 1847): 60–61.
"Deux rêves, par J.-J. Grandville," 15, no. 27 (July 1847): 210–14.
"J.-J. Grandville. Dessins inédits," 23, no. 45 (November 1855): 356–58.
"J.-J. Grandville. Dessins inédits," 23, no. 48 (December 1855): 380–82.
"Une scène de bal. Dessin inédit de J.-J. Grandville," 24, no. 52 (December 1856): 407–8.
"Dessins inédits de J.-J. Grandville." 25, no. 14 (April 1857): 111–12.

Newspapers and Periodicals Consulted

L'Artiste
Association mensuelle
Bibliographie de la France
La Caricature
La Caricature provisoire
Le Charivari
Le Corsaire-Satan
Figaro
L'Illustration
Journal des Artistes
Le Moniteur universel
La Silhouette

Other Sources

Adam, Victor. *Nouvel Abécédaire en énigmes.* Paris: Rittner et Goupil, 1833.
Adhémar, Jean, and Jacques Lethève. *Inventaire du fonds français après 1800.* Vols. 8 and 9. Paris: Bibliothèque nationale, 1954, 1955.
Adhémar, Jean, and Romi. "Grandville le maudit." *Bizarre,* no. 2 (1953): 11–16.
Album cosmopolite. Paris: Imprimerie de Béthune et Plon, n.d.
Alkan Ainé, Alphone, and Leprince. *Les Quatre Doyens de la typographie parisienne.* Angers: A. Burdin, 1889.
Appelbaum, Stanley. *Bizarreries and Fantasies of Grandville.* New York: Dover, 1974.
Balzac, Honoré de. *Oeuvres complètes de Honoré de Balzac.* 40 vols. Paris: L. Conard, 1912–40.
La Basilique de saint Nicolas en Lorraine. Saint-Nicolas-de-Port: Connaissance et Renaissance de la basilique de Saint-Nicolas-de-Port, 1979.
Baudelaire, Charles. *The Painter of Modern Life and Other Essays.* Translated and edited by Jonathan Mayne. London: Phaidon Press, 1964.
———. *Oeuvres complètes.* Paris: Éditions du Seuil, 1968.
Bechtel, Edwin De Turck. *Freedom of the Press and L'Association mensuelle: Philipon versus Louis-Philippe.* New York: Grolier Club, 1952.
Beik, Paul Harold. *Louis Philippe and the July Monarchy.* Princeton: Van Nostrand, 1965.
Bénézit, Emmanuel. *Dictionnaire critique et documentaire des peintres, sculpteurs, dessinateurs et graveurs.* New ed. 10 vols. Paris: Librairie Gründ, 1976.
Benjamin, Walter. *Charles Baudelaire: A Lyric Poet in the Era of High Capitalism.* Translated by Harry Zohn. London: NLB, 1973.
Béraldi, Henri. *Les Graveurs du XIXe siècle.* 12 vols. Paris: L. Conquet, 1885–92.

Bertier de Sauvigny, Guillaume de. *The Bourbon Restoration.* Translated by Lynn M. Case. Philadelphia: University of Pennsylvania Press, 1966.

———. *Nouvelle Histoire de Paris, La Restauration, 1815–1830.* Paris: Hachette, 1977.

Bezucha, Robert. "Discourses on Misery." In *A New History of French Literature,* edited by Denis Hollier. Cambridge, MA: Harvard University Press, 1989.

Blanc, Charles. *The Grammar of Painting and Engraving.* Translated by Kate Newell Doggert. New York: Hurd and Houghton, 1874.

———. *Les Artistes de mon temps.* Paris: Firmin-Didot, 1876.

Bouchot, Henri. *Les Livres à vignettes du XIXe siècle.* Paris: E. Rouveyre, 1891.

———. *La Lithographie.* Paris: Ancienne maison Quantin, 1895.

Boyé, Pierre. "Les Grands-Parents paternels de J.-J. Grandville." *Le Pays Lorrain* (1931): 281–89.

Brivois, Jules. *Bibliographie des ouvrages illustrés du XIXe siècle, principalement des livres à gravures sur bois.* Paris: L. Conquet, 1883.

Brownstein, Rachel M. *Tragic Muse: Rachel of the Comédie-Française.* New York: Alfred A. Knopf, 1993.

Buck-Morss, Susan. *The Dialectics of Seeing: Walter Benjamin and the Arcades Project.* Cambridge: MIT Press, 1989.

Buret, Eugène. *De la Misère des classes laborieuses en Angleterre et en France.* 2 vols. Paris: Paulin, 1840.

Cabanne, Pierre. *Les Bustes des parlementaires par Honoré Daumier.* Lausanne: Édita, 1980.

Cahiers de l'Institut d'histoire de la presse et de l'opinion, no. 7. Tours: Université de Tours, 1983.

Champfleury, Jules. *Les Vignettes romantiques.* Paris: E. Dentu, 1883.

———. *Histoire de la caricature moderne.* 3rd ed. Paris: E. Dentu, 1885.

Charton, Édouard. *Mémoires d'un prédicateur saint-simonien.* Paris: Au Bureau de La Revue encyclopédique, 1831.

———. "I.-I. Grandville." *L'Illustration,* March 27, 1847, 49–50.

Château de Blérancourt (Aisne), Musée national de la Coopération franco-américaine. *Sur le sentier de la découverte: Rencontres franco-indiennes du XVIe au XXe siècle.* Paris: Éditions de la Réunion des musées nationaux, 1992.

Chevalier, Louis. *Laboring Classes and Dangerous Classes in Paris during the First Half of the Nineteenth Century.* Translated by Frank Jellinek. New York: Howard Fertig, 1973.

Chu, Petra ten-Doesschate, and Gabriel P. Weisberg, eds. *The Popularization of Images: Visual Culture under the July Monarchy.* Princeton: Princeton University Press, 1994.

Clogenson, S. "J.-J. Granville [*sic*]." *L'Athenaeum français,* nos. 11 and 12 (March 12 and 19, 1853): 250–52; 273–75.

Collet, Dr. Georges. *Le Bressan Louis Desnoyers.* Vincennes: Impr. Rosay, 1938.

Collingham, H. A. C. *The July Monarchy: A Political History of France, 1830–1848.* New York: Longman, 1988.

Comte, Achille. *Règne animal de M. Cuvier disposé en tableaux méthodiques.* Paris: Crochard, 1832–41.

Cuno, James. "Charles Philipon, La Maison Aubert, and the Business of Caricature in Paris, 1829–41." *Art Journal* 43, no. 4 (Winter 1983): 347–54.

———. "Charles Philipon and La Maison Aubert: The Business, Politics, and Public of Caricature in Paris, 1820–1840." PhD diss., Harvard University, 1985.

Dardaud, Gabriel. "L'extraordinaire aventure de la girafe du Pacha d'Egypte." *Revue des Conférences Françaises en Orient,* 15th year, no. 1 (January 1951): 1–72.

Davenson, Henri [Henri Irénée Marrou]. *Le Livre des chansons.* 3rd ed. Neuchâtel: Éditions de la Baconnière, 1946.

Delteil, Loÿs. *Le peintre-graveur illustré.* 32 vols. Paris: Chez l'auteur, 1906–30.

Dérieux, Henry. "Joseph Guichard, peintre lyonnais (1806–1880)." *Gazette des Beaux-Arts,* 5th ser., 5 (March 1922): 181–94.

Desfeuilles, André. "Les Dessins de J. I. Grandville au Musée Carnavalet." *Le Vieux Papier,* no. 212 (1965): 249–54.

Deux siècles d'architecture sportive à Paris. Paris: Mairie du XXe arrondissement, 1984.

Dolléans, Edouard. *Histoire du mouvement ouvrier, 1830–1871.* 7th ed. Paris: Librairie Armand Colin, 1967.

Domaszewska, Helena. "Zbiór Rysunków Grandville'a w Muzeum Narodowym w Warszawie" [The Drawings of Grandville in the National Museum of Warsaw]. *Rocznik Muzeum Narodowego w Warszawie* 19 (1975): 537–74.

Du Camp, Maxime. *Souvenirs littéraires.* 2 vols. Paris: Hachette, 1892.

Dumas, Alexandre. *Mes Mémoires.* Annotated by Pierre Josserand. 5 vols. Paris: Gallimard, 1954–68.

Dupin, Marie-Pierre. "Un publiciste et homme politique saint-simonien: Edouard Charton." *Versailles, Revue des Sociétés des Amis de Versailles,* nos. 62 and 63 (1976 and 1977): 23–29 and 26–30.

Eitner, Lorenz, Betsy G. Fryberger, and Carol M. Osborne. *Stanford University Museum of Art: The Drawing Collection.* Stanford, CA: Stanford University Museum of Art, 1993.

Faber, Richard. "Paris, das Rom des XIX. Jahrhunderts. Eine Metacollage." In *Antike und Moderne: Zu Walter Benjamins "Passagen,"* edited by Norbert W. Bolz and Richard Faber. Würzburg: Königshausen und Neumann, 1986.

Felkay, Nicole. "Les Libraires de l'époque romantique d'après des documents inédits." *Revue française d'histoire du livre* 9 (1975): 31–86.

Frégier, H.-A. *Des Classes dangereuses de la population dans les grandes villes.* 2 vols. Paris: J.-B. Baillière, 1840.

Garcin, Laure. "Grandville: Visionnaire, surréaliste, expressioniste." *Gazette des Beaux-Arts,* 6th ser., 34 (December 1948): 435–48, 466–70.

Gasnault, François. *Guinguettes et lorettes: Bals publics et danse sociale à Paris entre 1830 et 1870.* Paris: Aubier, 1986.

Gautier, Théophile. *Histoire de l'art dramatique en France depuis vingt-cinq ans.* 6 vols. Paris: Magnin, Blanchard et Compagnie, 1858–59.

———. *Portraits contemporains.* Paris: Charpentier, 1874.

Getty, Clive F. "The Drawings of J. J. Grandville until 1830: The Development of His Style during His Formative Years." PhD diss., Stanford University, 1981.

———. "Opposition Caricature and Political Harassment." *Print Collector's Newsletter* 14, no. 6 (January–February 1984): 197–201.

———. "Physiognomy, Science and Romantic Visual Satire." In *Correspondances: Studies in Literature, History, and the Arts in Nineteenth Century France,* edited by Keith Busby. Atlanta: Rodopi, 1992.

———. "Max and J. J. Grandville." In *Twenty-First-Century Perspectives on Nineteenth-Century Art: Essays in Honor of Gabriel P. Weisberg,* edited by Petra ten-Doesschate and Laurinda S. Dixon. Newark: University of Delaware Press, 2008.

Goldstein, Robert Justin. *Censorship of Political Caricature in Nineteenth-Century France.* Kent, OH: The Kent State University Press, 1989.

Grand-Carteret, John. *Les Almanachs français.* Paris: J. Alisié et Cie, 1896.

Grandville, J. J. *Un autre monde.* Reproduction en fac-similé de l'édition originale de 1844 précédée d'un hommage à Grandville par Max Ernst et d'un texte de Pierre Restany. Paris: Libraries associés, 1963

Gusman, Pierre. *La Gravure sur bois en France au XIXe siècle.* Paris: Éditions Albert Morancé, 1929.

Hannoosh, Michele. *Baudelaire and Caricature: From the Comic to an Art of Modernity.* University Park: The Pennsylvania State University Press, 1992.

———. "The Allegorical Artist and the Crisis of History: Benjamin, Grandville, Baudelaire." *Word & Image* 10 (January-March 1994): 38–54.

Hatin, Eugène. *Bibliographie historique et critique de la presse périodique française.* Paris: Firmin-Didot frères, fils et cie, 1866.

Hillairet, Jacques. *Dictionnaire historique des rues de Paris.* 9th ed. 2 vols. Paris: Les Éditions de Minuit, 1985.

Huart, Louis. *Paris au bal.* Paris: Aubert, 1845.

Hugo, Victor. *Oeuvres complètes de Victor Hugo.* 45 vols. Paris: Ollendorff, 1904–52.

Kaenel, Philippe. "Autour de J.-J. Grandville: Les Conditions de production socio-professionnelles du livre illustré romantique." *Romantisme* 43 (1984): 45–61.

———. "Le Buffon de l'humanité: La Zoologie politique de J.-J. Grandville (1803–1847)." *Revue de l'art,* no. 74 (1986): 21–28.
———. "J.-J. Grandville et le *Magasin pittoresque* d'Edouard Charton." *Gazette des Beaux-Arts,* 6th ser., 115 (February 1990): 77–98.
———. *Le Métier d'illustrateur, 1830–1880.* Paris: Éditions Messene, 1996.
Karlsruhe, Staatliche Kunsthalle. *J. J. Grandville: Karikatur und Zeichnung; Ein Visionär der französischen Romantik.* Karlsruhe: Staatliche Kunsthalle, 2000.
Kerr, David S. *Caricature and French Political Caricature, 1830–1848: Charles Philipon and the Illustrated Press.* Oxford: Clarendon Press, 2000.
Lacordaire, Simon. *Vie et histoire du XXe arrondissement.* Paris: Éditions Hervas, 1987.
Ledré, Charles. *La Presse à l'assault de la monarchie, 1815–1848.* Paris: Colin, 1960.
Lemaître, Frédérick. *Souvenirs de Frédérick Lemaître, publiés par son fils.* Paris: Paul Ollendorff, 1880.
Lemaître, Henri. *Histoire du dépôt légal.* Paris: A. Picard et fils, 1910.
Le Men, Ségolène. *Les Abécédaires français illustrés du XIXe siècle.* Paris: Promodis, 1984.
———. "De l'image au livre: L'Editeur Aubert et l'abécédaire en estampe." *Nouvelles de l'estampe,* no. 90 (December 1986): 17–30.
———. *Grandville au Musée Carnavalet.* Paris: Paris-Musée, 1987.
———. "Quel est donc le livre qui peut les captiver ainsi?" In *Livres d'enfants, livres d'images.* Paris: Éditions de la Réunion des musées nationaux, 1989.
———. "De Jean-Paul Choppart à Struwwelpeter: L'Invention de l'enfant terrible dans le livre illustré." *Revue des Sciences Humaines* 99, no. 225 (January–March 1992): 45–59.
Lemoisne, Paul-André. *Gavarni, peintre et lithographe.* 2 vols. Paris: H. Floury, 1924–28.
Louis, Paul. *Histoire de la classe ouvrière en France de la Révolution à nos jours.* Paris: Librairie Marcel Rivière, 1927.
———. *La Condition ouvière en France depuis cent ans.* Paris: Presses Universitaires de France, 1950.
Lowenfeld, Viktor, and W. Lambert Brittain. *Creative and Mental Growth.* 8th ed. New York: Macmillan, 1987.
M., F. "Les Loisirs de Chatou." *L'Illustration,* October 7, 1848, 93–94.
Mac Orlan, Pierre. "Grandville le précurseur." *Arts et Métiers Graphiques,* no. 44 (1934): 19–24.
Martin, Henri-Jean, and Roger Chartier, eds. *Le temps des éditeurs: Du Romantisme à la Belle Époque.* Vol. 3 of *Histoire de l'édition française.* Paris: Promodis, 1985.
Massin, Robert. *La Lettre et l'image, la figuration dans l'alphabet latin du huitième siècle à nos jours.* Paris: Gallimard, 1970.
Meixmoron de Dombasle, Charles de. "J.-J. Grandville." *Mémoires de l'Académie de Stanislas* 11 (1893): 300–339.
Mirecourt, Eugène de. *Louis Desnoyers.* Paris: G. Havard, 1855.
Montigny, Louis-Gabriel. *Le Provincial à Paris, esquisses des moeurs parisiennes.* 3 vols. Paris: Chez Ladvocat, 1825.
Nadar [Gaspard Félix Tournachon]. *Quand j'étais photographe.* Paris: E. Flammarion, 1900.
Nancy. *Inauguration du monument de J.-J. Grandville.* Nancy: Imprimerie Coopérative de l'Est, 1893.
Nancy, Musée des Beaux-Arts. *Grandville: Dessins originaux.* Nancy: Ville de Nancy, 1986.
———. *Grandville: Les Métamorphoses du jour.* Nancy: Ville de Nancy, 2003.
Nancy, Société des Amis des Arts de Nancy. *Société des Amis des Arts de Nancy.* Exhibition catalogs. 1833–45.
Noblet, Charles. *Jules Claye, imprimeur.* Paris: Pillet et Dumoulin, 1886.
Nollet (Fabert), Jules. *Eloge historique de J. J. Grandville.* Antwerp: Max Kornicker, 1853.
Passeron, Roger. *Daumier.* Translated by Helga Harrison. Secaucus, NJ: Poplar Books, c. 1981.
Picot, Georges. *Le Dépôt légal et nos collections nationales.* Paris: A. Picard, 1883.
Porel, Paul, and Georges Monval. *L'Odéon, histoire administrative, anecdotique et littéraire de second Théâtre français.* 2 vols. Paris: Alphonse Lemerre, 1876–82.
Quantin, Albert. "M. Alfred Mame et la maison Mame." *Le Livre,* March 10, 1883, 65–72.
———. "M. Henri Fournier (1800–1888)." *Le Livre,* May 10, 1888, 133–39.

Ray, Gordon N. *The Art of the French Illustrated Book, 1700–1914.* 2 vols. New York: Pierpont Morgan Library, 1982.
Régnier-Destourbet, Hippolyte-François. *Recueil factice des livraisons de Un bal sous Louis-Philippe par l'Abbé Tiberge.* Paris: Dumont, 1831.
Renonciat, Annie. *La Vie et l'oeuvre de J. J. Grandville.* Paris: ACR Édition Internationale, 1985.
Rigaudias-Weiss, Hilde. *Les Enquêtes ouvrières en France entre 1830 et 1848.* Paris: F. Alcan, 1936.
Robert, Adolphe, and Gaston Cougny. *Dictionnaire des parlementaires français.* 5 vols. Paris: Bourloton, 1889–91.
Rosen, Charles, and Henri Zerner. *Romanticism and Realism.* New York: Viking Press, 1984.
Saint-Victor, Paul de. "Revue dramatique." *Le Pays: Journal de l'Empire* (September 18, 1854).
———. "2e Dizaine." In *D'après nature* by Gavarni. Paris: Morizot, 1858.
Sainte-Beuve, Charles-Augustin. *Nouveaux lundis.* 7th ed. rev. 13 vols. Paris: Calmann Lévy, 1890–94.
Seligman, Janet. *Figures of Fun. The Caricature-Statuettes of Jean-Pierre Dantan.* London: Oxford University Press, 1957.
Silvestre, Joseph Balthazard. *Alphabet-album: Collection de soixante feuilles d'alphabets historiés et fleuronnés tirés des principales bibliothèques de l'Europe, ou composés par Silvestre.* Paris: J. Techner, 1843.
Sorel, Philippe. *Dantan jeune, caricatures et portraits de la société romantique.* Paris: Paris-Musée, 1989.
Statisque de la France. Paris: Imprimerie Royale, 1837.
Stewart, John Hall. *The Restoration Era in France: 1814–1830.* Princeton: D. Van Nostrand, 1968.
Stoessel, Marlene. "Dans le demi-jour: Le même et le semblable, Deux contes en images de Grandville." In *Walter Benjamin et Paris,* edited by Heinz Wismann. Paris: Les Éditions du Cerf, 1986.
Thureau-Dangin, Paul. *Histoire de la Monarchie de Juillet.* 5th ed. 7 vols. Paris: E. Plon, Nourrit, 1911–14.
Très Beaux Livres et manuscrits. Catalog no. 8. Paris: Librairie Valette, n.d.
Twyman, Michael. *Lithography, 1800–1850.* London: Oxford University Press, 1970.
Tytler, Graeme. *Physiognomy in the European Novel.* Princeton: Princeton University Press, 1982.
University of Missouri. *The Art of the July Monarchy: France 1830 to 1848.* Columbia: University of Missouri Press, 1990.
Vicaire, Georges. *Manuel de l'amateur de livres du XIXe siècle, 1801–1893.* 8 vols. Paris: A. Rouquette, 1894–1920.
Vigier, Philippe. *Nouvelle Histoire de Paris, Paris pendant la Monarchie de Juillet (1830–1848).* Paris: Hachette, 1991.
Villermé, Dr. Louis-René. *Tableau de l'état physique et moral des ouvriers.* 2 vols. Paris: J. Renouard, 1840.
Wechsler, Judith. *A Human Comedy: Physiognomy and Caricature in 19th Century Paris.* Chicago: University of Chicago Press, 1982.
Wetzel, Luc. *Alexandre Bixio.* Montbéliard: Imprimerie et lithographie de Henri Barbier, 1869.
White, Harrison C., and Cynthia A. White. *Canvases and Careers: Institutional Change in the French Painting World.* Chicago: University of Chicago Press, 1993.
Wright, Beth S. "Henri Gaugain et le musée Colbert: L'Entreprise d'un directeur de galerie et d'un éditeur d'art à l'époque romantique." *Nouvelles de l'estampe,* no. 114 (December 1990): 24–31.
Zipes, Jack. *The Trials and Tribulations of Little Red Riding Hood: Versions of the Tale in Sociocultural Context.* South Hadley, MA: Bergin & Garvey, 1983.

Photographic Credits

All of the photographs of the drawings in the Missouri Album are published with the permission of Special Collections, Archives and Rare Books Division, University of Missouri-Columbia Libraries, Columbia, Missouri. The photographic credits for the figures not from the Missouri Album are as follows:

Cleveland, David M. Thum: 68
London, Hanover Studios: 51
London, Prudence Cuming Associates Limited: 91, 114
Lyon, R.M.N.- R.G. Ojeda: 59
Nancy, Bibliothèque municipale: 1, 4, 5, 10, 14, 22, 33, 57, 76 (photo G. Mangin), 112, 113, 118
Nancy, Musée des Beaux-Arts: 25; photos G. Mangin: frontispiece, 26, 40, 41, 42, 92, 98, 100, 111, 115
Nancy, Musée Lorrain/Photos G. Mangin: 38, 54, 116, 119
Paris, Bibliothèque nationale de France: 2, 3, 6, 7, 8, 9, 11, 12, 13, 15, 16, 18, 19, 20, 21, 23, 24, 29, 31, 32, 34, 35, 37, 39, 43, 44, 47, 48, 49, 52, 53, 56, 60, 62, 63, 64, 65, 69, 70, 73, 74, 75, 77, 78, 79, 80, 81, 82, 83, 84, 88, 89, 90, 93, 95, 96, 97, 99, 101, 102, 105, 107, 108, 110, 117, 121, 124
Paris, Photothèque des Musées de la Ville de Paris: 17, 45, 46, 72 (photo Ladet), 86
Photographs supplied by owners or previous owners of artworks: 27, 28, 30, 50, 55, 58, 61, 66, 67, 71, 85, 87, 94, 103, 104, 106, 109, 120, 122, 123

Index

Page numbers for illustrations are in boldface.